REACHING FOR THE SKY

THE MARINA BAY SANDS SINGAPORE

REACHING FOR THE SKY

THE MARINA BAY SANDS SINGAPORE

With contributions by
Sheldon Adelson
Peter Bowtell
Dr. Cheong Koon Hean
Adam Greenspan
Gary Hack
Brooke Hodge
Martin C. Pedersen
Moshe Safdie
Peter Walker

ORO Editions

PART 1
THE VISION
THE DESIGN
THE MAKING
PART 2
ARCHITECTURAL
DRAWINGS &
PLANS
PART 3
A CIVIC ICON
A DESTINATION
AN EXPERIENCE
PART 4
A CLOSER
LOOK
PART 5
A PLACE FOR
THE PEOPLE

Contents

06	**Part 1: The Vision, the Design, the Making**
08	Marina Bay: A New Waterfront for the Garden City by the Bay Dr. Cheong Koon Hean
16	The Making of Marina Bay Sands Sheldon Adelson in Conversation with Martin C. Pedersen
24	Rethinking the Public Realm Moshe Safdie
52	The Landscape of Marina Bay Sands Peter Walker and Adam Greenspan
66	Touching the Impossible Peter Bowtell
78	The Making of an Icon Martin C. Pedersen
94	**Part 2: Architectural Drawings and Plans**
122	**Part 3: A Civic Icon, a Destination, an Experience**
124	Visual Portfolio
136	The Architecture of Memorability Gary Hack
148	**Part 4: A Closer Look**
150	The Public Realm
172	Hotels, Atria, and SkyPark
198	Casino, Theaters, and Convention
208	Crystal Pavilions
218	ArtScience Museum
244	Art at Every Turn: The Marina Bay Sands Art Path Brooke Hodge
264	**Part 5: A Place For the People**
278	About the Contributors
280	Team Credits

PART 1

THE VISI

THE DES

THE MAK

MARINA BAY SANDS

ON
IGN
ING

MARINA BAY: A NEW WATERFRONT FOR THE GARDEN CITY BY THE BAY

DR. CHEONG KOON HEAN

A civic space, business center, and community playground in one, Marina Bay has put Singapore on the radar of investors all over the world. The development of this ambitious extension of the city center is the result of strategic, far-sighted, and meticulous planning, as well as coordinated implementation by the Urban Redevelopment Authority (URA). From the outset, Marina Bay was envisioned as a dynamic, waterfront "Garden City by the Bay," bustling with activities twenty-four hours a day, seven days a week. Surrounded by water and gardens, the area offers opportunities for further urban transformation, attracting new investments, visitors, and talents, and becoming a new destination for the local community.

In line with Singapore's forward-looking approach, the planning and design of the Marina Bay area started many years ago. Land reclamation from 1971 to 1992 created around 360 hectares in the bay area and 80 hectares in Marina Centre, in anticipation of economic growth and preparation for expanding the Central Business District. Two internationally acclaimed city planners—Kenzo Tange of Japan and I. M. Pei of the United States—helped develop the initial master plan for Marina Bay, which evolved substantially over time to keep pace with changing trends and market demands. In the 1990s, the idea gained traction for Marina Bay to be a major focus for city celebrations. Thus, the planners had to ensure that the bay have a human scale so that people could relate to activities on the water, and that any new development be in dialogue with existing buildings across the water. After studying various waterfront developments around the world, the government decided that the size of the bay should be reduced to about 48 hectares through further reclamation at Marina South and Collyer Quay. Also, urban design guidelines were developed to ensure a dynamic, "stepped" skyline profile, with low-rise buildings along the waterfront and skyscrapers in the background. This meant that tall buildings would not overwhelm the bay and the overall pedestrian experience around the waterfront would be pleasant.

The URA planned Marina Bay to grow seamlessly from the existing urban center by extending the city into this new area. One step in the process was the creation of a regular road grid for better traffic and pedestrian flow. This integration enables Marina Bay to tap the facilities and resources of the established

Historic image of Boat Quay, Singapore

Site map defining the Marina Bay District

downtown district at Raffles Place, Shenton Way, and Marina Centre. In addition, Marina Bay developers are encouraged to incorporate open spaces, visual corridors, and pedestrian links for physical access and visual connectivity. The land parcels are oriented to ensure that almost all new projects have water or garden views. Development proposals are reviewed by the URA's Design Advisory Panel, which provides input on building massing and layout, pedestrian access, and landscape design, as well as architectural elements such as materials, finishes, and lighting. The goal is to make sure that key developments are sensitively designed to fit into the wider city context.

Beyond giving Singapore a stunning new skyline, Marina Bay planners had environmental sustainability in mind. In 2007, Marina Bay was transformed into a freshwater reservoir, right in the heart of the city, to help increase water storage capacity. The Marina Barrage was constructed across the Marina Channel to act as a tidal barrier to keep out seawater and control flooding. Other sustainable features include a comprehensive rail-transit network, vertical greenery, and the use of district cooling (a centralized system that can serve many buildings) for better energy efficiency. All common services are housed within tunnels to minimize roadwork and traffic disruption during installation, repair, and maintenance. New project designs must achieve a minimum Green Mark Platinum or Gold^{plus} standard, Singapore's highest environmental ratings, which are more stringent than LEED standards.

The Development of Singapore's Downtown

Another goal of Singapore's expansion of the Central Business District was the introduction of mixed-use districts, which combine businesses, residential properties, hotels, and recreational amenities. Such districts not only reduce the need for people to travel long distances to work but also create a lively after-work atmosphere. Land parcels zoned as "white sites" give developers and designers the flexibility to incorporate a variety of uses based on business concept and market demand. The new Marina Bay was conceived as an international business and financial hub, complemented by condominiums, hotels, shops, restaurants, nightspots, and venues for large-scale outdoor events. The government envisioned a vibrant downtown—a great place to live, work, and play. In line with this, the land parcels allow for flexible adjustment of size, providing larger areas to developers who require more generous floor space, such as Marina Bay Sands with its convention facilities.

The new developments around the bay are really extensions of two existing precincts. One arm stretches from the Central Business District at Shenton Way. The other reaches to connect Marina Centre, which hosts exhibition and convention facilities, hotels, and entertainment uses, with the Bayfront area, which also features entertainment along with retail-oriented developments such as Marina Bay Sands. This approach, where expansion "embraces" Marina Bay gradually and systematically over time, has helped guarantee that each phase of development benefits from proximity to existing areas.

The Marina Bay Sands Integrated Resort: Building on the Legacy of the Garden City by the Bay

In 2004, Singapore started to explore the idea of introducing integrated resorts as part of a strategy to increase tourism by broadening leisure and entertainment options. Such resorts include not only casinos but also world-class recreational and entertainment venues. The gaming component helps support the viability of other facilities such as convention centers, hotels, and public attractions including museums and galleries. After obtaining more information about the conditions necessary for the feasible development of integrated resorts—and with positive response from potential investors—Singapore decided in April 2005 to proceed with plans for projects at Marina Bay and Sentosa. The resort at Marina Bay would be geared toward business visitors, while its counterpart at Sentosa would provide family-oriented attractions.

The waterfront at Marina Bay, with its excellent views, was identified as a strong location for the integrated resort. It was easily accessible from the Central Business District and could enhance the business and convention hub at Marina Centre. The resort was also viewed as a catalyst for a critical mass of additional development at Marina Bay.

Singapore decided to adopt an innovative approach toward choosing the integrated resort developer. The government established the land price up front to give potential bidders greater certainty, and focused on selecting the best combination of business concept and attractive design. A brief—including a master plan and urban design guidelines—called for an iconic development that contained a compelling mix

URA development model for Marina Bay and surrounding area

of unique anchor attractions, such as theaters and other entertainment, alongside convention and exhibition facilities, hotels, restaurants, and shops, as well as extensive public spaces.

The site was divided in two by Bayfront Avenue. To achieve a large contiguous site of about 16 hectares, the developer would be allowed to build extensive under- and aboveground links to connect the two halves. The brief also called for the construction of a new underground mass-transit rail line and station to link the development to Singapore's existing network.

To ensure that the design concept would be appropriate for the prime downtown location, the brief required the architectural treatment to be of a contemporary style rather than mimicking themed motifs of historic locations found in other cities. The portion of the development facing the waterfront promenade had to be low or medium rise to secure clear panoramic views of the water and skyline from key vantage points and other developments around Marina Bay. Beyond this, the building height was allowed to step up to provide a layered, three-dimensional profile. Also, URA guidelines encouraged the architect to provide public open spaces, as well as a publicly accessible observation deck within the high-rise elements of the scheme.

The master plan for Marina Bay called for "a necklace of public attractions," a string of landmark developments designed to draw in visitors. One such attraction had to be an iconic design of significant scale with world-class content, located on a promontory within the integrated resort's site. The URA intended the waterfront promenade to be a

Top and bottom:
URA development model

major civic space and large viewing area for events on the bay; an event plaza would be the focal point for staging activities and spectacles, with the city serving as a backdrop. The brief required the development of an upper-level promenade as well as a lower-level boardwalk with direct access to the water's edge. The promenade could also include refreshment kiosks and provide shade with plantings and built structures. The developer had flexibility in reshaping the seawall of the waterfront promenade to better integrate into the design of the resort.

In line with the larger plan for Marina Bay to be a pedestrian-friendly district, the integrated resort had to be a major hub with direct, weather-protected walkways to the new Bayfront Rapid Transit System station and open spaces and attractions along the waterfront promenade. In addition to ground-level connections, the development would ideally include under- and aboveground pedestrian links to allow for seamless movement between individual buildings within the resort. Given the long frontages of the site, it was important that the resort have open views of the bay and the city skyline across the water. The brief therefore called for a first-story through-block pedestrian link connecting Bayfront Avenue to the waterfront promenade. These spaces were to be publicly accessible at all times.

Building on Singapore's green legacy as the Garden City by the Bay, three world-class waterfront gardens have been planned for Marina Bay. The first of the three, Bay South Gardens, includes a conservatory complex with cool-moist and cool-dry biomes and man-made "supertrees," whose concrete trunks and metal branches support vertical greenery and provide shade from a 50-meter height no natural "tree" could achieve. Pedestrian routes to the gardens would be provided, including a wide, landscaped deck connected to the resort and an underground walkway to the new rail-transit station.

The URA also worked with the National Parks Board to develop the landscape master plan for the area. Roads and public open spaces were to have unique tree and shrub plantings, providing a wide variety of forms, colors, and fragrances. The integrated resort's landscape design and selection of plant species also were closely coordinated to reinforce the character of the district. Any development within Marina Bay, including the integrated resort, is required to provide greenery at least equivalent in area to the built footprint. Such spaces may take the form of sky terraces, vertical greenery, viewing decks, or rooftop gardens and must be well integrated into the overall architectural treatment. Besides enhancing Singapore's civic image, such initiatives help combat the "urban heat island" effect within the city and lower temperatures in the tropical climate.

The Winning Proposal

The URA received several development proposals and assessed them based on two broad criteria: the first covered the attractiveness of the business and tourism concepts. The second considered the architectural design and whether it contributed positively to the signature skyline of Marina Bay and the city as a whole.

The proposal put forth by the Las Vegas Sands Corporation best met Singapore's economic, tourism, and planning objectives. The Sands consultant team comprised Safdie Architects, Aedas Pte Ltd, PWP Landscape Architecture, Arup, EC Harris, and Master Chong. Their vision offered the potential of boosting Singapore's attractiveness as a premium destination for business and leisure visitors. It was also impressive in terms of overall design, planning, and layout. The Sands scheme successfully accommodated the vast space needed for retail, convention facilities, theater venues, and a casino by placing these amenities underground, resulting in a low-rise development along the waterfront. The three high-rise hotel towers were deliberately set back from the water, enabling panoramic views of the entire bay and city skyline. The sculptural, wavelike roof structure of the low-rise components, the iconic form of the ArtScience Museum, the hotel towers, and the SkyPark, with its dramatic cantilever, all combine to create a powerful silhouette and identity for the Bayfront area. The arrangement of the towers and SkyPark also provides a "gateway" view to the city.

The entire development adopted axial concepts along key pedestrian corridors, providing clear orientation and ease of movement throughout the large complex. The required "through-block pedestrian link" gave visitors a direct visual connection with the city across Marina Bay. The architect also responded to the need for an event space on the waterfront promenade by designing a highly adaptable plaza for large-scale public activities.

Top: Safdie Architects' competition model for Marina Bay Sands

Bottom: URA rendering from 2007 of the future Marina Bay, Gardens by the Bay, and Central Business District

Bringing the Plans to Life

Once Singapore awarded the project to the Sands team, the URA and its Design Advisory Panel carefully guided the development. To ensure continuity, the panel included some members who had been involved in the initial evaluation of the architectural concept and design. The process involved regular, detailed discussions with the architect about modifications to enhance the attractiveness of the proposal; the panel also provided feedback on the detailing of particular design features, the selection of materials and finishes, and landscape concepts.

Close cooperation between the Sands team and government agencies was necessary because other infrastructure projects were under way in the area, including the Common Services Tunnels, the Downtown Line Stage 1 rail transit, the waterfront promenade, the Helix and Bayfront bridges, as well as the interface with the Bay South Gardens. The URA facilitated the construction work by opening up the adjacent areas for supporting work sites.

A project of such massive scale required dedication and commitment from the Marina Bay Sands management and design teams and the Singaporean government. This unique public-private partnership was instrumental in guiding and facilitating the integrated resort development from its inception, through its design and construction phases to its ultimate—and very successful—completion.

View of Marina Bay site, 2004

THE MAKING OF MARINA BAY SANDS

SHELDON ADELSON IN CONVERSATION WITH MARTIN C. PEDERSEN

Being an entrepreneur is not for the faint of heart. Big visions, invariably, require big risks. Sheldon Adelson, the chairman and chief executive officer of the Las Vegas Sands Corporation, is more than comfortable with that equation: he breathes it like oxygen. In six and a half decades, he has by his own count started more than fifty businesses. He parlayed a relatively small investment in a computer magazine into a highly profitable—and prescient—business running computer trade shows. This venture became the financial building block for what is now the world's biggest resort empire, and Adelson today is one of the world's most prominent philanthropists. His multibillion-dollar net worth tends to fluctuate, depending on the stock performance of his company and the risk-to-reward ratio of his latest project (and he's always hatching a new one).

When I interviewed Adelson about Marina Bay Sands, I learned something about the character of successful entrepreneurs. They don't process fear the way we mere mortals do. Failure does not exist. Obstacles are temporary. Indeed, he seemed to enjoy talking about the project's difficult birth—calling it at one point "death by a thousand cuts"—perhaps because Marina Bay Sands is, in the end, a financial, architectural, and civic triumph. How it came to be is a fascinating and fearless story.

Let's start by talking about the beginning of the project. How did your company get involved?
We're always on the lookout for new opportunities. The government of Singapore put out a request for companies that were interested in participating in their tender. We call this phase of the process a "beauty contest." It's not an auction for money. We were one of the leading candidates, not just because of my good looks and charm but also because of our experience in the convention market. They conducted a tender for the location at Marina Bay. Nineteen companies participated in that, and we were one of them. We subsequently found out from them that they wanted us to win the tender because of our convention experience. I think 30 or 40 percent of their decision was based on the developer's business strategy. For us, that was simple. We were incomparable on the convention side. But a significant part of the decision was based on the architecture.

Miriam and Sheldon Adelson

Details of The Venetian resort-hotel-casino and its sister property, The Palazzo, in Las Vegas

How did you select Moshe Safdie?
At the time, Brad Stone ran our construction and development division, and he had appointed a firm that had worked for us in Las Vegas. They also did work for us in Macau. But they really weren't known as creative architects. And early on, I didn't think the work they were doing was good enough. So when it came time to select another firm, there was one architect—Moshe Safdie—for whom I had the greatest admiration.

Why?
Because he created the Children's Memorial at Yad Vashem, the most effective structure to communicate a message of any I'd ever experienced. Most people who walk through can't leave with dry eyes. The first time I went to Yad Vashem, I thought, "If I ever need an architect to do something unique, I'm going to call Safdie."

That's interesting. I interviewed Moshe and at the end, I asked him, "Is there anything you want me to ask Mr. Adelson?" He said, "I'd like you to ask him why he hired me." It's certainly a huge conceptual leap from Yad Vashem to the Marina Bay Sands. How did you make that leap?
He had done a number of great projects—Habitat in Montreal, Yad Vashem, the National Gallery of Canada. But here's the thing: there is nobody else with experience creating integrated resorts. We're the only integrated resort builders in the world. So when we do one, we can't compile a list of ten architectural firms and select one, because there aren't any. We have to teach firms what integrated resorts are about. We have to give them the programming, the adjacencies, the circulation. We have to, essentially, design it ourselves. The only thing that we can't do is to create a beautiful building. I have a building here in Las Vegas designed by Gensler. It's magnificent, but it's nothing like the Marina Bay Sands. People call that the Eighth Wonder of the World.

It's on postcards already, an icon. Was that the initial brief you gave Safdie?
I said, "Moshe, I don't know how iconic you can make the hotel, but why don't you make an iconic museum?" What the Singaporean government wanted, as part of the architectural charge, was to build an iconic structure that people would look at and immediately think *Singapore*. They used the Sydney Opera House as an example. I told Moshe, "That's what they want."

And yet it's the SkyPark that's become a new symbol for Singapore. At what point did it come into play as a design element?
After we came up with the scheme, I said to Moshe, "Look, there's something you missed—a swimming pool." We could have put it between the hotel and the low-rise podium (the theater, casino, and convention center) but we needed a road here. I think Moshe created the SkyPark because neither he nor I understood that there wasn't enough room at the top of a single building to put in a big enough pool. So he created a platform to place the pool on, and then took the SkyPark idea from there.

Talk about the challenge of building a project of this scale in, what was it, three years?
One word: whew! It was not easy. First of all, we ran into a number of obstacles. The government owns the land in Singapore. And for whatever reason, it decided to put up more parcels of land for public bid than any other year in its history.

How did that affect you?
It absorbed all of the available contracting. When we put out requests to construct different parts of the resort, we couldn't get any local bidders to do the towers. A Korean company did them. We also had a shortage of materials and labor. That increased the cost. It had nothing to do with the architecture. Then, another problem popped up. All the sand to make the concrete was supposed to come from Indonesia. But Indonesia got into a dispute with the Singaporean government and put an embargo on sand. And it's still in effect today. They haven't resolved it, as far as I know.

So what did you do?
We had to bring in barges from China or Myanmar. I think the sand came from the Indochinese peninsula. It came from somewhere other than Indonesia. Then, we had a third problem. We were not allowed on the land to test it. They had given us some information. They gave us borings, which didn't show any problems. But the borings only accounted for the perimeter of the parcel. They did two or three on the edges, and the borings didn't reveal the extent of the problem. And there were two major problems with the land. It turned out that the borings failed to reveal seawalls that had been placed there by the British before World War II. The whole area is reclaimed land. They put all of that land on top of seawalls. So we had to pull out the seawalls, which were made up of incredibly large, room-size boulders. We dug holes to take the boulders

out. And what happened? The fill was like jelly. We had to build enormous circular concrete walls—125 meters across and 2 meters thick. We lost about six months in the process.

Just to do the footings?
Oh, no, no, just to clear the land so we could take out the seawalls and build the big circles to create retaining walls.

Did the low-rise convention center, theater, and casino need the same thing?
Yes. We couldn't put in footings on seawalls, because eventually the pressure would break them down. We had to get it off that rock. And in taking out the seawalls, we ran into marine clay, a sort of gelatinous material, that kept on sliding in. Once we cleared the land and put in the retaining walls, the buildings began to go up. Then, in late 2008—pretty much in mid-construction—the world financial meltdown occurred.

How did you deal with that?
It was troubling, but we had already put the money aside for that.

The National Geographic documentary made it seem as if the meltdown imperiled completion of the project. Was that an exaggeration?
We didn't have enough money in late 2008, and I personally infused almost 500 million dollars into the company. It was actually 475 million. A few months later, I put in another 525 million. The project was not stopped or slowed down, because we had a lot of the money already committed. We put most of our equity in before the banks; that's the way it's normally done. But there were a lot of unforeseen events—the seawall, the clay, the sand embargo—that increased the budget.

How much did the design change once construction got under way?
There were constant changes. One of the towers became a four-star facility, which meant that certain areas took up more room than expected. But the building department in Singapore refused to change our floor allowances, because they were concerned that our competitors who lost the bid would complain: "OK, you established certain criteria from the outset. I met the criteria. They met the criteria. Now, after you give them the concession, you're changing all the rules?" So they refused to change one square meter of our allowances.

Is that unusual?
Very unusual. All we had previously submitted were general plans. And we were held to them. No other property owner that I'm aware of would say, "The plans you submitted five years ago—which were not detailed—you can't change them by a fraction of 1 percent." Everybody gives you 5 or 10 percent leeway. But there was no leeway here. Obviously, it was a pain the butt. But in a way, it was good. When you deal with the Singaporean government, what you see is what you get. There is no corruption whatsoever. No one changes their mind. No one presses their own agenda. The government's view is supreme. In development, you can't have anything more valuable than certainty.

Moshe talks about how quickly this project got built, even with the obstacles. He called your construction team the best he'd ever seen.
We have an excellent team, and it was built by osmosis. Matthew Pryor had a lot of experience with high-rise construction in Hong Kong. He helped us build the Sands and the Venetian in Macau. When we started work in Singapore, John Downs was in charge of construction, but he worked through Matthew. Both of them are extremely talented and unflappable.

Matthew has an encyclopedic knowledge. He seems to know every detail of this very big project.
Yes, but the problem was, although he made every effort to contain costs, we went two and a half billion dollars over budget. It was death by a thousand cuts—an accumulation of all of the problems and changes.

Through all these struggles, did you ever experience any doubts?
Never. I never experience doubts. We must finish the project, at whatever cost. It's not very encouraging to work your tush off and then find out that it will cost an extra half-billion dollars. It's not fun. Now, I know a billion dollars doesn't buy what it used to…

It still buys plenty.
It still buys a lot. And that was a big blow. But I always knew in the back of my mind that if push came to shove, I had several billion dollars in cash and was prepared to use it.

And during this process, weren't you anxious, worried?
No. Never.

You are just wired differently. I would have been a wreck.
A lot of people are wired differently, but I'm a risk taker in life. We ran into obstacles on this project, but, as it turns out, instead of earning

The Adelsons preside over opening festivities at Marina Bay Sands

the money back in five years, it looks like we could earn it back in three and a half years. I've been in business for sixty-six years. I've learned certain things that are irrefutable. Unless you design something that's against the law of physics, there is no project in the world that can't be completed.

And when does a challenging project like this one become real?
When I put the first shovel in the ground. Once you plan it, there is nothing stopping it from being built. The shortage of materials, labor—it's all solved with money. There's no reason that something can't get built. There is always a way to solve a problem.

How often did you visit the site during construction?
Every couple of months.

Did you have a routine? Did you start at the top of the buildings and work your way down?
No, I met with people in our temporary offices and we went over plans. An entrepreneur cannot tell a lot by looking at a construction site. Construction is a prescheduled performance similar to, say, a Broadway play. Every day the people get on stage, they put on their costumes, they execute their parts—they sing, they dance, they talk. They start off at six or seven in the morning and work all day. We had three shifts a day, working twenty-four hours. What am I going to tell a guy pouring concrete? I looked at the plans. They told me where we were in the process.

And when it's finally done, what does that feel like?
It's a tremendous feeling, because it's a physical manifestation of the accomplishment.

Are there any new projects on the horizons?
Hopefully, we go to Japan, Korea, Taiwan, Vietnam, and Thailand. Everybody is calling for integrated resorts. We're the integrated resort company. We're leading the pack in terms of emerging markets. Steve Wynn does a good job designing his buildings, but nothing can compare with the Marina Bay Sands. He can't say, "I'll build you a more beautiful building." I can't even say that.

And is the Singaporean government happy with the building?
Thrilled. Well beyond their expectations.

One final question: Would you work with Moshe again?
Absolutely.

He said the same thing.
But I'm going have a cat-o'-nine-tails with me, because when he proposes things that I know are going to cost twice as much to build, I'm going crack down on him.

Don't worry, Mr. Adelson. Moshe wouldn't want to do the same thing again anyway.
I'd love to do the same thing, but I can't. Number one: I don't want to spend the six billion dollars. And number two: I can't reproduce that building. It's become the most important reference point in the world. I couldn't build one in another city. It would be immoral. This building belongs to the people of Singapore. It's part of their skyline.

RETHINKING THE PUBLIC REALM

MOSHE SAFDIE

The realization of the Marina Bay Sands integrated resort depended on the convergence of five unique circumstances. First, there was the city-state of Singapore, which had launched an ambitious program to encourage tourism. Toward that end, it created new landfill and a large enclosed bay, converted the sea into a freshwater reservoir, and issued an international call for proposals from the world's most able, experienced architects and developers, seeking designs to help bring Singapore's dream to realization.

Second, Singapore had evolved in its forty-five-year history into an extraordinary public planning authority; its staff of high-quality professionals set out to define the greater public purpose and urban design guidelines, not just for the integrated resort but for the entire Marina Bay and downtown. These guidelines were clearly articulated in the documents presented to the competing developers and architects. Moreover, positioning to optimize program and design, the government set a fixed price for the land so that the selection criteria could be solely qualitative.

A third element was the presence of a developer and operator, in the form of the Las Vegas Sands Corporation, with the proven capacity and experience for integrated resort megaconstruction projects, both in Las Vegas and Macau. The Sands group assembled an extraordinary construction management team, one with the track record to tackle a project of this unprecedented scale. Moreover, Sands chairman Sheldon Adelson had pioneered the use of convention centers as a fundamental ingredient of the Las Vegas experience, broadening the program of integrated resort activities. Las Vegas Sands came to the table with the vision and capability to realize the multifaceted aspects of Singapore's ambitious agenda.

Fourth was the booming world economy of 2005, the culmination of consecutive bull markets, continuously rising real estate prices, thriving retail business worldwide, and the general sense that the "sky was the limit." Whereas this situation had dramatically changed by 2007, the bidding and the decisions for Marina Bay Sands were made in the context of this sunny economy.

The final component was an architect in the prime of his career—with extensive experience creating iconic buildings as well as carrying out major urban design assignments—and one intimately familiar with Singapore: my professional trajectory seemed to have specifically prepared me for this unusual assignment. The absence of any one of these ingredients would probably have given the project a different path and character. It was the unusual combination of people and events that resulted in a project that seemed almost too good to be true.

Moshe Safdie's concept sketches for Marina Bay Sands

Marina Singapore

Top: Aerial view of Yad Vashem Holocaust History Museum, Jerusalem, 2005

Right: Northern view of the Jerusalem pine forest and hills from the end of the Yad Vashem "prism," 2005

Day one: it was March 15, 2005—the ides—at the end of a long day of official opening ceremonies for the Yad Vashem Holocaust History Museum, in Jerusalem. Two of the major players in what would become Marina Bay Sands were there—Sheldon Adelson in his capacity as one of the prime benefactors of Yad Vashem, I as the architect of the new history museum. As it would later unfold, this fateful meeting had even earlier origins. In 1976, Yad Vashem asked me to design a museum dedicated to exhibiting objects and material connected with the 1.5 million children who perished in the Holocaust. After a six-month struggle, I came to the conclusion that a museum presenting information about the children, which would follow in sequence a general historic museum, would saturate the visitor. I proposed an alternative concept: an abstract memorial in which a single candle was reflected into infinity, transformed by optical devices into millions of floating flames in an underground chamber. This would be a place of contemplation and reflection.

The Yad Vashem board rejected the design, fearing people would misunderstand such abstractions. "They might liken it to a discotheque," it was said. But in 1986, the memorial was realized after Abe Spiegel, who lost his two-year-old son in Auschwitz and was moved by the rejected model, provided funds for its construction. As I was to learn much later, Adelson visited the Children's Memorial and was deeply affected; he considered it to be one of the most moving architectural experiences he had ever had. It was this, and the history museum we designed that opened in 2005, that led Adelson to approach me that day at Yad Vashem. "We are working on a major project in Singapore, an integrated resort. I am looking for an architect. Would you be interested?" And, of course, I was. A few weeks later, responding to a phone call from Jim Beyer, Adelson's in-house chief architect, I arrived in Las Vegas. I did not bring a formal presentation, just some brochures of different projects. I realized that, with the exception of Adelson and Beyer, the others present were not familiar with my work; I also learned that a design by a Las Vegas–based architect had already been prepared and submitted to the government of Singapore. It was very much in the spirit of Vegas: a themed facility with a single large tower in the center, somewhat introverted in character. As I discovered later,

Left: Ardmore Habitat Condominiums, Singapore, 1985

Right: Model of Tampines prototype housing development, 1982

Upper: Site model of Tampines, 1982

Lower left and right: Cairnhill Road Condominiums, 2003

it was with the encouragement of Singapore's Urban Redevelopment Authority (URA) that Adelson began seeking a replacement architect. The government explained it was not looking to imitate Las Vegas; rather, it wanted a contemporary, bold design representing the spirit of Singapore.

Unknown to Adelson and his team when we met in Nevada was that I had a thirty-year history of working and interacting in Singapore. In 1978, a major Singaporean-Indonesian shipbuilder, Robin Loh, approached me about developing applications of my Habitat concept for Southeast Asia. The idea was to create prefabricated housing for Singapore and elsewhere in the region utilizing the 3-D module technology I developed for Montreal's Habitat '67. Loh hoped to use his shipyard's surplus capacity to fabricate three-dimensional shipping modules for different locations and conditions. We developed prototypes intended for a large site near Singapore's new Changi Airport. We also developed designs for a downtown project, known as Ardmore, at the head of Orchard Road. The project near the airport was not constructed, but Ardmore Habitat, a two-tower complex, was completed in 1985. Ironically, Loh had also commissioned us to design an integrated resort for Gold Coast, Australia, where he had major land holdings. A program rather similar to that of Marina Bay Sands, incorporating an arena, convention center, grand casino, several hotels, and public gardens, was conceived as part of a large new town to be called Robina (for Robin Loh). The scheme was well received, but the political mood in Australia at the time did not favor granting a casino-operating license to a Chinese-Singaporean, and the project faltered.

There was more involvement in Singapore in the 1990s. We constructed another residential complex, the Cairnhill Road Condominiums and, at the invitation of the Singapore Housing and Development Board, developed plans for a model town at Simpang. In sum, I had worked with Singapore's private and public sectors; I was intimately acquainted with the URA and its urban design objectives, and, of course, fully familiar with the tropical city-state's culture and physical context. I say all this because, while it was not a requirement for being selected for the project, my experience nevertheless proved extremely helpful in developing a design that, as it turned out, had to be produced in an impossibly short period of time.

The call for proposals for the Marina Bay integrated resort came approximately one year before the final deadline. Based on interim submissions, Singapore narrowed a field of ten competing developers to a short list of four. It was then that Adelson was told he could seek another architect. By the time I met Adelson in Las Vegas, we had four months to develop a detailed concept design to a schematic level; carry out

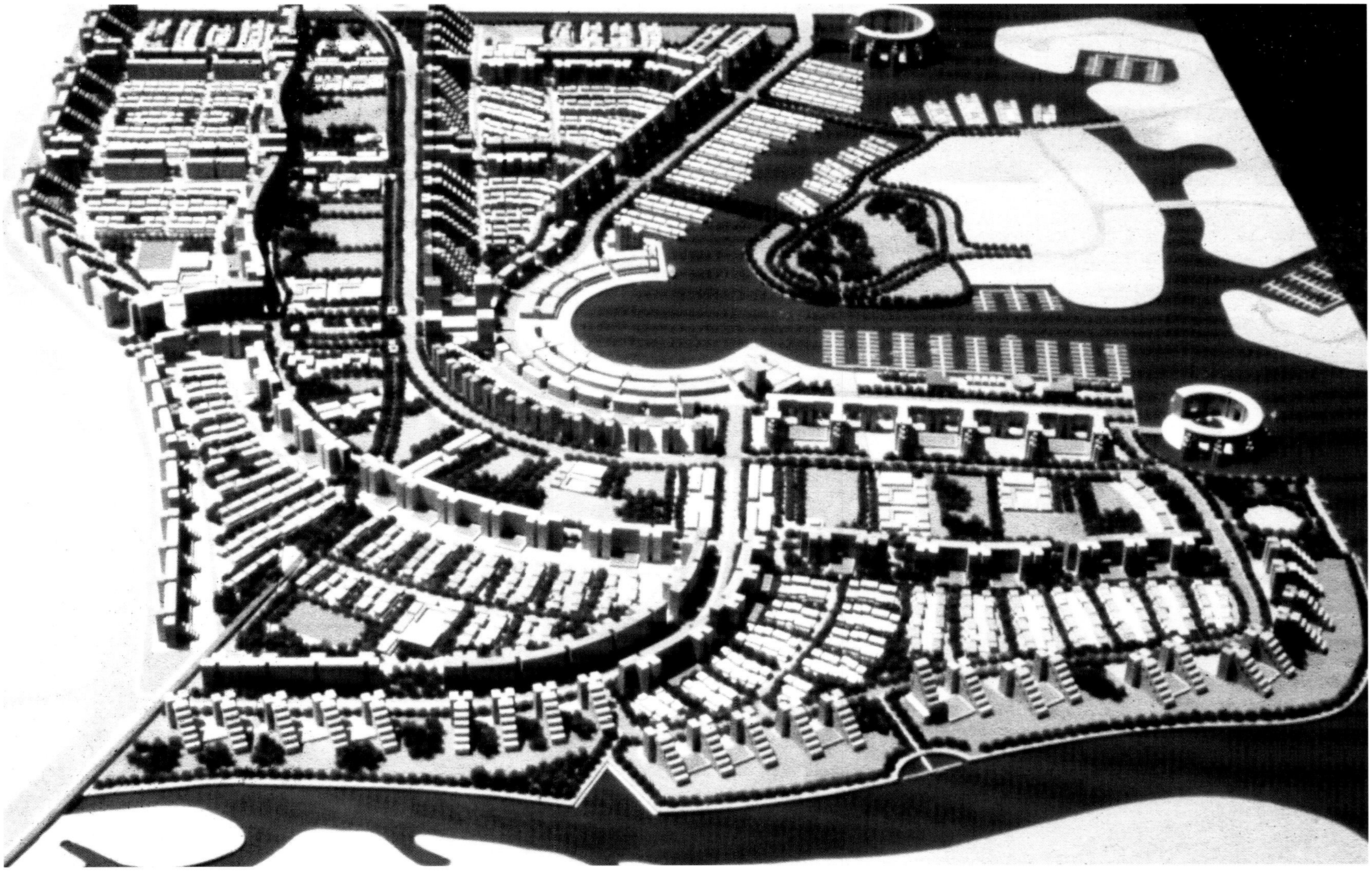

Top row: National Gallery of Canada, Ottawa, Ontario, 1988

Middle row: Ben Gurion International Airport, Tel Aviv, 2004

Bottom row: Columbus Circle, New York City, 1987

basic engineering to enable the confirmation of feasibility and pricing; and present these plans elaborately, with renderings, films, and models accompanied by a four-volume printed report. It would normally take four months just to produce the presentation material, let alone develop a concept.

During that preparation period, we were to have two workshop sessions with the URA's chairman, staff, and Design Advisory Panel, presenting our work in progress and getting feedback. I explained to Adelson that to meet the submission deadline—and, if awarded the contract, to tackle the enormous undertaking of building the resort—I would need to mobilize a substantial portion of my sixty-person staff in Boston, as well as delay or postpone many other activities. The resources required would be substantial. This was well understood, and the client gave us full design freedom to partner with a team of world-class consultants.

It would be naive to think that design happens in a vacuum, through the exploration of issues from scratch. Architects clearly draw on their personal sensibility and past experience. In the case of Marina Bay Sands, our firm's project history contributed greatly to our ability to conceive a concept for it. Clearly, if you're hired to design an airport and have done two or three others, you bring along knowledge of the building type. The same goes for a museum, library, or courthouse. Yet, I often tell clients that it is not important to select an architect on the basis of his having designed the building type before. Our first museum, the National Gallery of Canada, in Ottawa (1988), and our first airport, Tel Aviv's Ben Gurion International (2004), benefited from the fact that we started with design principles: we researched the building type inside out and were able to see things freshly because we examined them critically. But such research takes time, and the construction of Marina Bay Sands had a tight schedule. We had three years—a timetable set by Singapore, in line with its renowned efficiency, and by the Sands Corporation, a famously profitable enterprise eager to showcase this new addition to its luxury franchise. With the clock ticking from the moment we were awarded the contract, we dug deep into our experience, drawing on past designs but also innovating and reinventing at an unusually fast and exhilarating pace.

Mixed-Use

Perhaps the most complex aspect of Marina Bay Sands is that it is a mixed-use project. It calls for the juxtaposition of many different functions—a large-span convention center, high-rise hotel towers, a linear retail mall, and a stand-alone iconic museum, all served by an infrastructure of parking, truck docks and routes, and other services. Mixed-use is most difficult and complicated when it involves a high-density, high-rise, megascale development. Vertical elevator cores must be stacked and entrances and security zones differentiated. Common infrastructure must facilitate every component. We tackled such a mixed-use structure at Columbus Center in New York, in the mid-1980s. Working with Boston Properties, we accommodated more than 275,000 square meters in gross floor area (about half the size of Marina Bay), including Salomon Brothers' headquarters, offices, and trading floors, an Intercontinental Hotel, luxury apartment towers, a cinema complex, and a major shopping galleria. The seventy-four-story structure incorporated two towers over a common base of shopping and other public areas. At Columbus Center, we learned about articulating the different flows of users, giving identity to individual components while rendering them complementary to each other. Similar but smaller-scale projects followed.

I have come to believe that mixed-use is the future of dense, urban development. It is easier to meet environmental requirements and amenities when one juxtaposes a variety of uses, as opposed to constructing single, mono-use buildings, be they giant office developments or thousand-room hotels.

Humanizing the Megascale

One of my obsessions—or, say, commitments—over the decades of my practice has been the need to humanize the megascale. The Marina Bay Sands integrated resort was a megascale project par excellence. If any project ever was worthy of this adjective, this was it. As we set out to strategize the disposition of and relationship between the parts of the design, it was important to recall what measures were available to us. First and foremost was the need to make a large-scale project legible, self-orienting, clear: in other words, to give people the capacity to know where they are and understand the parts so they can easily move about, use, and inhabit the project.

Top row: Aerial view and terraced gardens, Habitat '67, Montreal, Quebec, 1967

Bottom row: Aerial view of rooftop garden, Salt Lake City Main Public Library, 2003

Yet megascale projects can often wind up being giant piles of buildings, denying daylight and views to many inside. The art of humanizing the megascale lies in the ability to evolve an arrangement of parts that maximizes penetration of daylight, contact with nature, and openness to views and, at the same time, avoids a sense of crowding to make people feel more comfortable and less overwhelmed.

I've come to generalize this effort as "seeking the sense of garden," a notion we first embraced at Habitat '67. Though stacked vertically on top of each other, each house—in other words, each family—possessed its own roof garden. Each would be served by an elevated walkway, forming a network of streets that stretched from the ground into the air. Each had the qualities of a stand-alone dwelling, open in several directions to light and the outdoors. We also employed aboveground gardens at Columbus Center, in our public libraries, and in many residential and office projects. The permeation of plant life and the connections between indoor and outdoor spaces have been underlying themes in all our projects, no matter the density or locale.

Belonging to Place

Finally, we had a deep conviction that buildings generally and major urban complexes specifically should be designed to resonate with their physical and cultural settings. The Marina Bay Sands integrated resort was to be built in a place without seasons, consistently hot during the day and sometimes cool in the evening, a place battered by torrential rains and unforgiving sunlight. Singapore's historical architecture, with its pitched, overhanging roofs, shuttered porches, and screens for cross-ventilation, is the legacy of European colonists struggling to survive in the pre–air-conditioned tropics.

The design for Marina Bay would need to incorporate particular qualities of traditional tropical architecture such as generous shade and overhangs. It would have to open up to the outdoors, allowing people to migrate from air-conditioned comfort during the day to cool waterfront breezes at night. At the same time, the design would have to aim for a high level of sustainability, recognizing the extraordinary amount of energy it takes to run air-conditioning. The goal would be to minimize the absorption of heat, provide protection from the sun, and infuse the architecture generously with plant life.

Tabula Rasa: The Site

There was literally nothing on the site but grass. The seawall created by Singapore's reclamation project was visible, and the land was completely flat. The call for proposals came with URA guidelines that would have great impact on the design. To summarize: there needed to be a landscaped promenade at least 25 meters wide, stretching along the entire waterfront and connecting with other promenades around the bay to form a unified whole. The government would build what would be called the DNA Bridge to link the Marina Bay segment of the promenade to the Marina area and around to downtown, forming a loop. A cultural building, its specific purpose yet to be defined, was to stand on the promontory on the northwest corner of the site, facing the city; this structure was to be a symbolic and "iconic" representation of Singapore. Two view corridors cutting back from Bay Boulevard, 30 and 15 meters wide, respectively, would link the subway to the waterfront. There would be a large, waterfront event piazza no smaller than 5,000 square meters. Finally, there would be two connections between the resort and the planned Gardens by the Bay to the east, one an elevated walkway spanning Bay Boulevard and Shears Avenue, the other a tunnel from what would be a new mass-transit rail station. There were many other finer details to be met, but these guidelines played a major role in generating the urban design scheme.

Working on a project of this complexity, we always begin by making a large site model at a scale ratio between 1:500 and 1:100, so that the volumes for the proposed program are substantial. For Marina Bay Sands, we first cut large blocks of foam plastic to represent the hotel, the convention center, and the casino; when we build a model, we often cut its components into smaller pieces so we can cluster and move them around as we try to understand the optimal massing and disposition of parts. This is frequently accompanied by the parallel processes of 3-D computer modeling and working with smaller models made from clay, wood, and any other malleable material around.

But while we were given a detailed program, it soon changed. First, we were told to propose a single hotel with 1,000 rooms. Within two weeks, this became 3,000 rooms. The component parts featured a convention center, shopping center, museum, casino, and two theaters. Additional requirements included some 4,000 parking spaces, several trucking docks, and an extensive infrastructure network with a district cooling plant and distribution

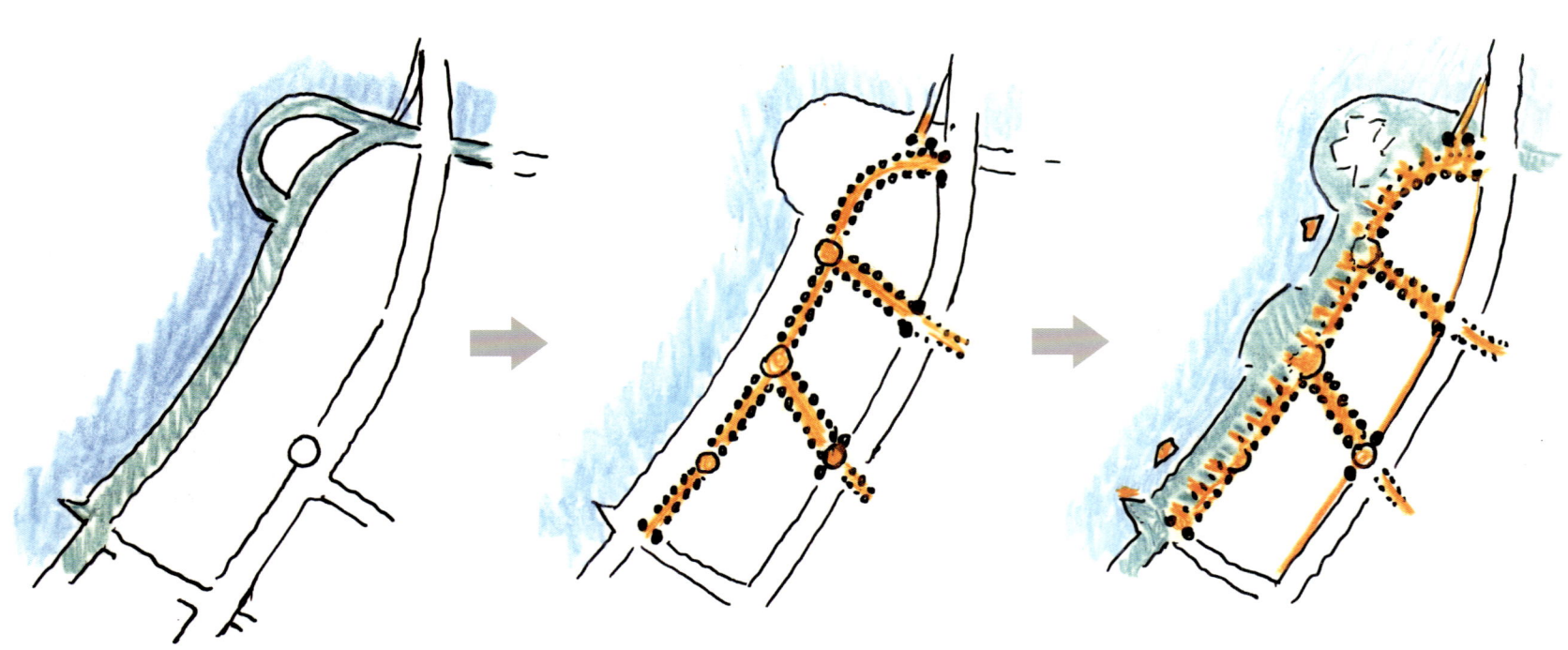

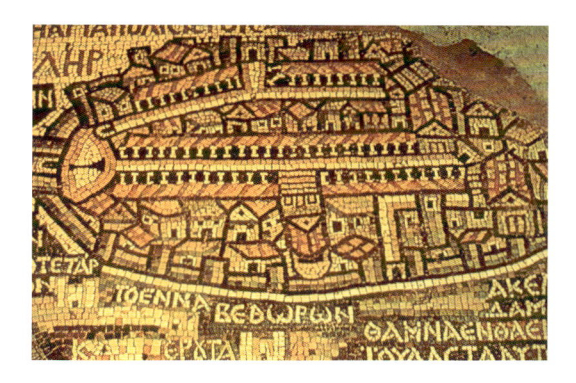

Madaba Mosaic Map of Byzantine Jerusalem, sixth century AD

Upper left: Marina Bay site with Central Business District beyond, 2006

Bottom: Urban diagram showing key axes of Marina Bay Sands

tunnels. We would need to excavate, and, with the site being landfill on the bay, the water table was practically at the surface.

A Town, Not a Building

As we reviewed the program of 581,400 gross square meters, the 15.4-hectare site, and the multiple uses to be accommodated, it dawned on us that we were actually designing a small town. This was perhaps one of the most important insights of the entire process. The problems of designing a town are fundamentally different to those of designing a large building. A town plan designates the locations of various uses and activities. It defines a network of movement and infrastructure for services, pedestrians, and vehicles. It often defines masses and densities. Yet the disposition of different functions is not the prime objective. Instead, one looks for a sense of hierarchy, the strategic placement of uses, to give a town its sense of orientation and location.

Philadelphia is a good modern-day example of a gridded town that seeks to achieve a hierarchy by creating a primary axis on the diagonal, differentiating it in scale and character from the rest of the grid. But the Greeks and Romans were the real masters of giving clarity through hierarchy to their relatively small cities. The typical Roman city, as exemplified by the plan for Roman Jerusalem, was defined by its walls, its gates, and the *Cardo Maximus* and *Decumanus*—the crisscrossing roads that formed the spines of urban activity. The famous Madaba Mosaic Map of Byzantine Jerusalem shows a *Cardo Maximus* extending north from today's Damascus Gate to Zion Gate; a double colonnade of shops, primary public buildings, churches, and palaces were all attached to this core artery. The *Decumanus*, running east to west, crossed the *Cardo* at midpoint. In such a plan, the most significant activities are always on the main path, which is distinguished by its scale. There is never any question of where you are. Beyond the *Cardo* are more intricate casbahlike alleys and paths leading to individual houses, domestic and altogether different from the monumental boulevard.

It was this kind of plan, with its clear hierarchy of spinelike roads, that inspired the design for Marina Bay Sands. But where should such a spine be placed? Traditionally, the *Cardo Maximus* ran through the heart of a development, symmetrically and equally serving the surrounding central areas. Some cities have developed their spines at the edge—Edinburgh is one example—but main streets on a perimeter always suffer from being single-loaded, restricting activity to one side.

As we examined the URA guidelines requiring a major promenade at the water's edge and two view corridors connecting to the subway perpendicular to the promenade, I realized that here was a clue. Why create another spine independent of the promenade? Why not integrate our *Cardo* with the promenade to form a single, grand indoor-outdoor urban space of unprecedented scale, partially air-conditioned, partially open to the sky? The view corridor perpendicular to this spine would connect the site with the view of the bay and the downtown to the mass-transit rail station.

As in Edinburgh, this would be a spine at the edge rather than the center of the development. Not unexpectedly, Adelson's first response was: "That would mean the retail is going to be single-loaded. Single-loaded retail does not work!" But being cognizant of the issue, I had a solution: create a multilevel spine with two levels of double-loaded retail under the proposed promenade and a single-loaded stretch along the promenade itself, complemented by a row of kiosks. The belowground shops on one side could be tucked immediately under the promenade, thus expanding the land available to us for development and reducing the overall density of the project. At the promenade level, the convention center, casino, and theaters would hover overhead, with views down into the Grand Arcade and across to the bay and skyline.

We immediately made a cross-sectional model showing the hustle-bustle of multilevel retail. I flew to Singapore to show Adelson the model, having checked it as baggage, and then the model missed the connection in London. I had to walk into the meeting without it. Drawings pinned to the wall showed only the promenade and spine integrated along the waterfront. "This will not work!" Adelson repeated. I had difficulty explaining the new concept. We were at an impasse, when someone walked in with a box from British Airways. Unpacked, the model showed the cross-section through the mall. It clearly indicated that, by stacking the lowest mall and depressing it two floors under the promenade, we could have our cake and eat it too. We would have a double-loaded mall with three levels of retail, integrated visually into the whole along with the other program components. The top level would be accessible from surrounding streets and the promenade. The middle level would connect to the subway and extend under the road toward the

- louvered canopy
- shading sails
- connection to street
- connection to subway

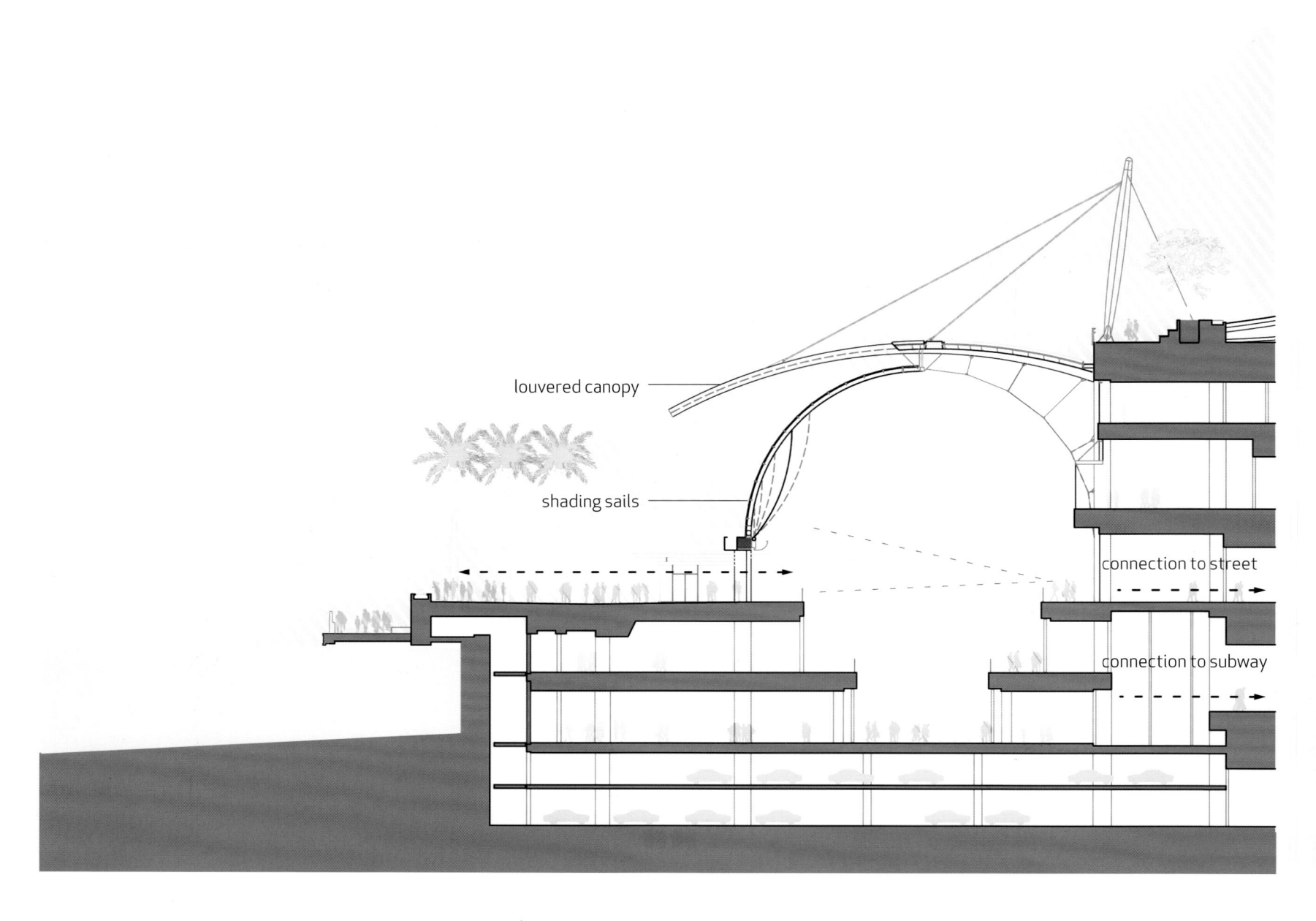

Grand Arcade section showing relationship of waterfront promenade to retail spaces

hotel. The bottom level would connect to the subway as well as the two parking levels underneath it. Thus, all levels were vitalized by different entry points. Adelson's response was instant. As he viewed the model, he fully supported the design.

Curving the Seawall

With the location of the principal spine and its cross-section behind us, we rapidly proceeded to construct a model following the straight alignment of the waterfront, which was impressive in its length but oppressive in its relentlessness. It lacked mystery. We saw immediately that we would have to reshape the bay to make it more dynamic. Otherwise, the promenades—the upper, which the URA required to be at least 25 meters wide, and the lower, by the water—would lack the magic that occurs when a sweeping bend foreshortens perspective. We envisioned a gentle curve, such as one might find in a natural bay, and a Grand Arcade that echoed this shape. With our decision to excavate the lower promenade and accommodate several levels of retail and parking belowground, we had assumed that the existing seawall, constructed by the government as part of its land reclamation, would need to be rebuilt in any event. Realigning the waterfront property line was not likely to have major financial consequences. But it would certainly require the approval of the URA.

Two workshops were scheduled for us to review the progress of our design with the architects on the URA's Design Advisory Panel so we might benefit from their input. In our first meeting, we presented models and drawings of the reshaped waterline. The URA quickly gave its consent: so long as we placed the curve across the straight line of the existing seawall, achieving

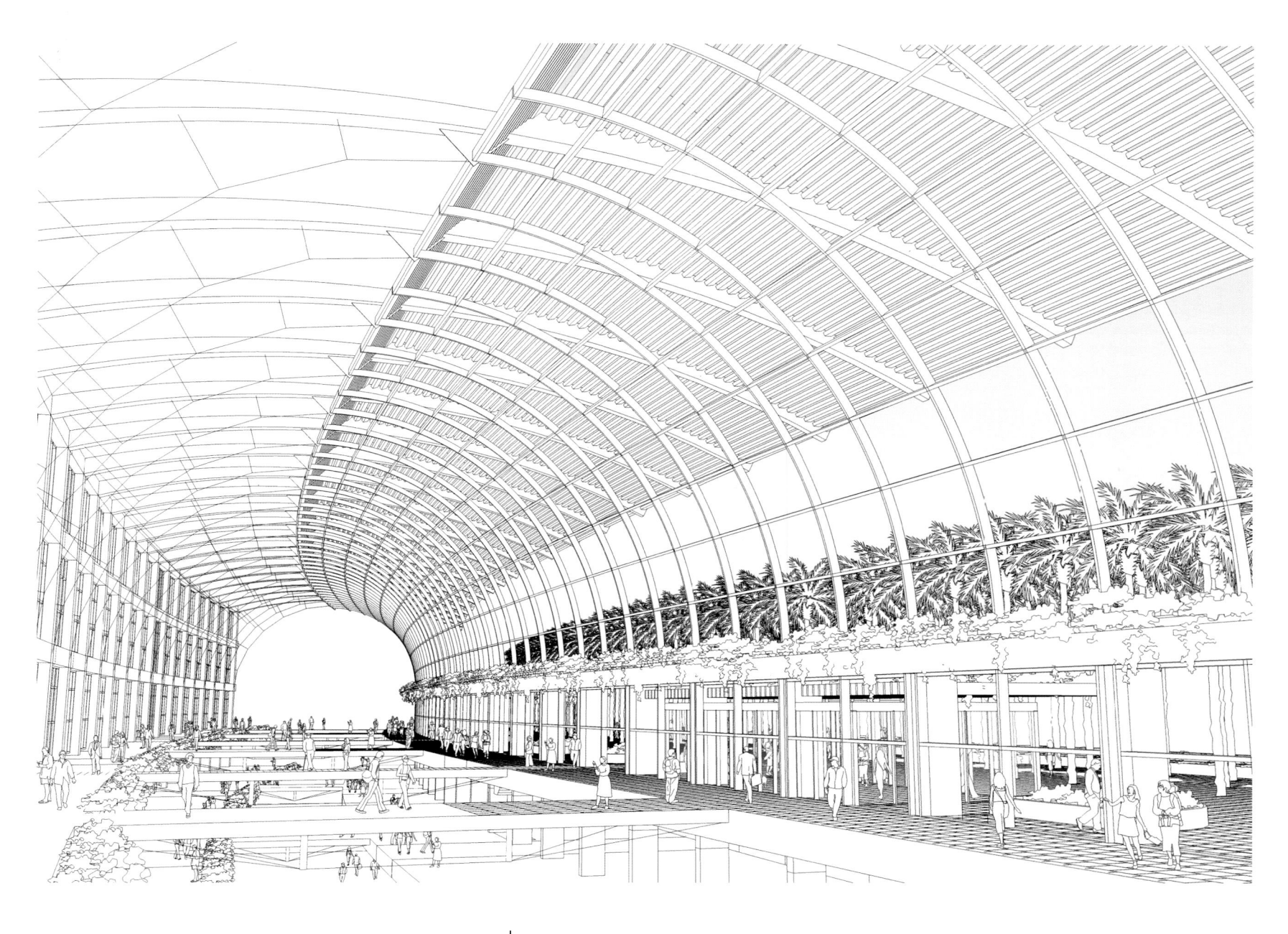

3-D sketch of Grand Arcade retail area

a balance between added and subtracted land, and maintained the volume of water in the bay, we could do it. Delighted, we proceeded to redraw the entire project.

Crystal Islands

As we started reconstructing the model, we wanted to further enliven the waterfront, and, in this spirit, we jokingly placed a couple of glass blocks in the water—floating crystal islands. These could be nightclubs, accessed by tunnels from the lowest retail level, bobbing in the water and offering magnificent views of both downtown and the resort. What could be more exciting? The client team responded enthusiastically. Nightlife was a major component of the project, and everyone embraced the idea of the Crystal Pavilions, as they came to be known, which flank the Event Plaza to the north and south.

But while we had free range to be playful in our conception of these glittering islands, certain aspects of the site, flood levels in particular, curtailed our options. I had initially hoped to open up the middle retail level to the lower promenade, thus providing views to the water and downtown. That conflicted with the absolute need for us to provide a 4-meter-high protection barrier against a potential surge of water. There was no compromising here, because any breach of water would infiltrate the subway system and cause devastation across the island. In the end, we set the flood level as high as the upper promenade and gave up on creating other openings to the bay—with the exception of the well-protected underground tunnels to the Crystal Pavilions.

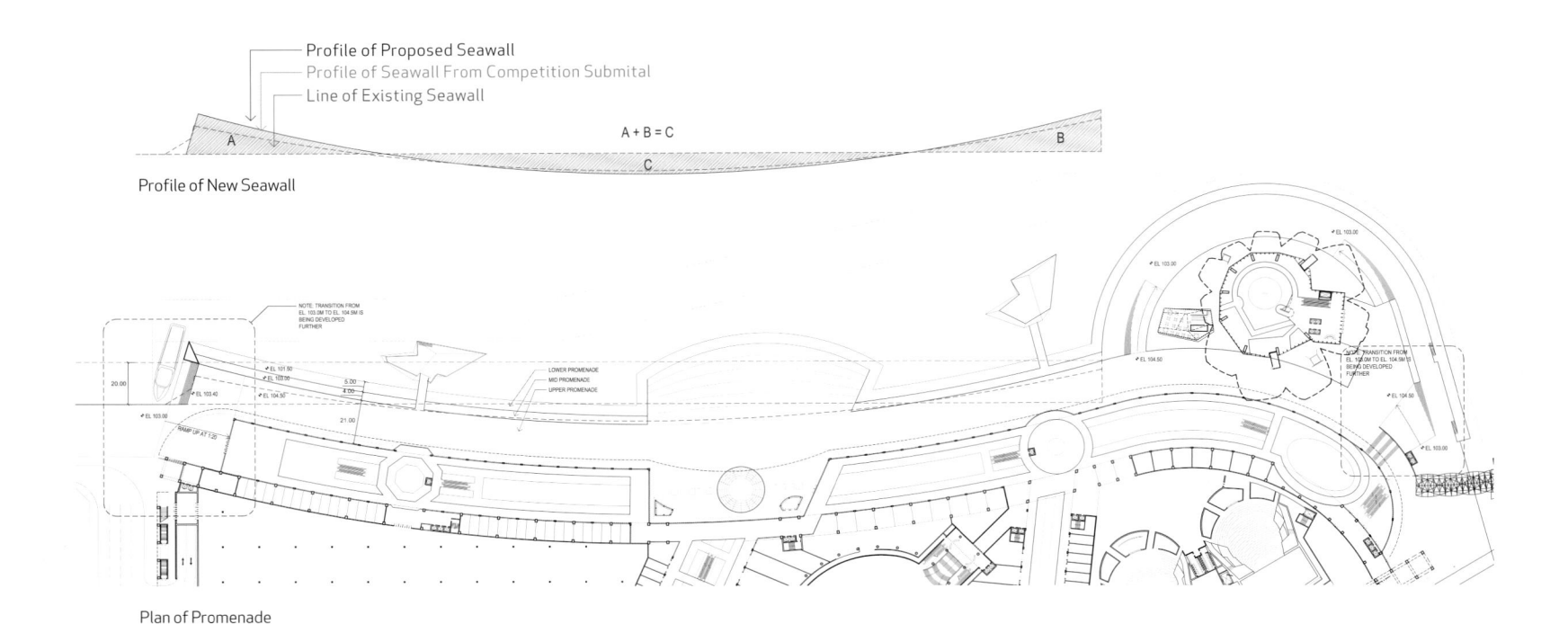

Profile of Proposed Seawall
Profile of Seawall From Competition Submital
Line of Existing Seawall

Profile of New Seawall

Plan of Promenade

Sketch diagram of proposed reshaping of waterfront seawall

One or Three Towers?

The initial Marina Bay Sands program called for a 1,000-room hotel, but the client team quickly revised this to take advantage of the maximum number of rooms the site could accommodate. After the approximately 253,000 square meters required for the convention, retail, casino, and theaters, about 266,000 gross square meters was left for the hotel, roughly translating into 3,000 rooms (about the size of the Sands Corporation's Venetian hotels in Las Vegas and Macau). But 3,000 rooms in a single tower would have resulted in a building stretching north-south across the entire property, forming a massive wall facing east toward the sea. Despite the relatively lower efficiency of breaking up the hotel structure, I proposed that we build three towers of about fifty-five stories each. The two large gaps between the towers would form a welcoming gateway, framing the view of the sea from downtown and vice-versa, from the water and new Gardens by the Bay toward the city. Each double-loaded tower would spread at its base to form a giant atrium at the lower levels, with glazed connections in between. As the parcels varied in width, the size of the atrium would decrease from tower to tower. The hotel's eastern facade, gently sloping outward, would be terraced, with balconies on each room supporting a planter of bougainvillea. The western facade, curving outward at the higher floors, would be glazed to maximize the magnificent view of the bay and Singapore skyline. And there was one further refinement: with each tower made of two slabs of east- and west-facing rooms, we twisted them slightly to create a dancelike relationship between the two parts, expressing the thinness of each slab in a dynamic connection to the whole.

Finally, the SkyPark

In the spirit of building an integrated resort—and in celebration of Singapore's tradition as the Garden City of Asia—we had hoped to develop extensive gardens, with swimming pools and jogging paths appropriate to a facility of this caliber. I had fond memories of my earlier years in Singapore, when I would stay at the Shangri-La at the top of Orchard Road, with its beautiful gardens overlooking town. But by the time we had satisfied the entire development program, there was literally no vacant land left. One possibility was to create gardens on the roof of the casino and convention center, but these vast spaces would lack views, overshadowed and overpowered by the adjacent hotel. With the model in front of us, now articulated into three towers, an idea gradually emerged: the SkyPark. We cut a slab of wood and placed it on top of the towers, cantilevering outward at both ends. The 1-hectare space could support several pools, gardens, and restaurants; it was truly a park in the sky. We were all excited by the potential yet concerned by its possible impracticality. Still, the idea had taken hold, and in the days to come we verified, step-by-step, its feasibility.

Safdie sketchbook with early SkyPark concept

The URA and MBS design teams held several workshops between 2005 and 2011.

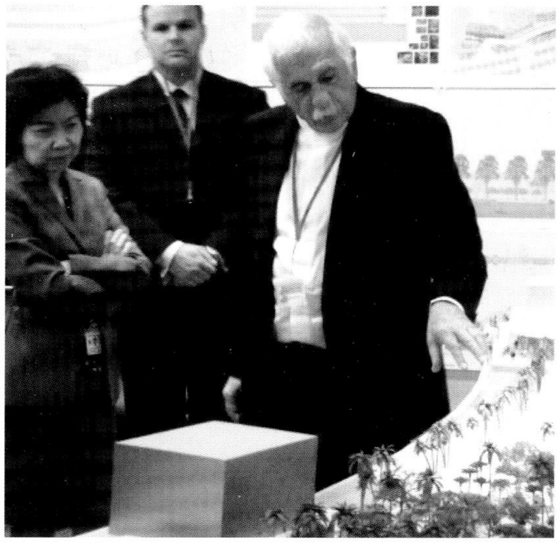
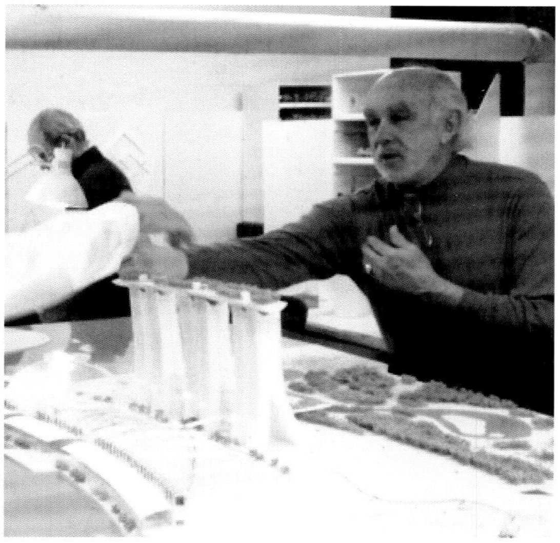
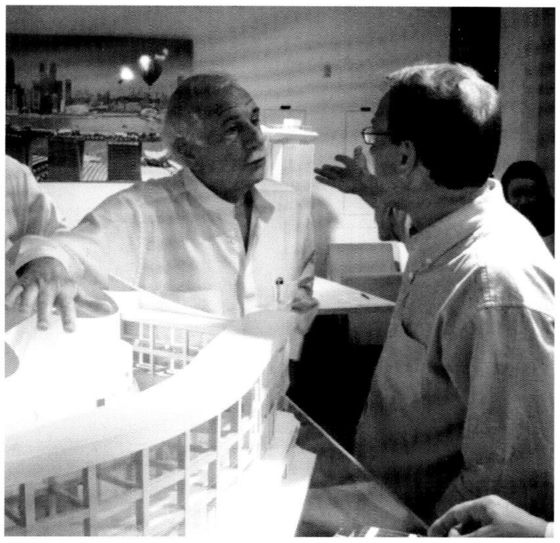
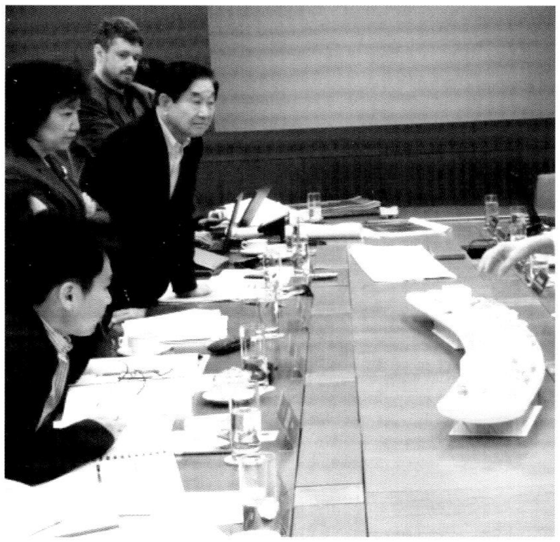
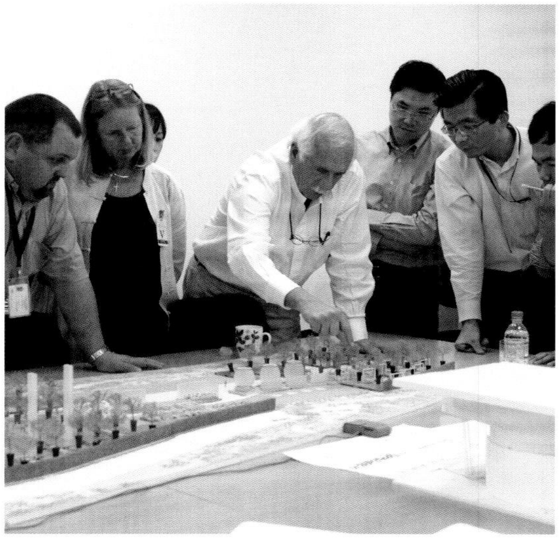
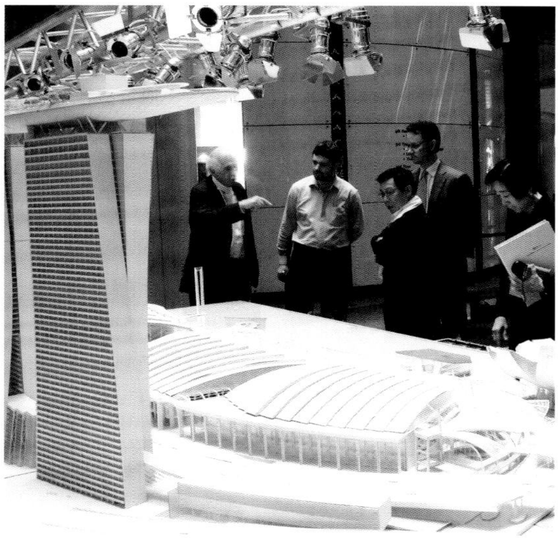
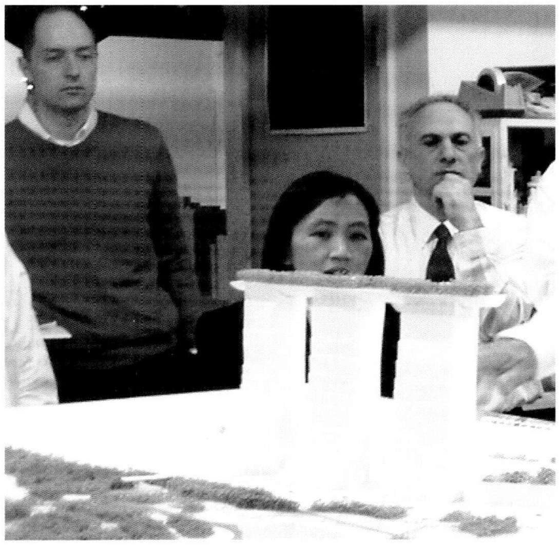
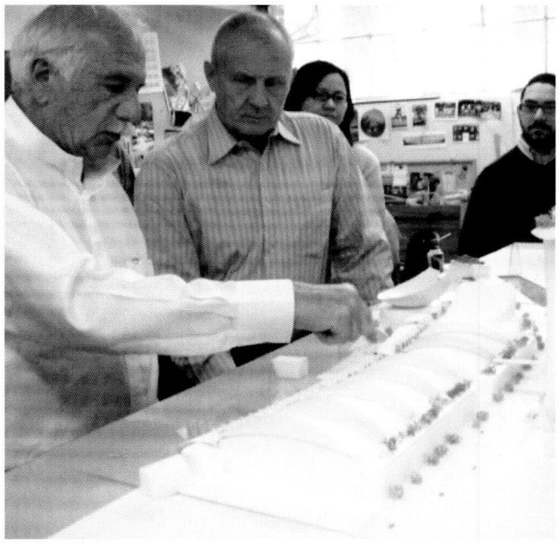
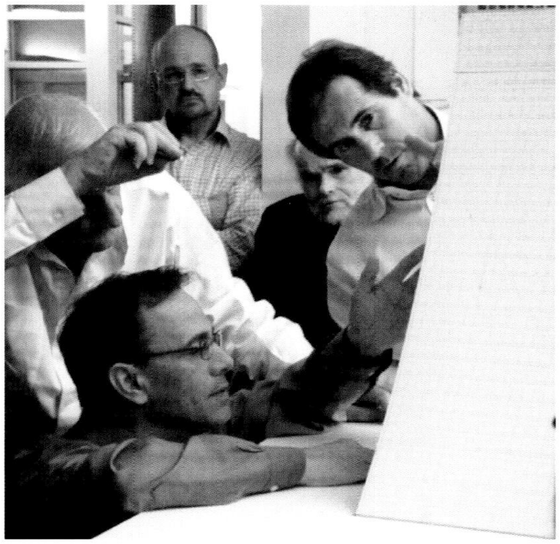

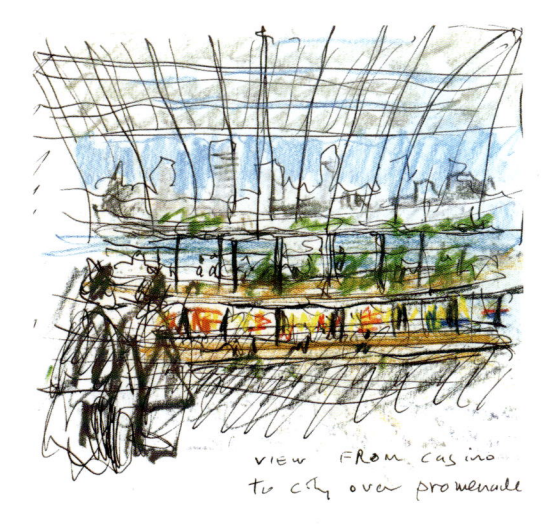

Top: Safdie sketch of retail arcade and waterfront promenade facing the city

Bottom: Safdie sketch of Grand Arcade

The Podium

Our "small town" was taking shape. The promenade and retail arcade served as the resort's *Cardo Maximus*. The two east-west view corridors formed the intersecting *Decumanus*. And the bay-front promenade and view corridors became the backbone of a single, great public space, into which we could "plug in" the following crucial elements: the convention center, the two theaters, the casino, the ArtScience Museum, and the diverse retail facilities. Each a complex structure on its own, these parts are all accessed from the central spine, which integrates them into a whole.

Meetings, Incentives, Conferencing, Exhibitions (MICE)

The program of required MICE spaces was substantial in relationship to the available land. The solution was to stack two levels of exhibition space (32,000 square meters) and two levels of flexible meeting rooms (20,000 square meters), with Asia's largest ballroom (8,000 square meters) on top. The MICE also provides a complex network of services including direct truck access to the exhibition floors. It also contains commercial kitchens large enough to serve some of the biggest meeting venues in the world.

The MICE at times must accommodate 45,000 people at once, so the public flow must be intuitive and self-orienting. We explored many models for arranging the spaces. Initially, we placed the prefunction and public-access areas along Bay Boulevard, thinking that the activity within would animate the building's facade on the public thoroughfare. Upon further analysis, we realized that exploiting the extraordinary views of the bay and skyline could make this convention center a unique experience. By placing the lobbies along the water to the west, we were able to adjoin a grand, public outdoor terrace that also overlooks the city.

Simultaneously, we tweaked the detailing of the promenade's long west facade to further maximize views of the city and bay. We gave the enclosed areas of the Grand Arcade glass walls and designed large canopies for the arcade overall, shading indoor and outdoor spaces from the tropical heat without obstructing the view. The louvered canopies hang from a network of masts and cables, evoking a marinelike architectural vocabulary. The west edge of the podium roof, just above the canopies, forms a continuous, landscaped walkway that runs the length of the entire project and connects to the convention center terrace. Both the walkway and the terrace serve the dual function of providing emergency egress. Most challenging for the MICE was its structural design, which had to provide vast open spaces for the expo floors, ballrooms, and meeting rooms, with the enormous ballroom on the upper level. For speed of construction and flexibility of use, we conceived of the entire structure in steel trusses and columns, complemented as needed by sections of reinforced concrete.

The Casino

I had, of course, visited Las Vegas more than once and was familiar with the typology of its casinos—expansive, low-ceilinged spaces stretching at the base of large hotels, with walls just 5 or 6 meters high and sometimes a hectare in floor area. This model forces public circulation to the hotel through gaming venues often surrounded by food facilities and entertainment. Going this route in Singapore would have required an enormous footprint, big enough to accommodate a sophisticated gaming program and a gross floor area of about 350,000 square meters. Moreover, the Singaporean government forbade forced circulation through the casino; in fact, it required the casino to be contained, hidden from sight from the perimeter of the public concourses. It made perfect sense to conceive of this introverted, internalized space as multileveled.

By a stroke of luck, I was invited during my second trip to Singapore to travel back to the United States with Sheldon and Miriam Adelson on their private plane. We stopped in Macau, because Sheldon Adelson wanted to visit the Sands complex there and review plans for the company's Cotai Strip resort, then under construction. To my surprise, I discovered that the Macau casino, which opened in 2004, was a multilevel facility centered on an atrium that opened up to hotel floors above. We began exploring a concept for the Marina Bay casino in which a ground-floor gaming space would be surrounded by three tiers of undulating mezzanines, accommodating more gaming; an exclusive club for VIPs and high rollers; and celebrity-chef restaurants. The giant, central atrium would be roofed by a complex, three-dimensional lattice, which, in turn, would contain the world's largest "chandelier"—a stretched, suspended net supporting LEDs and crystals. The chandelier took

Wind Screen
Sky Park
Rib Structure

Restaurant

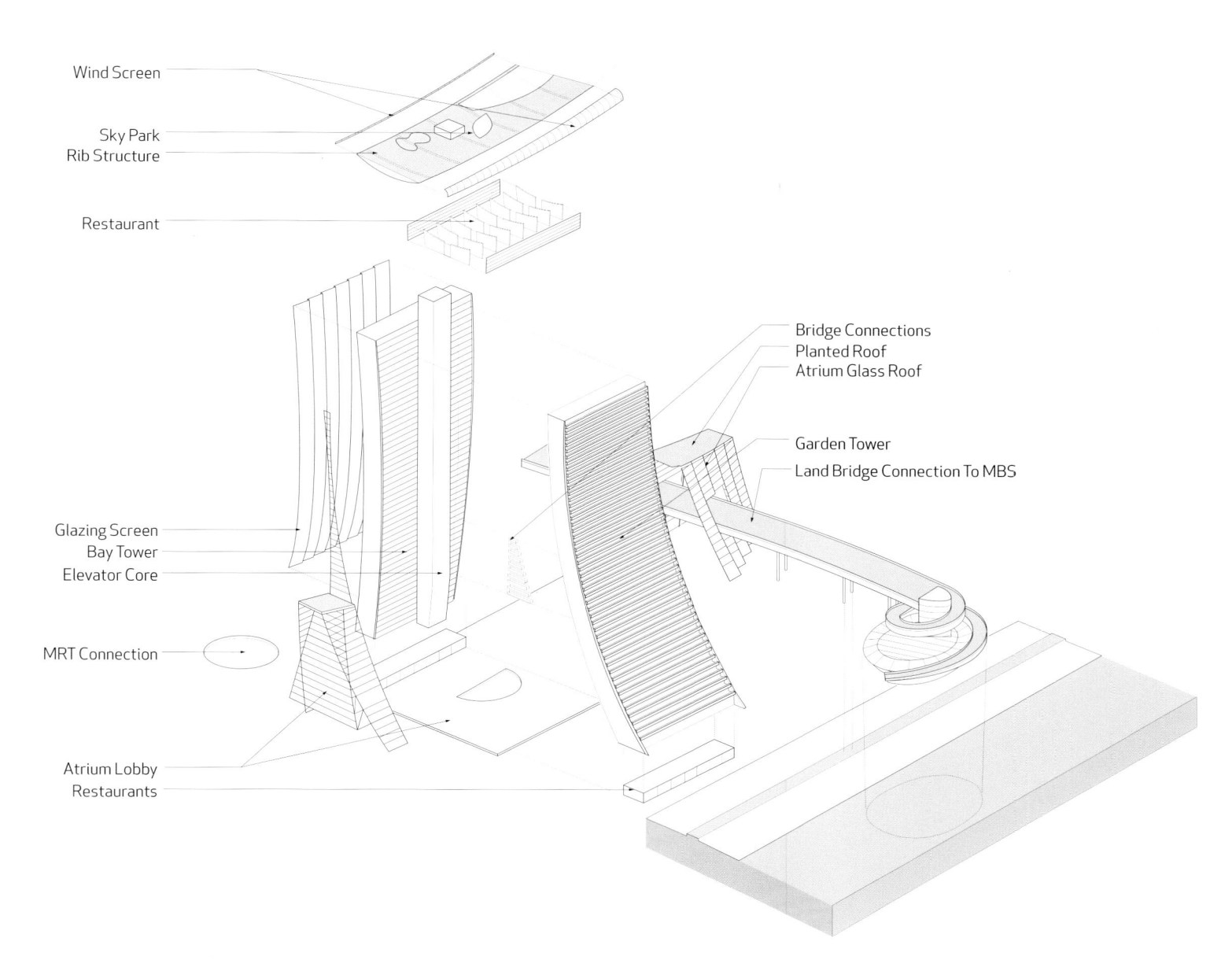

Bridge Connections
Planted Roof
Atrium Glass Roof

Garden Tower
Land Bridge Connection To MBS

Glazing Screen
Bay Tower
Elevator Core

MRT Connection

Atrium Lobby
Restaurants

Exploded axonometric showing hotel components

six months for our team to design, including functionality tests with life-size mock-ups in a Singapore warehouse. To satisfy the requirements for direct lighting and surveillance on each gaming table, we created a network of stainless steel treelike elements, forming a kind of abstract orchard that accommodates cameras and lighting yet remains open so viewers from above can see the action below.

The result is unlike other gaming venues in its being a huge space that nonetheless creates intimacy and a sense of orientation. It channels the old-world festivity, richness of texture and color, and element of ritual that we associate with the grand casinos of Monte Carlo or Montenegro. Yet its scale manages to accommodate the state-of-the-art equipment and amenities expected of a Las Vegas Sands establishment.

The Theaters

The URA program called for two theaters of 2,200 and 2,000 seats, each with a full proscenium stage and complete array of stage facilities. Singapore's marketing team expressed a strong preference for a single-balcony design rather than a multi-tiered horseshoe auditorium, which I would have preferred. We followed the precedence of Las Vegas and Broadway theaters in attempting to design a flexible auditorium, easily adaptable for a variety of kinds of performance. We worked to create not only excellent sight lines but also well-organized storage and backstage spaces for technical and other equipment, all served by underground trucking docks that further support rapid transitions from show to show. Inside, each theater has its own identity, distinguished by color (one red, one blue), size, seating capacity, and type of entertainment to be accommodated. Outside, the theaters share a large lobby inspired by our design

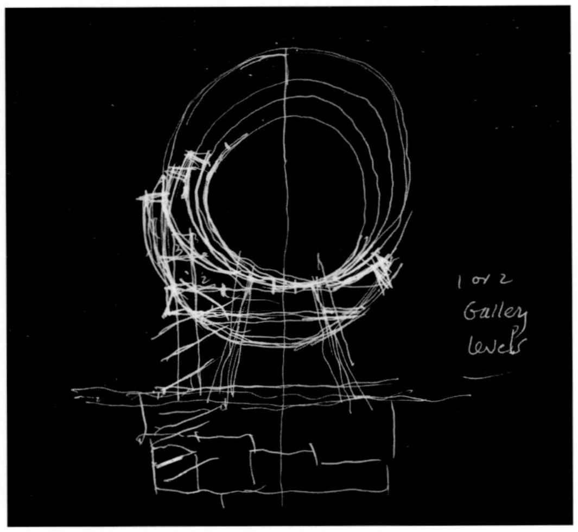
1 or 2
Gallery
levels

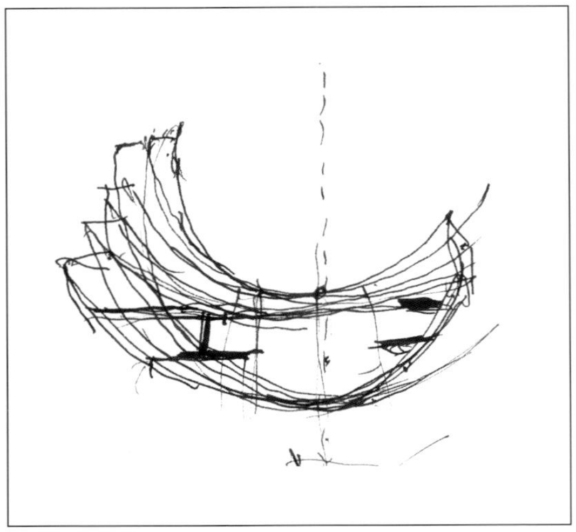

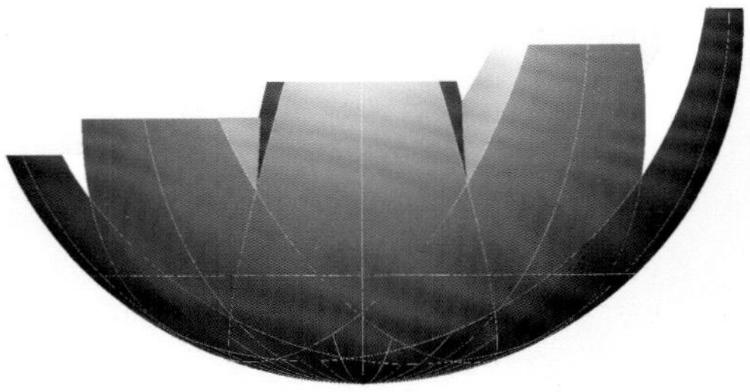

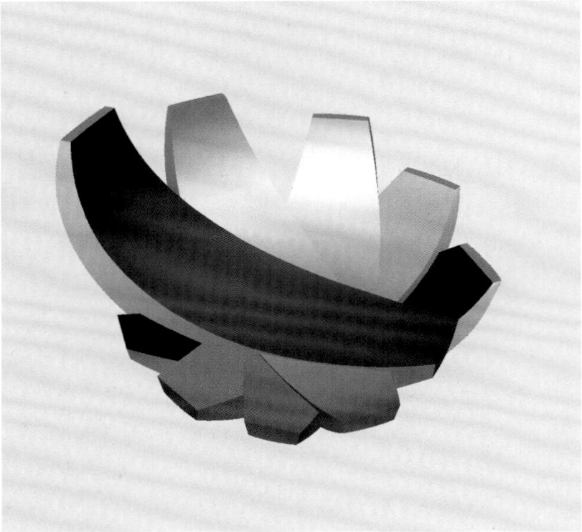

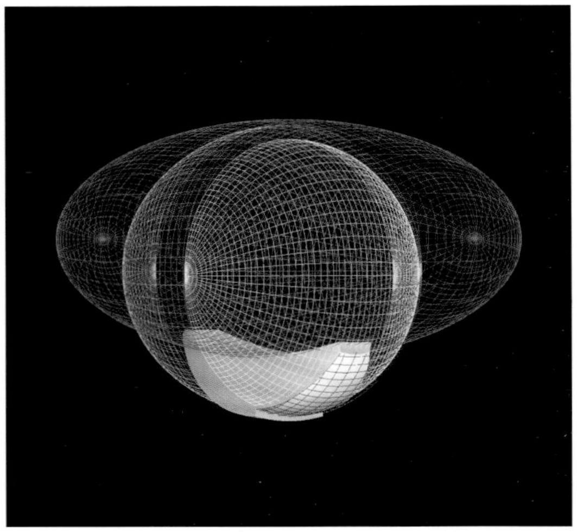

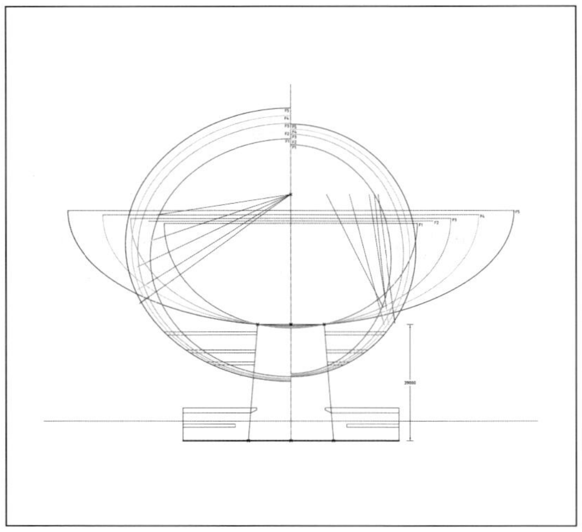

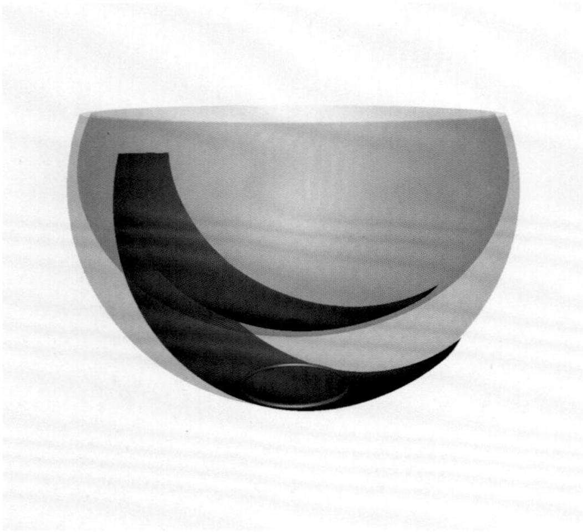

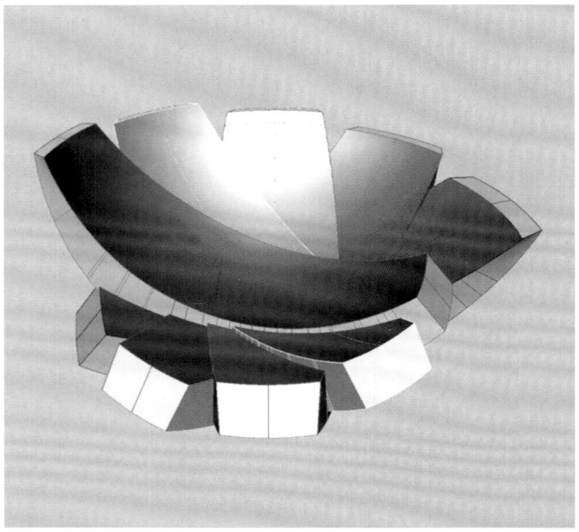

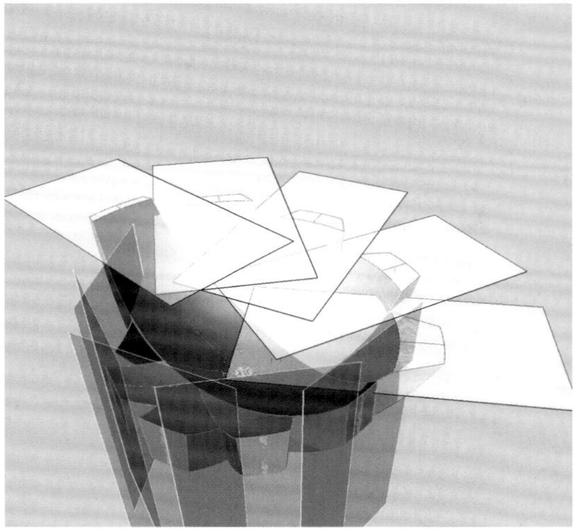

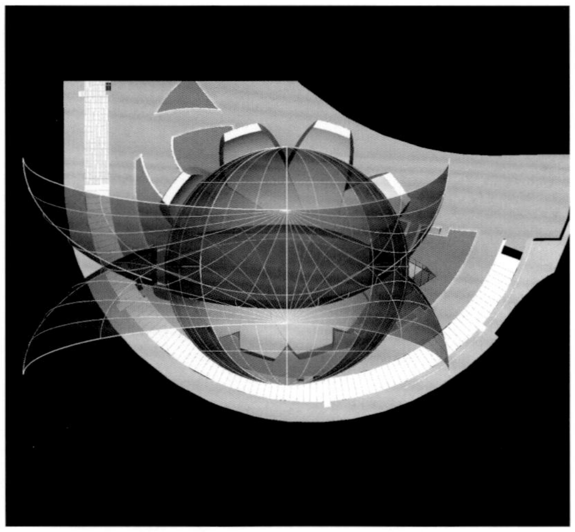

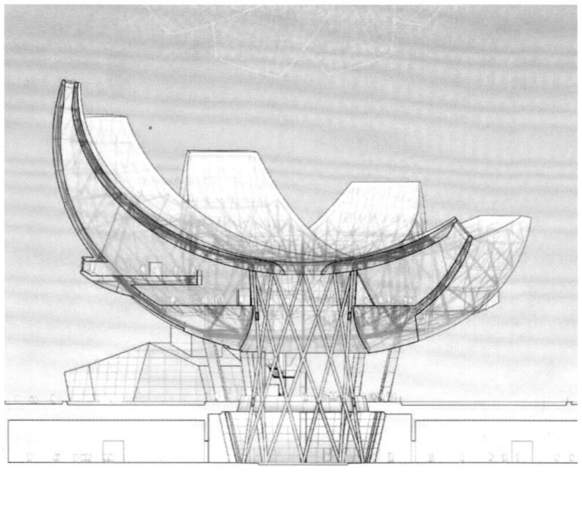

The ArtScience Museum design evolved from an initial sphere into a detailed exploration of spheroid geometries. The final compressed-sphere geometry features a slightly different radius for each of five volumes, creating ten petals of varying height and width arrayed on a central axis.

for the Ford Center for the Performing Arts in Vancouver (1995), with a giant, segmented mirror wall facing the galleries leading to the balconies, reflecting and multiplying the activity and feeling of excitement.

The ArtScience Museum

For the promontory at Marina Bay—the culmination of the waterfront promenade and the centerpiece of the expanded downtown Singapore—the government mandated an iconic cultural building. We proposed a new kind of museum, one that explores the quest for knowledge and the passion for innovation that form the shared foundation of art and science. In its celebration of creativity, the new ArtScience Museum would also express the spirit of Singapore and its citizens.

The design that emerged has two principal parts. One is the base, embedded in the earth and surrounded by bay waters and a large lily pond; the other is a flowerlike structure of ten petals, generated by spheroids of varying radii, that seemingly floats above the landscaped pond base. The petals—or fingers, as some refer to them—rise skyward in varying heights up to 60 meters, each crowned by a skylight that illuminates the galleries within.

Visitors enter the museum through a freestanding glass pavilion and travel to the upper and lower galleries via large elevators and escalators. In total, the three gallery levels contain 6,000 square meters. An elaborate, internal, steel lattice structure supports the asymmetrical flower, which is anchored at its core by a basketlike diagrid—a sculptural centerpiece that balances the opposing forces generated by the irregular form. This efficient structural solution gives the museum its weightless, hovering quality. The dishlike roof collects rainwater and drains it through an oculus, creating a waterfall through the center of the building that feeds the interior pond.

The museum's envelope is made of double-curved fiber-reinforced polymer (FRP), a material typically used at this scale in the construction of boats and yachts. The vertical sides of each petal are sheathed in bead-blasted stainless steel panels. This unprecedented use of FRP made possible the building's jointless, continuous skin and sense of lightness, its gleaming petals juxtaposed with areas of exposed white polymer that seem to swell, sail-like.

This unique structure has already stimulated the public imagination; many refer to it as the "symbol of Singapore," fulfilling the expectations of the government and the goal of our design. Some liken it to a welcoming hand, others to a lotus, while still others see in it the richness of geometry and mathematics—the integration of order and complexity. In this manner, the museum's form stands as a strong symbol of its function: an institution promoting a deep understanding of the relationship between art and science.

Public Art at Marina Bay

The URA's Art Incentive Program encouraged the remarkable site-specific art at Marina Bay Sands in two ways. First, it gives additional development rights to developers who provide public art. Second, like government agencies the world over, the URA mandates that a percentage of a project's budget be devoted to public art. The client team was eager to maximize the possibilities of every possible square meter of development, and, in the end, we were authorized to direct approximately 50 million dollars toward artwork. The URA guidelines allowed for the architect to select artists whose work made them desirable for collaboration on site-specific opportunities. We then submitted the artists' credentials to the URA for approval.

What I would like to highlight here is the methodology we followed in seeking to integrate art and architecture, a process whose roots stretch back to antiquity. In Gothic times, art and architecture were inseparably conceived as a single experience. The soaring, carefully balanced structure of the Gothic cathedral creates large windows adorned with stained glass. Sculpture over archways and on flying buttresses celebrates a variety of architectural components, integrating conception and execution in a unified whole. With the Renaissance, such integration often gave way to a more "applied" approach, in which frescoes, ceiling paintings, or sculptures were placed within the architecture as objects or events unto themselves, thus diminishing the sense of collaboration.

Our objective at Marina Bay was to recapture, conceptually, a Gothic-style integration. For example, Ned Kahn's *Wind Arbor* is an inseparable component of the large window-wall of the hotel atrium. The work, which the viewer perceives as part of the architecture, provides essential shading from the western sun and creates a rippling visual effect as

The seamless integration of art and architecture is experienced in Gothic cathedrals.

Axonometric detail of ArtScience Museum steel structure

aluminum flappers move with the breeze. The *Rain Oculus*, also by Kahn, enhances the great inverted dome that spans a key intersection of the retail mall. Swirling water fills the dome like a whirlpool; eventually, a burst of "rain" falls through the dome's oculus into a pond one story below, which feeds into the canal running through the mall. It makes the observer aware of the physical laws at hand. It also draws the eye toward the sky and creates a dynamic sense of anticipation.

In total, there are eleven different art installations by seven internationally known artists. To cite just two more examples of the synchronicity of art and architecture: Zheng Chongbin's *Rising Forest* is a series of ceramic pots that forms the base for an orchardlike tree canopy that stretches in- and outdoors through the hotel atrium. In the upper half of the atrium, Antony Gormley's *Drift* hovers over and occupies, as well as amplifies, the cavernous space. Bouncing light, it is visible from multiple vantage points, transforming and enriching our experience of the space.

Epilogue

From the perspective of the client (the Las Vegas Sands and Marina Bay Sands Corporations), the integrated resort at Marina Bay presented the challenge of creating a multiuse facility that combines tourist, retail, and entertainment attractions and is functional and profitable. Profitability would undoubtedly benefit from an exciting and memorable design, one that would draw public attention. Yet an underlying priority was the operational efficiency of an intricate machine, a complex of hotels, theaters, convention facilities, and gaming that employs some 10,000 people.

From the perspective of Singapore, the objective was to enhance tourism by offering a heretofore unavailable range of venues and amenities. At the same time, the URA and government clearly aimed to create yet another segment of vital, downtown urban design, animating the waterfront and serving not only visitors but also citizens from all walks of life.

As architects, our mandate was to meet the needs and objectives of our immediate client, Marina Bay Sands, as well as the government. Yet, there was another, more personal, agenda to be explored in the design. From the outset, I viewed this project as an opportunity to demonstrate how one can create a new kind of twenty-first-century urban meeting place. Unlike shopping malls, suburban or urban, this would be a place not for commerce alone but for multiple activities, fusing commerce with culture and entertainment in a single complex. Also, unlike the introverted malls that proliferate in Asian as well as Western cities, this place would reach out to the surrounding urban network and infrastructure. The flow of the building along the bay would encourage a sympathetic pedestrian flow along the promenade, and the entire resort would connect to surrounding districts via subway and roadway.

This new kind of extroverted complex would weave protected, air-conditioned public spaces with outdoor, nature-connected plazas, promenades, and rooftop gardens—including, at Marina Bay Sands, the unique amenity of the SkyPark. This seamlessness of indoor and outdoor public space, which offers options depending on the season or time of day, is a hallmark of Marina Bay Sands and a major factor in its success. The hotel atria, shopping promenades, and arcades have proven, over the first two years of operation, to be truly public in character. They encourage, indeed, they invite the unrestricted movement of all visitors, whether they be customers or curious bystanders.

I have often stated that the challenge of the architectural profession today is to humanize the megascale, to demonstrate that the great densities of mixed-use development, which are becoming the norm in many big cities, can be made intimate, comfortable, and accessible through design intervention. One strategy for humanizing the megascale has to do with clever manipulation of sunlight, direct and indirect. This position allows different uses to complement, harmonize with, and reinforce each other, creating an infrastructure that becomes self-orienting by recognizing people's desire for the outdoors, density notwithstanding. The design for Marina Bay Sands has been a laboratory for exploring these issues, and the SkyPark is perhaps our most dramatic design response. Its magic resides not just in its physical, iconic character but also in the fact that it provides a hectare of landscaped, outdoor space. The SkyPark functions as an observatory, perched atop the fifty-seventh floor with a dramatic view of Indonesia and Malaysia across the water. It also is a public facility. This becomes the legacy of Marina Bay Sands. It is an idea destined to perpetuate itself elsewhere as we discover how to create, within the high-density urban environment, public gardens and parks for all to enjoy.

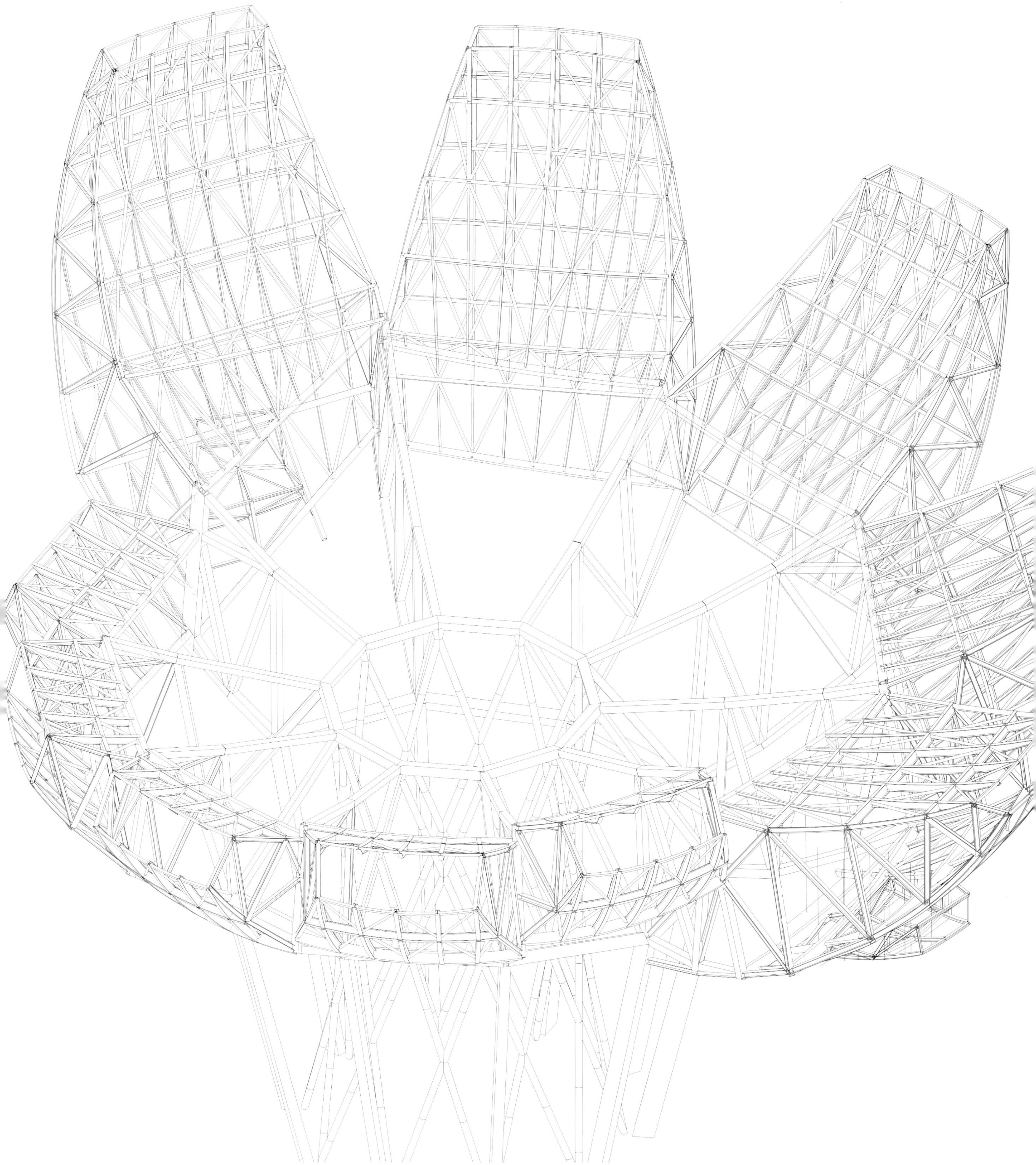

West elevation of
Marina Bay Sands Hotel

49

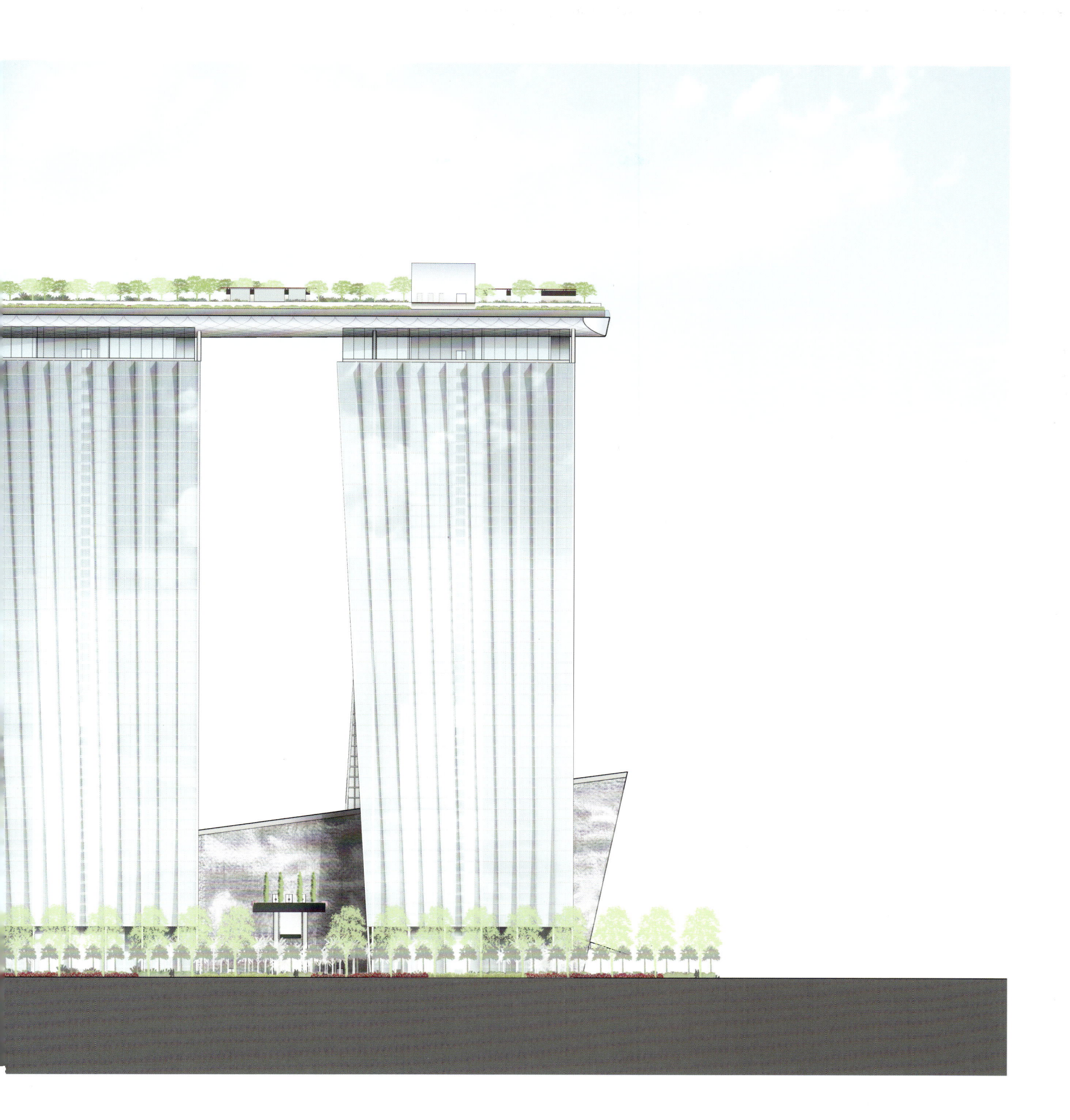

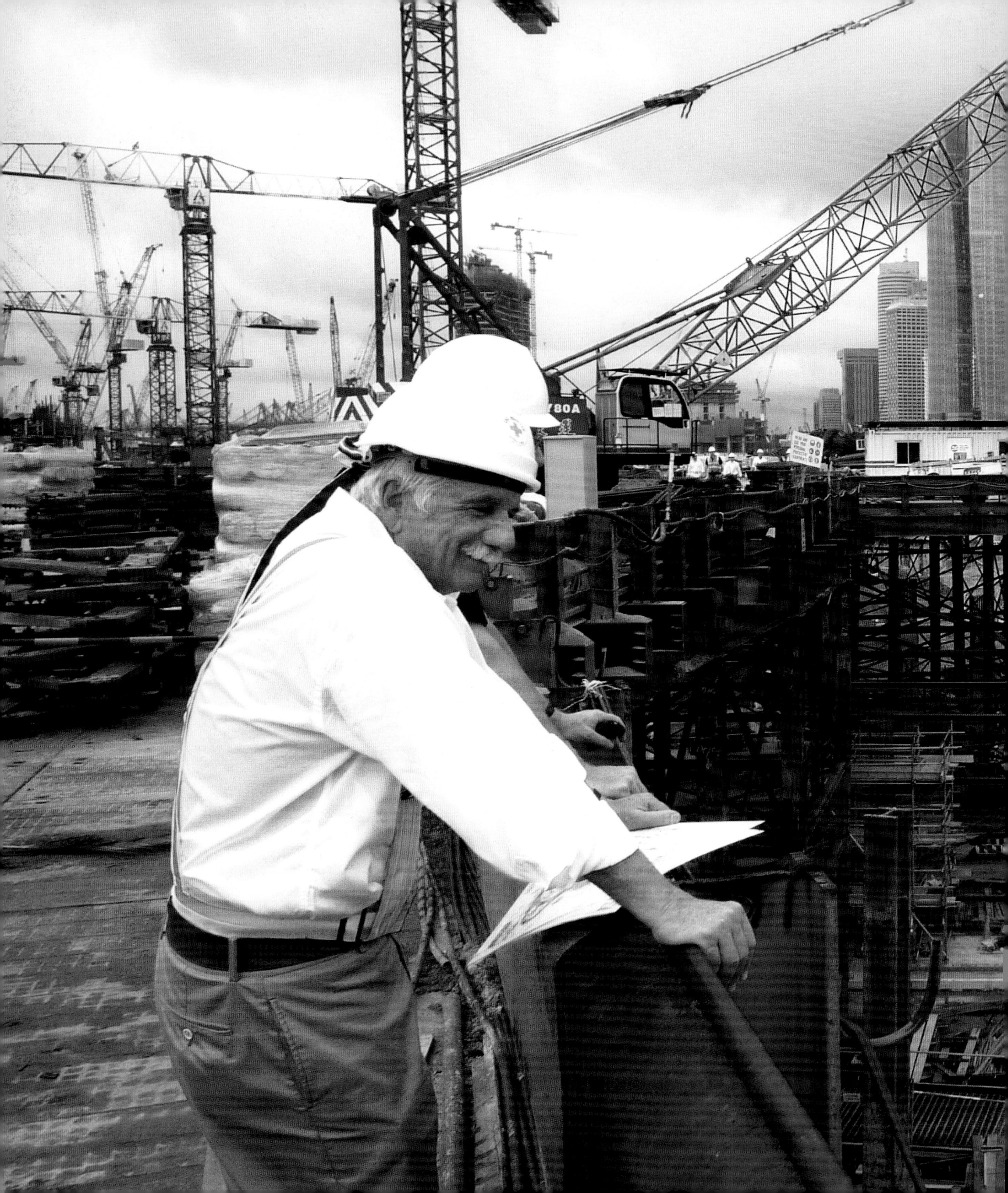

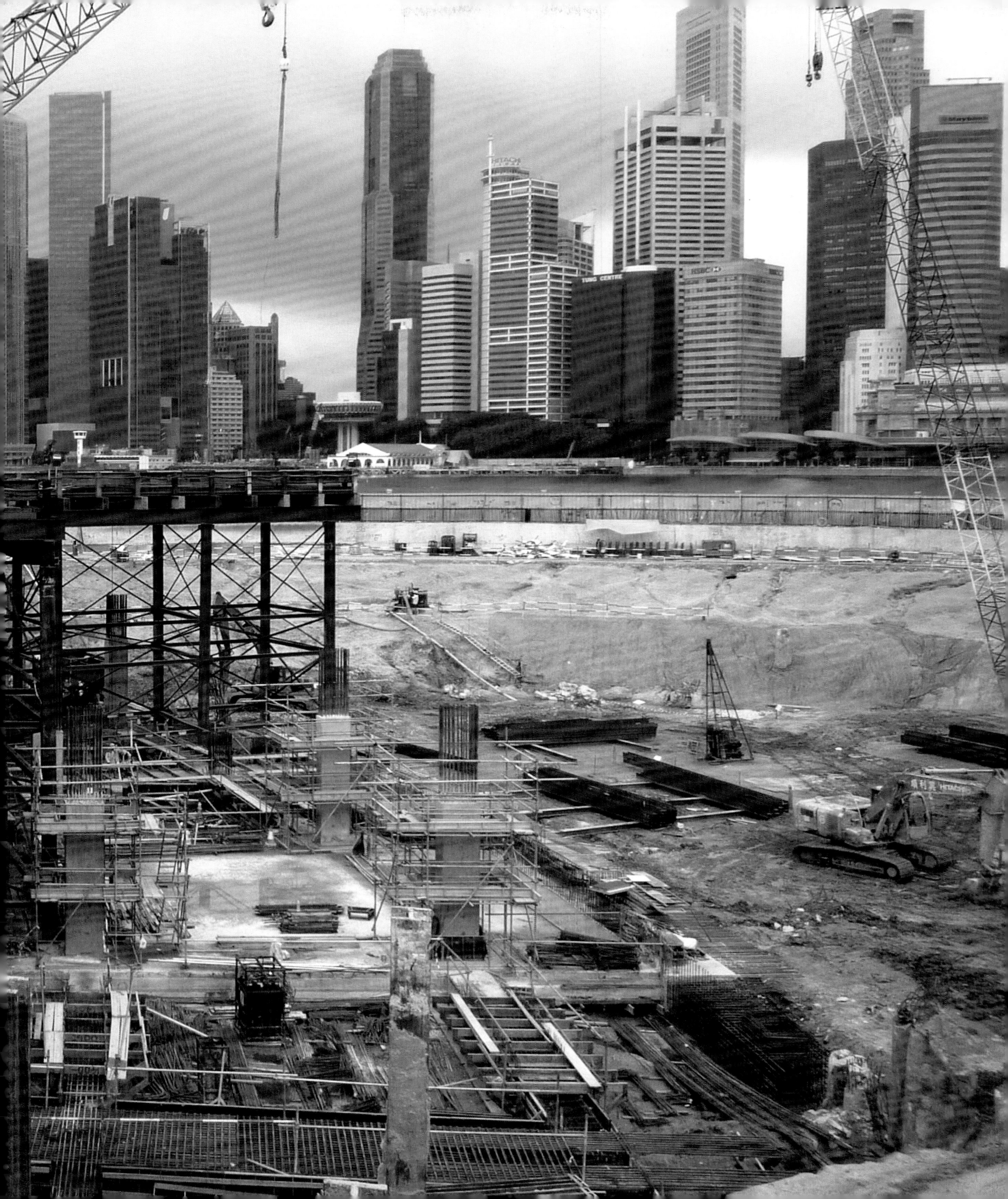
TUNG CENTRE
HSBC

THE LANDSCAPE OF MARINA BAY SANDS

PETER WALKER AND ADAM GREENSPAN

Singapore: The Garden City

Singapore's first prime minister, Lee Kuan Yew, conceived of his island as the Garden City, a moniker made official in 1968, soon after independence. Through incredible political will and sustained physical efforts, Singapore today is simultaneously one of the world's greenest and most urban cities. The Garden City identity and Singapore's geography have fostered an institutional attitude toward land and the landscape quite unlike that in any other place. For these reasons, the landscape associated with the Marina Bay Sands integrated resort is more than a mere recreational destination or a garden amenity to a development: not only does it tie into the infrastructure of this megaproject, it also advances the urban design of the city of Singapore and supports the character of the nation.

Singapore sits at the southern tip of the Malay Peninsula, 37 kilometers from the equator. It has a tropical climate conducive to plant growth, though available land for planting is limited. Since the early 1960s, the Singaporean government has engaged in land reclamation, filling adjacent waters to create room for expansion. Singapore's borders contain a substantial amount of topography, with hills that can be leveled yielding earth for fill. The city-state also has urban development and infrastructure and easy access to seabed sand. These facts allowed for the creation of nearly 700 square kilometers of new surface, and the reclamation process has fostered incredible achievements toward progressive engineering, sustainability, and social goals. Singapore's active engagement with its landscape thus generated a governmental culture focused on the interaction of all the systems and inhabitants—humans, flora, and fauna—that make up its dynamic urban ecology. With each new landscape project in Singapore, the government and its Urban Redevelopment Authority (URA) have reached toward higher levels of innovation and effect.

The site of Marina Bay Sands was the product of land reclamation yet remained relatively untapped for years, occupied with various interim uses. Ultimately, the URA intended the integrated resort, as well as Singapore's new botanical garden, the Gardens by the Bay, to inaugurate the development and growth of downtown Singapore around Marina Bay. Therefore, in concept, the architecture and landscape of the

Waterfront promenade

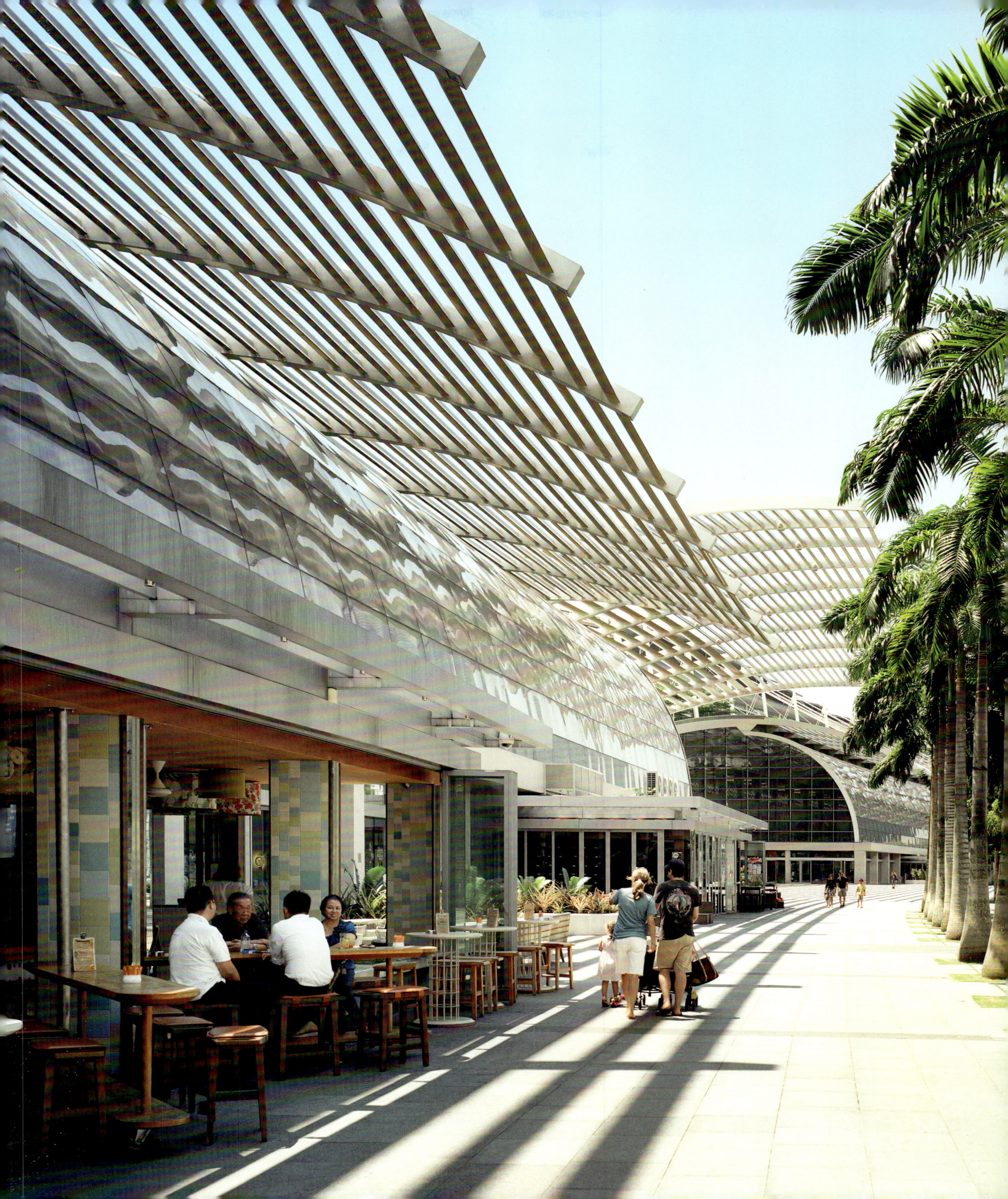

PWP mock-up of royal palm spacing along the promenade

integrated resort had to reach ambitious urban design goals, serving the needs of both visitors and the Singaporean public as a whole.

Over the past twenty-five years, PWP Landscape Architecture has worked with Moshe Safdie on many occasions and on other projects in Singapore. None of those endeavors matched the scale or speed of Marina Bay Sands. We were captivated by Moshe's vision, and when he invited us to join the project after he won the competition in 2006, we eagerly agreed. We first visited the site that same year, when we traveled to Singapore to review final competition entries for the Gardens by the Bay, to be built adjacent to the resort. (Peter Walker was on the jury; Adam Greenspan accompanied him to review the Marina Bay Sands location.) Our interaction with the Singapore Botanic Garden executives and staff, as well as our tours of the renowned, colonial-era botanic gardens themselves, made a lasting impression on us both. The potential for synergy between the integrated resort and the Gardens by the Bay—combined with the government's support for landscape and the vigor of the tropical plant life all around—buoyed us as we began to conceive of a design scheme.

The Landscape of Marina Bay Sands

The landscape master plan for Marina Bay Sands aims to connect the existing city to this new site. Based on urban design guidelines set out by the URA and the National Parks Department (Nparks), the streetscape planting agenda for the precinct provides for varied experience and horticultural discovery as one moves through the streets around the resort. Of the nearly 12 hectares of landscape area at Marina Bay Sands, 75 percent is public space, encompassing the 1.5-kilometer-long public waterfront promenade; the Level 4 sky promenade and garden walk; and the landscape bridges over Bayfront and Sheares avenues that connect the hotel with the new Gardens by the Bay. Other landscape components include the streetscapes and plazas at Level 1; the hotel lobby gardens; the 3,100-square-meter hotel vertical garden; and the SkyPark. While the components of the resort are destined to be icons of Singapore, the landscape on, around, and through those buildings situates the architecture and helps create identity. These are both the civic landscapes and gardens that Singaporeans and visitors see from across the bay and the environment that people inhabit when they enter the resort.

Tree selection and tagging in Malaysia

Scale and the Civic Landscape

Singapore has numerous gardens and planted landscapes that deeply affect visitors and citizens alike. Some of these plantings have achieved a masterful level of integration between horticulture and urban design, with vegetation defining the city and shaping the urban experience. These remarkable installations are planting designs of true civic scale and proportion, from the rain trees that line the streets between downtown and Changi Airport, to the bold displays of plant form and color at the airport itself. Other gardens and urban plantings of note usually occur at a much smaller scale and are experienced best at close range. Yet the landscape design for Marina Bay Sands had to have the size and energy to both match the architectural strength of the development and play an active role within the dynamic urban setting. Our goal was for these new landscapes also to become touchstones of the Garden City, parallel to the remarkable civic plantings that Singapore already has fostered and continues to maintain. At the same time, we saw the need and opportunity to create garden installations of varying scales that register with residents and visitors from different distances and in different ways.

Planted Infrastructure

In addition to the landscape design's aesthetic and orienting roles, all the vegetation on the project is a form of ecological infrastructure. Every plant on the site is actually growing on structure, at ground level or above. Thus, the vast volume of soil and plant life serves the development as a sponge for rainwater and as a heat sink. The streets were designed in sections as integrated urban infrastructure: they create identity, but their components also provide for shade, storm-water management, pedestrian and vehicular movement, as well as a level of district security.

We selected primary and secondary tree species for each street in the resort, creating a coherent identity for these corridors. For the large Bayfront and Sheares avenues, which run north to south, we chose *Hopea odorata* and *Samanea saman*. These plantings stretch south to knit Marina Bay Sands back into the existing city fabric. Similarly, we created a palette of two or three palm species for the east-west access roads, which connect the resort to the new Gardens by the Bay. All of the east-west roads in Marina Bay are, essentially, galleries of palms that visitors experience by car and on foot. In addition to the visual and horticultural impact of these landscaped walks, the integrated planting and paving design of the streetscape has practical uses. The shade and shadow created by the colonnade of street trees will greatly lessen the heat one experiences from paving in the tropics. The planted colonnades that run alongside the colonnades of the buildings create a comfortable pedestrian environment. And the paving itself is perforated around each tree's root zone, which allows the tree to get water and helps reduce storm-water runoff.

Iconic Landscapes

From the first, we considered the promenade and SkyPark to be the project's landscape icons. The SkyPark was conceived of as distinctive, specific only to Marina Bay Sands. The plantings for the large-scale promenade, on the other hand, needed to connect the resort to all other waterfronts around Singapore Bay—and therefore, needed to make a bold statement at a civic scale. The challenge was to design something unique to Marina Bay Sands yet cohesive with the rest of the Garden City's horticultural framework. We worked with Safdie and his office to simplify the relationship between the upper and lower promenade levels, developing an undulating edge at the lower that played against the long curve of the upper. The result is a sequence of curved, medium-scaled spaces where people can congregate while others stroll by. When selecting plants, we initially proposed tall cabbage palms installed in tightly spaced rows of three to form a kilometer-long triple allée. During the URA design review meetings, questions arose about whether the palms could provide enough shade during the hot Singapore days and whether the close, 4-meter spacing would allow for adequate movement. Through research and multiple full-scale mock-ups constructed in Berkeley, California, we determined that the design satisfied both requirements. Ultimately, however, we decided to interrupt the allée with informal groupings of wide-spreading shade trees to create a more dynamic interaction of planted systems and shadow. The URA Design Advisory Panel felt that this final design provides a more varied pedestrian experience as well as a more interesting juxtaposition against the architecture when viewed from across the bay. The canopy trees add shady areas at key junctures along the promenade where people can enter the retail mall.

Landscape plantings are used to articulate scale and sequence throughout the Marina Bay district.

57

Street-level landscape plan

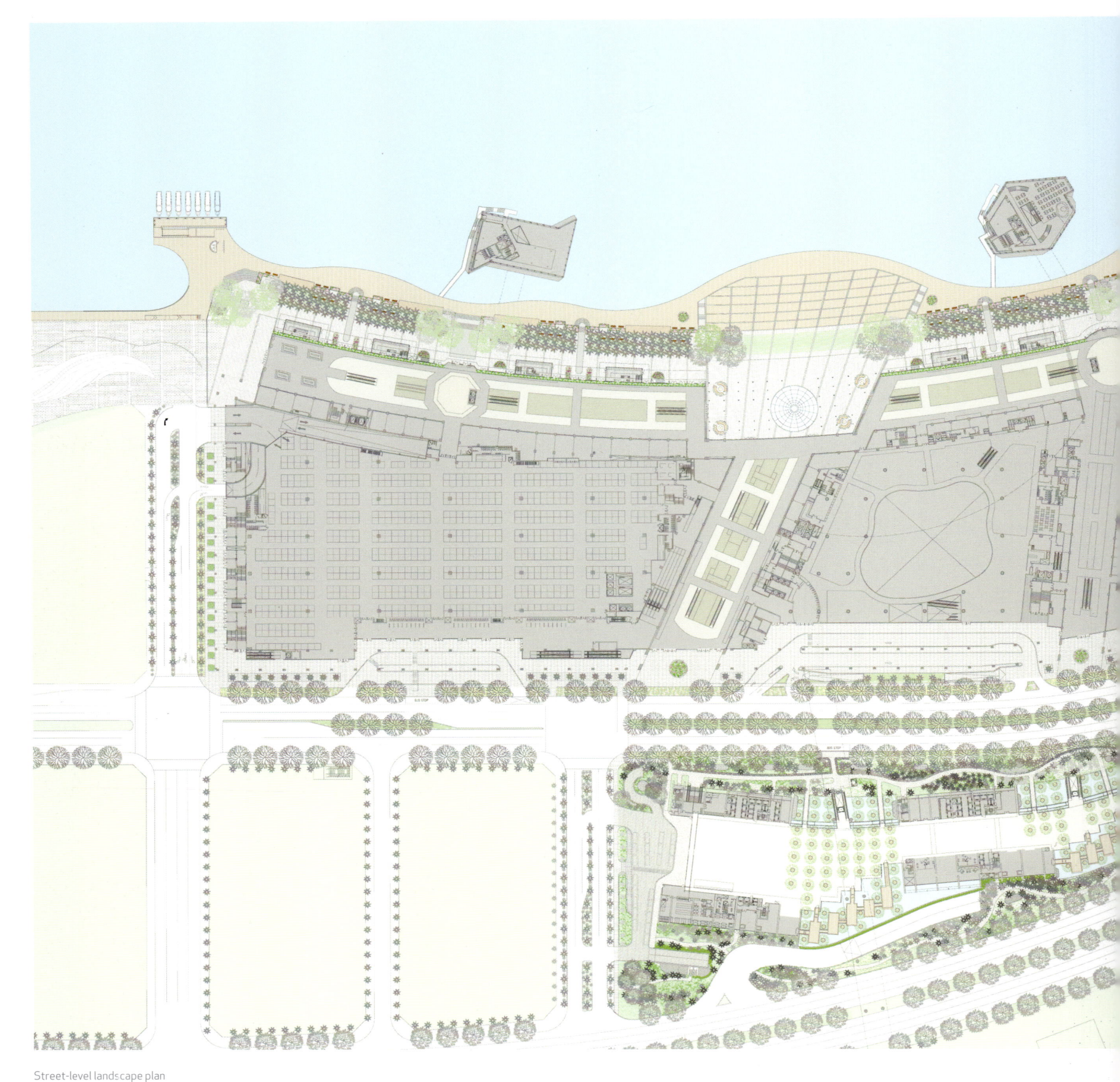

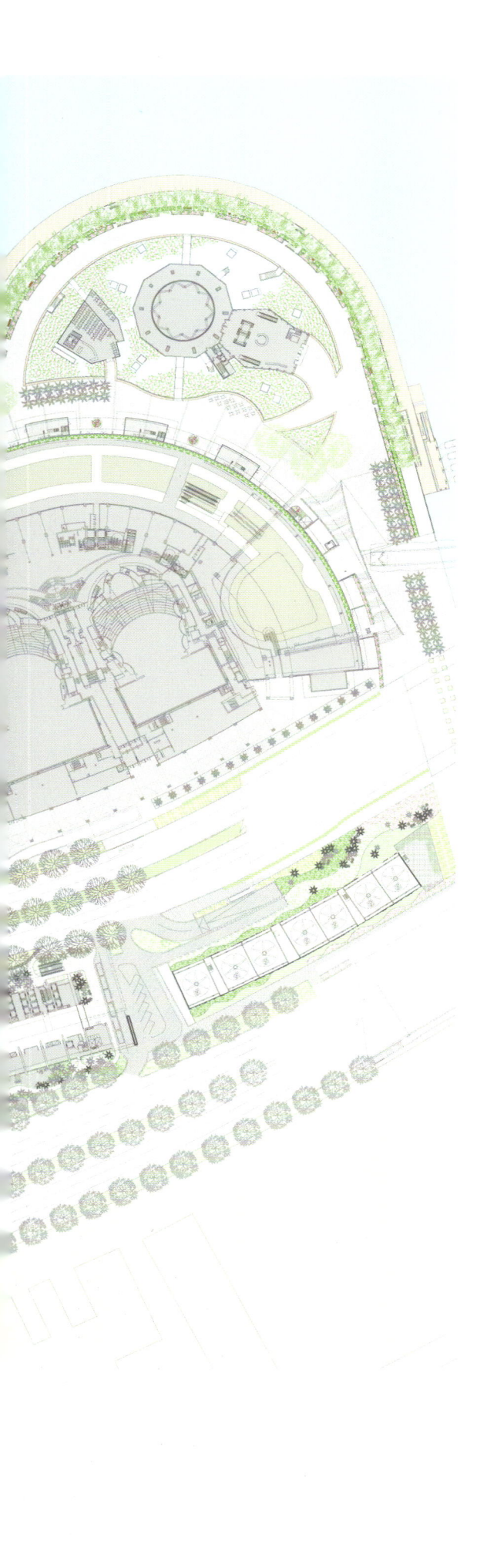

The Instant Forest: Advance Tree Procurement and the MBS Nursery

Early during our work on the project, it became clear that the magnitude of the planting we were describing in our drawings was immense—more than 50,000 vines, palms, and trees, some as tall as 15 meters, the equivalent of four stories. We became focused on the importance of obtaining large-scale plant material, the largest imaginable, and creating a pregrow environment in which to nurture those plants so the landscape would have a strong impact on opening day. Still, the scale of this development would dwarf even the biggest trees that anyone could buy. That realization led us to focus also on creating outdoor spaces in the resort through the massing and volume of plants and the shade they provided.

When we first came to Singapore for this project, in 2006, the interactions between our office and the Singapore Botanic Garden visionaries and procurement staff helped shape our understanding of large-scale plant sourcing in the area. There were no production nurseries in Singapore that could supply anything close to the size and amount of material we would need. Our contacts also cautioned us that nurseries throughout Southeast Asia were getting down to limited stock because of development booms in southern China and the Middle East. The implications of this situation were familiar to us, because we had recently finished a long-term sourcing and pregrowing plan for the World Trade Center Memorial in New York City. More than 300 oaks for the design had to come from five states and be purchased young, so that they would eventually match each other in form and size. We gathered the trees at a nursery in New Jersey to be grown and shaped until their installation at the site's Memorial Grove three to five years later.

On that initial trip, we began planning for a temporary Marina Bay Sands nursery that could receive plants from many overseas sources and grow them into larger specimen material. We relied on lessons learned from other pregrowing projects, but there were significant differences between our work in temperate climates and the process in tropical Singapore. We proposed the nursery to the Las Vegas Sands team, and the idea met with general approval. Yet buying and growing trees for future use seemed a bit less urgent than the immediate challenges facing designers and engineers, such as how to contain water while excavating thick black clay to form a foundation, or how to construct a swimming pool fifty-seven stories above ground. Our challenge became to convince the development team that, although the Marina Bay Sands opening was three years away, we needed to start looking for and growing plants immediately so they would be ready in time. In the end, the project built a nursery about a half-hour from Marina Bay on land the government made available for our temporary use. Trees from four countries—most from Malaysia, others from Thailand, Australia, and China—were brought into Singapore as early as two years before installation.

The process of locating, hand selecting, and transporting some of the world's largest trees and palms was a painstaking endeavor that involved not just PWP but also Marina Bay Sands and Las Vegas Sands executives; Singaporean horticulturists; arborists; the local landscape architects Peridian Asia; the landscape contractor; and many nurseries. PWP representatives reviewed each of the more than 750 trees and 2,400 palms on the project individually, first by photo, then in person. The variety of species and the unusually large sizes that we needed are available only from a select subset of nurseries dedicated to growing very tall trees. Specimens of this scale are grown not in containers, like smaller plants, but directly in the ground or in bags. For this reason, we hired tree hunters to locate abandoned, out-of-business nurseries in the area, where young trees that were cast off years ago were still growing. Trees that fare well in these situations, with little oversight, often reach magnificent size. Our tree hunters were local landscape architects and plant growers who knew what we wanted and which sources to tap on our behalf. Often, landscape contractors have to search hard to find a specific plant. Random substitutions, especially on a project like Marina Bay Sands, are unacceptable. So we started building our contact network in Singapore early on. That way, when the time came, we had guidance as well as an understanding of what was possible and how to obtain prime specimens.

With information from our scouts, we set off to search for and mark the trees we wanted. These adventures meant spending anywhere from a day to a week on the back roads of southern Malaysia, often picking through overgrown swamps and fields. To mark a tree, we wrap a numbered plastic tag around a branch or trunk; these tags are designed to break when removed, which prevents someone else from transferring them to a different, undesired specimen. While we have vast experience tagging in all sorts of climates and conditions, one special difference in the tropics was the bats

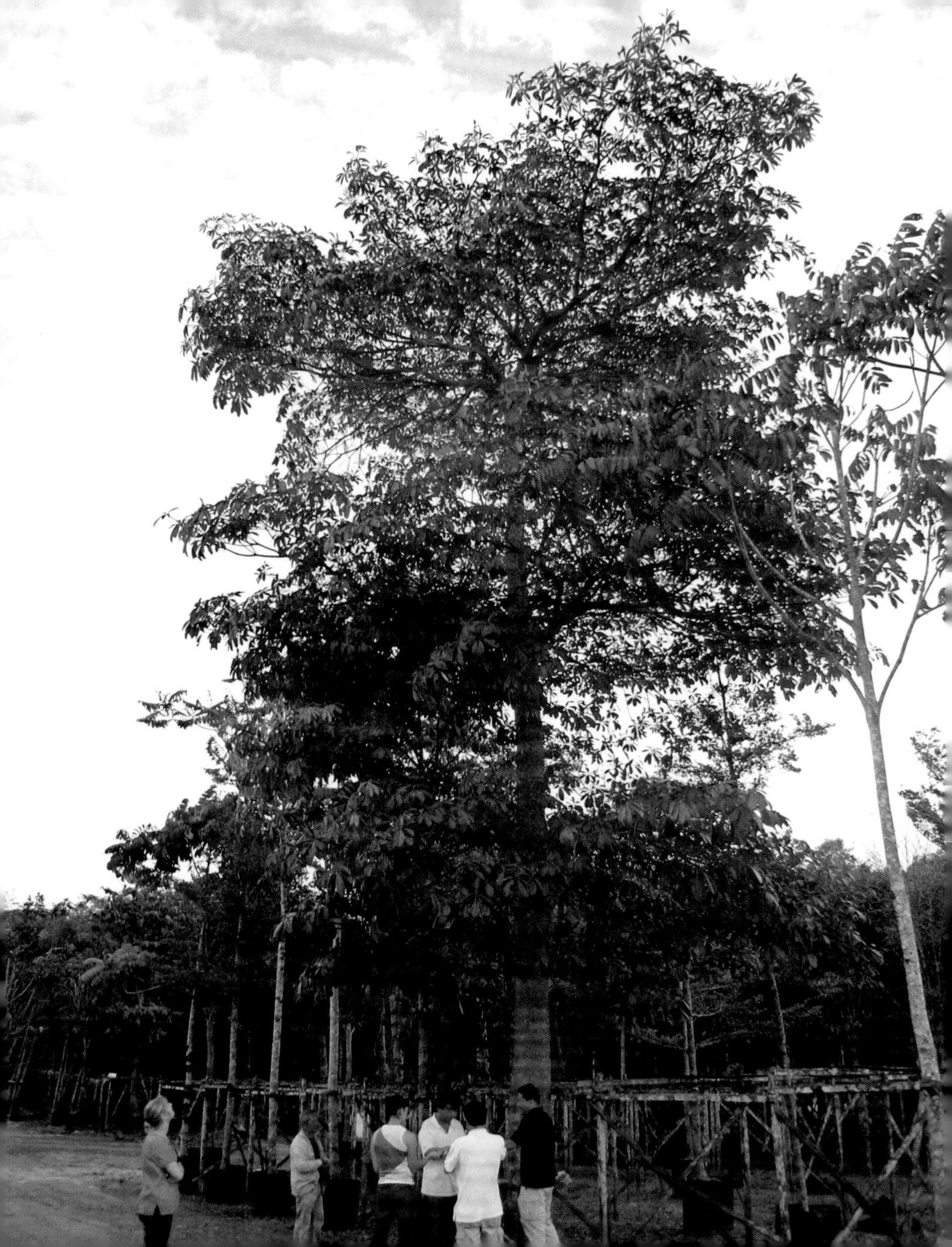

that sleep hanging upside-down in the leaves of certain trees. We often check the height of a tree using a 6-meter measuring pole. Knocking the silver fronds of Bismarck palms with the pole woke the shaggy brown bats and caused colonies to swoop down from their daytime shelter. (They later returned.) Needless to say, this was a startling addition to our process. We also had less dramatic wildlife encounters, with geckos, monitor lizards, frogs, monkeys, dogs, and plenty of mosquitoes.

Out tagging, we looked for particular species for each installation at Marina Bay Sands, checking each plant for health and uniformity in height and shape. We then reassessed them at the pregrow nursery. For example, we needed 200 matching cabbage palms for the triple allée down the promenade, because we wanted the trees to function visually as a planted extension of the grand arcade. The trunks of these palms can differ in structure: some are straight like poles, some taper, others are bulbous. We noted all these differences, so when planting the kilometer-long allée we could do a phased installation of nonidentical trees, achieving the illusion of uniformity by avoiding abrupt shifts in trunk shape.

Uniformity was less of an issue for the shade trees interspersed among the palms, which we intended to create wide crowns at the mall junctures along the promenade. We chose three canopy tree species that were irregular and different from, though complementary to, each other. The Alstonia has sinewy branches and palmate, handlike leaves. The golden flame tree creates wide dappled shade, with delicate light green leaves and yellow flowers. The khaya, from the mahogany family, has a dark trunk that develops an orange cast over time. This tree, with its medium-size green leaves, was already a familiar sight in Singapore, where builders in the colonial era used it to shade streets.

When selecting all the trees, we considered not only individual form but also the implications of transport on shape. Because the promenade trees came from outside Singapore, they had to be brought across the border on tractor-trailers. To fit through the customs gantry, the trees could be no longer than about 15 to 17 meters, including their roots and surrounding soil, and no wider than 4 or 5 meters, meaning most had to be severely pruned. We felt that the drastic pruning common in the Southeast Asian landscape industry often led to unsightly trees at installation. This was another reason we fought hard to have a nursery built early on: bare and truncated trees would need time to grow new limbs and achieve renewed health and beauty before delivery to the site. The phenomenal growing conditions in Singapore resulted in mature and vibrant trees unusually soon, after only eighteen months in the pregrow nursery.

A Number of Firsts

While developing the design for Marina Bay Sands, we were able to draw on our past experience, having worked on many domestic and international projects of similar scale and with related goals and programs. The integrated resort landscape, however, gave us some unique opportunities and resulted in a number of firsts for our office: the SkyPark, a 1.2-hectare rooftop garden; the "skyscaping" achieved on the fifty-story hotel facade; and the 152.5-meter-long modular green wall within the hotel atrium restaurant. Each of these unusual landscape installations took hours of detailed design and very particular construction coordination.

The vast green wall that became a backdrop to the atrium restaurant was, in part, a collaboration between our design team and Nparks, Singapore's National Parks Department. During our meetings with the URA's design panel, we discussed the government's and our mutual interest in green walls and green roofs, which provide both aesthetic impact and ecological benefit. In our past investigations, green walls had not proved sustainable for the specific projects we were working on. They require a large amount of water, which can make them taxing to maintain in Mediterranean or temperate locales. But the idea of a green wall in tropical Singapore—with its host of native epiphytic species, which can grow vertically on rock or in trees—was exciting. We learned that Nparks was staging trials of different green-wall systems. This was a wonderful opportunity and, to us, quite remarkable: the government had built cutting-edge mock-ups of different technologies and plant palettes for us to review before we proposed a design. This information was invaluable. It led to a custom green-wall system created with a series of small, square panels containing between two and fifteen species each. Our intention was for the pixilated installation of the panels to create a pattern when viewed from afar that dematerializes up close. Standing in front of the wall, the viewer encounters each square meter as a miniature garden.

Another new challenge for us was the hotel's eastern aspect, which Safdie's design conceived of as a living facade. When his concept drawings came to our office, we were instantly captivated and considered many provocative

SkyPark cross-section

planting schemes. Finally, given the breezy and somewhat dry conditions that likely faced the elevated planters and the fact that the sun would set behind the hotel buildings, we developed a 3,100-square-meter tapestry of bougainvillea cultivars. We chose bougainvillea for its great adaptability to containerized culture in the tropics as well as its subtle differences in hue. For the hotel, we selected a floral palette of deep magenta, light pink, and a white bloom with green-and-yellow leaves. When one views the facade from a distance at sunset, its colors echo the hazy, painted layers of clouds in the western sky beyond.

Our most visible project in the resort, the SkyPark, is like no other garden we know. At first, we were concerned that without protection this elevated landscape would be wind whipped. Our initial concept paired plantings with generous lengths of clear, reflective glass walls, shielding greenery from racing winds. As the design developed, however, wind-tunnel studies for the resort overall showed surprisingly little wind at the SkyPark. This freed us to develop our gardens in the sky with the expectation that plants and pedestrians would be comfortable there. Still, we assessed every plant for its ability to handle periodic gusts. Plants not evolved to live in windy conditions might dry out. On the other hand, some trees equipped for wind wouldn't work either, because their branches break off easily to spare their trunks. In the final design, a generous use of stone, timber, and plant materials indigenous to the region aim to create a grounded feeling for SkyPark visitors. The sensation, combined with the sight of swimmers gliding through water with the Singapore skyline below, is both comforting and startling.

In many ways, the SkyPark encapsulates the variety and excitement of all our work on this unique project: it was collaborative, a challenge, and an opportunity to work on scales both grand and intimate. It is at once an icon of Marina Bay Sands but also a very visible expression of Singapore as the Garden City. In its entirety, the integrated resort also exemplifies an integrated approach to design. Because of the combined efforts of architects, developer, government, retailers, nurseries, and many others, this project enhances the identity of Singapore as a civic environment that is "green" in both senses of the word. We feel lucky to have been involved in the creation of Marina Bay Sands.

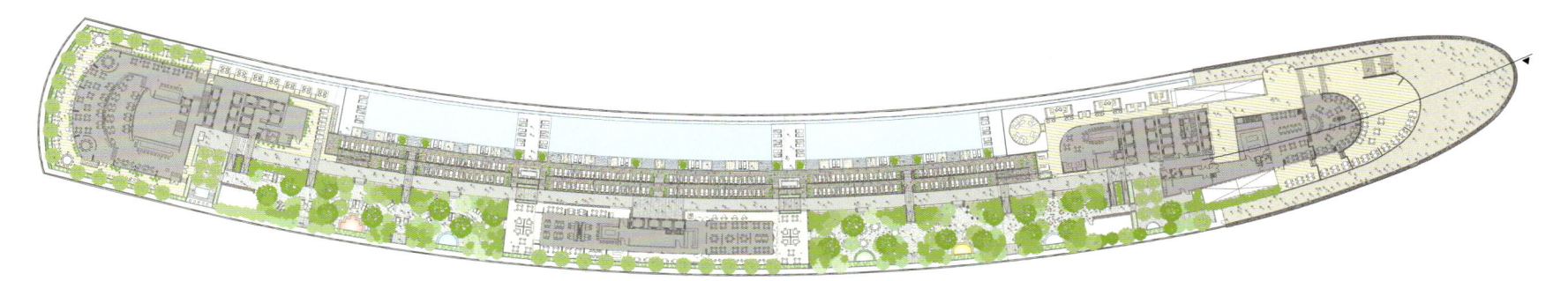

Top: West elevation with green facade

Middle: Section through Infinity Pool

Bottom: SkyPark Landscape design plan

Hard- and softscape materials reflect
Singapore's identity as the Garden City by the Bay.

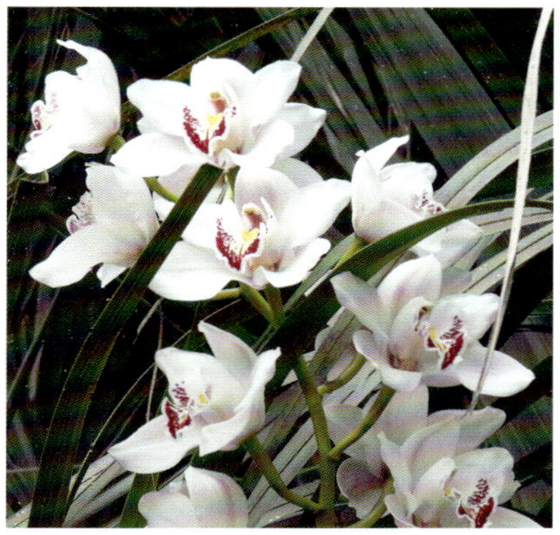
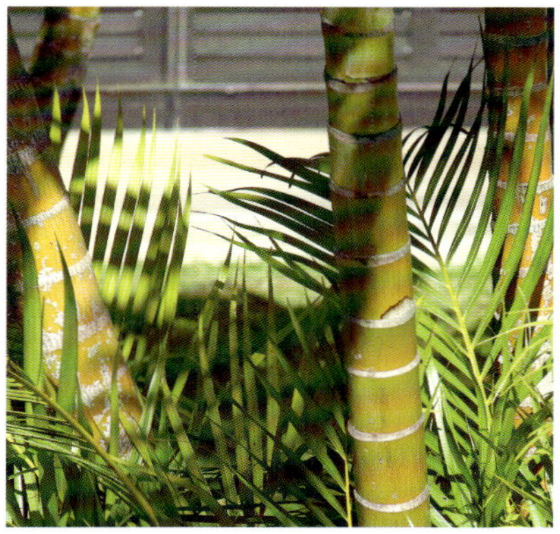
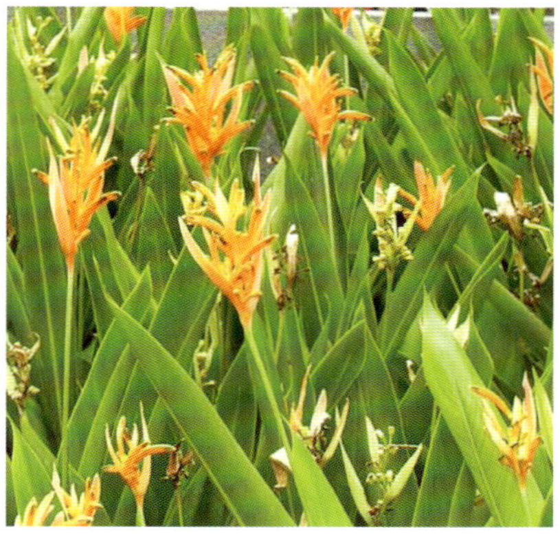
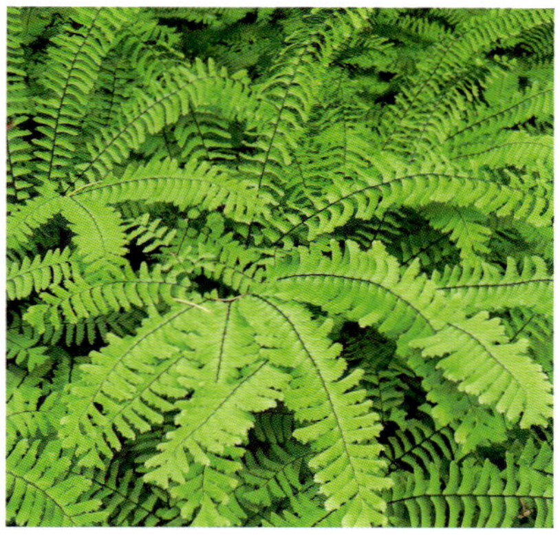
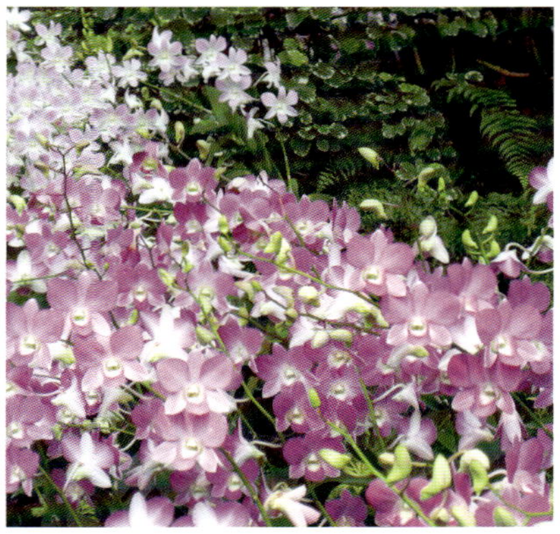
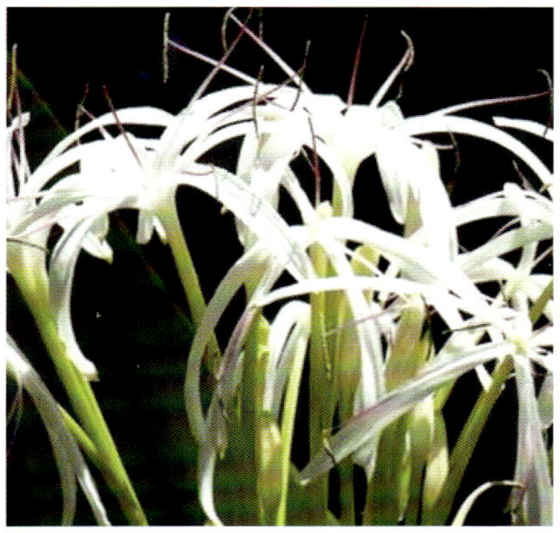
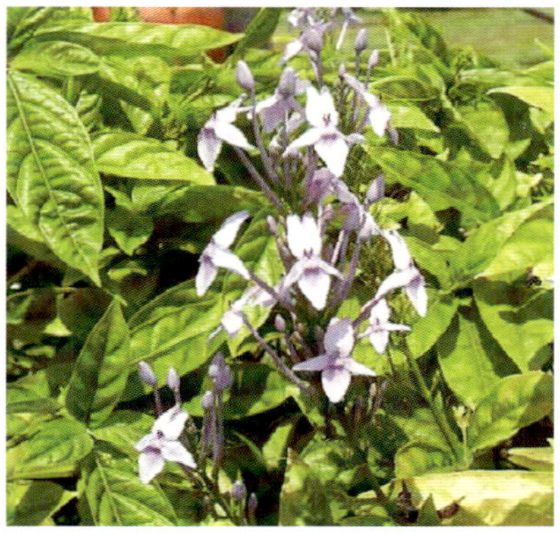
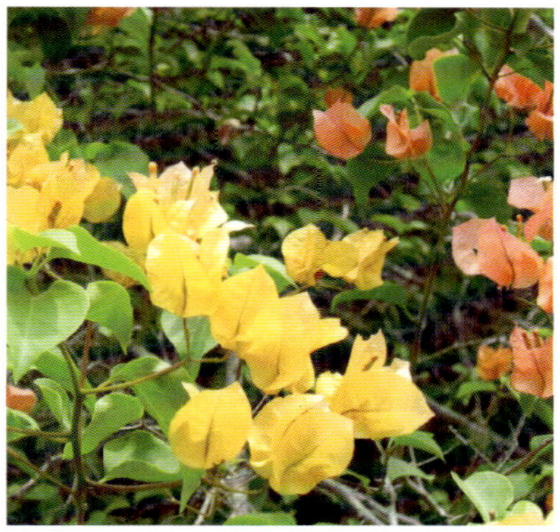
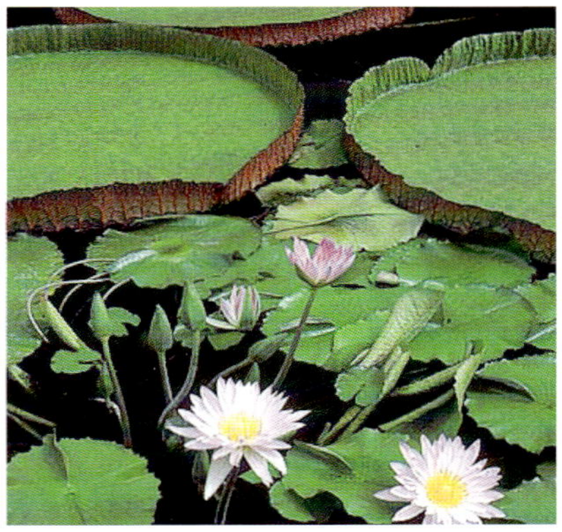
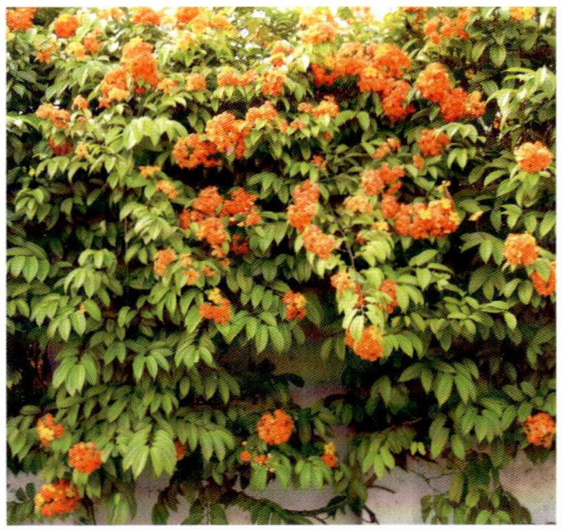
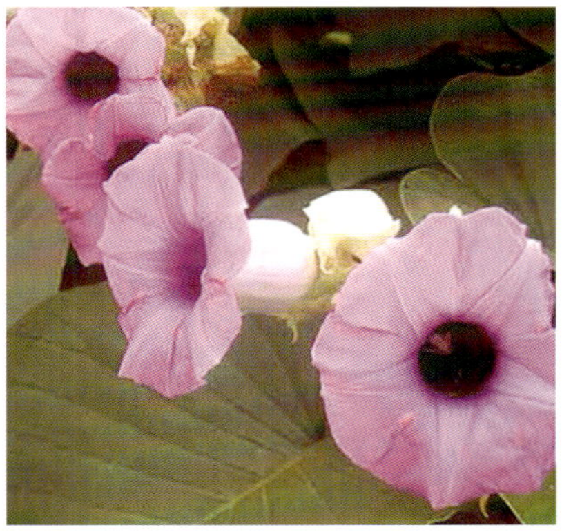
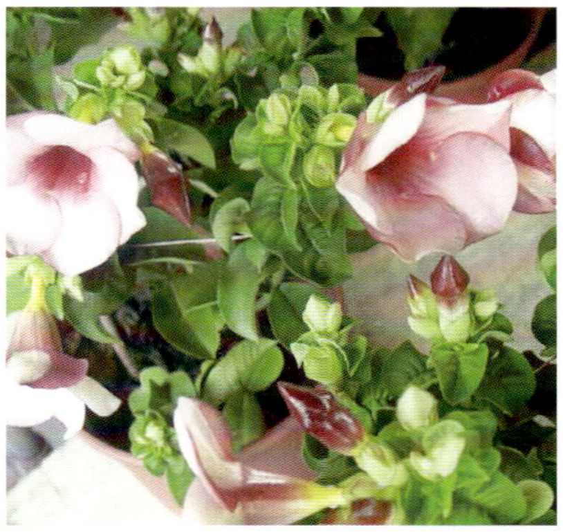
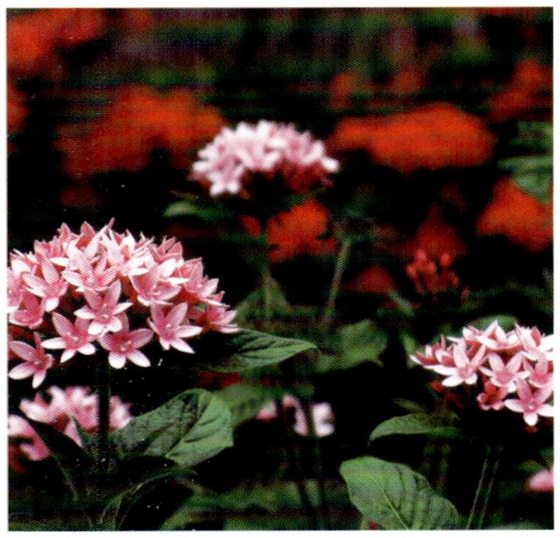
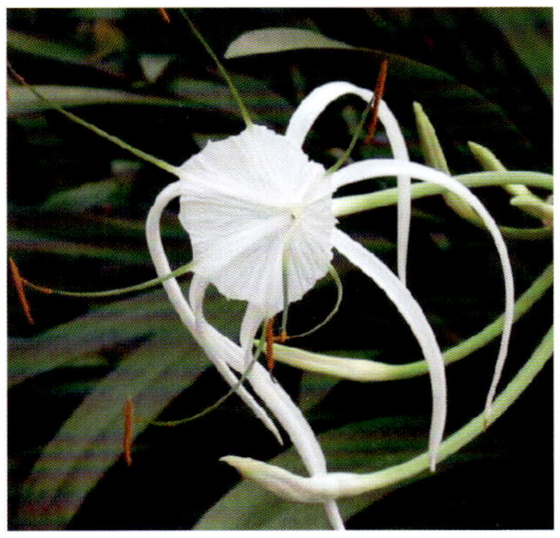
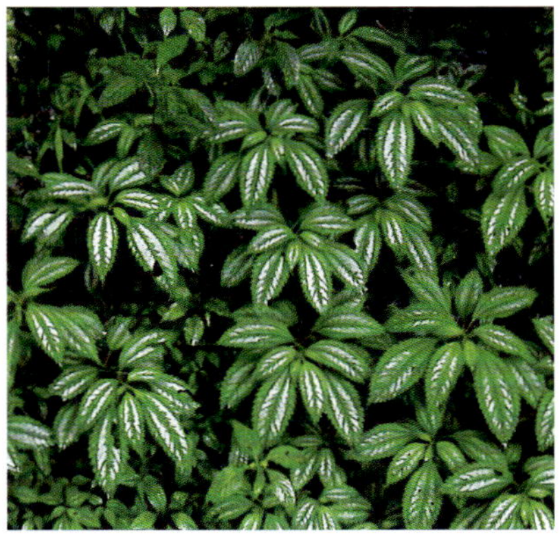
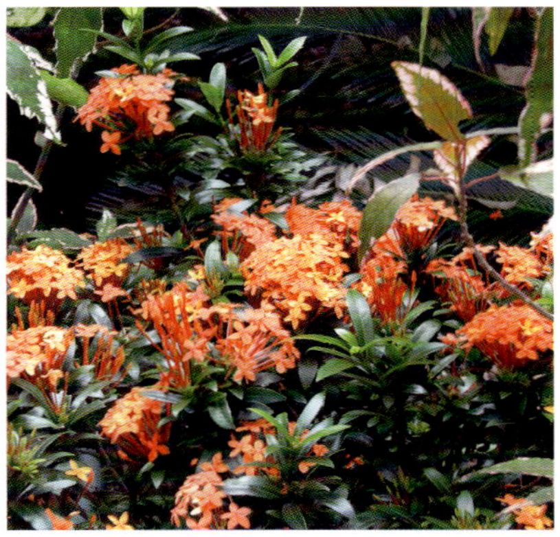

TOUCHING THE IMPOSSIBLE

PETER BOWTELL

Even now, the very idea seems breathtaking in its ambition. Longer, higher, faster, deeper: in its conception and completion, Marina Bay Sands was and is all these things and more. In every aspect, the final building is a testament to the men and women who participated in this piece of unconventional construction. Some said it could not be done, but they were outnumbered by those who had the determination to see it through! Marina Bay Sands has been a journey into the unknown, propelled by the ambition and spirit of people who believed enough in their mastery of those most elemental materials—steel and concrete—to craft a landmark out of a dream.

Lao Tzu observed that the journey of a thousand miles begins with a single step. As I experienced it, my first step was a thousand-mile journey—from Melbourne to Singapore, then to Boston and 100 Properzi Way, the office of Safdie Architects. This was July 2006. Moshe Safdie and developer Sheldon Adelson had just won Singapore's competition to build Marina Bay Sands. Warm and tranquil, bathed in midsummer sun and sheltered by a wall of ivy, the architectural studio had a serenity that belied our urgency. We had to find a starting point for building an integrated resort that so far existed only in models, watercolors, and digital renderings. Experts from around the globe gathered. And for five days we concentrated on mud.

Turn back the clock twenty-five years. The city-state of Singapore, wanting to extend its commercial center, decided to reclaim land from its river port at the rim of the Singapore Straits. They created a freshwater harbor and the new Marina Bay building surface, shrinking the river basin and pushing the colonial-era Beach Road—and the front door of the famed Raffles Hotel—back from the water's edge. Yet underneath the sandy landfill lay a bed of marine clay and silt, the residue of years of tropical rain. Fifty meters thick and soft as black putty, this was to be the foundation for our project. Our task was to create an icon, a structure whose image, whether printed on postcards or posted on Facebook, would become synonymous with Singapore. Now, an engineering challenge complicated this already daunting job because of Safdie's daring scheme to bury parking, enough for

Concept sketches, ArtScience Museum structure, courtesy of Arup

Diagram of Ideas

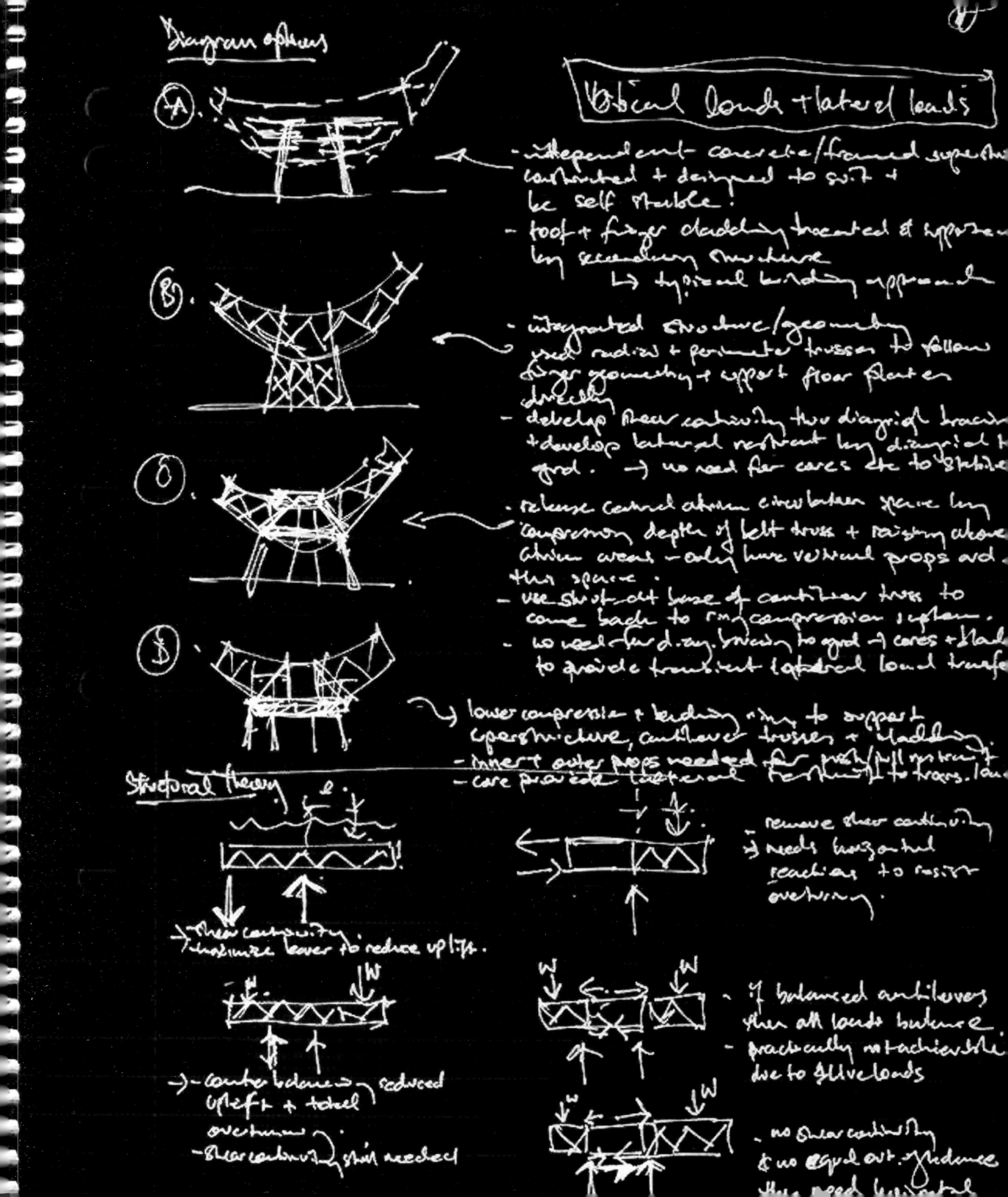

A. [sketch]
→ - independent concrete/framed superstr. constructed + designed to suit + be self stable
- roof + finger cladding transmitted & supported by secondary structure
  ↳ typical building approach

B. [sketch]
→ - integrated structure/geometry — used radial + perimeter trusses to follow finger geometry + support floor plates directly
- develop shear continuity thro diaph'l bracing + develop lateral restraint by diaph'l + grid. → no need for cores etc to stabilise

C. [sketch]
← - release central atrium circulation space by compression depth of belt truss + raising above atrium areas — only have vertical props arnd this space.
- use shortend base of cantilever truss to come back to ring compression system.
- no need for diaph. bracing to grid → cores + blade to provide transient lateral load transf.

D. [sketch]
→ lower compression + bending ring to support superstructure, cantilever trusses + cladding
- inner + outer props needed for push/pull restraint
- core provides lateral restraint to trans. lat.

Vertical loads + lateral loads

Structural theory

[sketch]
- shear continuity
- maximise lever to reduce uplift

[sketch]
- counterbalance → reduced uplift + total overturn
- shear continuity still needed

[sketch]
- remove shear continuity
  → needs horizontal reactions to resist overturning

[sketch]
- if balanced cantilevers then all loads balance
- practically not achievable due to ½ live loads

[sketch]
- no shear continuity & no equal out. goodness then need horizontal

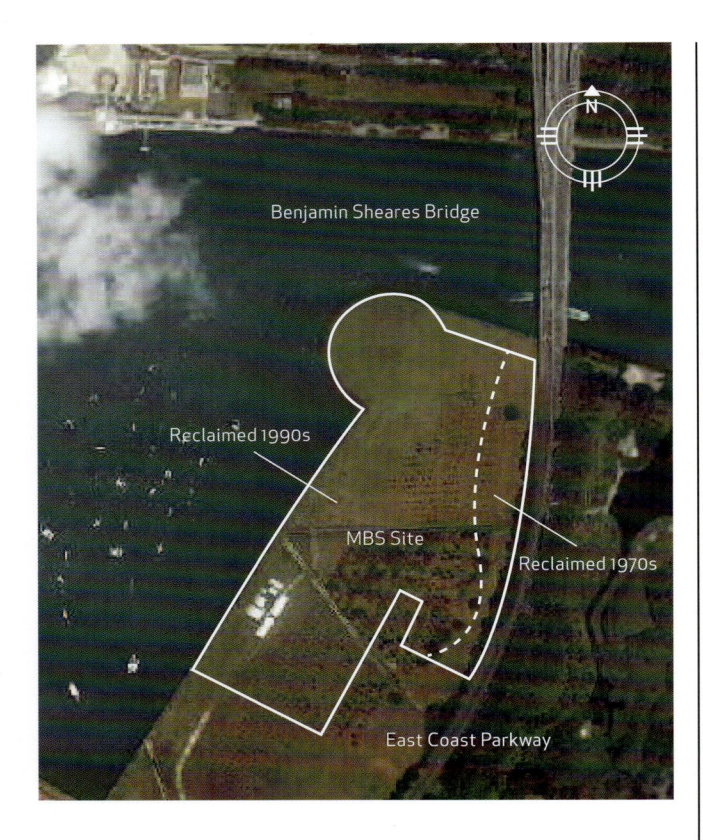

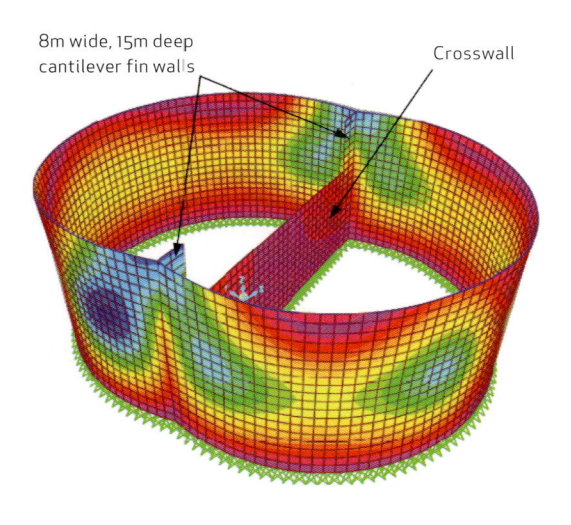

Top: Marina Bay Sands site plan showing reclaimed land

Bottom: Stress diagram showing "peanut" foundation wall

more than a thousand vehicles, within the soft maritime belly of the site. We needed to excavate at least 15 meters deep across the entire area, in some places as deep as 35 meters. But the solution to this complex problem lay in simplicity: doughnuts and peanuts. These were not edible confections but circles and figure eights of reinforced concrete, built with the support of piles driven deep through the clay into the bedrock below. Up to 125 meters in diameter, with walls up to 2 meters thick, these single and double rings had the circumferential strength to resist the weight of earth and water pressing in from all around as the clay was excavated. Some of the largest ever built, these cells enabled construction to commence unobstructed by steel props, speeding the process by as much as six months over the more traditional methods of strutted excavations.

Remarkably, the yellow traces from those early frantic days of sketching came to define the final project. Fast ideas established the ground rules on which the architectural design could proceed. Tapping the best talent in the Arup world, we toiled day and night for eight months, working with designers and engineers from every corner of the globe—Hong Kong, New York, Boston, Singapore, Melbourne, Brisbane, London—to tackle the challenges of this unprecedented project. Our team gathered monthly to share the development of our thinking with our client. Some solutions came quickly. The curvaceous blade walls that defined each of the three hotel towers were an obvious choice from day one. On the other hand, the ArtScience Museum—how to match its asymmetrical design with structural feasibility—went through relentless testing against exacting architectural requirements. And yet time was precious. Our deadline for delivery of this megalith was only three years away, and the first soil was already turning as we decamped from Boston and moved our teams to Singapore. There was no time, and there would never be any time. We just had to draw it, deliver it, build it!

Complex in design, every element of Marina Bay Sands is also complex in its engineering. Setting a backdrop to Marina Bay are the three hotel towers—named simply Tower 1, Tower 2, and Tower 3. Over fifty stories high, each tower peels apart at its base to straddle the atrium, which also serves as a public pedestrian thoroughfare open twenty-four hours a day. Looking along this axis, the structure of the towers reveals itself. Walls rise from the plaza base and curve gently together to kiss near the middle and embrace through the remaining height of each building. These walls, 600 millimeters thick, repeat every 6 meters along the length inside each tower, with hotel rooms nestled in the protected, in-between spaces. Linking the towers where they "kiss" are steel bracing frames cast into the walls. With no plate thinner than 100 millimeters, these elements are huge when viewed in isolation but merge seamlessly within the walls once encased.

There are many good reasons why you don't see a lot of buildings like these hotel towers. They require special support before being linked to achieve self-sufficiency and stability, and they move in ways that other, more rectilinear, buildings do not. Imagine, if you can, the sway of each tower at its hip, bearing the weight of more than twenty stories of concrete above. The resulting lateral load bends and shapes the tower in search of equilibrium, causing the concrete to move gradually over time, slowly relaxing through a process known as creep. For the most part, this movement is a minor fraction of the entire building's dimension and has little impact overall. But for the fast-running elevators that ferry people up and down each tower, this poses a major engineering challenge. Digital modeling of the highest accuracy was required to calculate and estimate the likely movement. Running tracks were preinstalled with adjustment in mind, allowing, in advance, for shifts that were certain to occur. The result runs smooth, with high-speed transport shuttling people through the buildings with silent precision.

Sixty meters from ground plane to roof, the three hotel lobbies act as a central orientation space and, taken as one, have a grand scale. Fire engineering skills sublimely accommodate life safety within this formidable, conjoined space. The facades are light and open, carefully integrating engineering function within support systems for the glazing. This is not a space where each component performs a single task. Every element has multiple uses, each acting in composition to reinforce the others. For example, the mechanics in the atrium ceiling designed to extract smoke during an emergency also perform the more ordinary service of ventilating hot air, a routine problem specific to Singapore's tropical climate. Beauty serves function, and function belies elegant simplicity. It is a space to be experienced not observed.

From inside the hotel axis, shimmering facades reflect the city lights over Marina Bay. Bowed sweeps of glass fins reinforce the curvilinear geometry of the architecture, and in the

Labels on top image: Peanut, Circular, Semi-Circular, DCS Box, Circular, Circular, Circular

Top: Diagram of main excavation areas

Bottom: Panoramic view of excavation inside "doughnut."

69

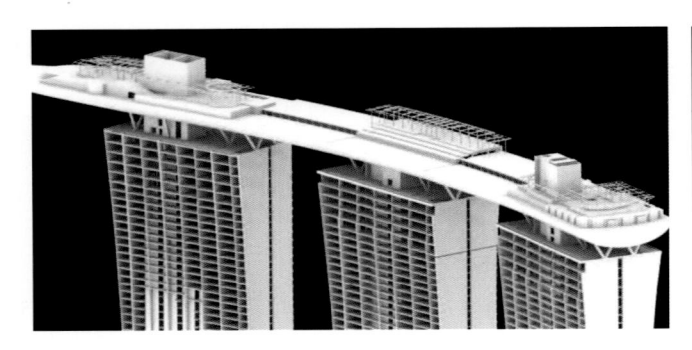

Digital images of BIM structural model

Clockwise from upper right:
Shear walls diagram, Hotel Tower 1; temporary bracing during construction Hotel Tower 1 lower levels; 3-D model of theater podium-roof steel structure; 3-D model of casino podium-roof steel structure; temporary props and link truss; sketch of shear walls and link truss

oblique rays of sunset they twinkle and glimmer, setting the walls aglow. The walls come alive, too, on the west face of the atrium in between the towers, with artist Ned Kahn's *Wind Arbor* installation, a sheer curtain of tensile wires and lightweight aluminum tiles that waft in the breeze. Here is another example of design and engineering in harmony and mutual service: as eddies shift and flow across the facade, the aluminum moves in ripplelike waves that not only delight the eye but also reflect 50 percent of the western solar heat. Shading the cathedral-like space inside, Kahn's *Arbor* reduces the air-conditioning load for the interior street running the full length of the three hotel towers. It is amazing that something so delicate can have such a substantial impact.

And yet all the while the eye is drawn upward. Little can prepare visitors for the thrill of the SkyPark, perched above the concrete plinths of the hotel. From below, it appears to float separate from the towers, thrusting toward the city and cantilevering 65.5 meters beyond the last hotel wall. The drama of the engineering resolve to achieve the SkyPark is palpable. This is no ordinary structure. At its core are two huge, steel box girders over 10 meters tall that reach forward like the jawbones of some prehistoric fossil. Yet for all its bulk, this steel 3,500-tonne skeleton is delicately balanced. Like any inhabited cantilever (and there are few), the issue is not so much about strength but ultimately about the individual user's experience. Do I feel safe? Is it too bouncy? Can I feel other people walking or dancing? These are all questions an engineer must resolve, and yet these are questions of perception: how much movement is too much? Will visitors feel uncomfortable? Unsafe? Inevitably, no two people will answer the same. The solution to this problem must be active, and ours started with a study of pedestrian comfort with shift and vibration. Going forward on this information, we placed a 5-tonne steel plate, or damper, at the tip of the cantilever and tested the result ourselves by playing music and having engineers jump to the rhythm of the beat. Perfectly tuned, this weight counterbalances every movement. The cantilever goes up, the damper moves down; one twists, the other twists back. For each action there is a perfect and opposite reaction. Physics tames physics. Is it any wonder that each visit is sheer excitement?

But to focus only on the cantilever is to ignore the other marvels of the SkyPark. There's its construction, which took not years but months, aided by a megalift of gargantuan proportions. Then there's the flexible, articulated spine, which links the towers but allows them to move independently, a solution devised under the consultancy of wind engineers. Especially spectacular is the 151-meter-long Infinity Pool, its side edge seeming to vanish into a sweeping view of Singapore. And, because Singapore is a city with very little space, the entire SkyPark offers relief—relief not only from the tropical heat, provided by the air currents wafting over this garden in the clouds, but also from the crowds and bustle of this island state, the density of an Asian metropolis of global importance. The SkyPark is both a haven and a marvel.

If Marina Bay Sands were a play, it would have five acts. So far we've seen the first three: the basements, the towers, and the SkyPark. The final elements of the performance are the podium and the museum. Yet, like any good drama, the plot is complex and interwoven. The podium has not one subplot but four, each with its own characters and events. Clearly visible are the convention center, casino, and theaters, each nestled below its own clamshell-like roof. Woven around and between these large venues is "subplot" four: the retail mall.

The centrally located, four-story casino is curvilinear and sumptuous. Its roof is complex, supported on a sweeping truss that divides the space, creating a home for a chandelier that covers the whole ceiling, simultaneously mesmerizing and discreet. To the south, the roof is stepped, with each leaf sitting on the shoulders of its partner. To the north, the roof form is concave and shell-like, a single plane draped effortlessly to meet the edge of the building's concrete frame. In the spaces below, sweeping, curved railings at each level create dynamic strata while focusing attention on the main playing floor below. In its final form, there is something restful and relaxing about the space, a calm that belies the frenetic activity that transpires within.

The five-level exhibition and convention area anchors the integrated resort at its western end. Columns infrequently puncture this large and highly flexible space, making it adaptable for a wide range of uses. At the upper level, the ballroom is column free but subdividable by a giant, collapsible air wall. Here, the structure is beholden to the space, with trusses that allow for dividing the hall. The seemingly simple has been made complex, with the geometry of the interior forming a contrast to the geometry of the roof overhead. Farther to the east, a pair of

71

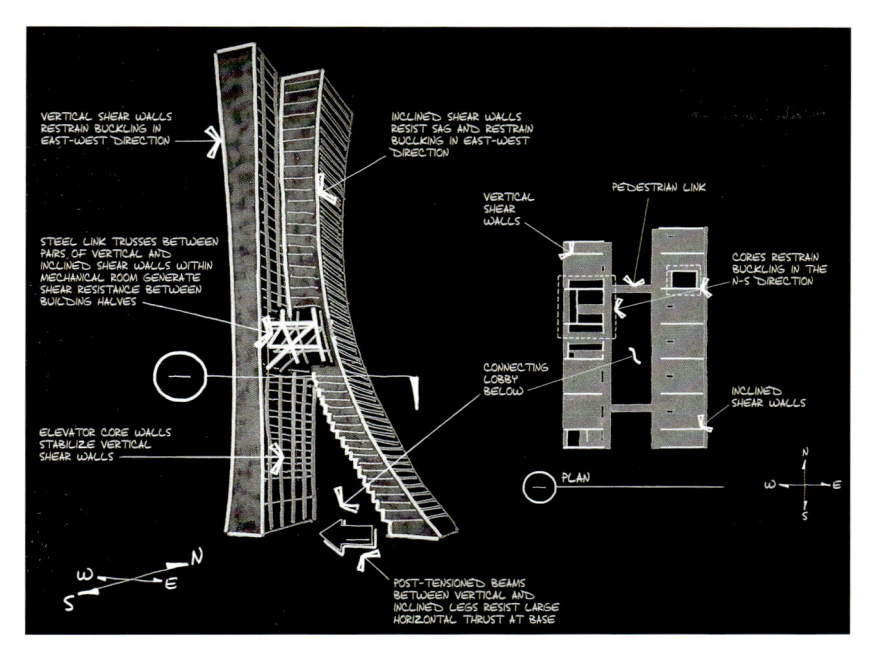

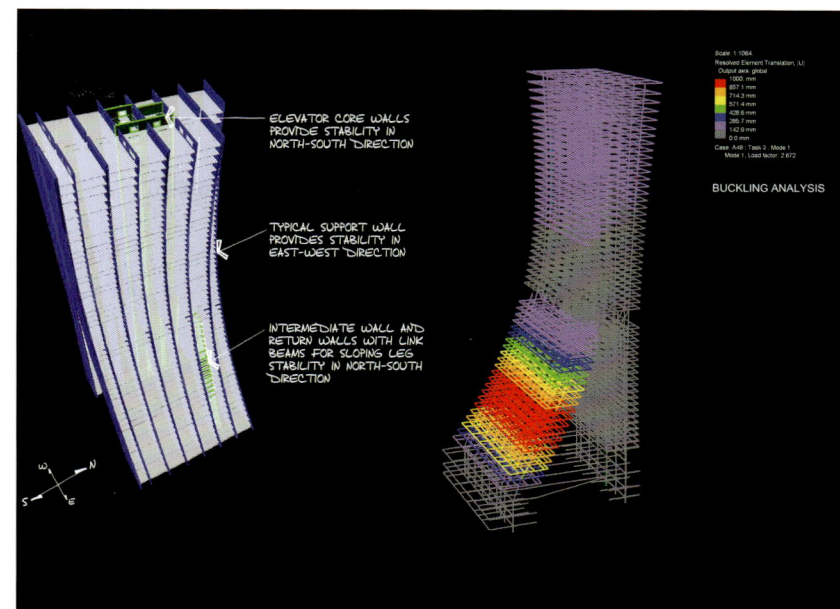

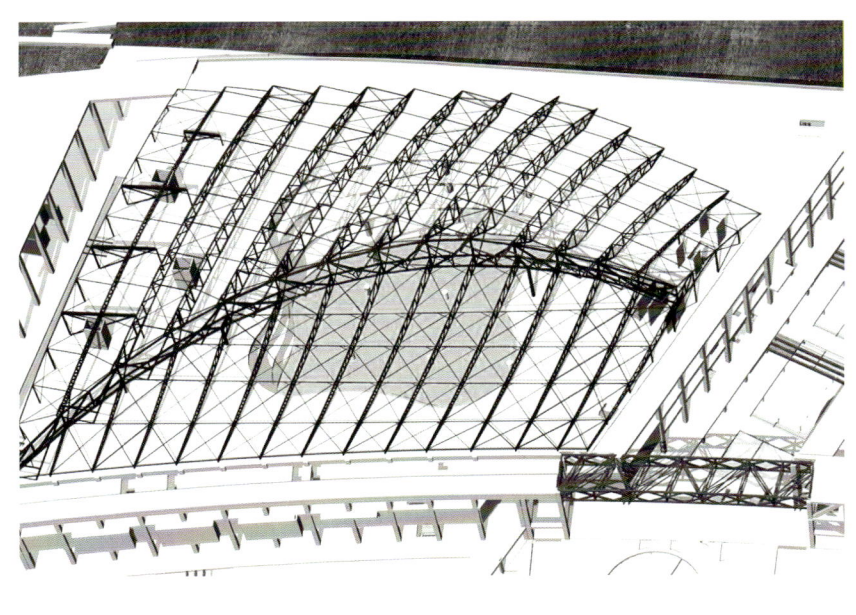

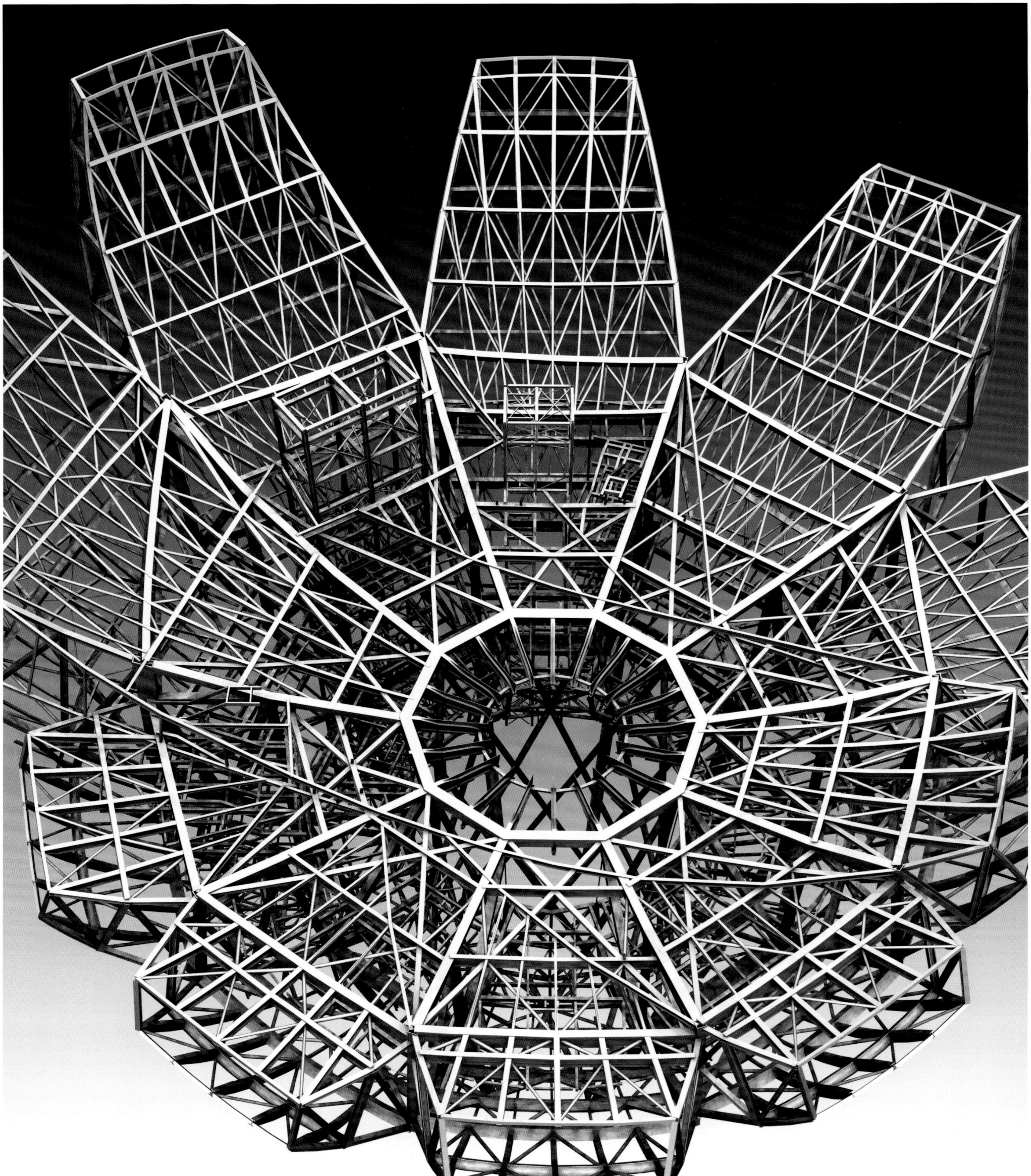

Three-dimensional image showing structural steelwork of ArtScience Museum

concrete boxes house theaters for the performing arts. Separated but interconnected, these theaters nestle below a third shell-like roof.

Integrated within these three spaces are the retail malls, each individual in character but clearly part of the same family. The arcade mall wraps around the theaters on their west side, while the corridor malls snake on either side of the performance venues, between the convention center to the south and the casino to the north. The corridors stretch beneath arched, barrel-vaulted glass ceilings. At each end, glass walls span from floor to ceiling, supported by no more than cables stretched between the buttressed bulk of concrete-framed building blocks. However, with the Grand Arcade mall, which faces the waterfront, the retail space takes on a life of its own. Sinewlike, it shelters beneath louvered roofs, some as large as football fields, cable supported and tensioned in a perfect counterbalance to the arched framing of the glazed enclosures below. Where facade stops and structure continues is for only the most knowledgeable to comprehend.

At last, we come to the final act: the ArtScience Museum. Complex in every detail, the museum matches its name in being a perfect blend of art and engineering. In concept, the museum has two sections. In the podium, large gallery spaces surround a central courtyard and tranquil lily pond, filled and replenished by rain filtered though a roof oculus some 60 meters above. While the lower level literally grounds the building, anchoring it in concrete, the upper galleries define the museum visually. Perched on sticks, they seem to defy gravity, reaching to the sky in a welcoming gesture of openness, like a lotus or a hand outstretched to the city and the world beyond.

At the very earliest stages of design, a problem must be broken down into component parts. For the museum, it was vital that the upper galleries appear to stay aloft effortlessly, as if by magic. Each space had to be connected yet defined by the boundaries set by each of the ten petals or fingers. Free-flowing stairs had to provide access between floors, enabling patrons to follow a linear path.

Through rigorous testing and modeling, we created a structural puzzle elegant in its simplicity. Cantilevered trusses radiate from a central steel core, separating the galleries and then splitting to define the edge of each "finger" as it curves skyward. At the top and bottom of the central core, two rings carry opposing forces of tension, balancing the structure. Still, the galleries are asymmetrical, and without a second intervention the building would lurch sideways to the ground. Enter the diagrid, a helixlike central stabilizing element. Connected only to the upper tensile ring, the diagrid resists any imbalance from the different sizes of the ten galleries. Next, ten steel megacolumns positioned around the central void provide vertical support to the upper galleries. Finally, the framing to the lift shaft acts like a stake driven solidly to ground, anchored to prevent rotation. Each piece of the puzzle is vitally important to the integrity of the whole, all in perfect harmony to complete the composition.

Achieving this kind of integrated solution—where the structure becomes the design, which in turn reinforces the structure—required empathetic and mutual collaboration between architect and engineer. This level of cooperation underpinned the entire engineering drama of Marina Bay Sands: complex in execution, exciting in delivery, unique on a global platform. It could only be built now, and only in Singapore. We were all lucky to have been part of its realization.

The Observation Deck is the largest occupiable cantilevered structure in the world. To test calculations for pedestrian comfort, Arup's structural team conducted a dynamic-loading test with people jumping to different musical beats.

75

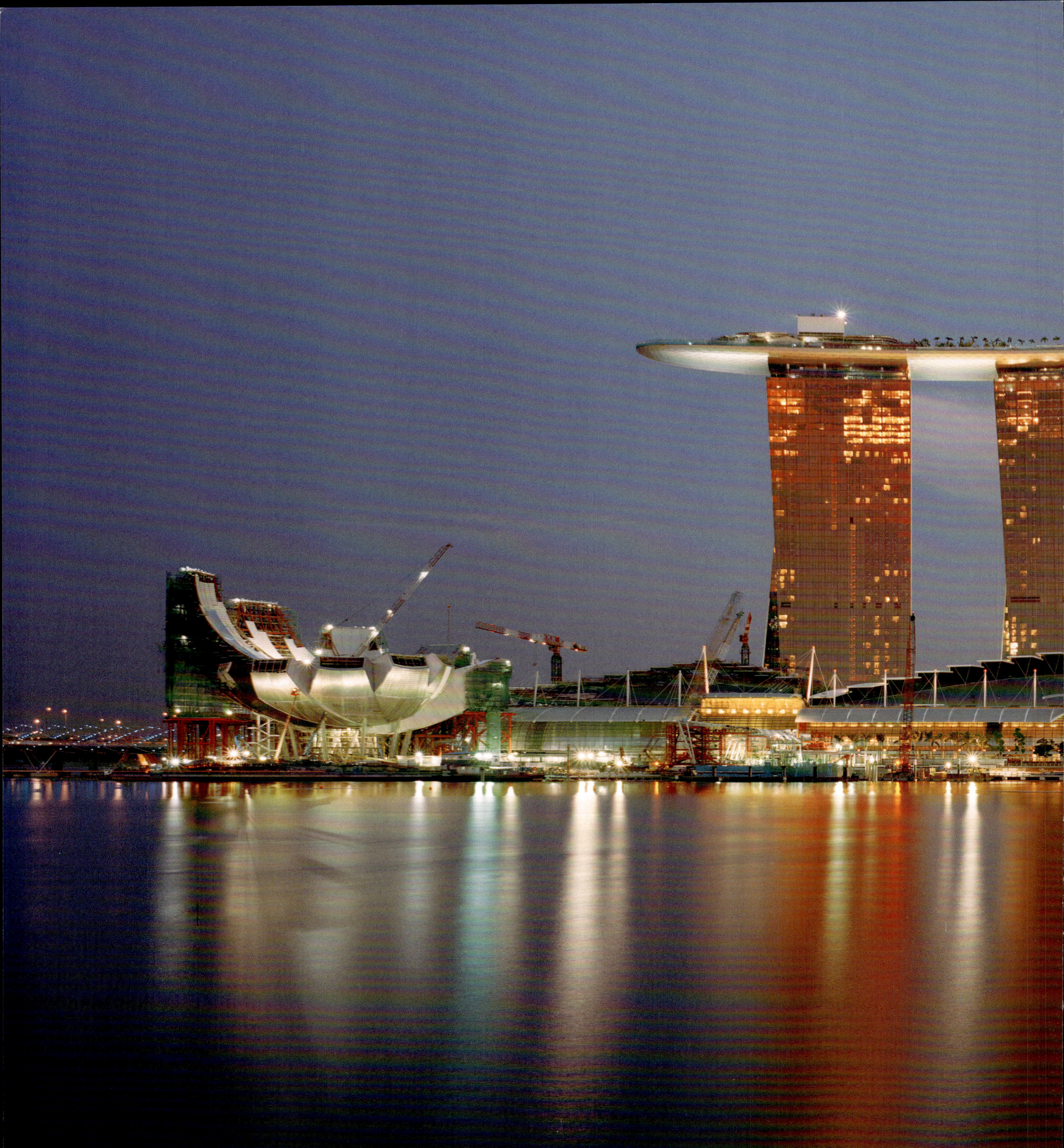

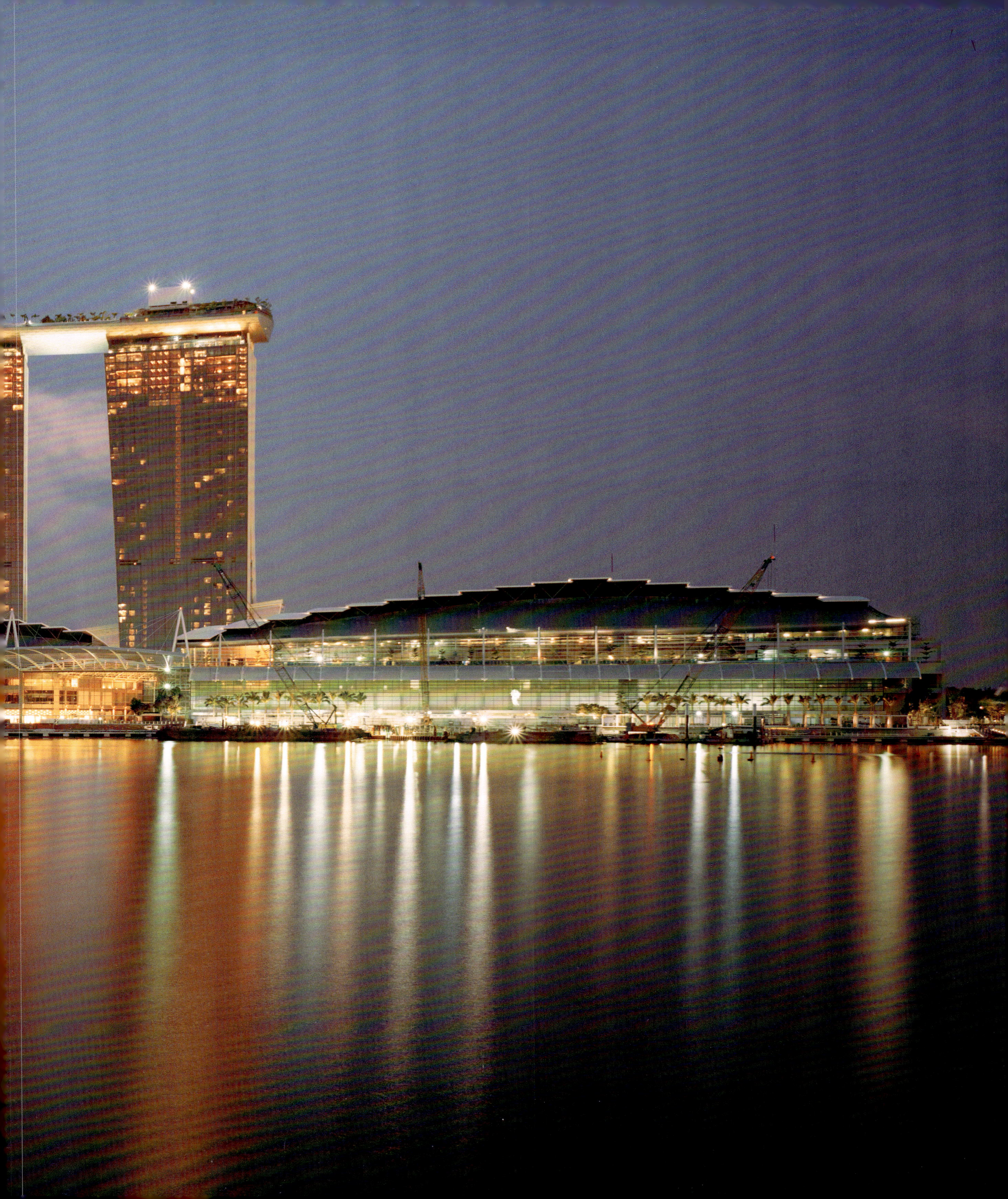

THE MAKING OF AN ICON

MARTIN C. PEDERSEN

When George Tanasijevich received news that his Las Vegas Sands Corporation team had won the development rights for Singapore's Marina Bay integrated resort, he didn't have much time to celebrate. Less than twenty-four hours, in fact. But given the pace of the project so far, this was no surprise. The company had created and scrapped its original hotel and convention center scheme, then hired the renowned architect Moshe Safdie to create an entirely new one in three months, all the while preparing an elaborate, six-volume, thousand-plus-page proposal. "These were coffee-table-style books," Tanasijevich says. "They had French silk covers, fine Japanese paper, with computer renderings and full-color illustrations. But really, it was a deep dive into what the property would look and feel like, the way we'd program it, the impact it would have on the economy, the number of jobs it would create. It covered everything you could imagine."

On the morning after the big announcement, Tanasijevich received a call from government officials in Singapore. "As soon as we won, they were ready to run with this thing," he says. Indeed, the development and construction teams began forming almost immediately.

Tanasijevich worked with local officials on fast-tracking the approval process—something the government had already anticipated. Matthew Pryor, the company's former vice president for construction in Asia, assumed responsibility for building the 9-million-square-foot project. Already working in Macau, on an even bigger but less architecturally ambitious project, Pryor tapped John Downs, his right-hand man, to oversee the day-to-day construction of Marina Bay Sands. Very quickly, the effort became an exercise in rapidly morphing construction and design teams. "It was like a pyramid," Pryor explains. "I sat at the top, and then you start building out the layers below until you ultimately get to 16,000 workers on site."

For now, though, there was just a small team trying to unravel and anticipate all the problems and challenges ahead: how many contractors did they need? Why weren't the local companies interested? How many workers would they need to hire? Where would they come from? How much temporary housing would they need to build? What about raw materials? Access roads? Those three sloping, fifty-seven-story towers? And how on earth would they build the SkyPark? The list was both head spinning and

Excavation work begins in 2006

BACHY
BAUER
BACHY SOLETANCHE
CAT
CAT
DANGER-KEEP OUT!
BAHAYA-JANGAN DEKAT!

80

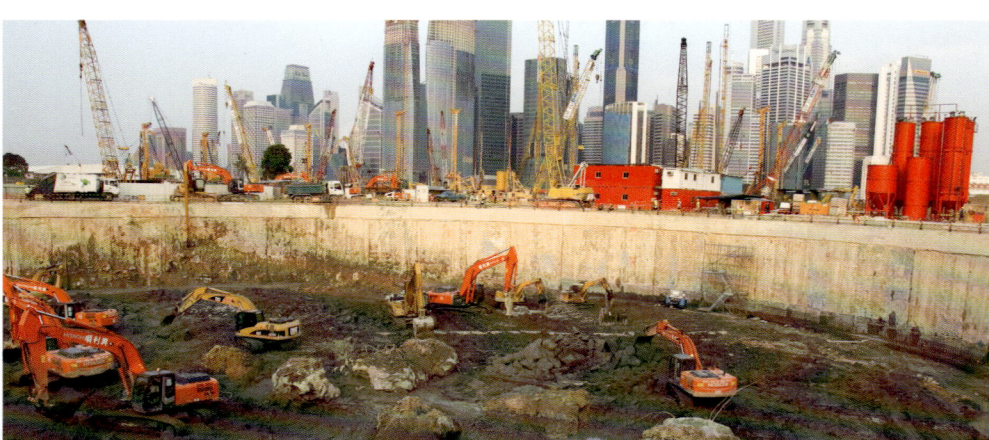

A last look at the site
before excavation

Excavation site in 2006

book length. There would also be thousands of unforeseen dilemmas they couldn't begin to predict. "To organize it, we broke the project into four parts," Downs says. "A tower team, two podium teams—one for the casino and the theater, one for the convention center—and the infrastructure team, which managed the museum, the two crystals, the roadways, and the rail tunnels underneath."

The Singapore Urban Redevelopment Authority (URA) had shrewdly bundled a new subway tunnel and station into the development package, ensuring that Marina Bay Sands would eventually become the heart of a new twenty-first-century business and entertainment district. The Sands project was part of a larger, city-created master plan for Marina Bay, the reclaimed parcel of land in the Singapore Harbor located directly across from the Central Business District. Eventually, a botanical garden and a cruise ship terminal promise to funnel thousands of tourists through Marina Bay Sands. At the same time, the subway should make the site accessible to the public and spur the development of office towers nearby. A 3.2-kilometer tunnel will replace an existing highway. It's the kind of coordinated effort that makes Singapore the envy of urban planners everywhere. "The government is decisive and proactive," Tanasijevich says. "It's one of the advantages of investing here. There is a real alignment between the government and the private sector."

One of the first of many unforeseen challenges emerged early on, during site analysis. The design and construction teams knew that Marina Bay was the product of a large dredging operation that had closed off the mouth of the Singapore River and created a freshwater harbor. The feasibility of building on the resulting land, however, was a question mark. A few ramshackle restaurants had been located out there, but they sat lightly on what the site team discovered were 9 meters of sand—and underneath that, an almost unimaginable problem for a project of this size. "When we started driving the piles down to hit bedrock, or good ground," Pryor says, "we found a seawall which literally ran the length of the hotel." Constructed decades ago by the government, the seawall, hidden under the landform, had been largely forgotten. "They basically built a platform on top of that seawall," he says. "And we didn't know about it. It was a challenge that took months to overcome at substantial cost."

The solution? Pryor and Downs tapped into the collective expertise of dozens of civil, technical, and structural engineers, who suggested building the kind of diaphragm wall often used for tunnels. The wall would essentially rest on good ground and encase the foundation. "We brought in a different piling system and drilled down through the rock," Pryor explains. "The diaphragm wall is more or less the footprint of the building. The foundation is under that, encased in it, and then you have a whole grid of pilings that take the actual load. We started building the wall, and then parallel with that, we dug down and began clearing out the rocks as much as we could. It is what's known as top-down construction, going up and down at the same time. Those diaphragm walls essentially became the hotel tower's basement wall. You form the wall and then dig out inside it, and there's your basement."

Except, of course, it wasn't that easy. Because they were building on reclaimed land in the middle of a harbor, there was another complication: marine clay. Sometimes known as "black toothpaste," this loose substance is the bane of coastal builders the world over and the cause of many structural failures, including the 2004 collapse of Nichol Highway in Singapore that killed four people. Here, it was especially maddening. As the team drilled and dug its way to good ground, marine clay kept sliding into the newly created void. So for twenty-four hours a day, six days a week, the project became a kind of mechanized juggling act—dig, drain, build— performed by hydraulic pumps, pile drivers, cranes, and hundreds of workers, dedicated to holding back not just the hugely inconvenient slop but really the sea itself. They built more than 3.2 kilometers of retaining wall, some of it as thick as 1.5 meters. "It was crazy, absolutely nuts," Pryor says, clearly relishing the experience in retrospect. "There is nothing else like it from an engineering perspective. Forty percent of the volume of the building is below-ground. The basement in places is 50 meters deep. We were in the ground for a year."

The collaboration between Las Vegas Sands and Moshe Safdie was a curious one from the start, and once the bid was won and work commenced, an interesting dynamic evolved. They were engaged in the ultimate challenge: creating architecture (with a capital A) on a massive, arguably unprecedented, scale. It was unfamiliar territory for everyone involved. Pryor and Downs had worked on bigger projects but not at this level of refinement. Safdie lived in a world of architectural refinement but had never done a project of this size, a resort, or even a

Top: Cranes and heavy equipment at site excavation

Bottom: Steel fabrication of SkyPark begins in 2008

commercial building. "When we came on, they had no confidence in us," Safdie recalls. "John Downs knew my reputation but not in terms of production capabilities, response to detailing, sensitivity to the developer. We had to gain their confidence. We performed, and slowly their confidence grew. Technical issues were solved, needs were addressed. We discovered together how to transform the project. And John—who's an architect by the way—also realized this was different from Macau. They were an amazing team."

And they had to be, since they were building a one-off—a series of one-offs, actually—and those are always fraught with difficulties. Some problems emerged during construction: unstable land, a spike in the cost of raw materials, a sand embargo, a global banking crisis. Major complications, to be sure, but as the irrepressible chairman and CEO of the Las Vegas Sands Corporation, Sheldon Adelson, says, "Once you decide you're going to move forward with a development, the rest is only money."

One big hurdle was evident from the model early on and didn't have an immediate solution. Safdie had boldly proposed taking all of the amenities usually found in luxury resorts—pools, spas, nightclubs, restaurants, bars, and green space—and housing them in a sculptural structure that would span the three fifty-seven-story hotel towers. The 1.2-hectare SkyPark would be about as long as an aircraft carrier and feature a 66.75-meter Observation Deck cantilevered at the north end, offering panoramic views of Singapore, the Indian Ocean, and Malaysia. If it was executed at anywhere close to the elegance suggested by Safdie's renderings, it would surely become the new symbol for Singapore.

Wild, audacious, breathtaking, stunningly simple in the purity of its conception—it now needed to be built. Figuring out how became a series of questions answered by a small army of structural experts. "Arup did all of the engineering, and it's very much on the cutting edge," Pryor says. And what did they make of those three sloping towers connected at the top by a linear park more than 304 meters long? "They looked at it long and hard and scratched their heads, but said, 'This can be done,'" he says. "From an engineering point of view, you can pretty much build anything these days. It's just a matter of how long it takes and how much it costs. Here, they had to come up with a good solution that was buildable within a certain time frame and relatively cost-effective."

The test wasn't just in devising a way to construct the SkyPark 198 meters in the air. The three hotel towers, which look like gigantic A-frames, were equally quixotic. Though at first glance they appear identical, they are in fact distinct structures, with different footprints and wildly different structural loads. Each tower is, in essence, two buildings joined at the top, with the two halves gracefully peeling away from each other at the twenty-second floor to create a vast, connected cathedral-like space in the lobby below.

The south tower, Tower 1, which has the widest footprint and most complex geometries, was particularly vexing. "Basically, you have one straight leg and another one that kicks out at about 45 degrees, leaning against it," Pryor says. "When that happens, it puts eccentric loads on that straight leg. The 45-degree leg is trying to push over the straight one. So what we had to do was tie the two legs together where they began to meet, at the twenty-second floor. This joint is called a link truss, and it spans four or five stories, creating a very rigid right-angle triangle."

Before reaching the magical inflection point, a huge web of steel scaffolding propped up Towers 1 and 2. "Working with the contractor for the hotel towers, Ssangyong Engineering and Construction, we created almost a building within a building," Pryor says. "It was about a thousand tonnes of temporary steelwork, which we used to lie the towers on until we tensioned them up. Until you got to the kissing point and linked them up, those two towers were very unstable." Once the link trusses had been installed—a process that took about four months—they were ready to remove the temporary steel and test the viability of the towers. With a large team of engineers on-site, and a heavy load of building monitors measuring movement, the team over the next thirty-six hours slowly removed the steel web. "That was the first major engineering test," he says.

After the tower legs had been secured—or "tied-off," in engineer-speak—it was a straight, somewhat conventional sprint to the top. The real fun would commence up on the structurally reinforced roof slabs. "To design and engineer and plan the SkyPark took almost a year," Pryor says. During this lengthy process, he and Downs were in constant contact with engineers and consultants, leaping across time zones to push the project forward. "We were following the sun using Arup's Boston, New York, London, Hong Kong, and Singapore offices," Downs says.

HSBC
CSC L&M FS
CAT KKL
KOBELCO

XCMG
QUY150
DANGER
LIFTING
IN
PROGRESS

Construction activity on the site
between 2006–11

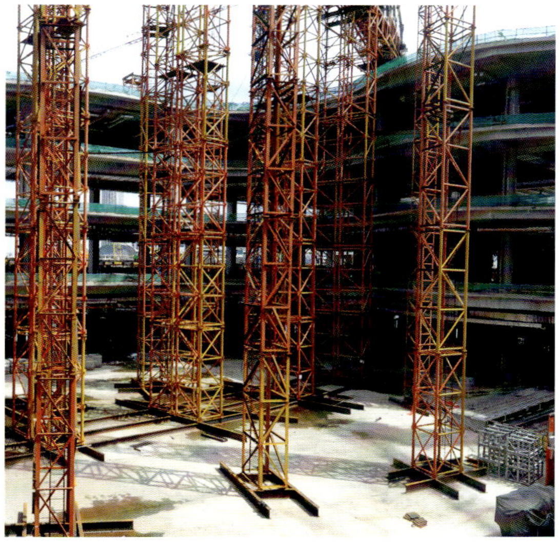

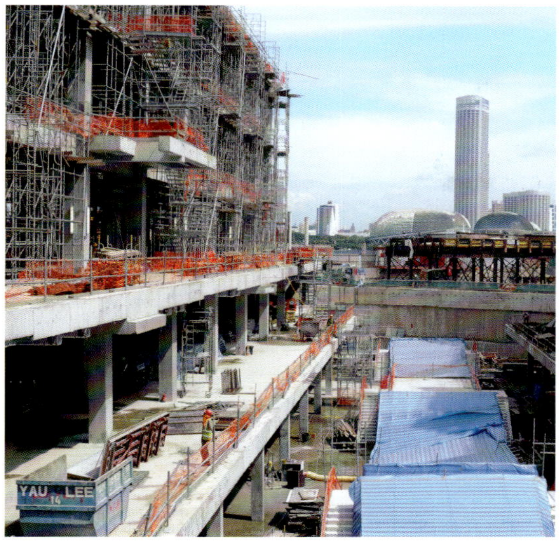
YAU LEE

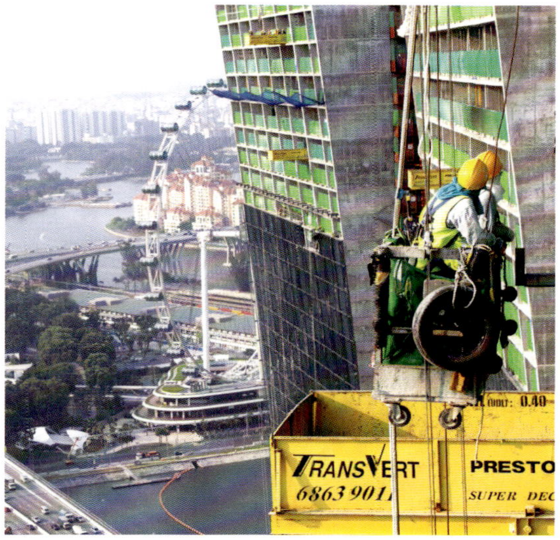
TRANSVERT
6863 9011
PRESTO

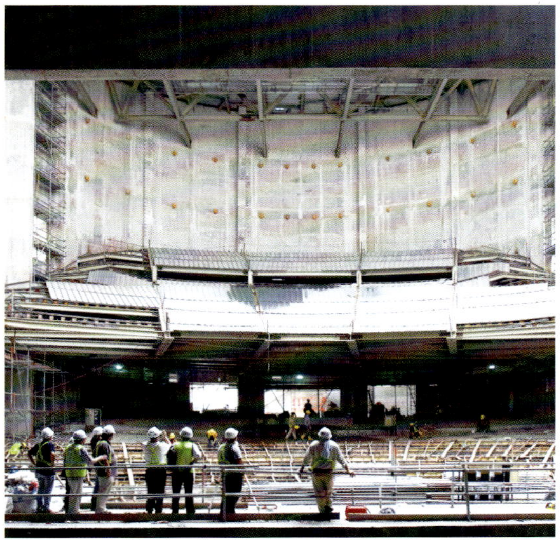

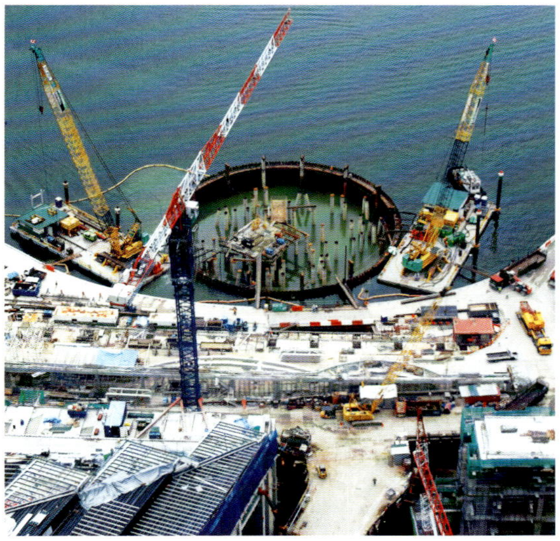

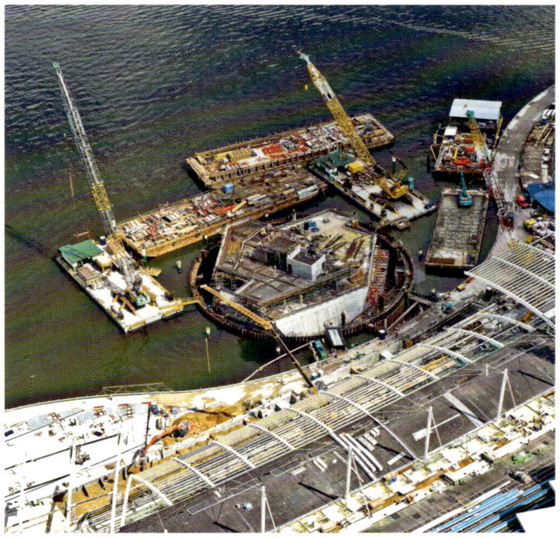

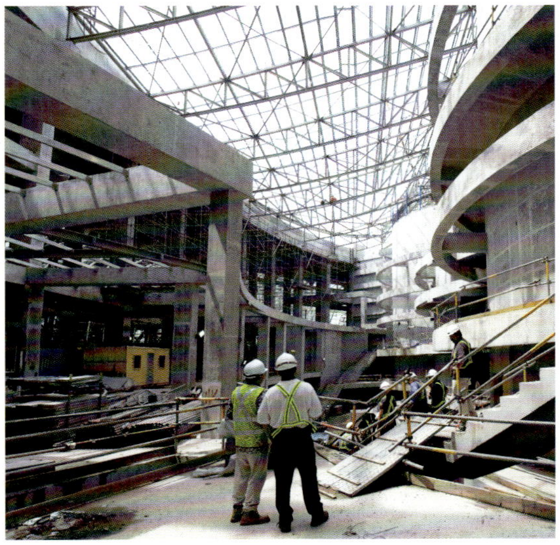

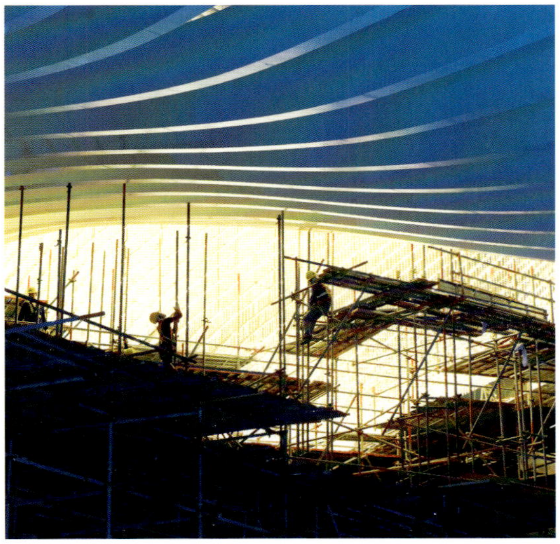

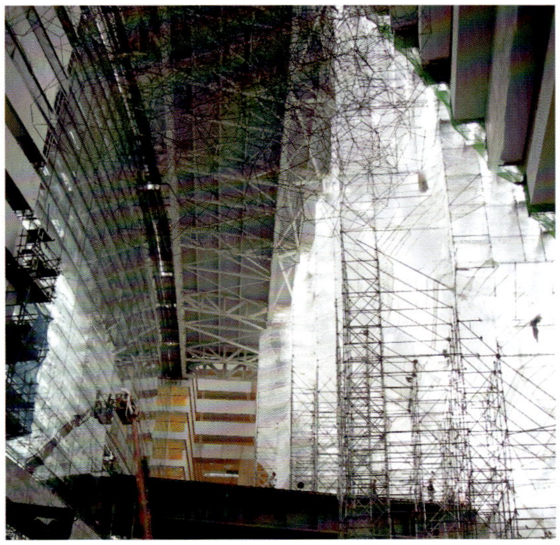

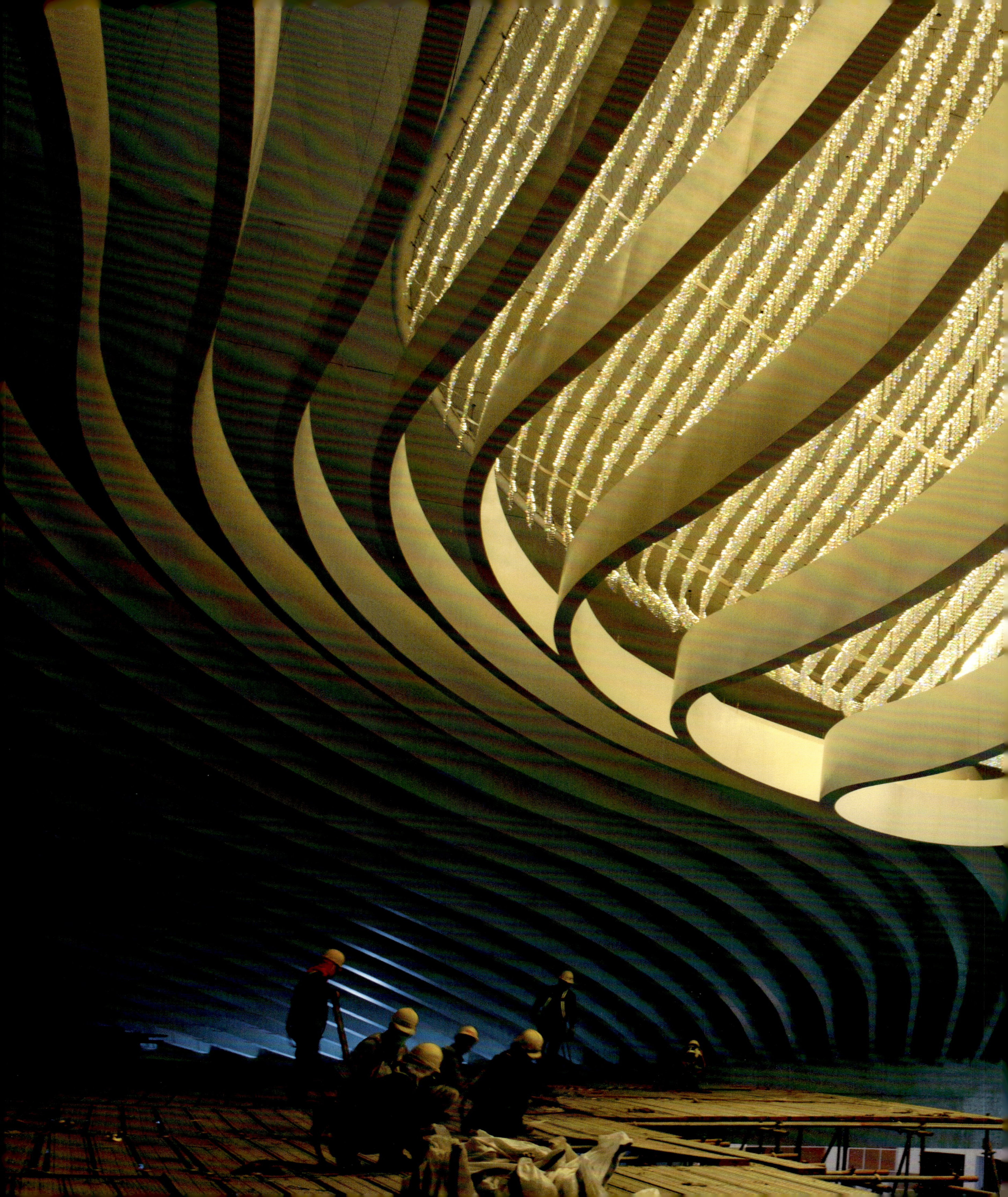

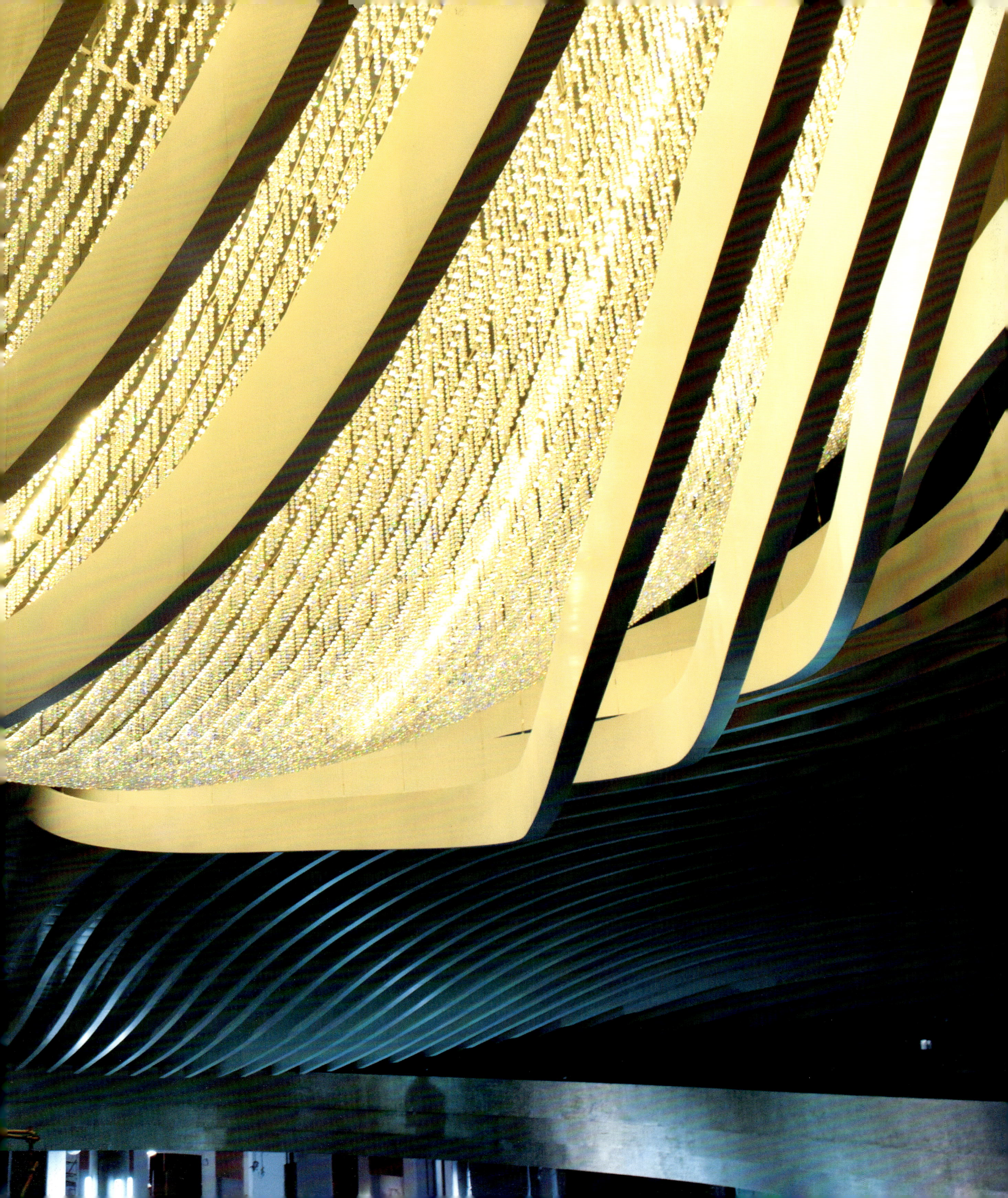

88

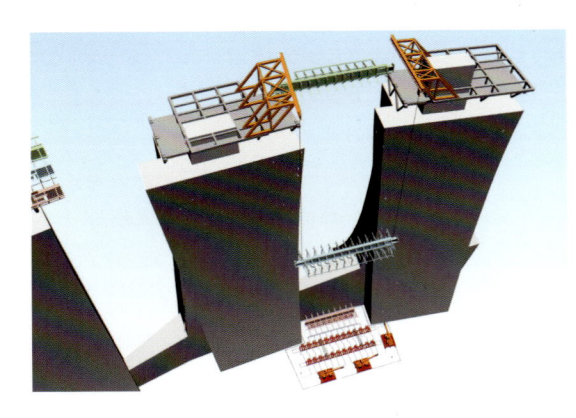

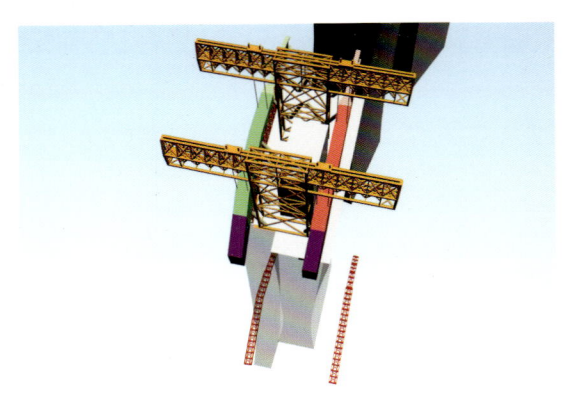

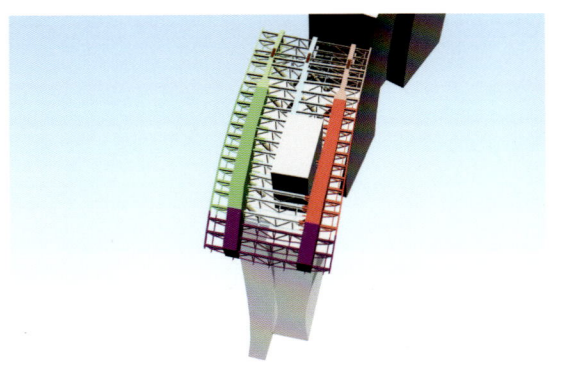

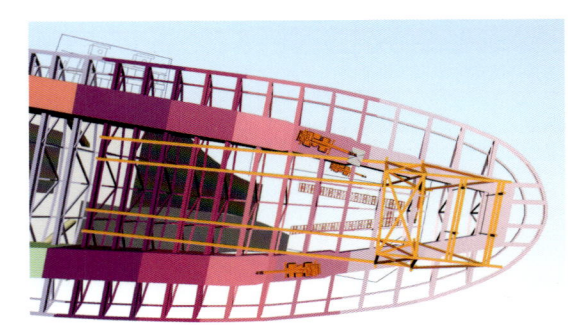

Engineers used bridge-building technology to lift more than 8,000 tonnes of steel components for the SkyPark.

The engineering solution for the SkyPark utilized prefabrication on a massive scale. Eventually, the structure would weigh more than 8,165 tonnes, so the engineers broke it down into component parts, which were fabricated at local shipbuilding yards and then trucked to the site in pieces. On the roof of each tower, they created a series of steel supports. Each piece would be lifted in the air a distance equivalent to the length of two soccer fields—beginning with the three huge, 816-tonne box trusses that would connect the towers—and then maneuvered into place with cranes and welded together. "Our first instinct was to build the whole structure in steel, including the sections above the hotel towers," Pryor says. "Instead, we decided to complete the towers in concrete, and then 'infill' with steel. This allowed us to complete the towers as we were fabricating the steelwork. What we did, essentially, was build a steel ship, and plunk that down on top of the three towers."

The logistical challenge here was a primitive one. "The strongest cranes can lift 40 or 50 tonnes, but to try even twice that would be very high risk," Pryor says. The SkyPark's biggest pieces, the box trusses, were many times heavier than that and required a sophisticated lifting system called strand jacking. "These are a series of high-tension cables fixed to the towers, which travel down to the ground on both sides. It's very tightly controlled computer technology. There are only two companies in the world that can do it. They attached the trusses to the cables. Then, as they rose—very slowly, 8 to 10 meters an hour—they had to carefully synchronize the tensioning of them, and lift at exactly the same speed." The first hoist was almost performance art, done on a civic scale. Like building the Golden Gate Bridge, it was a public high-wire act that played out over several weeks and immediately transformed Marina Bay Sands from a mammoth Asian construction site into an international icon.

As the final form began to take shape, Singaporeans across the harbor began posing for pictures with the SkyPark prominently in the frame. Meanwhile, despite the obstacles, the rest of the huge project buzzed to completion in just thirty-nine months, a testament to perseverance and teamwork. "It was a very collaborative process, on an expedited basis," says Tanasijevich, named president and CEO of Marina Bay Sands in July 2011. And he would know: he was the one who organized the original bid and brought together a development team that called upon the expertise of a multitude of consultants, bankers, lawyers, and staff members. "Moshe's original concept is this building, I can tell you that," says Tanasijevich. "The concept was there, day one. But for those of us who are not architects and engineers, it can be hard to tell what a building will look like from a drawing. I don't think any of us had the ability to really understand what this would feel like. Even to this day, I'll walk around and think, 'Wow, I never anticipated that.'"

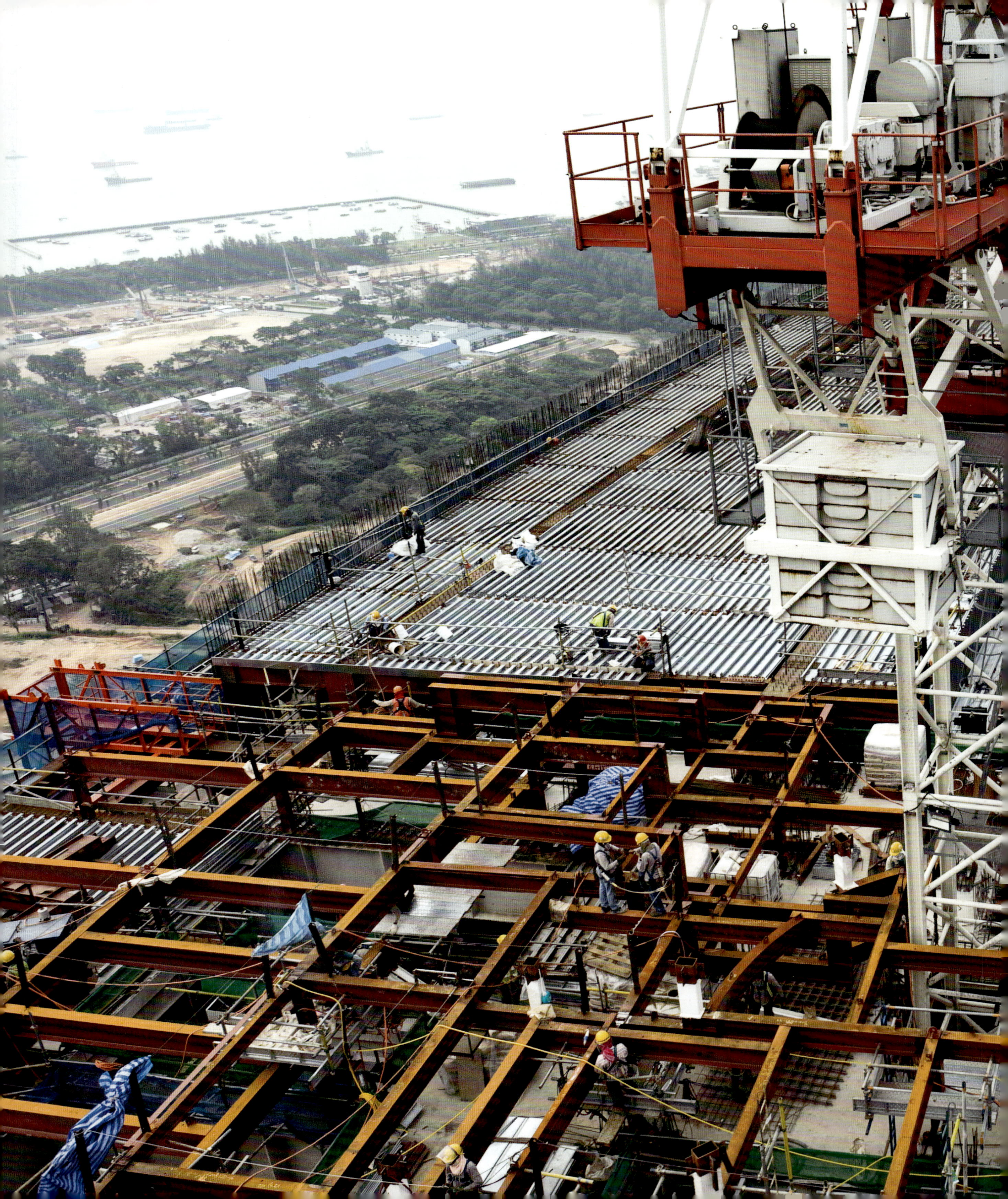

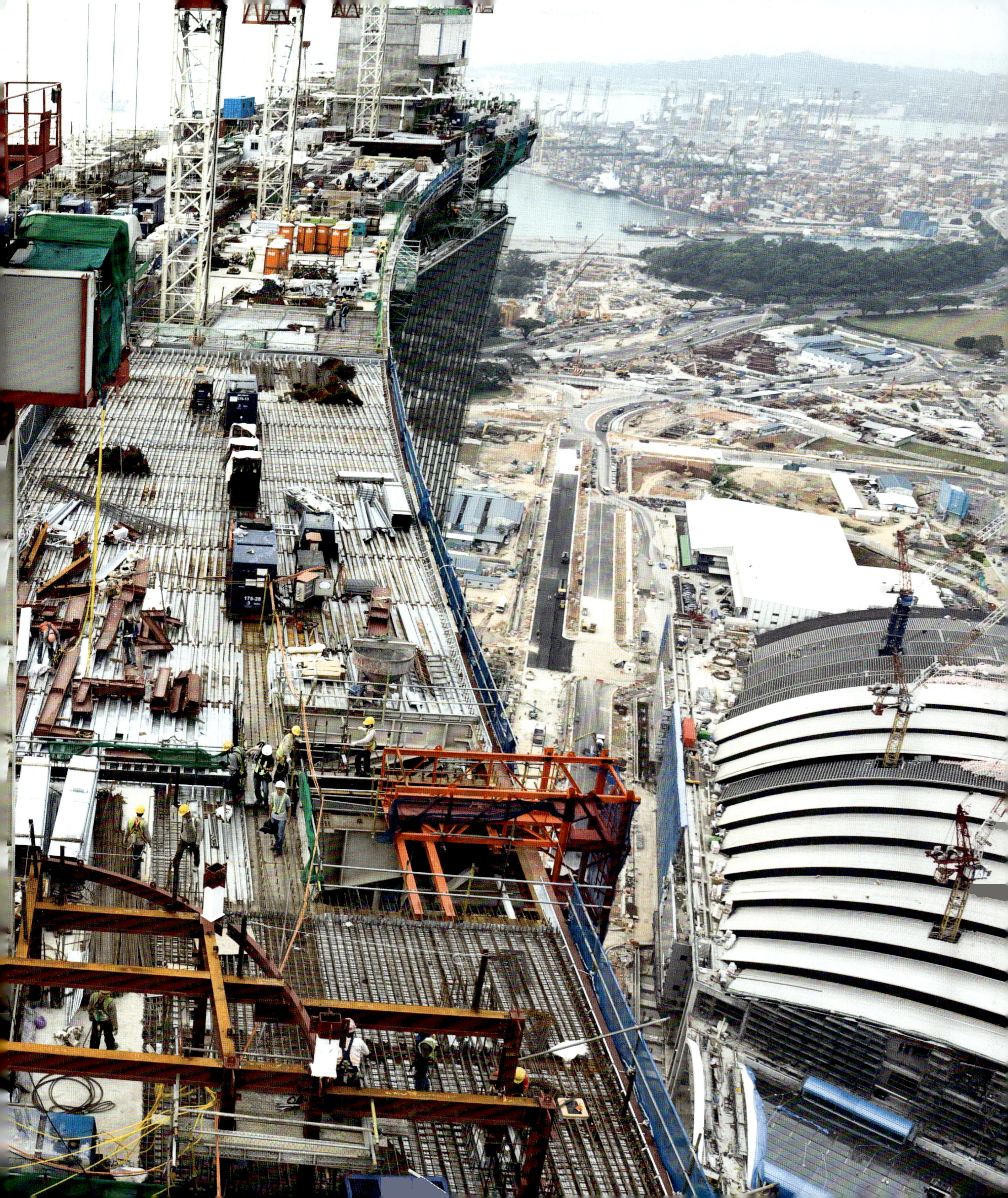

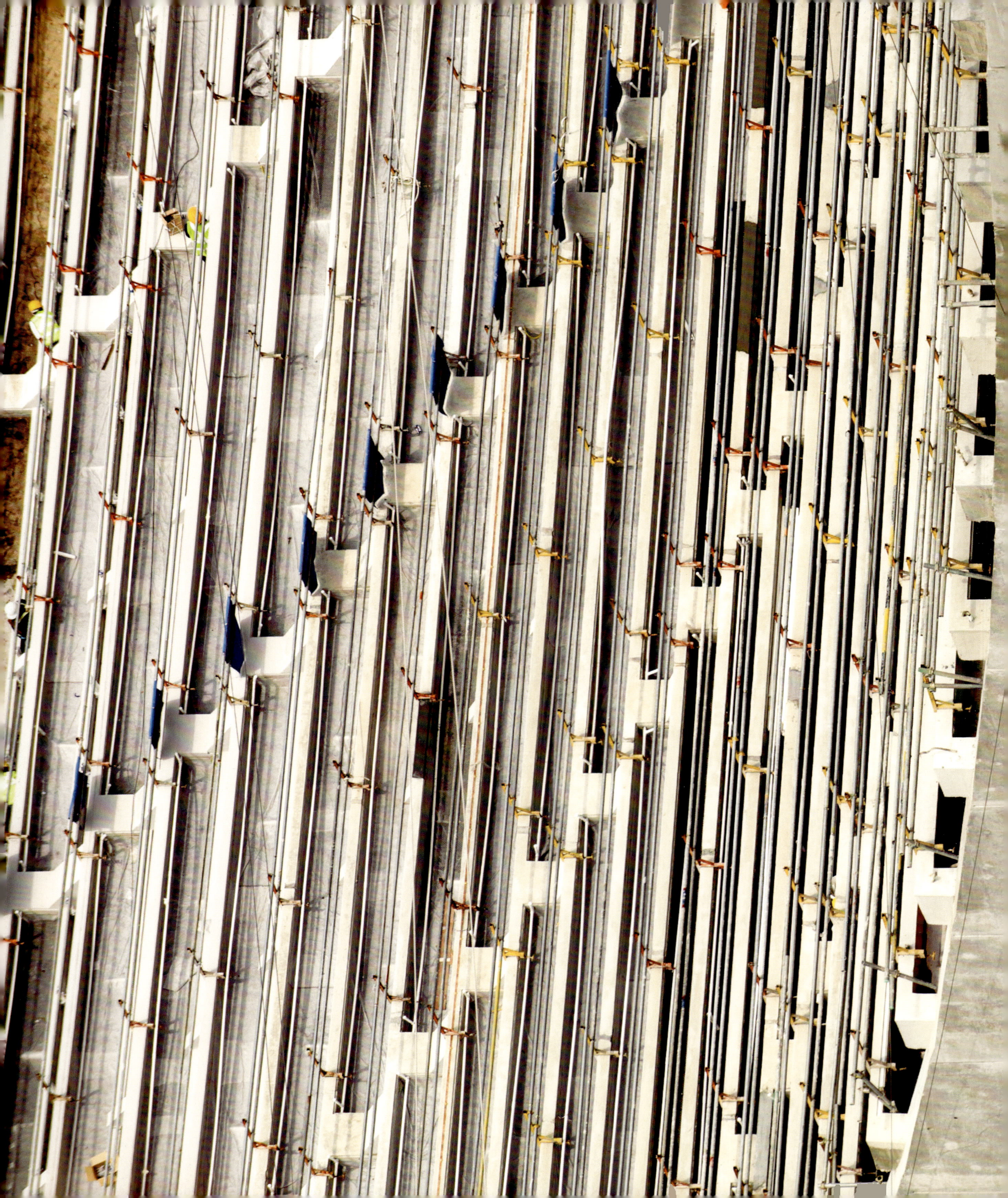

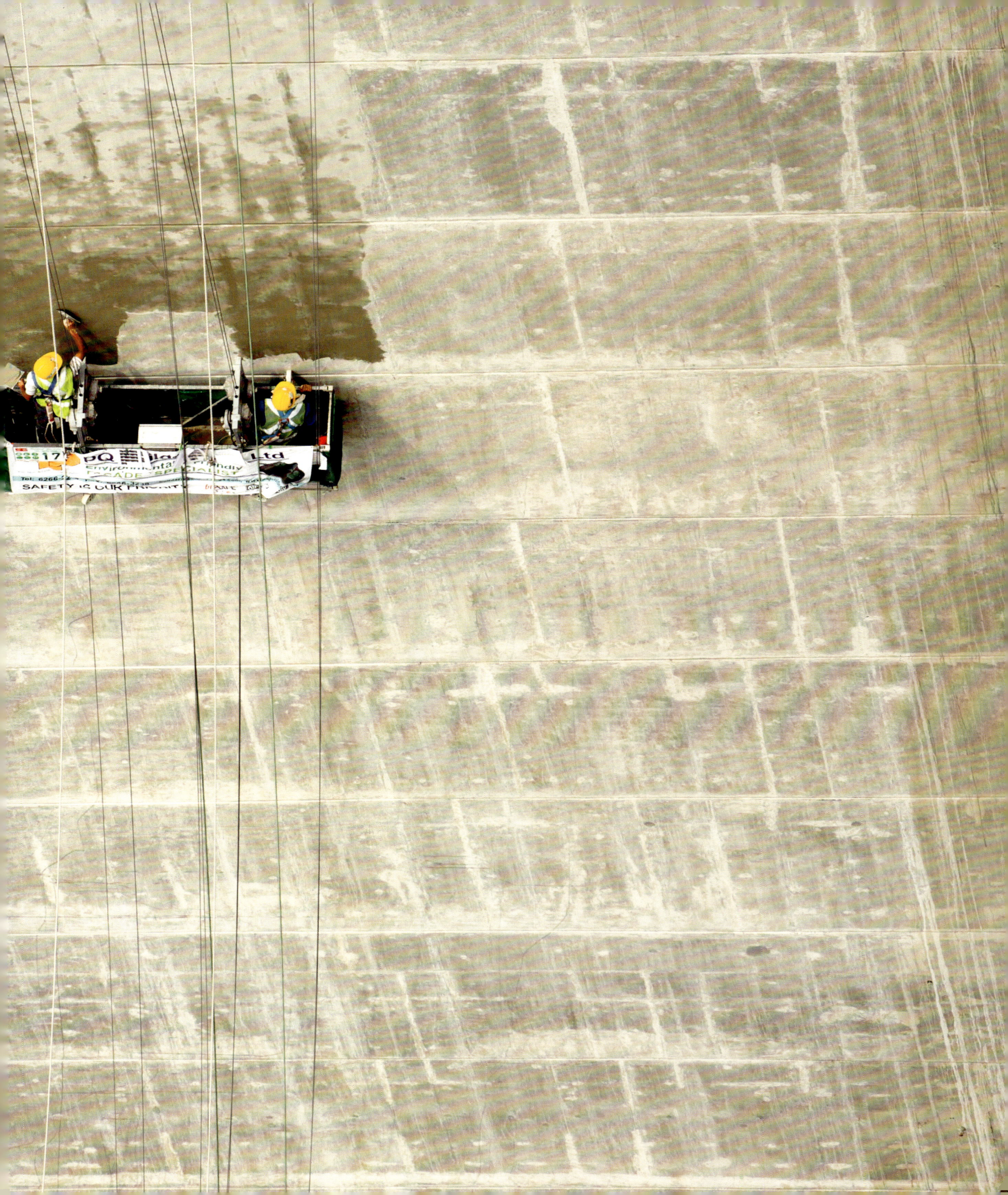
Ltd

PART 2
ARCHITECTURAL DRAWING PLANS

MARINA BAY SANDS

CTURAL

S &

SITE PLAN

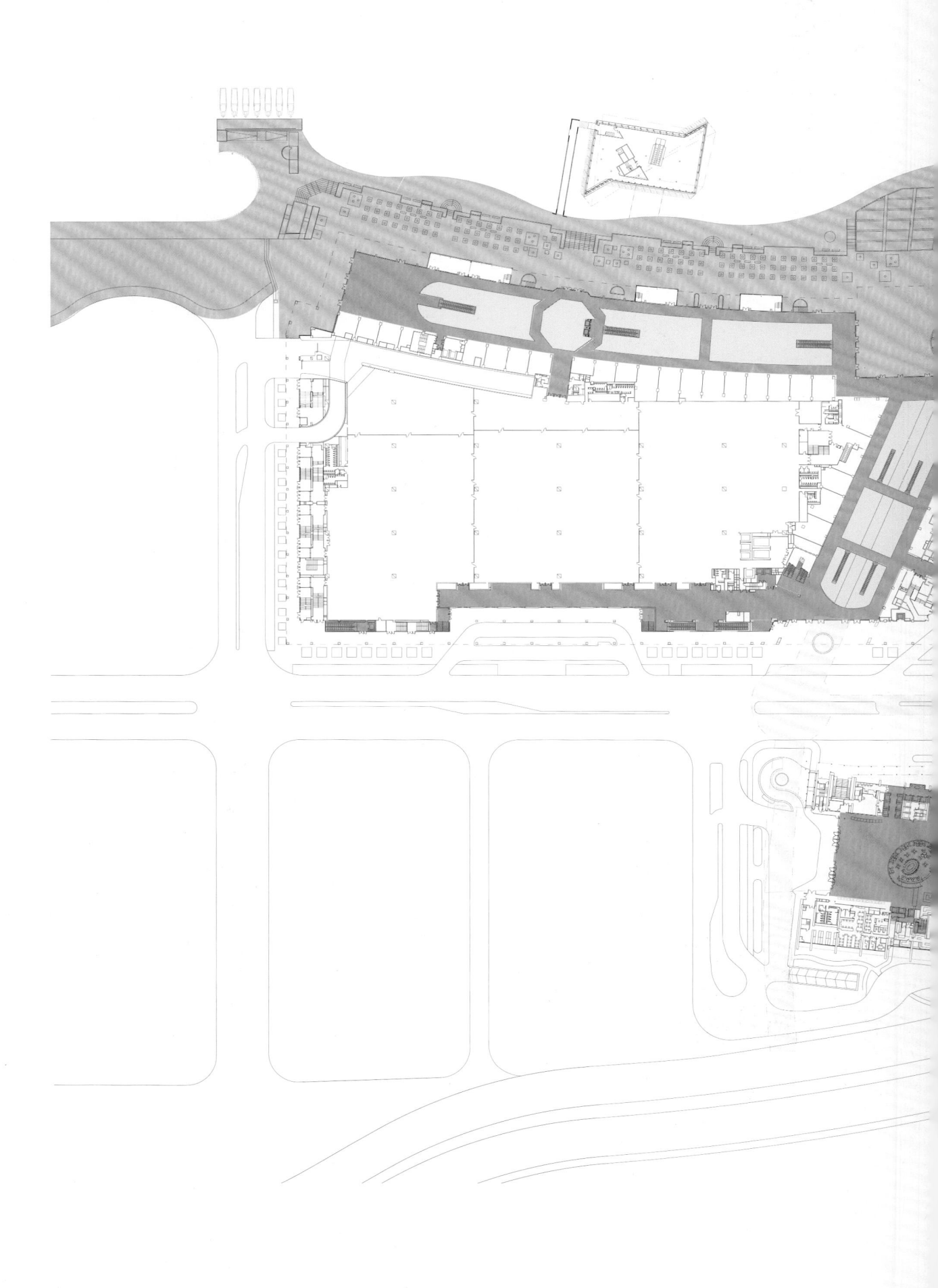

0 20 50 100m

N

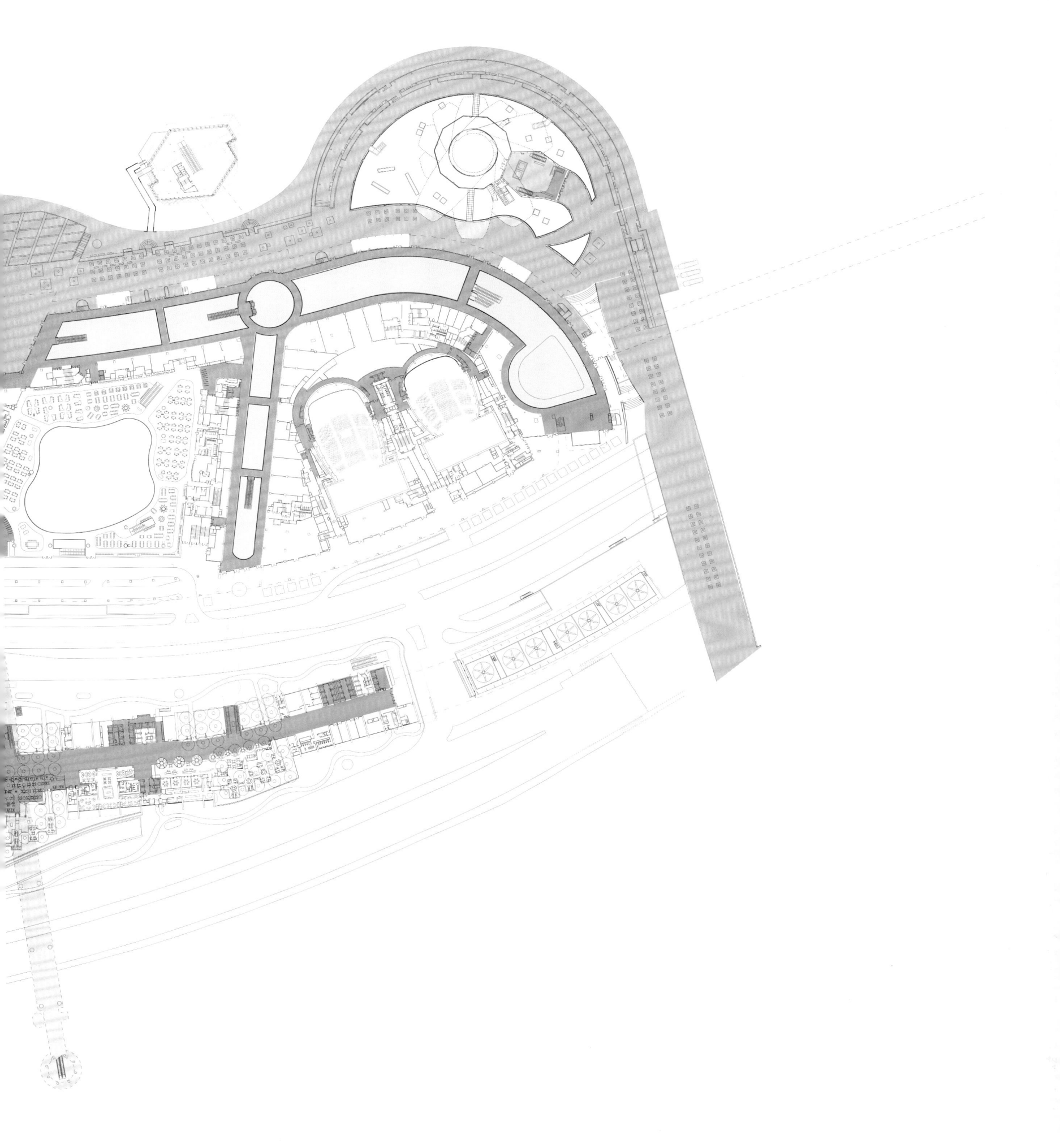

SITE ROOF PLAN

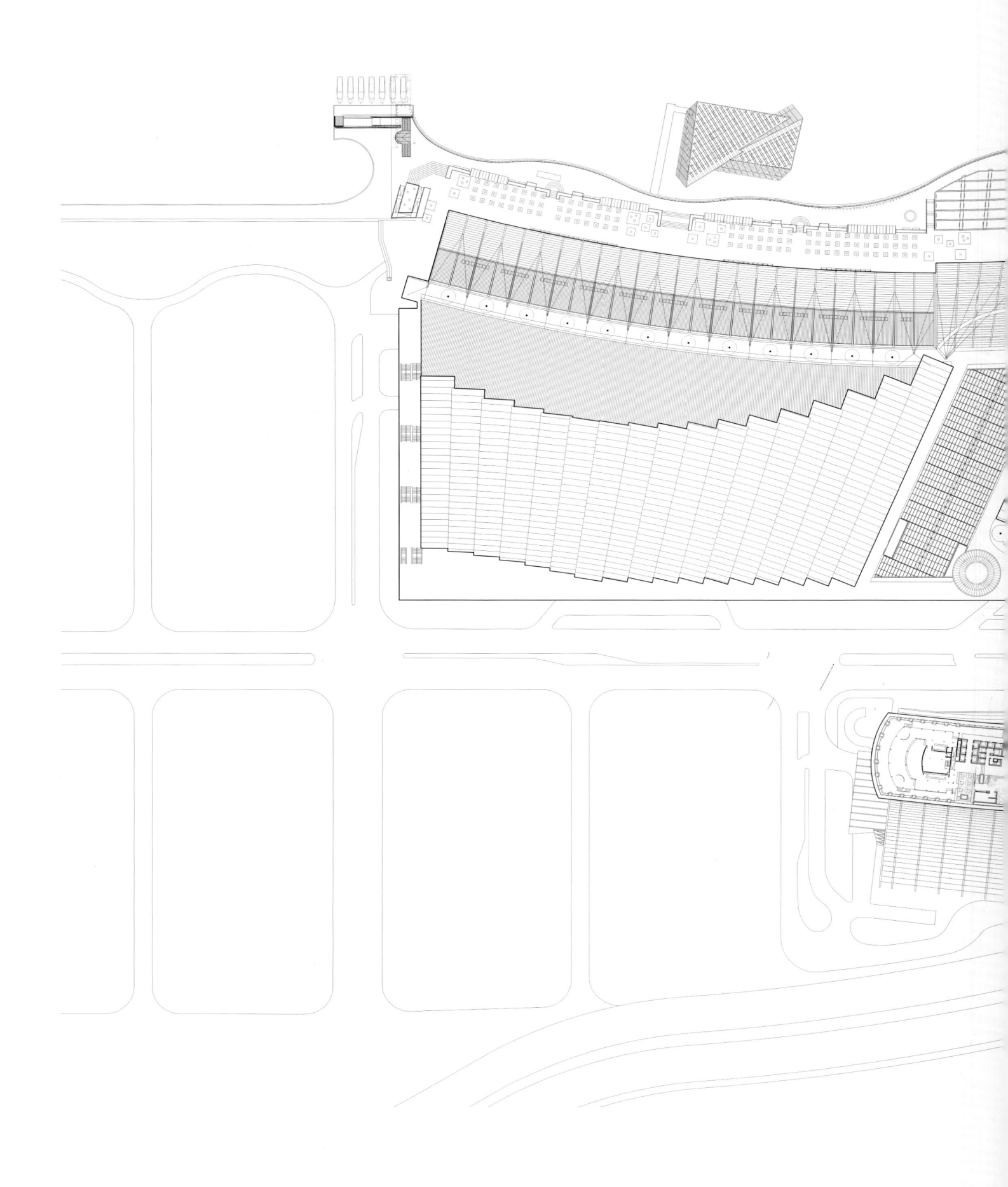

98 0 20 50 100m

N

SKYPARK PLAN

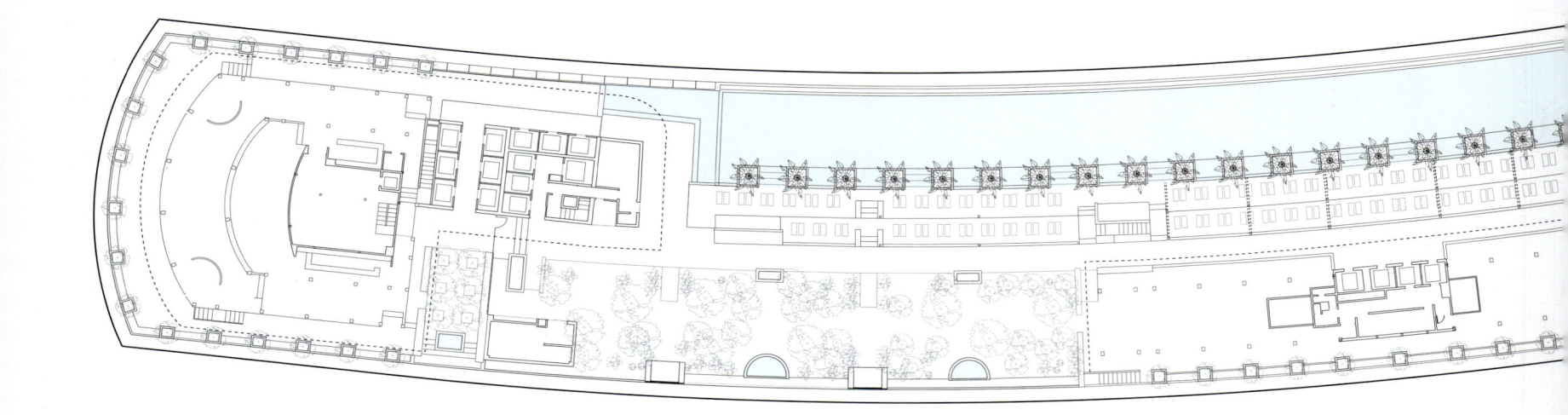

0 10 25 50m

N

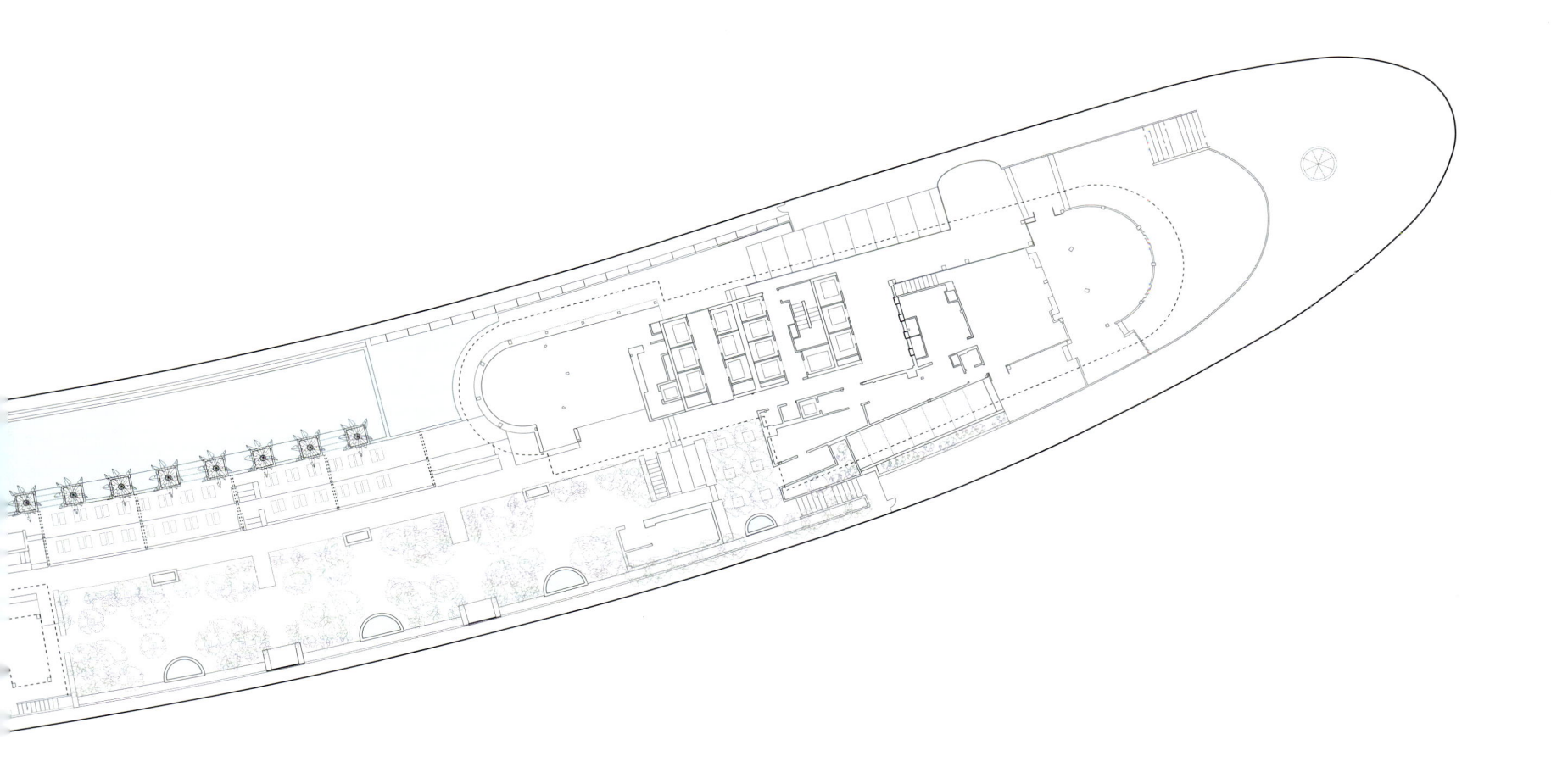

SITE SECTION

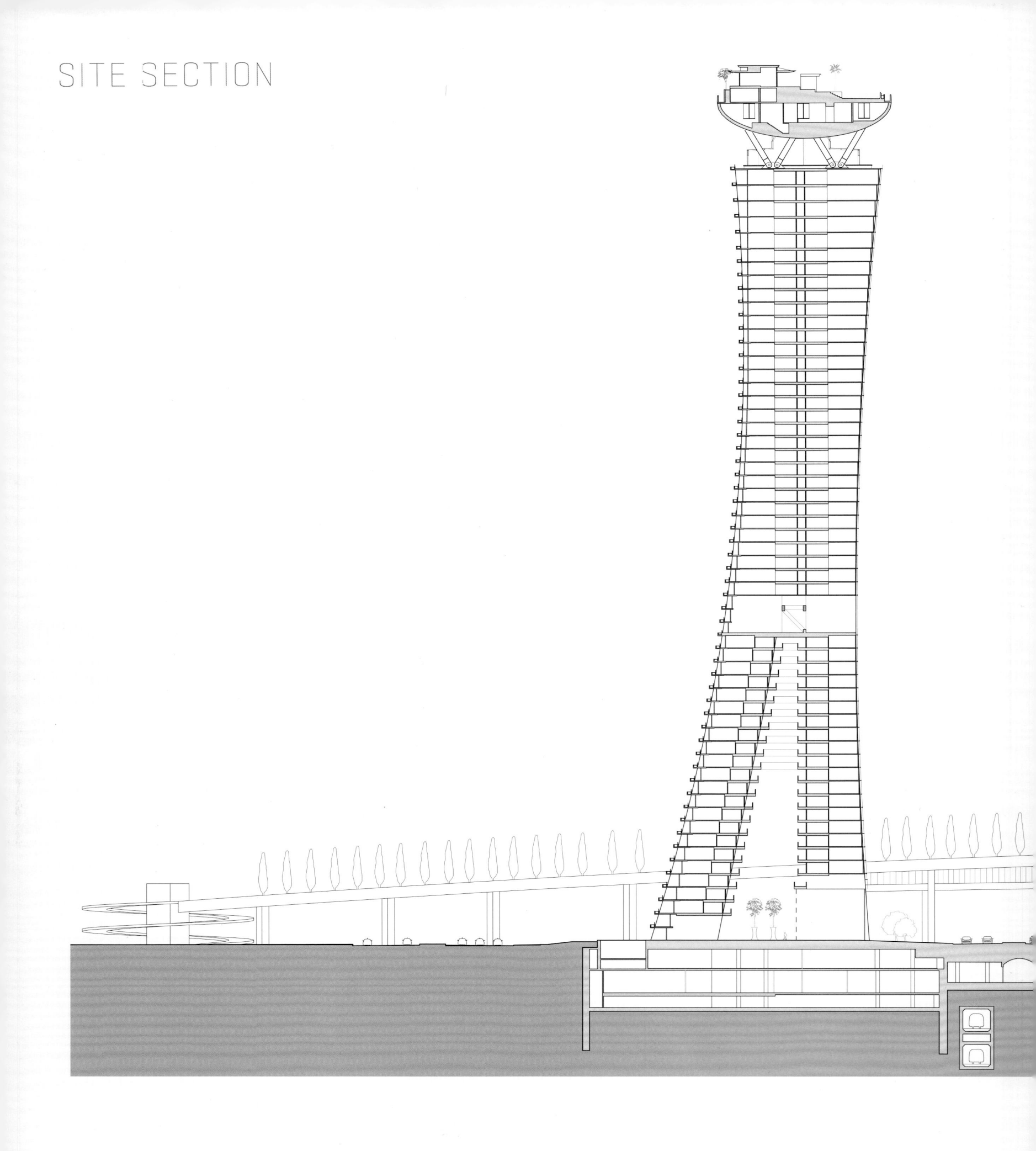

BAYFRONT AVENUE ELEVATION

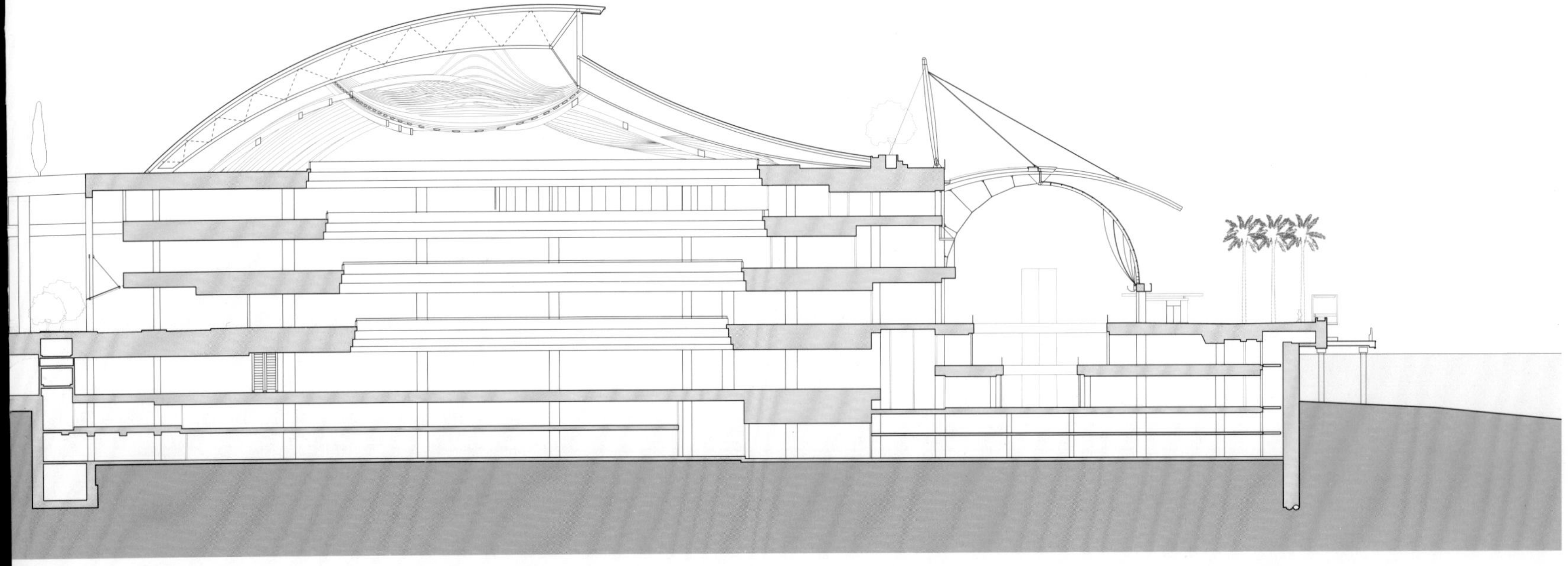

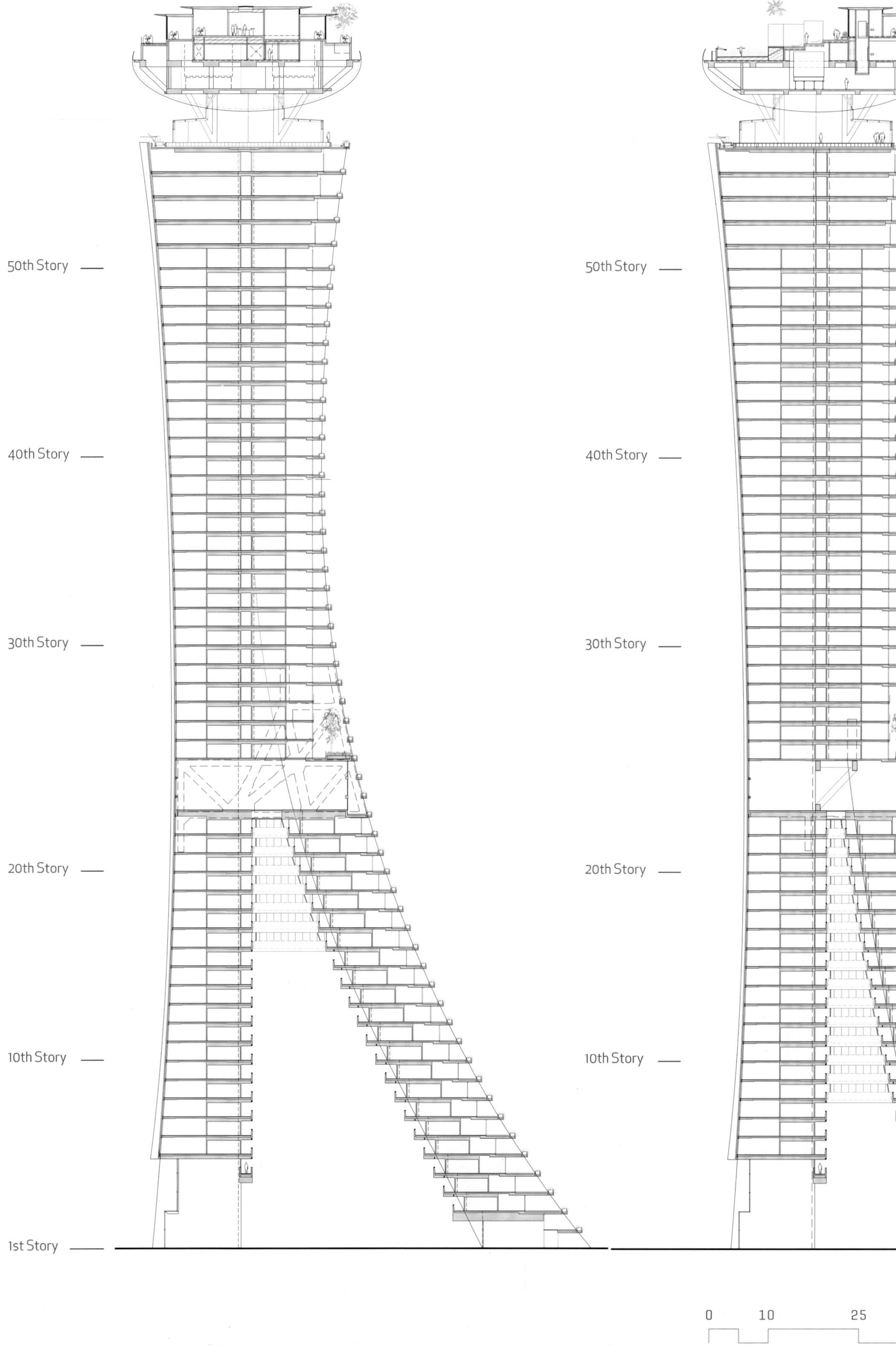

50th Story

40th Story

30th Story

20th Story

10th Story

1st Story

0 10 25

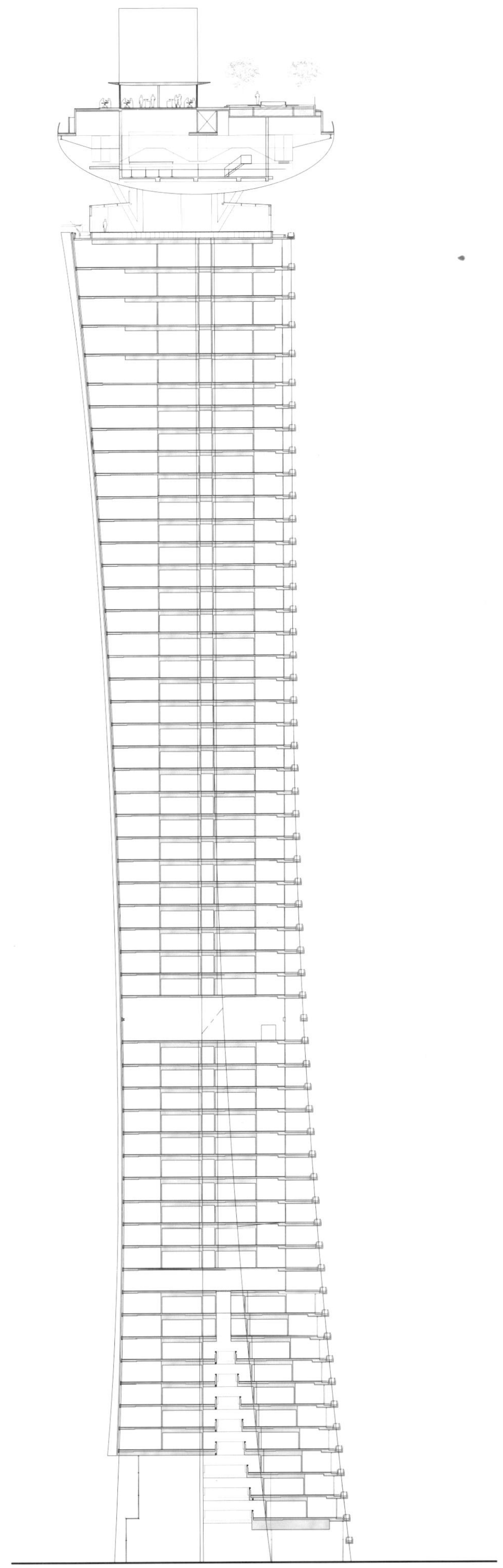

3

CASINO ROOF AND CHANDELIER

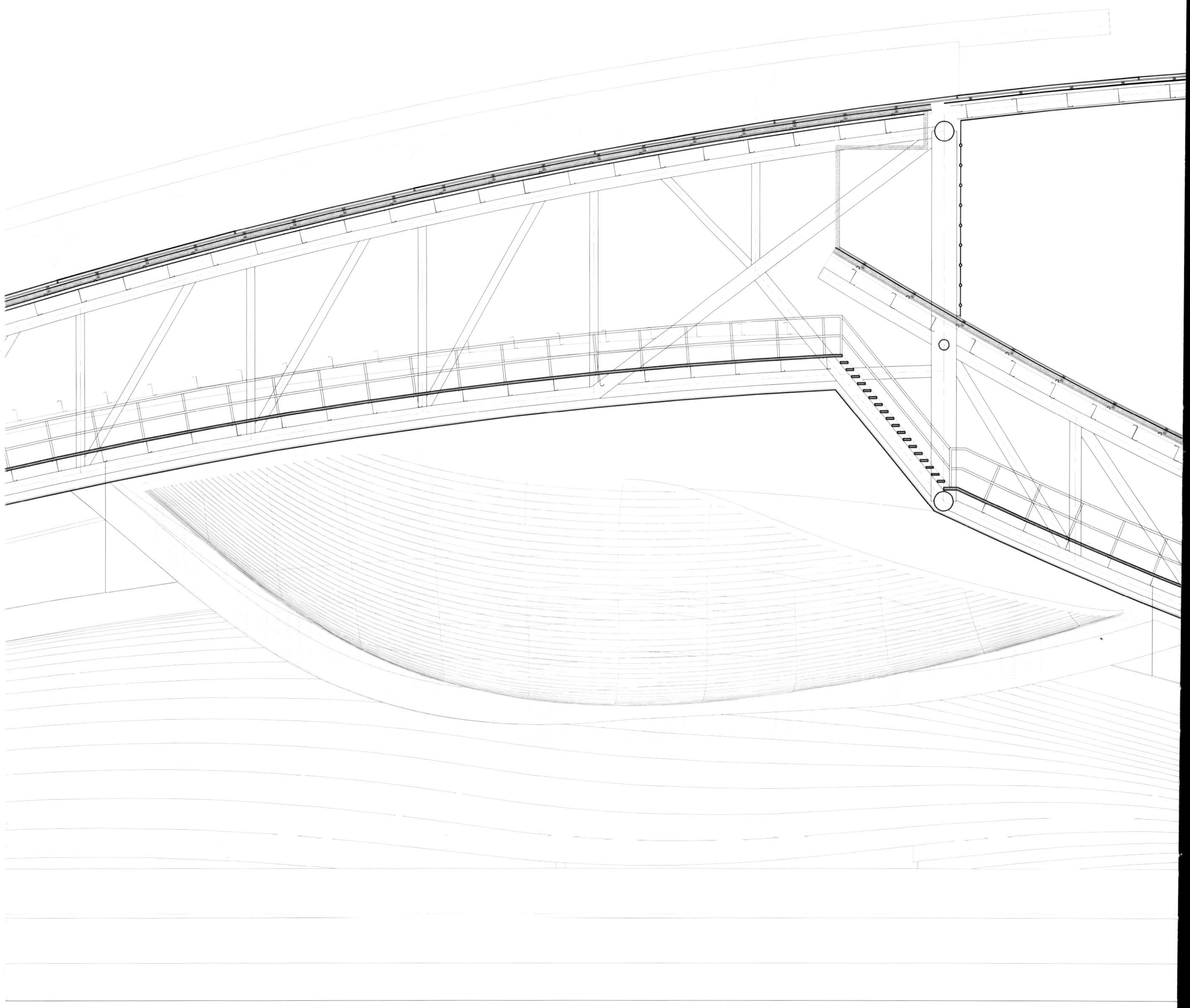

50th Story
40th Story
30th Story
20th Story
10th Story
1st Story

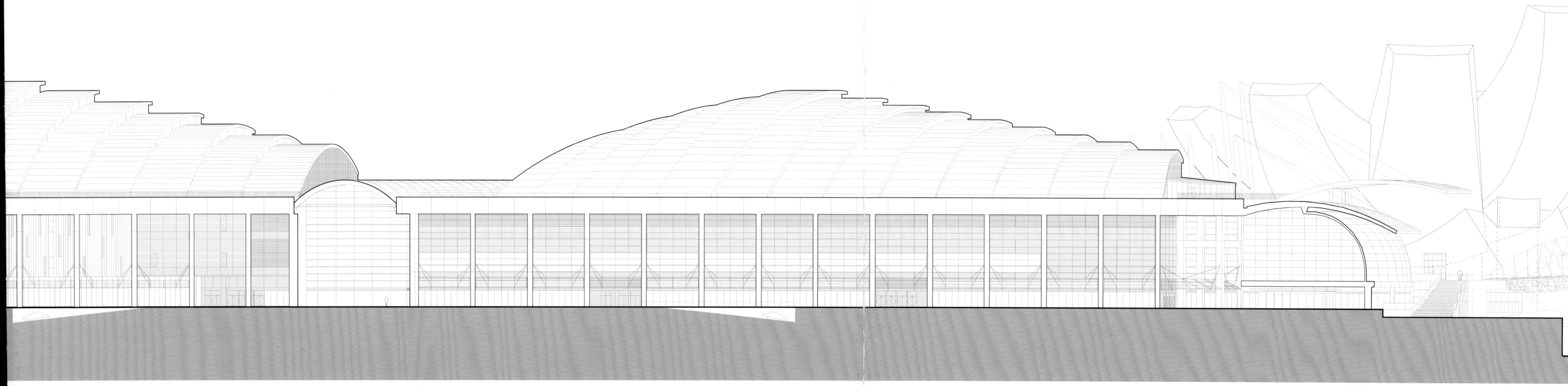

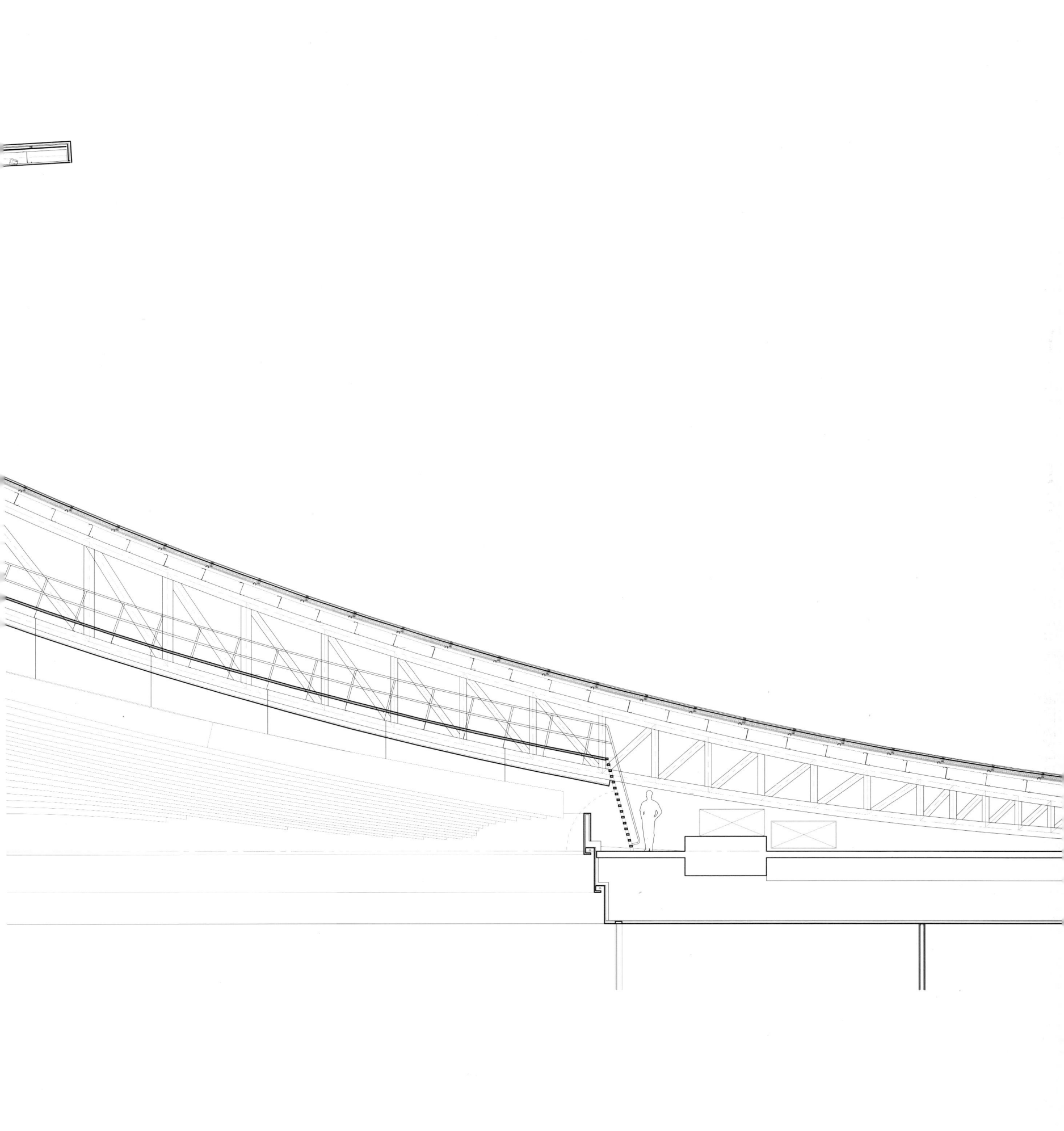

VIEW CORRIDOR SECTION

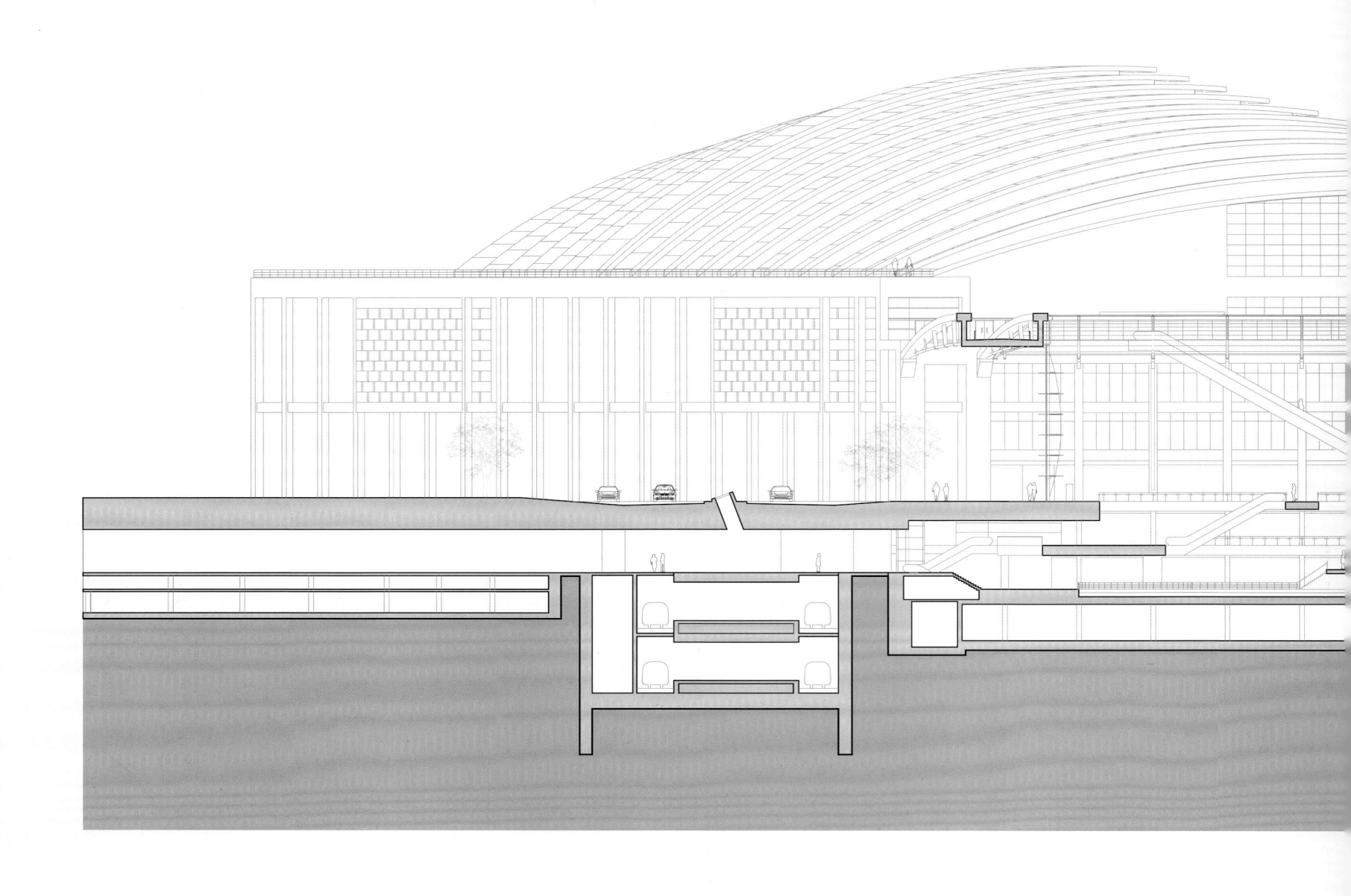

0 10 25 50m

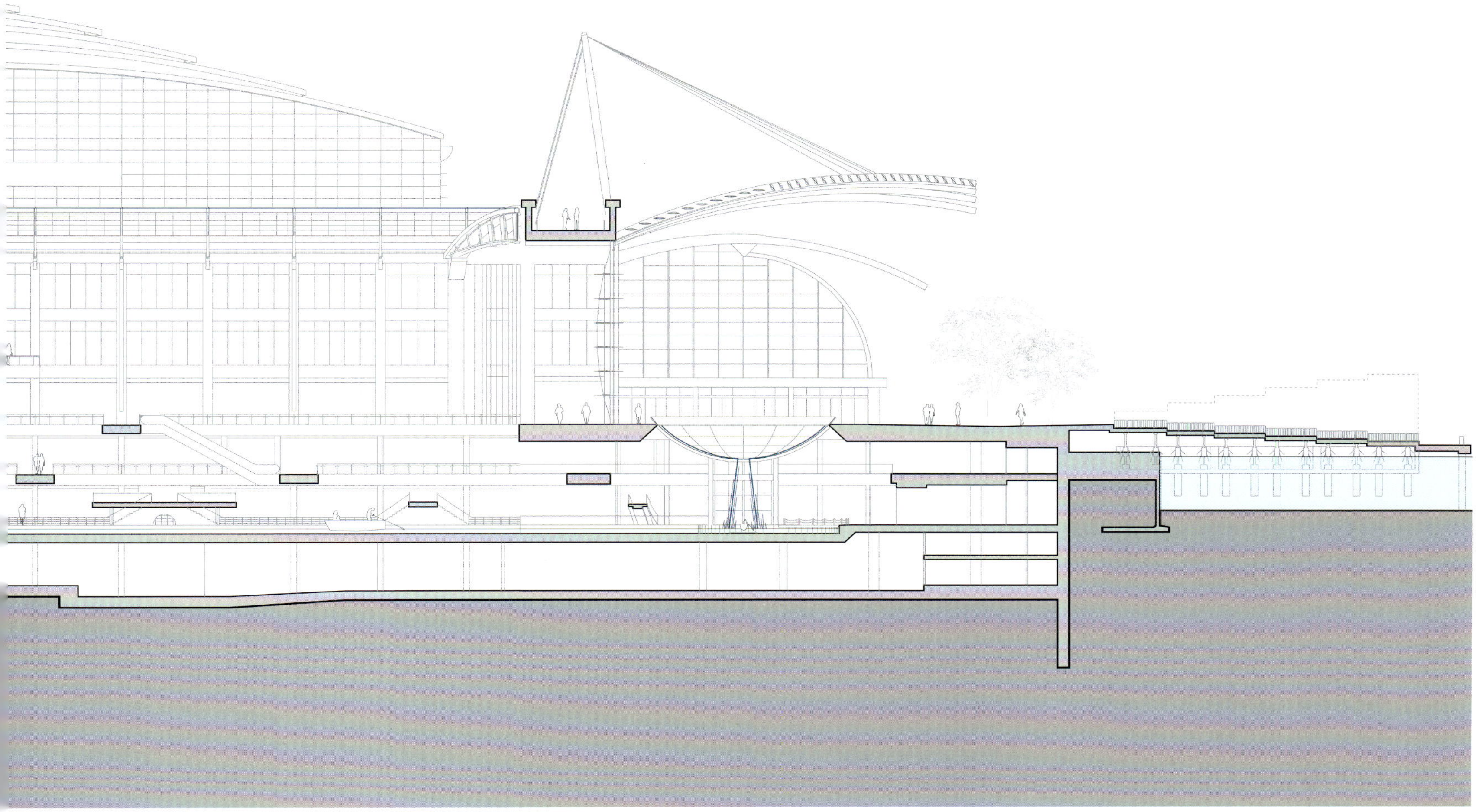

ARTSCIENCE MUSEUM PLANS

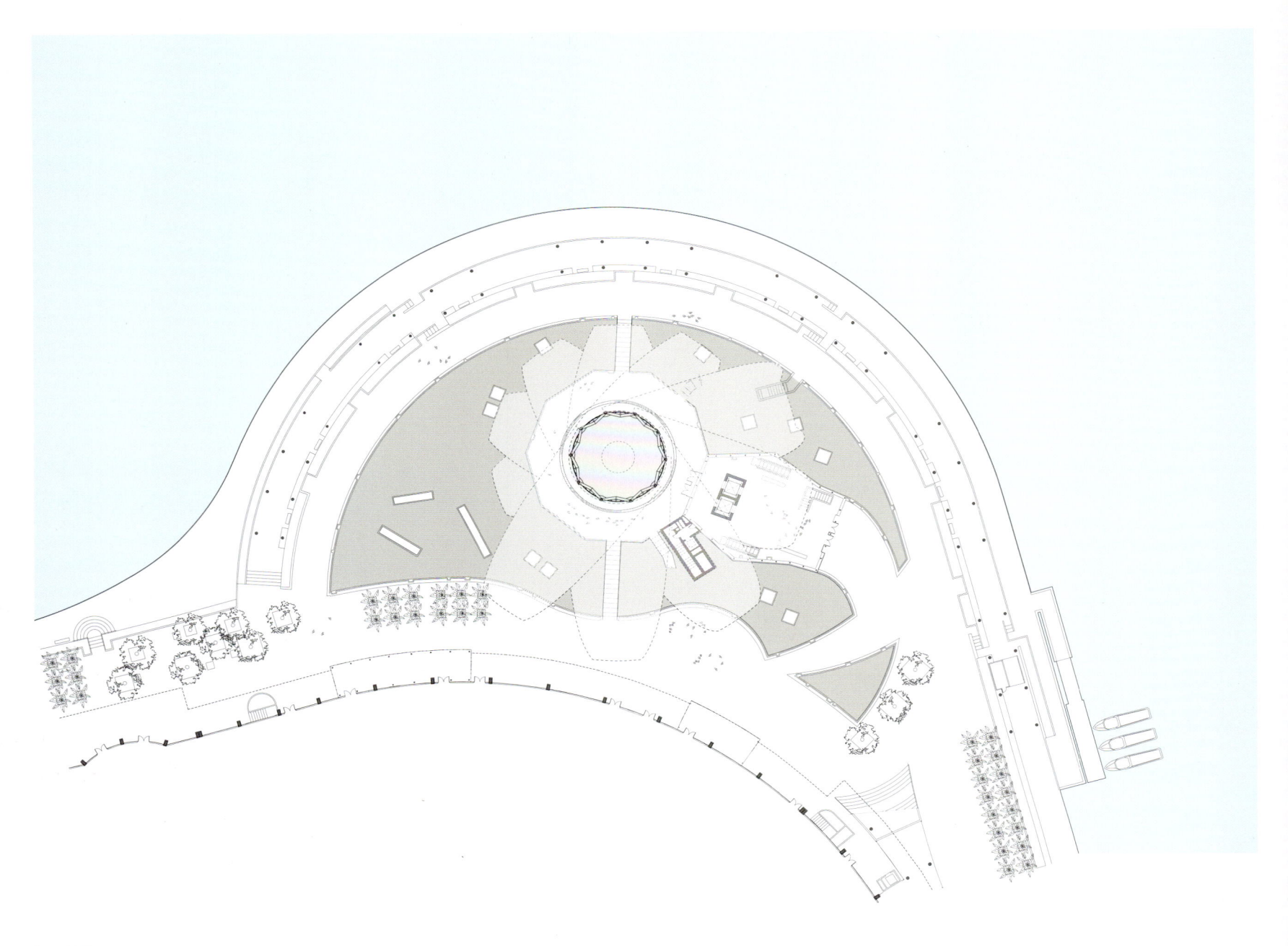

Level 1 Plan

0 10 25 50m

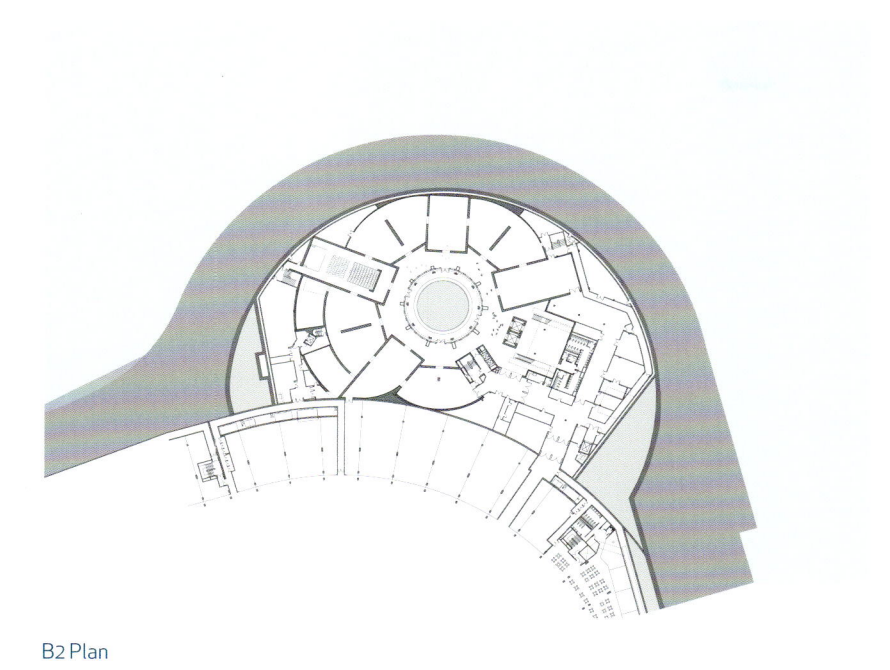

B2 Plan

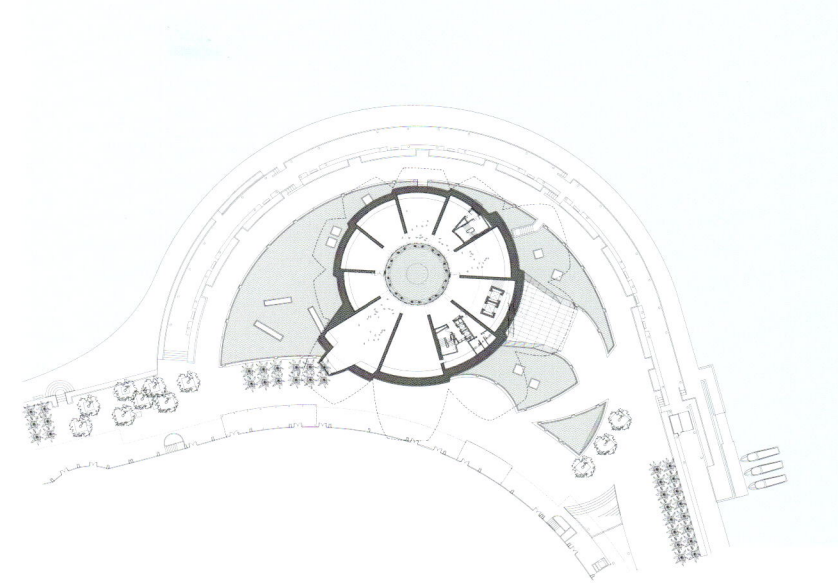

Level 2 Plan

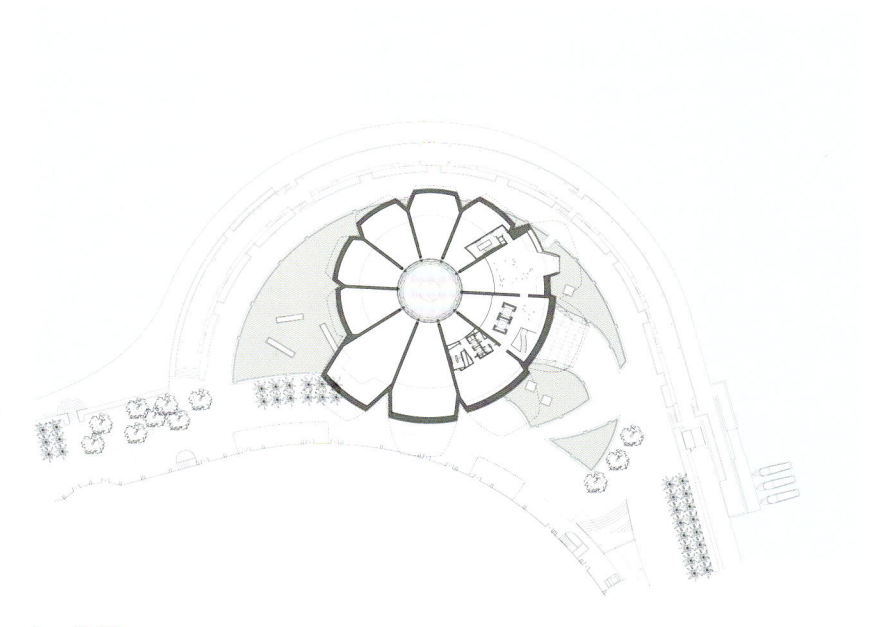

Level 3 Plan

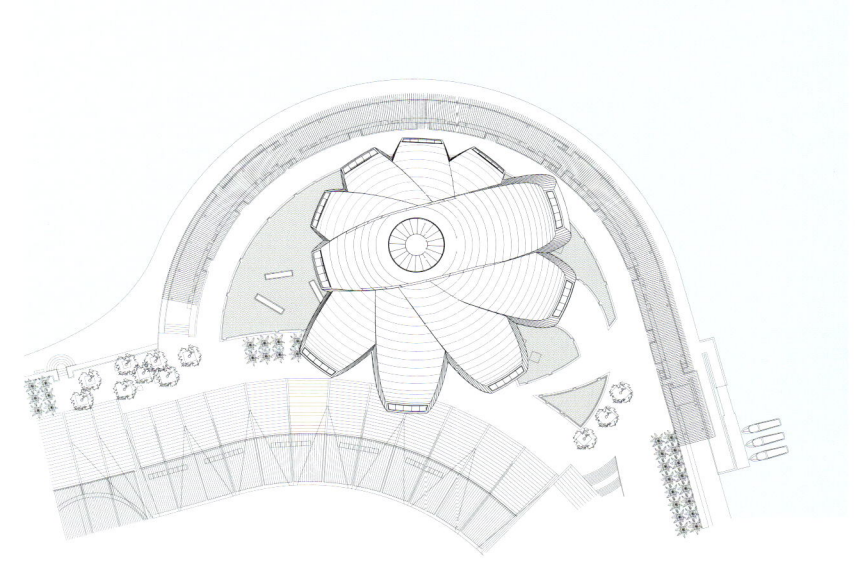

Roof Plan

0 10 25 50m

N

ARTSCIENCE MUSEUM SECTION

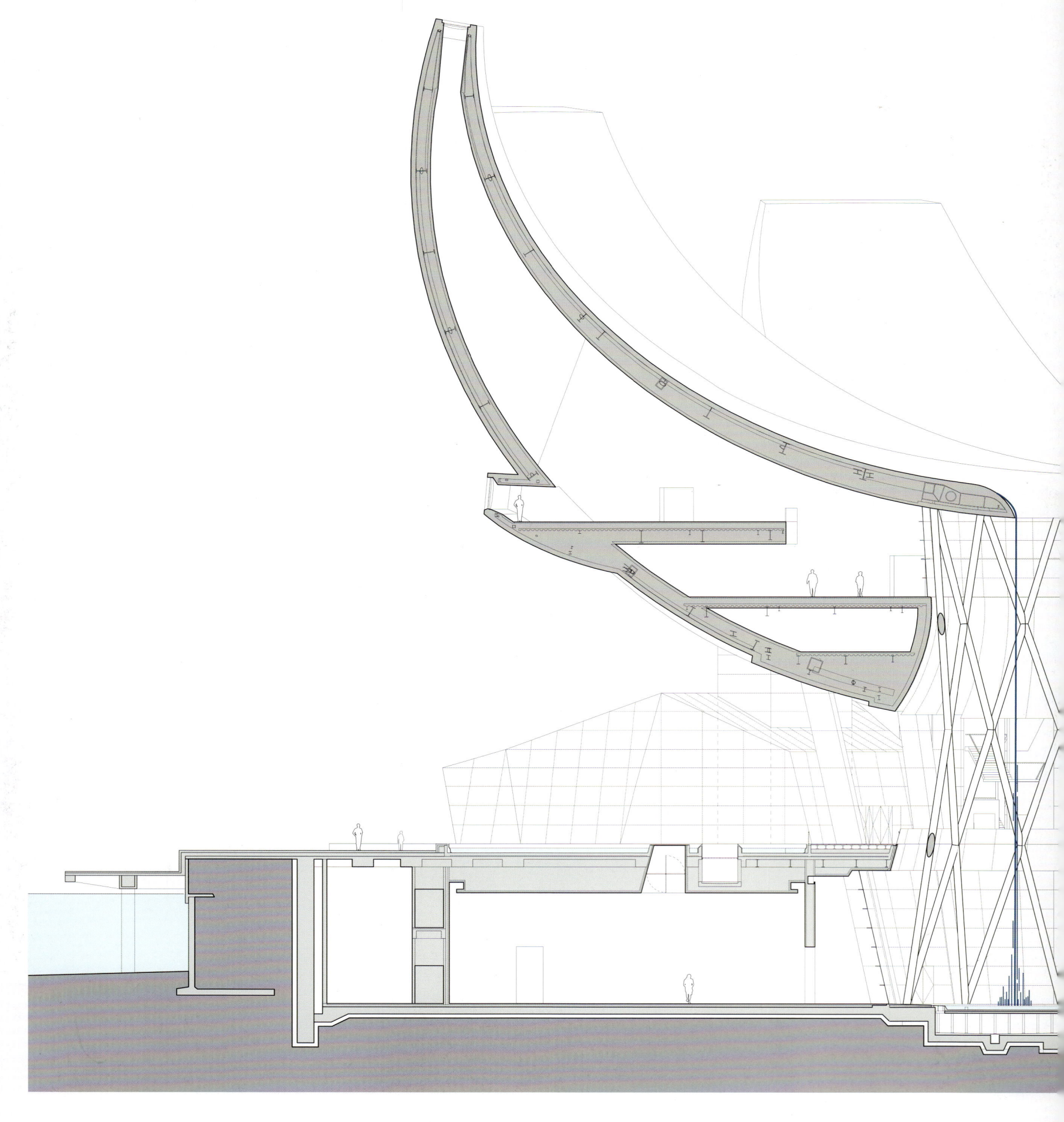

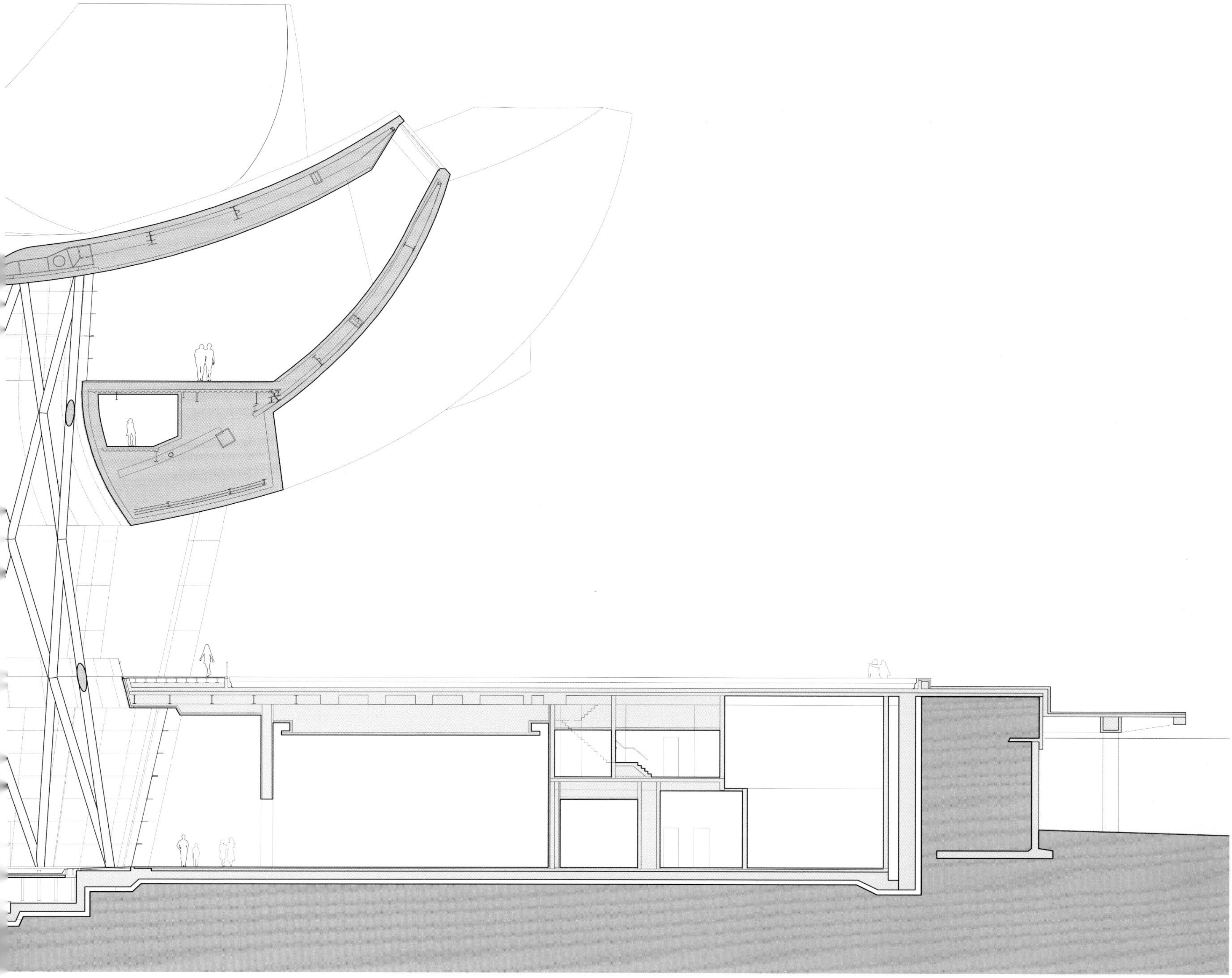

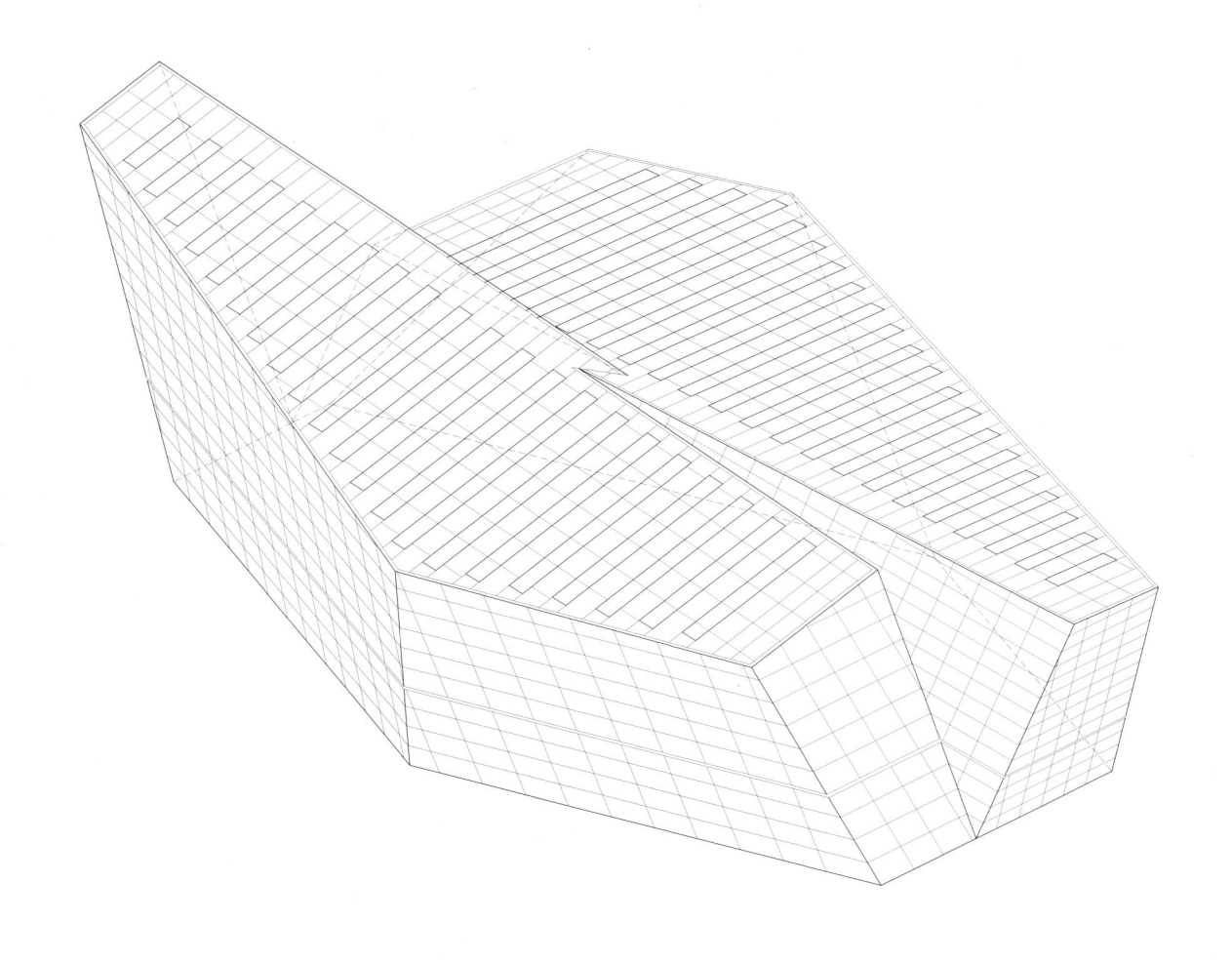

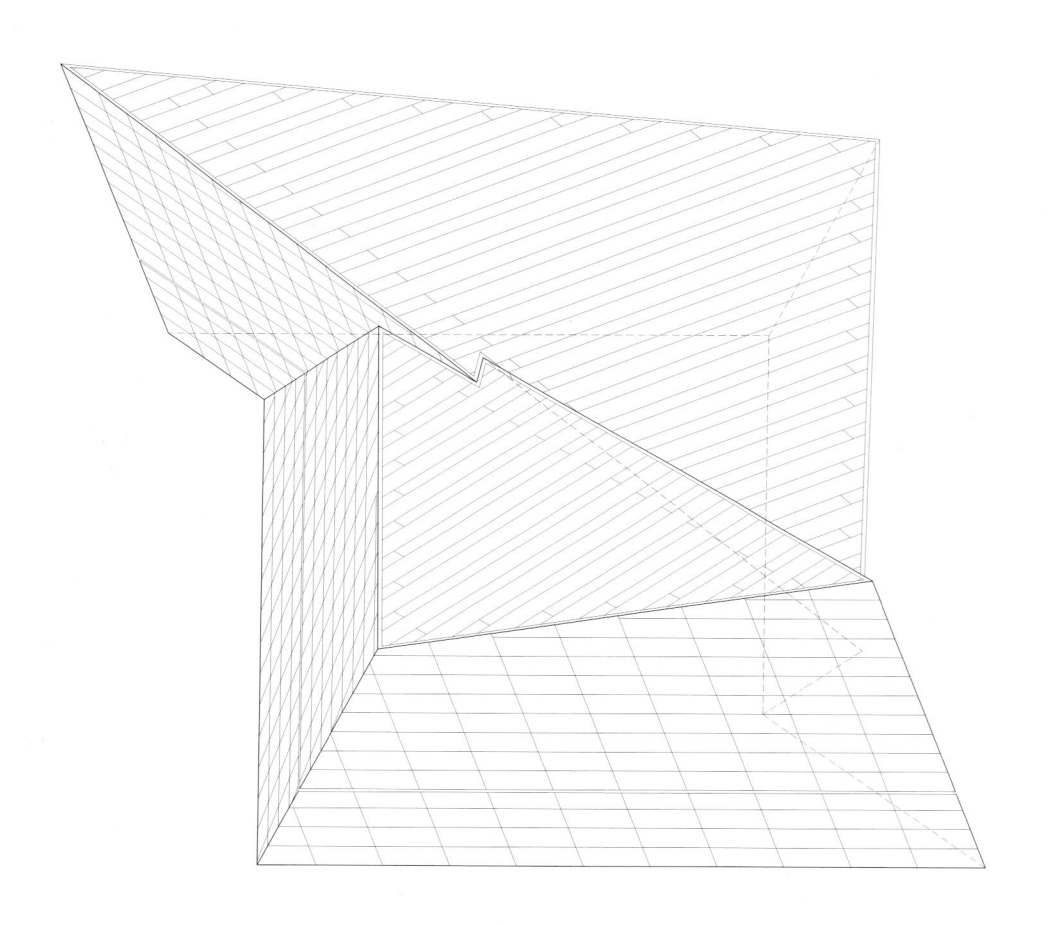

CRYSTAL PAVILIONS

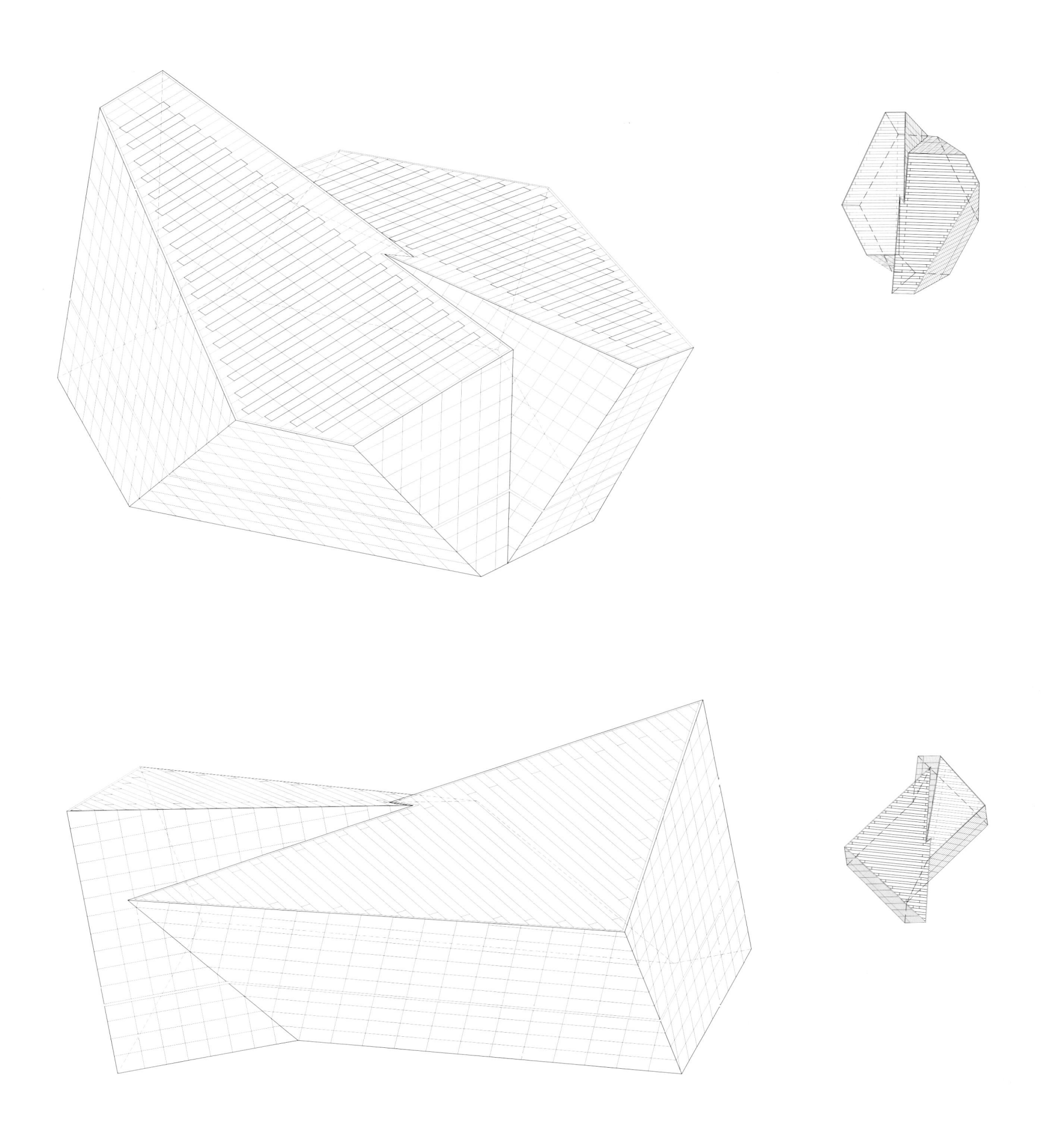

CRYSTAL PAVILION SECTION

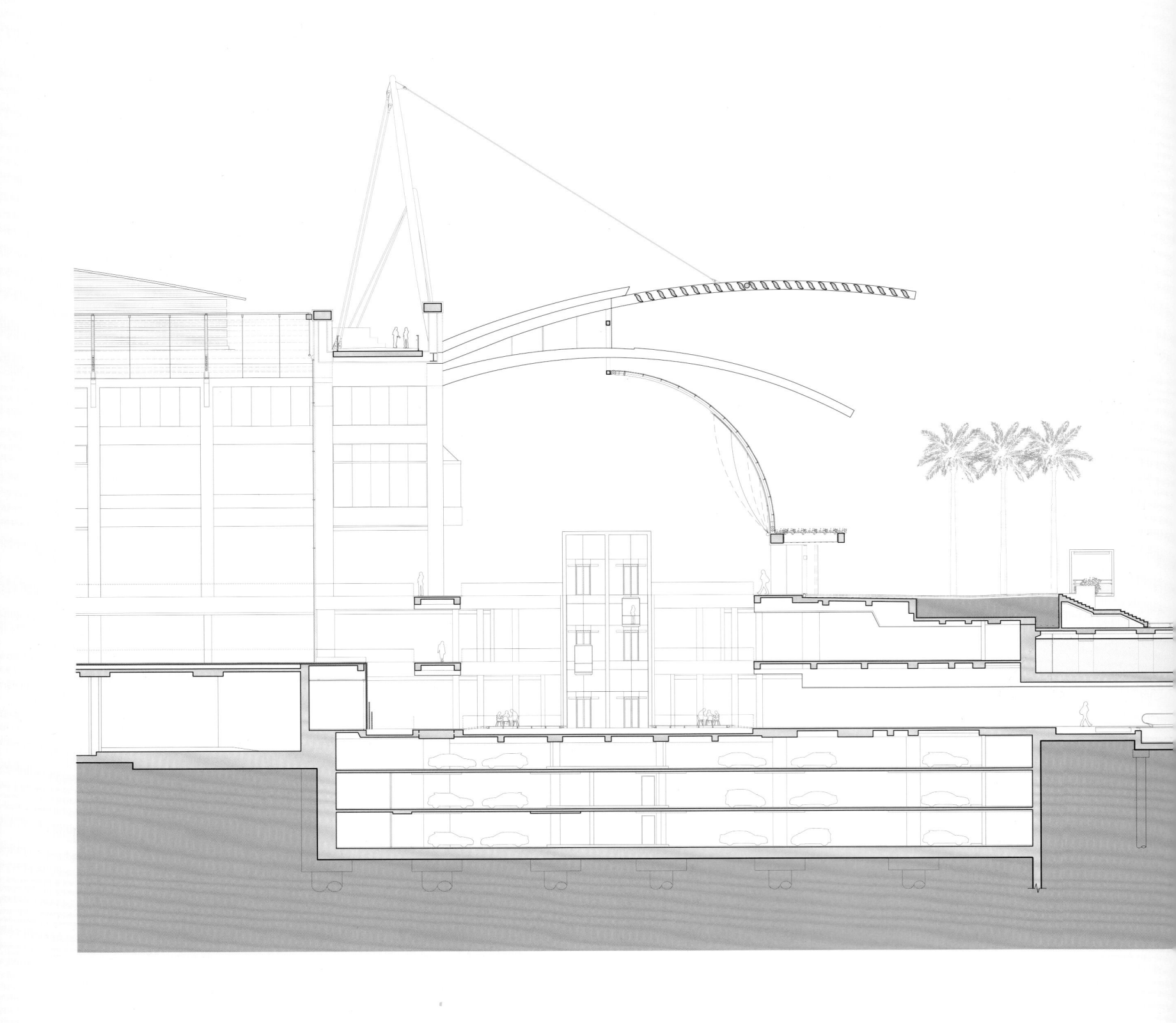

0 10 25m

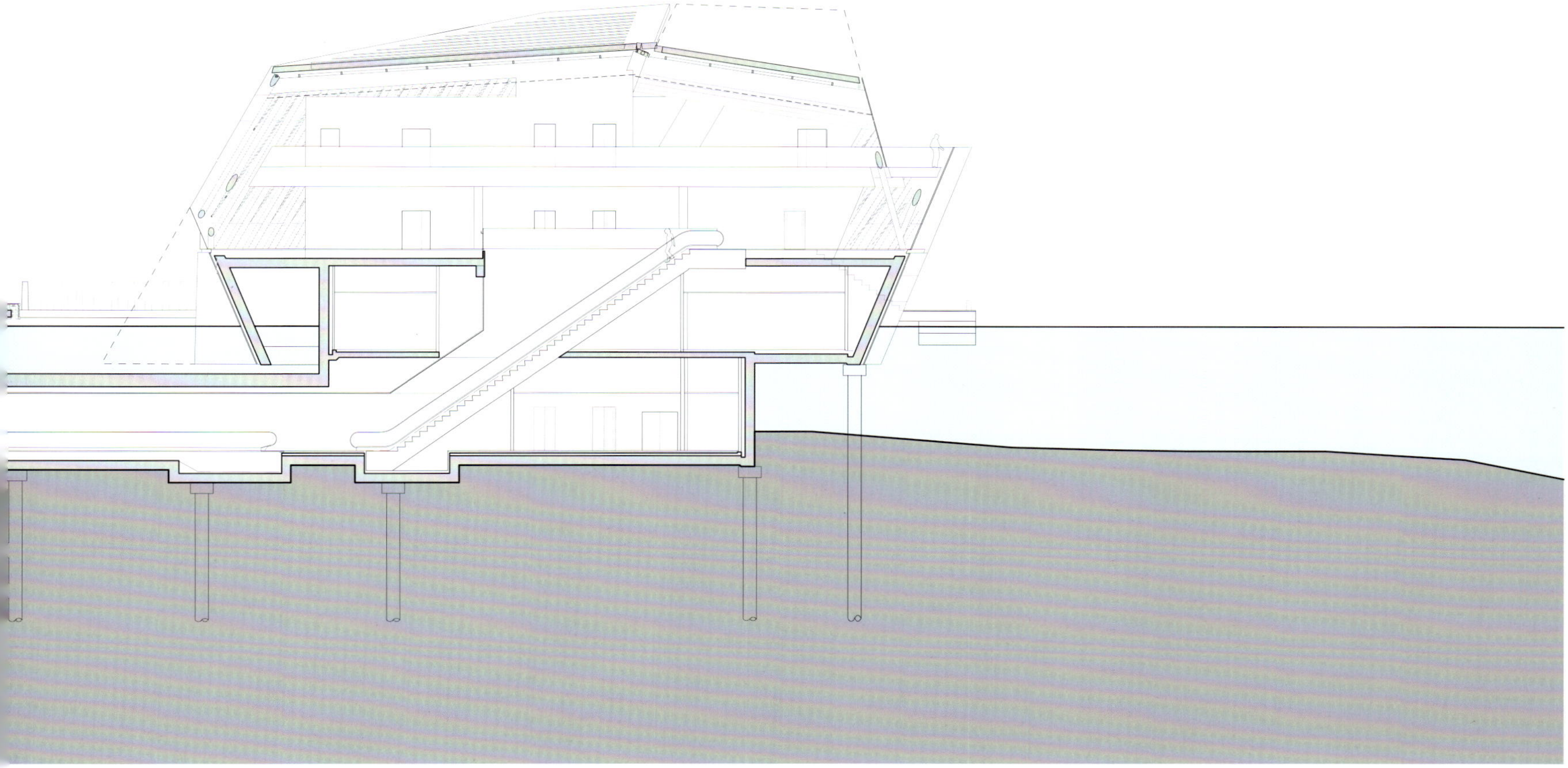

PART 3
A CIVIC IC
A DESTINA
AN EXPER

MARINA BA

ON

ATION

IENCE

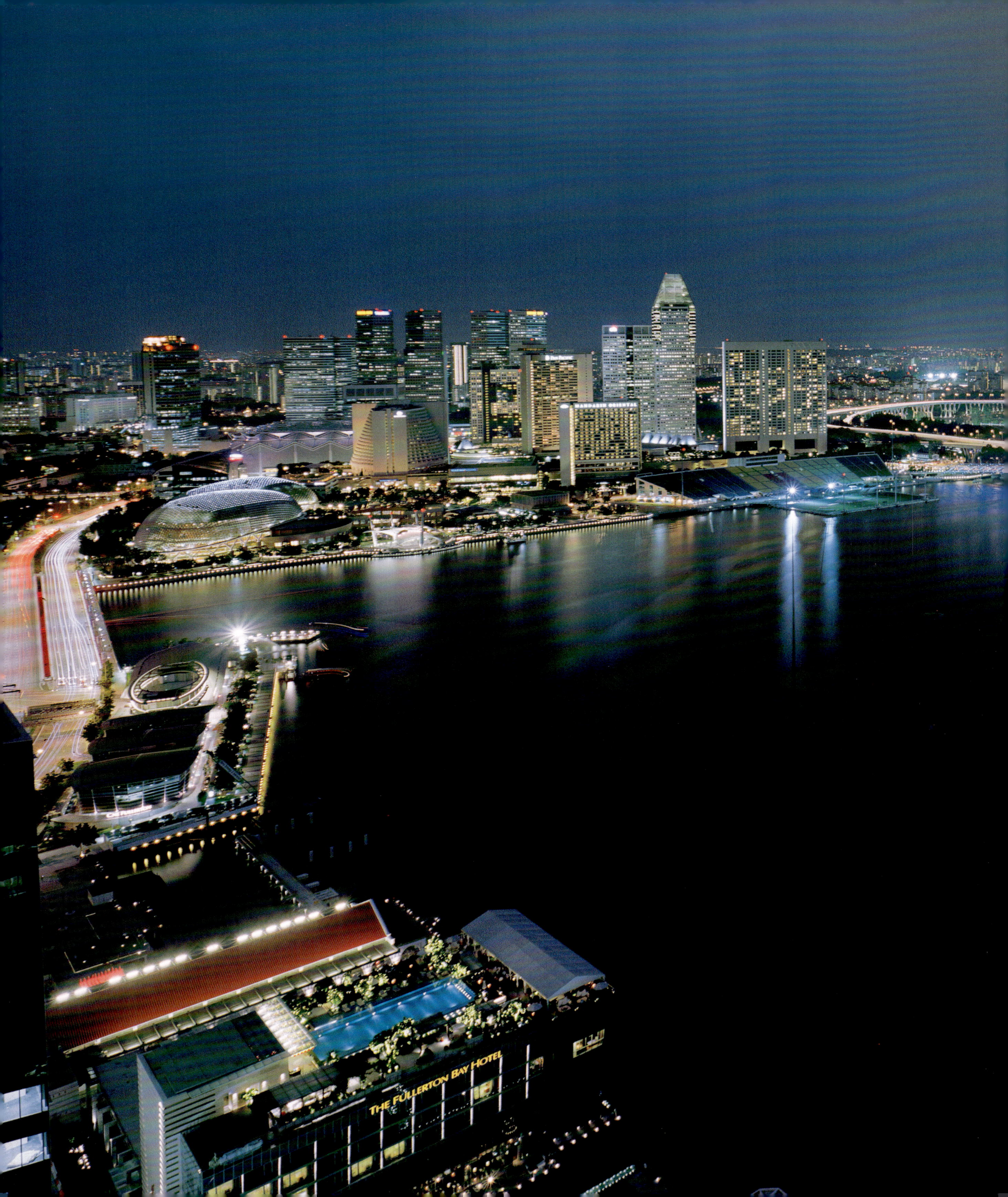
THE FULLERTON BAY HOTEL

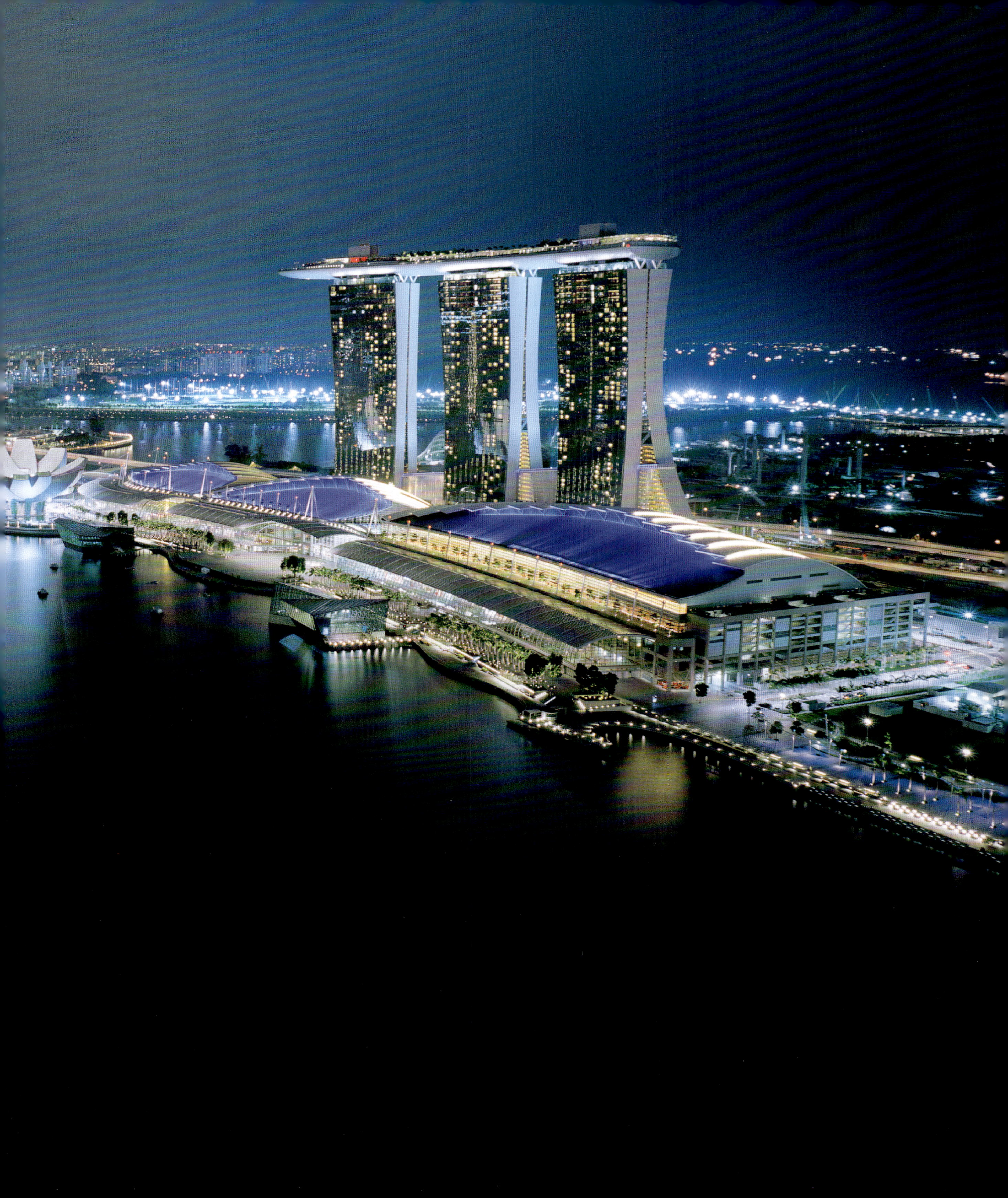

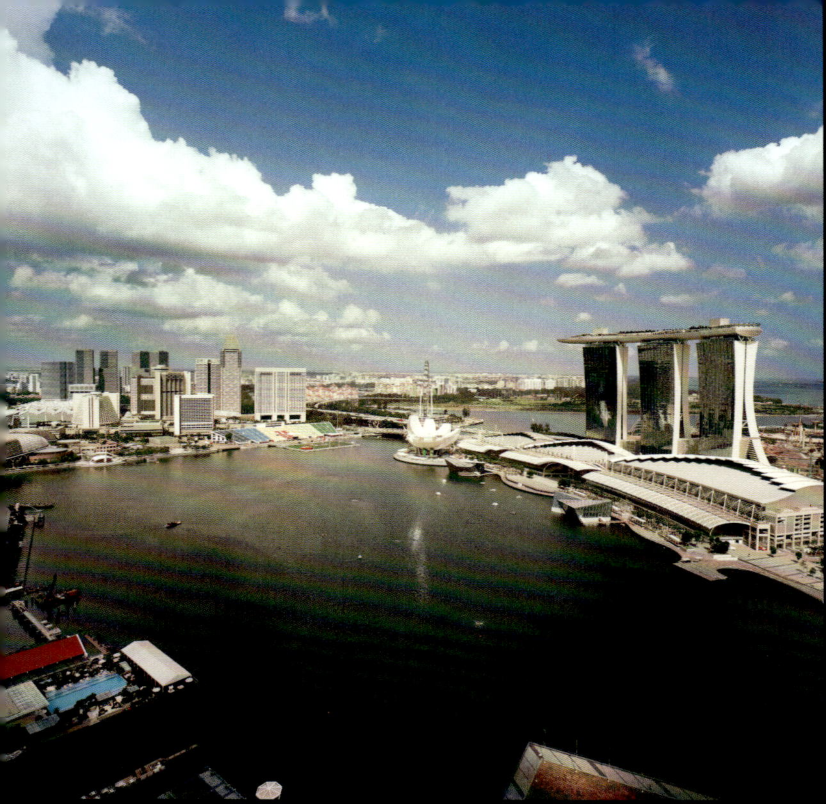
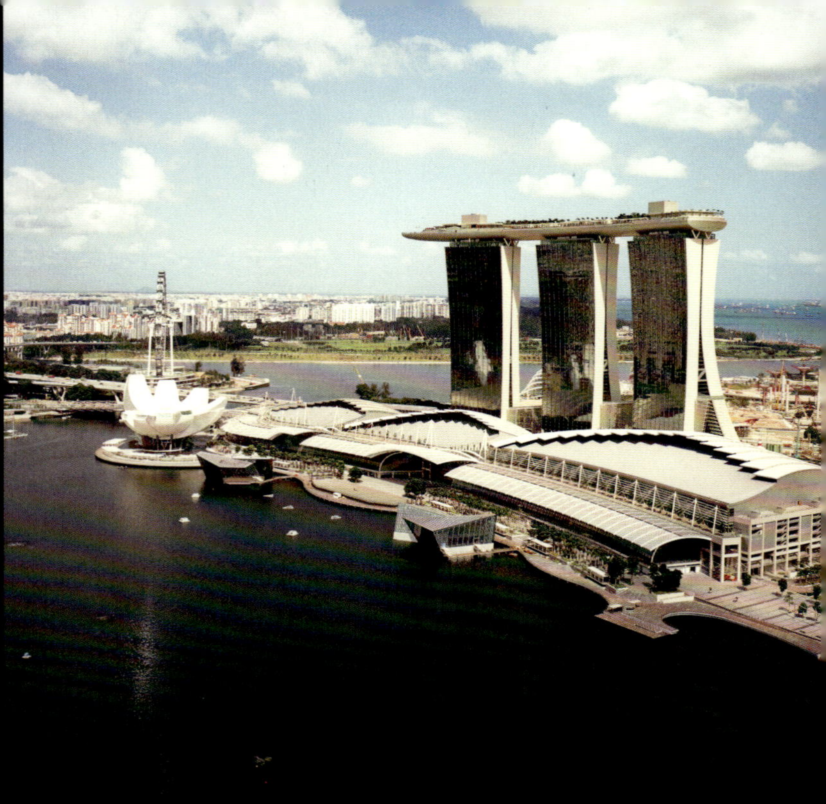
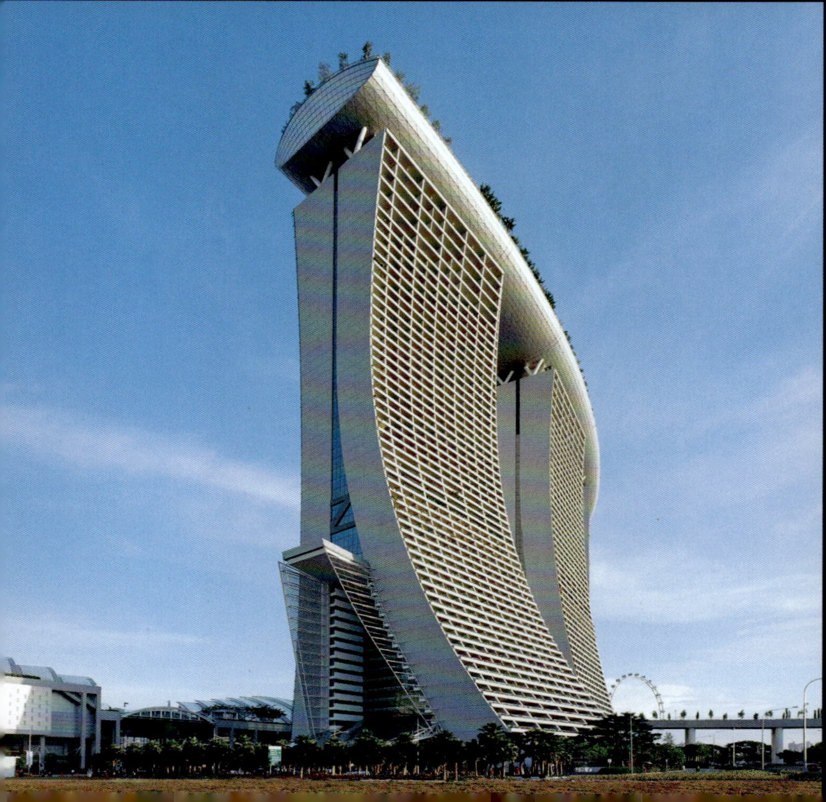
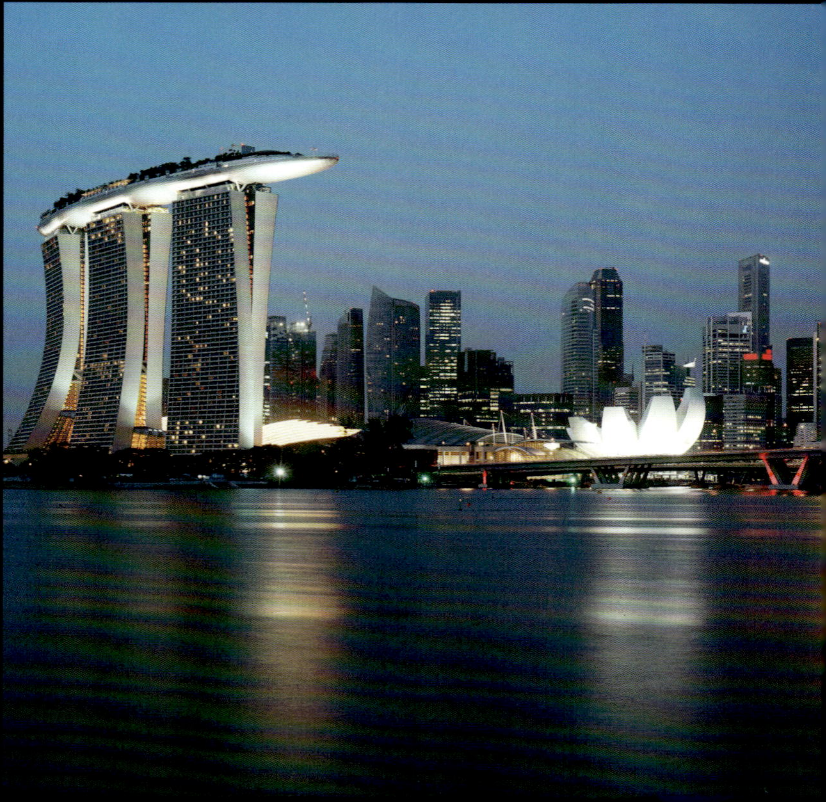

Marina Bay Sands transforms Singapore's skyline.

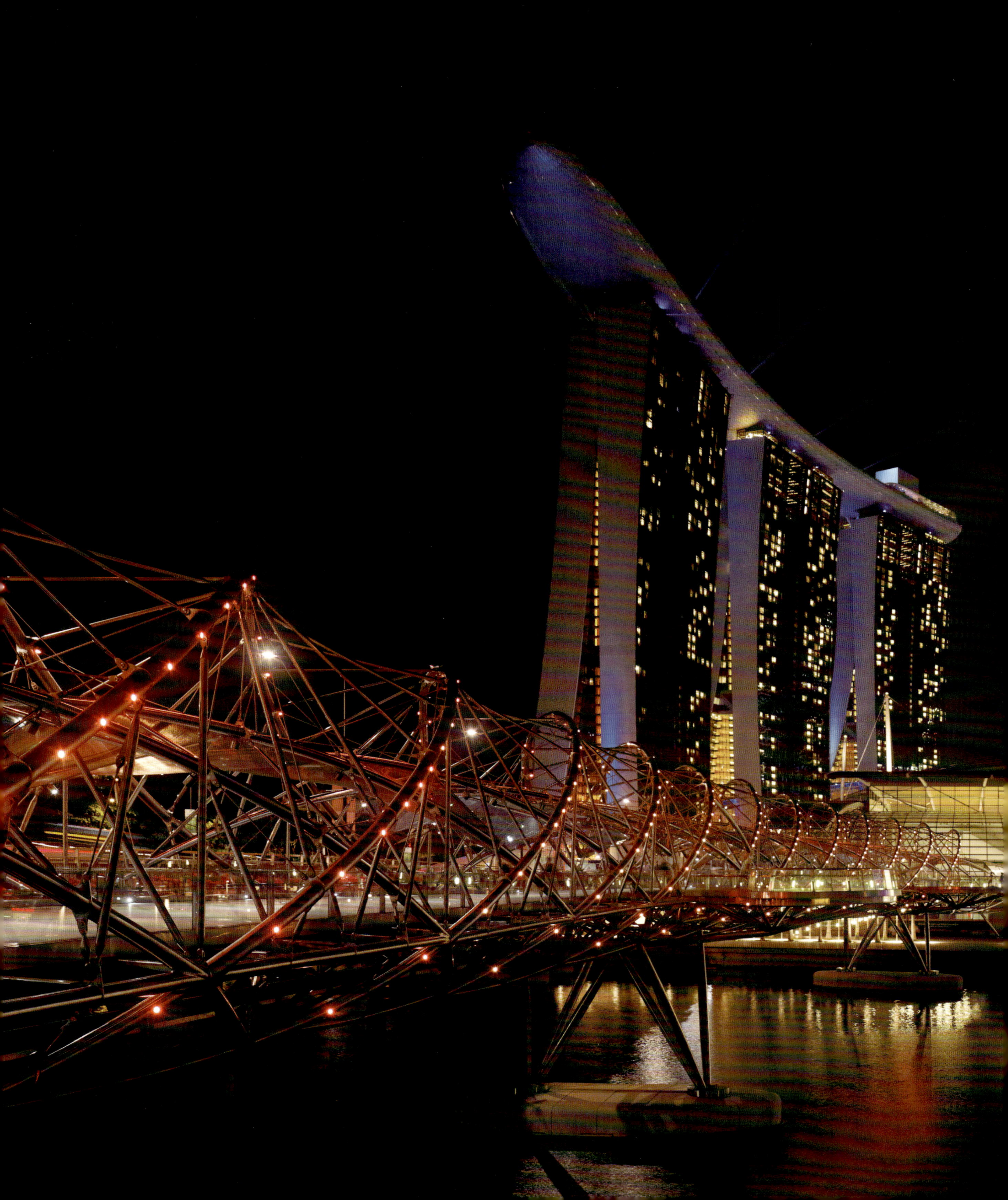

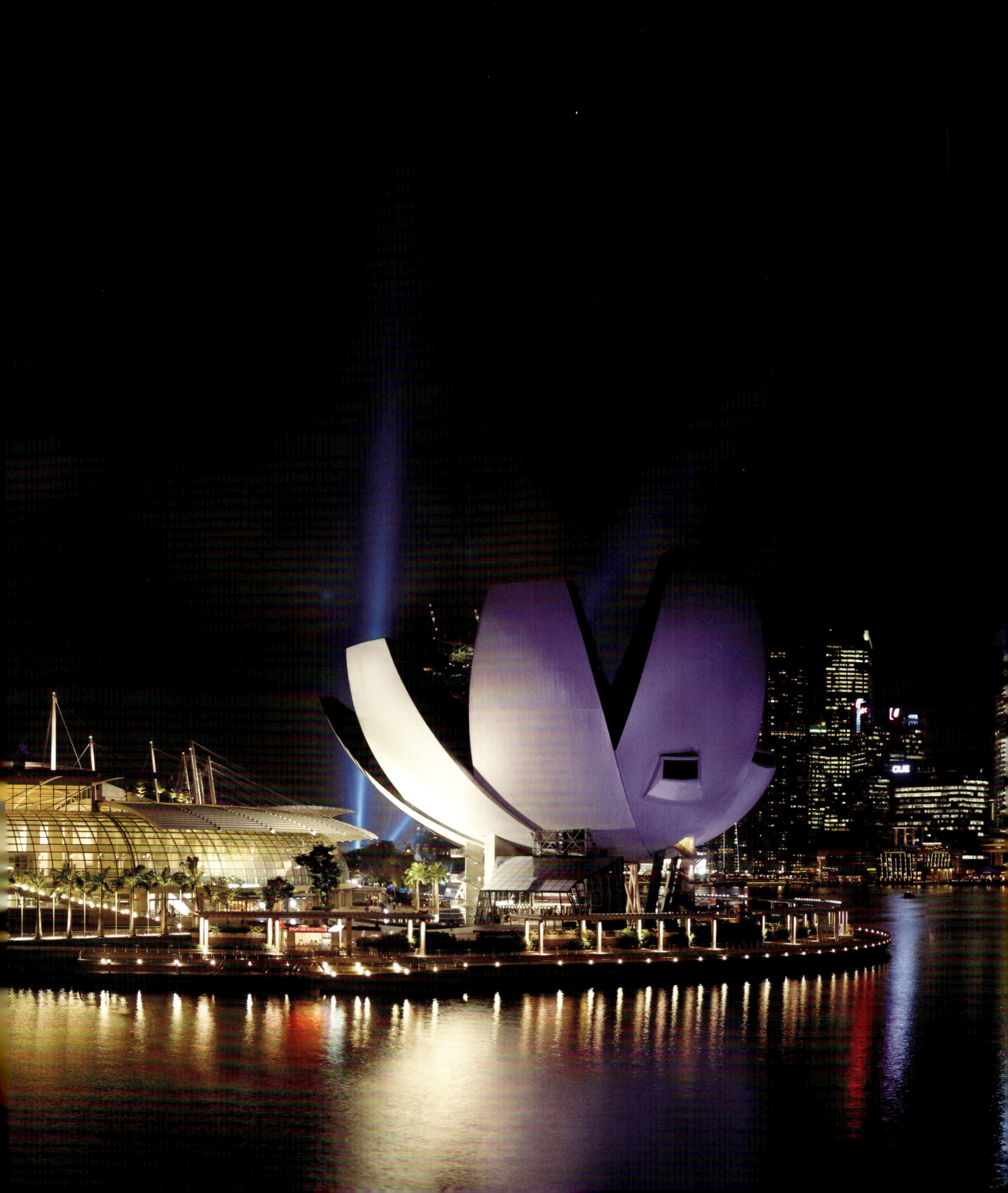

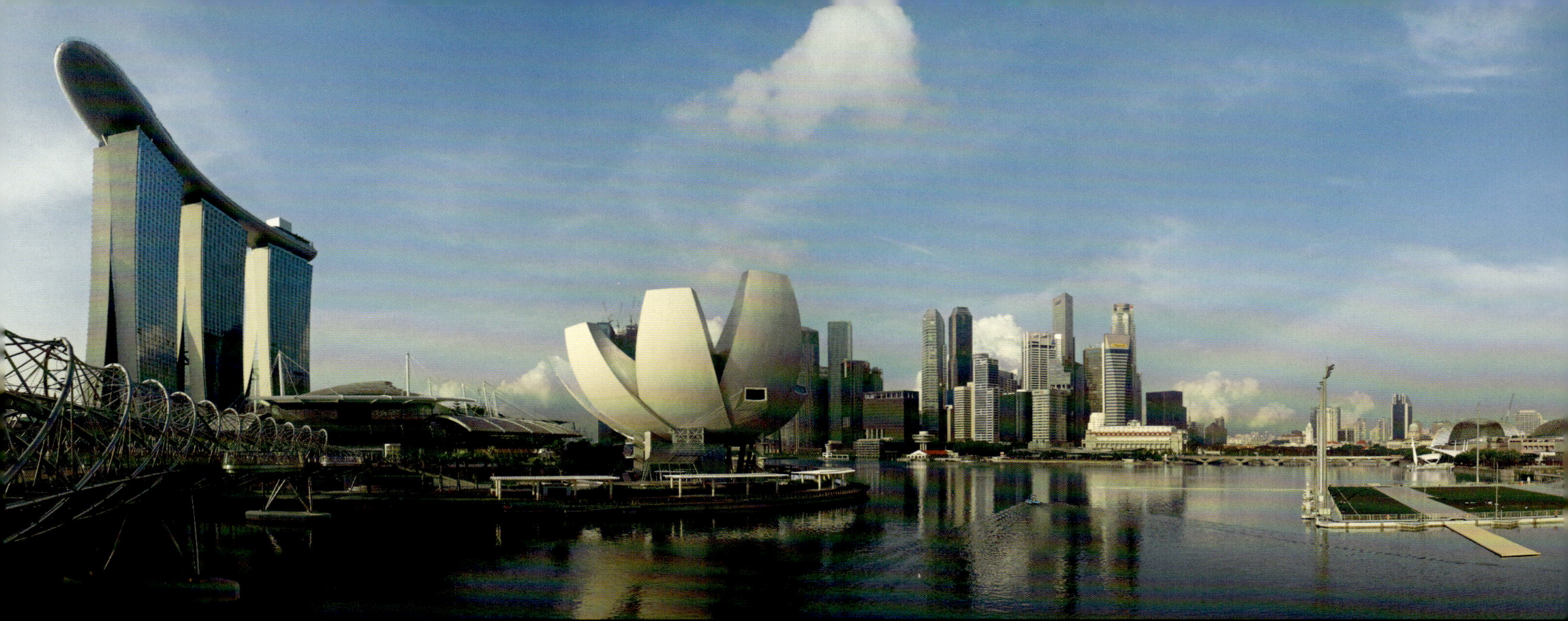
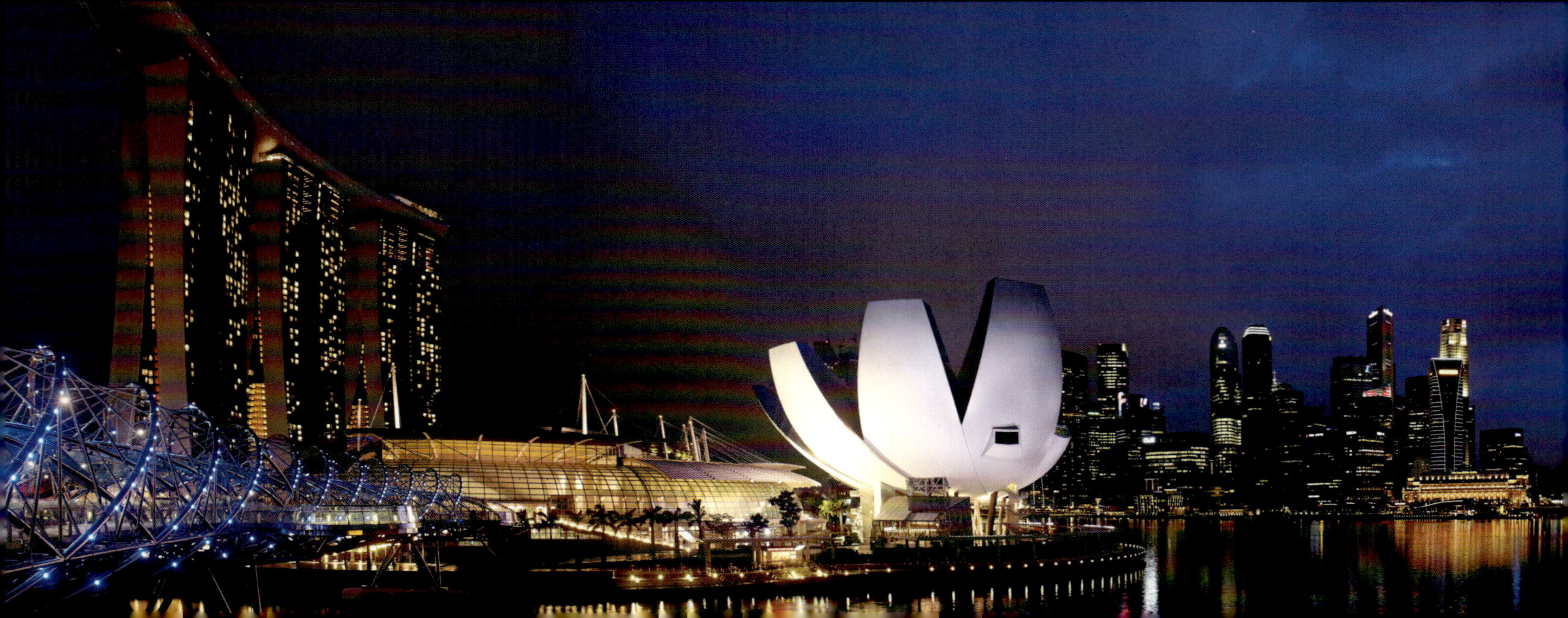

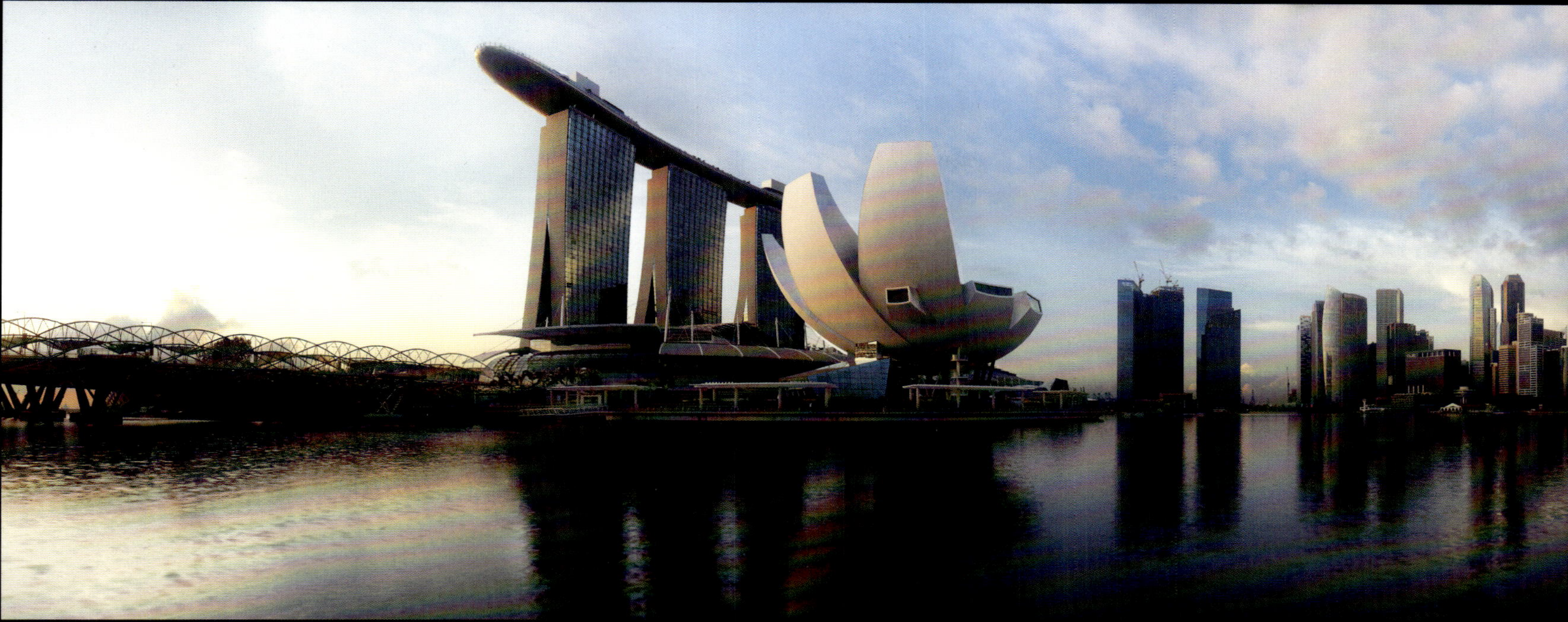

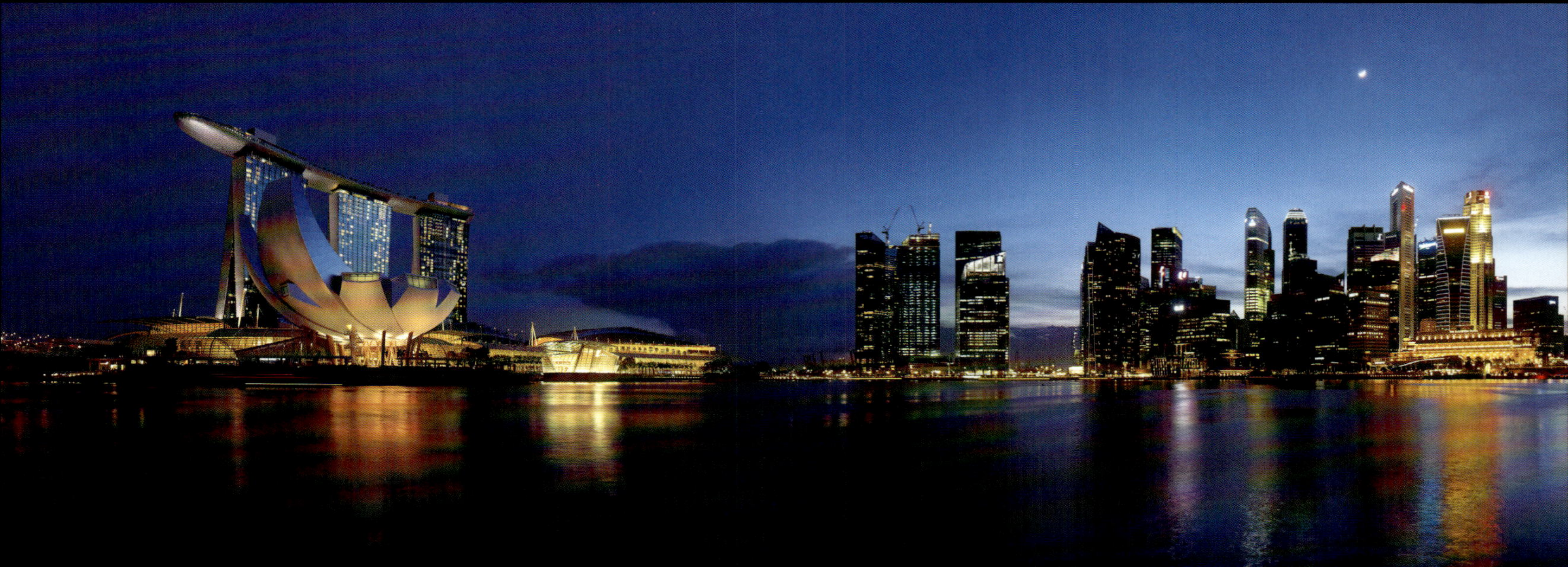

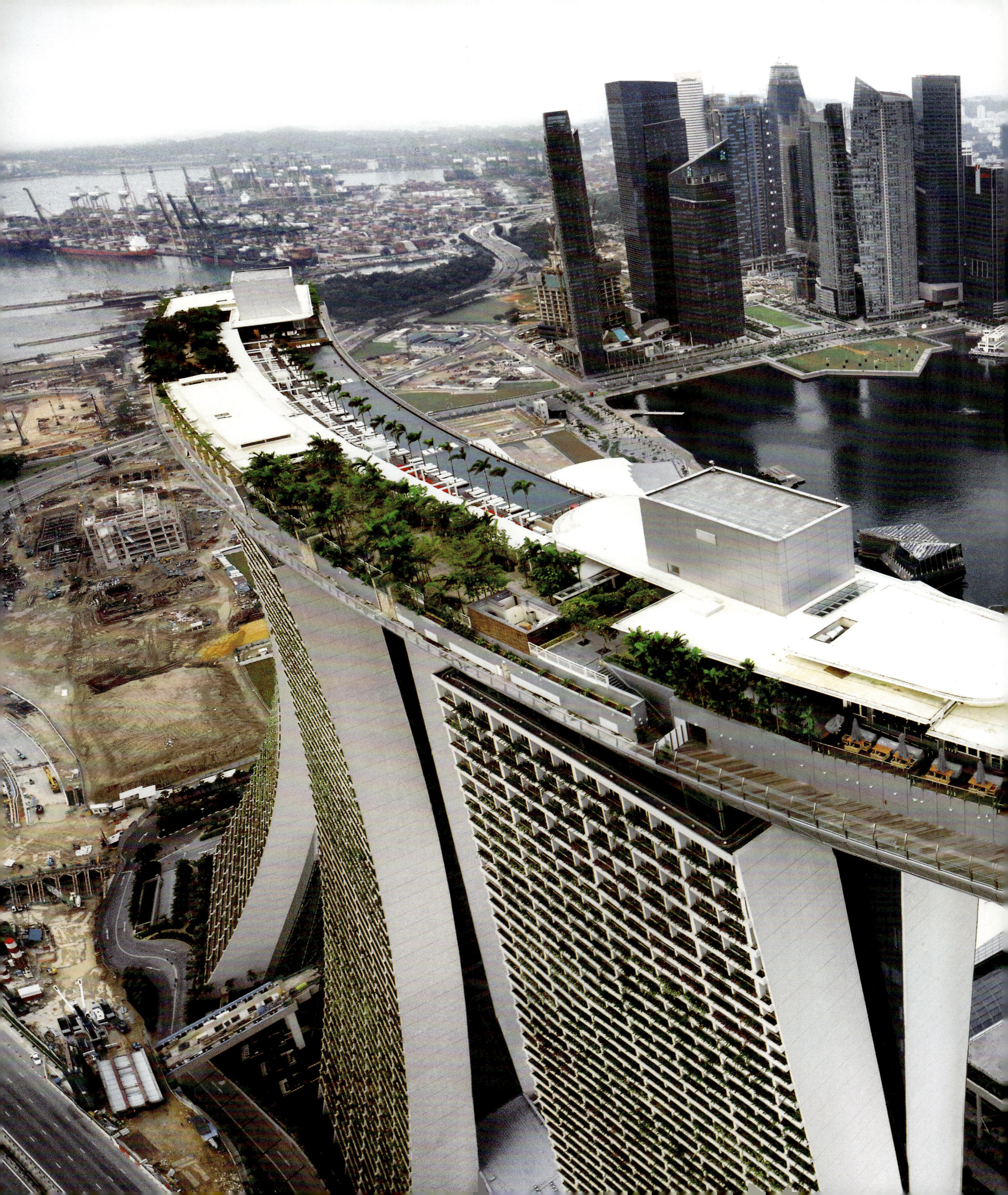

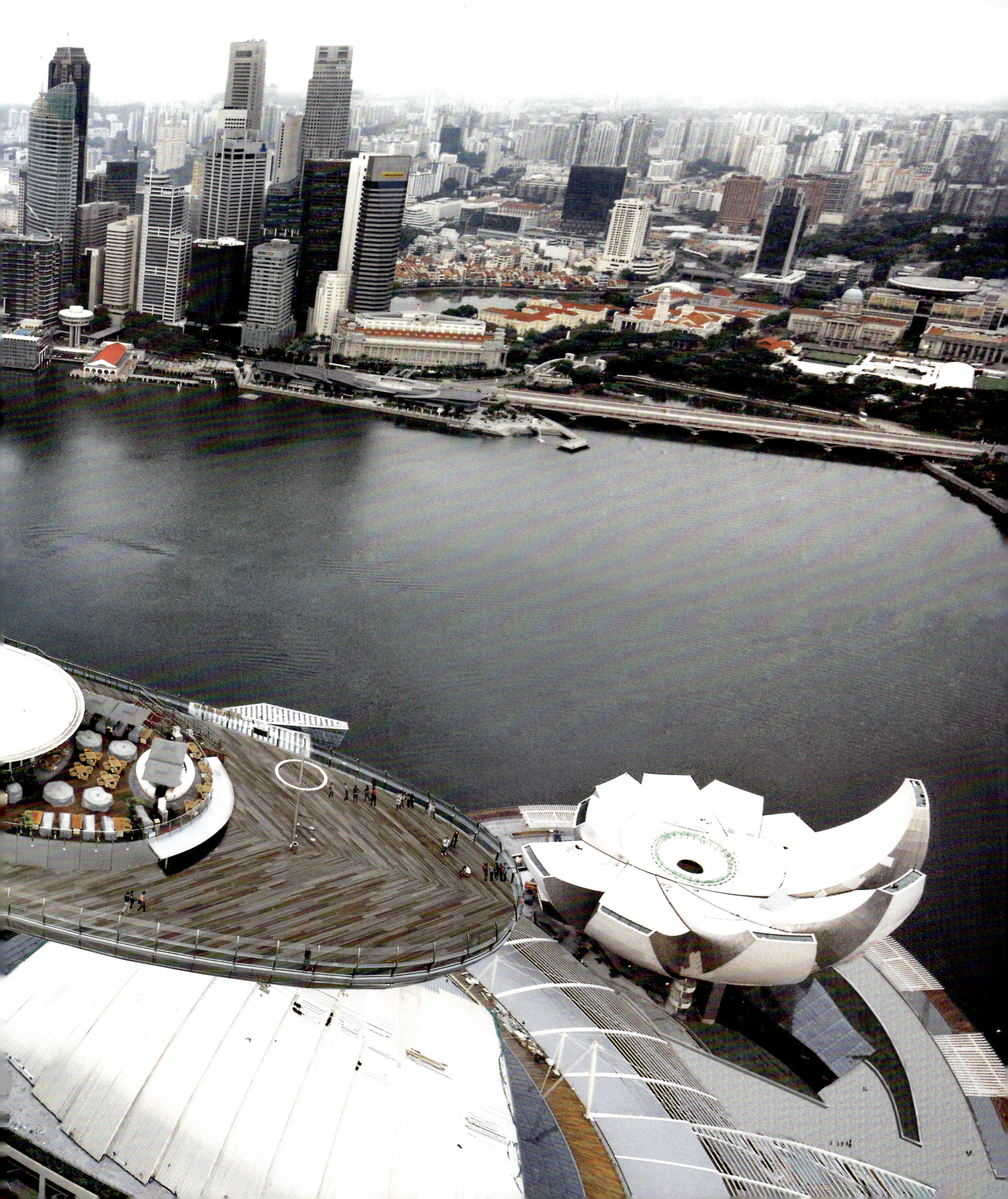

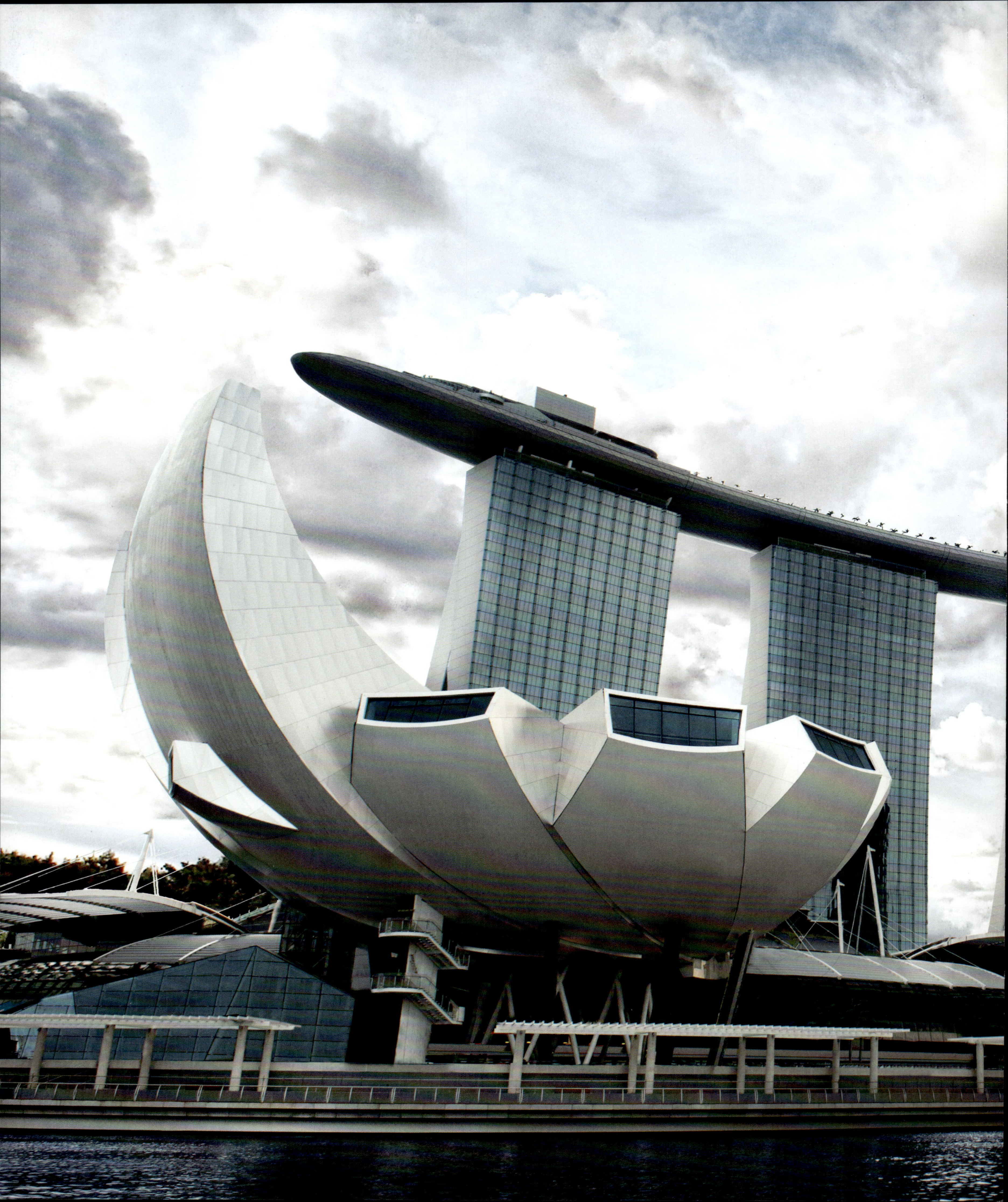

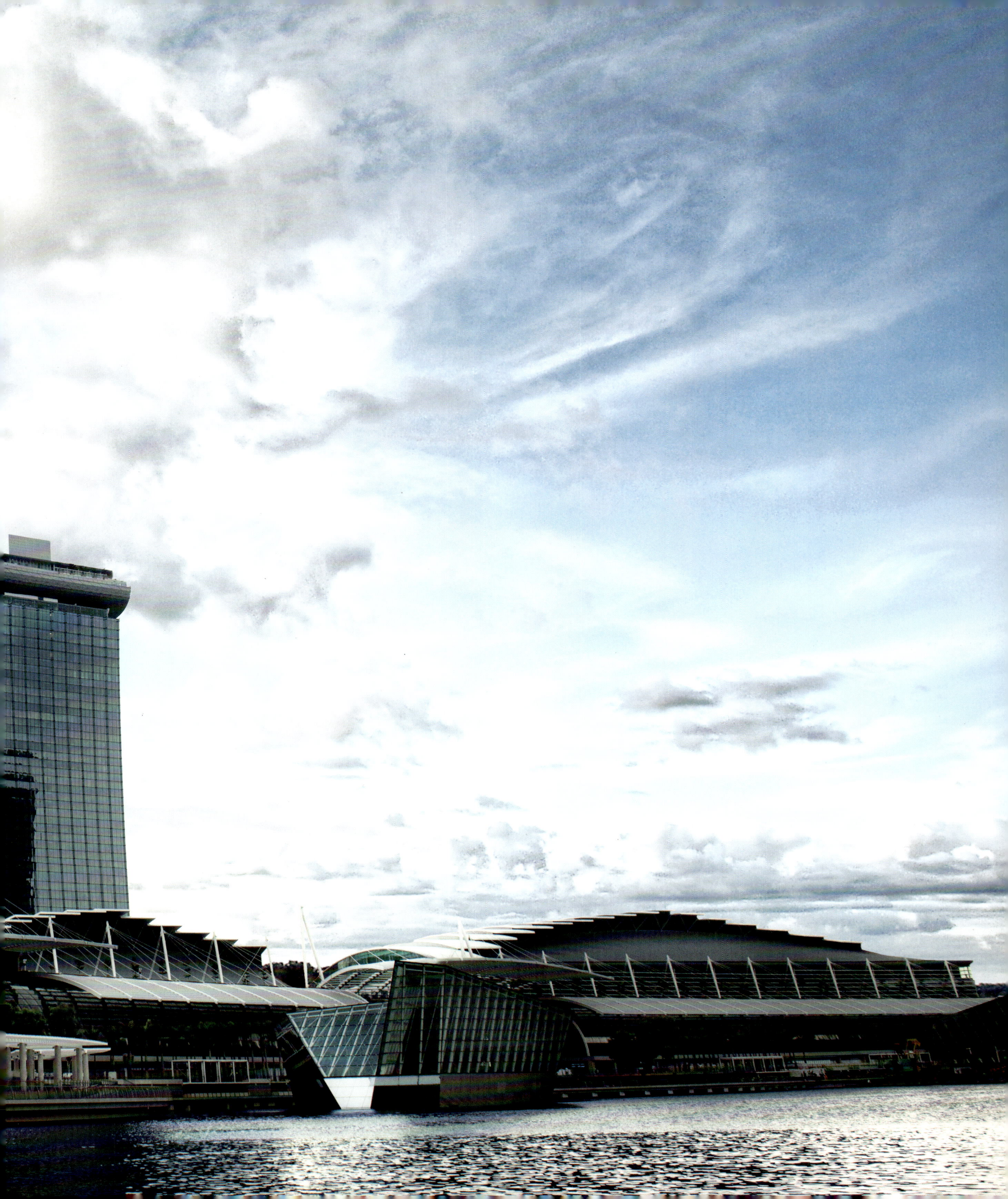

THE ARCHITECTURE OF MEMORABILITY

GARY HACK

The scene has quickly become famous among resort aficionados: couples talking quietly at the razor's edge of an outdoor swimming pool fifty-seven stories above the ground, with Singapore's skyline across the bay seemingly almost close enough to touch. It sends chills down the spine of anyone with even a hint of vertigo. The Infinity Pool at Marina Bay Sands combines total calm in the midst of one of Asia's most dynamic cities with the thrill of vulnerability—the illusion of danger while being safely immersed in still waters under a bright tropical sun. And this isn't the only experience to be had at the world's highest rooftop garden. Other vacationers lounge in the dappled shade below palms and trellises, while children play in a wading pool. As day turns to night, underwater lights transform the water into a shimmering transparency, the city beyond sparkles, and the air fills with the happy voices of revelers on the terraces of the SkyPark's restaurants and clubs. It is truly a magical place.

How does one create an environment for lasting memories in a world of cities where every building, public space, and designed object seems to be shouting for attention? Some famous structures are known mainly for their iconic shapes, the Eiffel Tower and Empire State Building among them. Others, such as the Sydney Opera House, serve as a metaphor for their special setting, impressing at a distance, even at the expense of cramping the activities within. Still others, including the Guggenheim Museum in Bilbao, Spain, are instantly recognizable and seem to capture the spirit of a new age, but their shapes are too complicated for even professionals to reproduce. The Marina Bay Sands offers another way of being memorable, rooted in unique possibilities of both place and program. Its memorability is built on the many ways in which it can be seen and experienced.

Asian Urbanism

Singapore is by common consent the most intelligently planned and best managed city in Southeast Asia; it has a sophisticated energy that belies its reputation for being merely buttoned-down. It shares with other emerging cities the issues of dealing with explosive growth, rising wealth, and fast-changing economies, but unlike its counterparts, it has managed to stay one step ahead. It followed Tokyo's lead and pinned its future on mass transit, and it has a long history of shaping development patterns for livability and economic

Illustration of hotel towers viewed from the future Gardens by the Bay

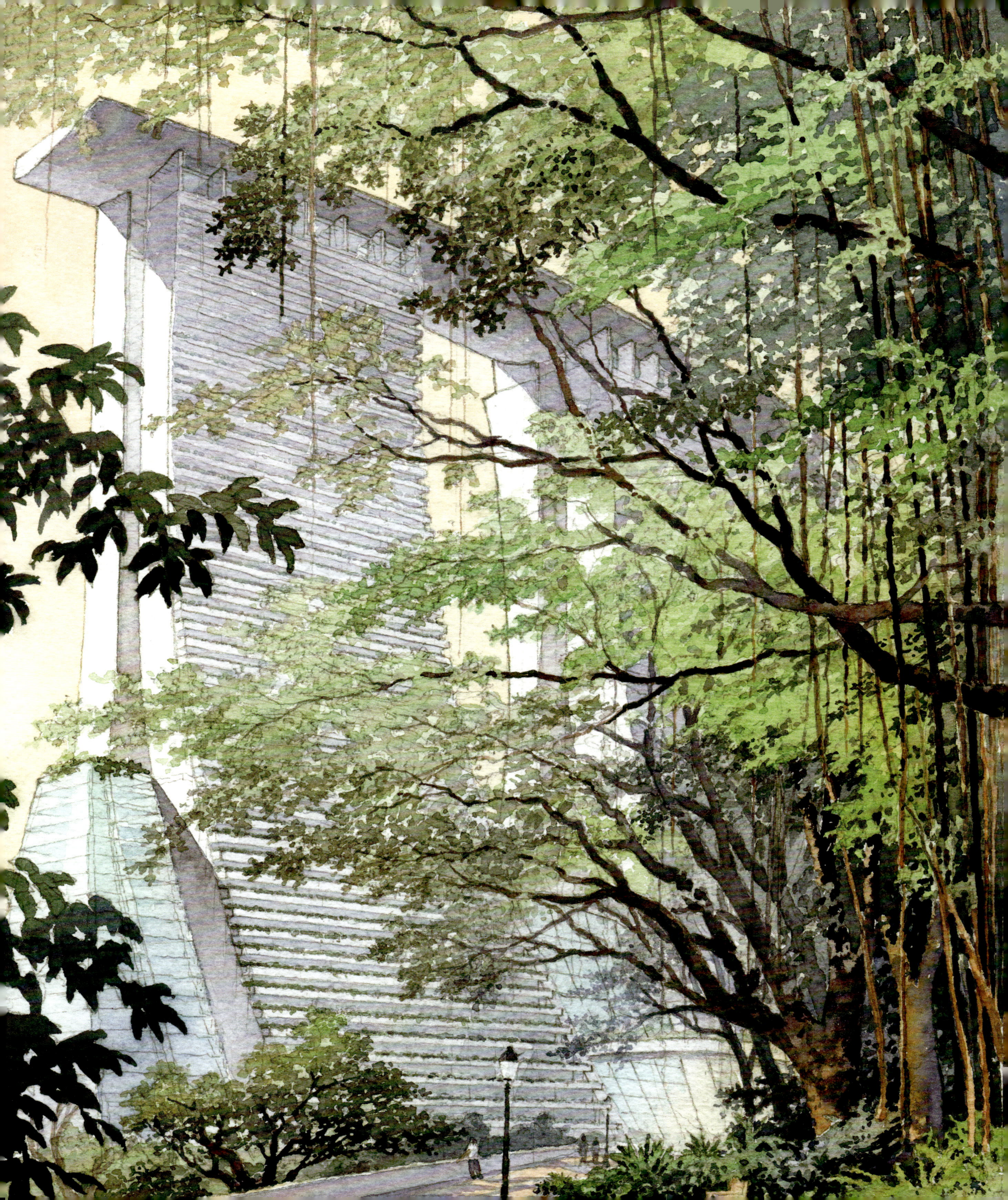

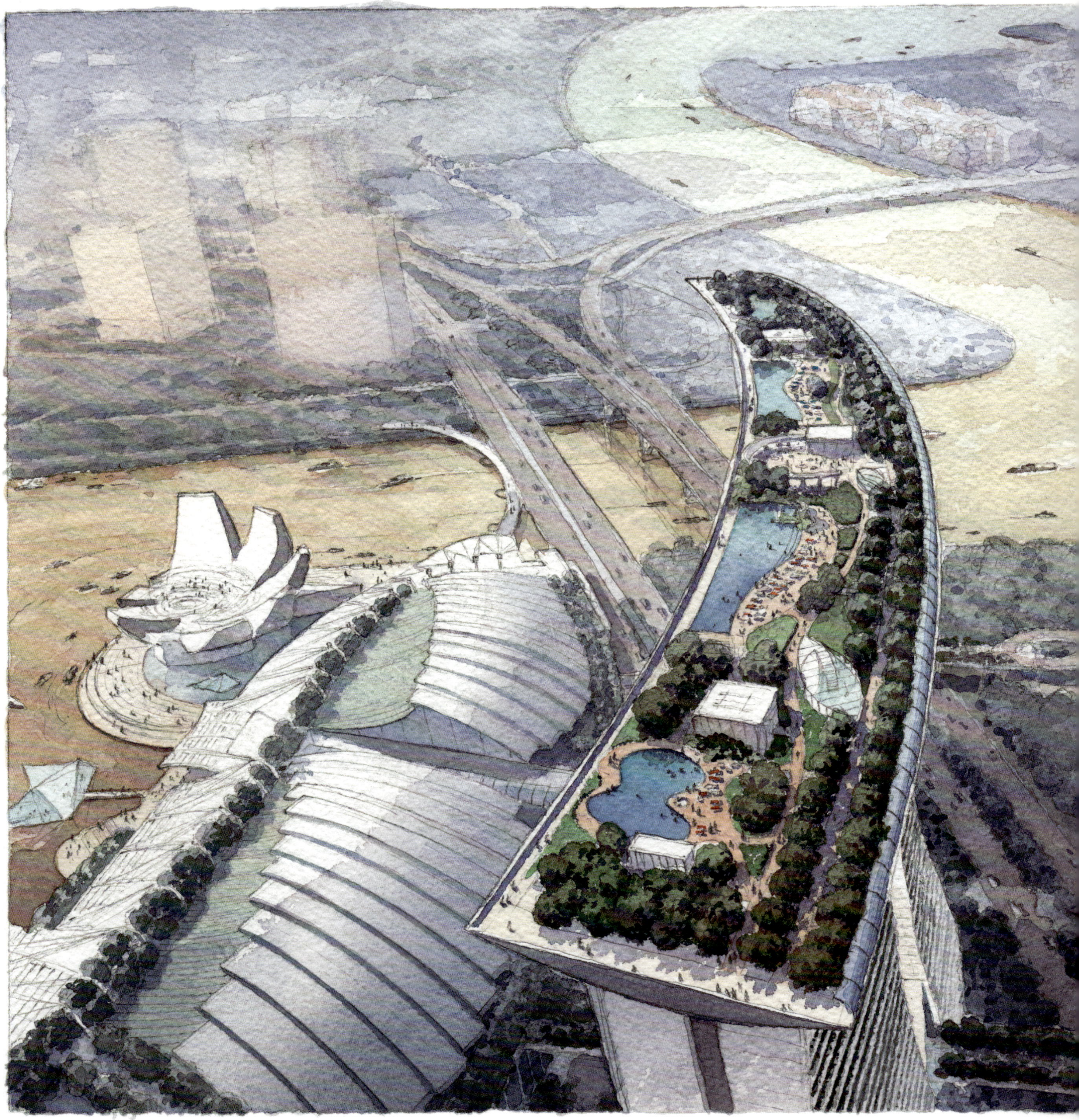

advancement. For many years, Singapore's slogan has been the "Garden City," evidenced by generous parks and open spaces that relieve the densities of a compact urban core. More recently, as wealth increased and the cost of doing business threatened traditional industries, the government has invested heavily in making Singapore a focus of the knowledge economy and tourism, diversifying to tap the rising prosperity of Southeast Asia.

Marina Bay Sands resulted from two important policy decisions the Singapore government made in the 1960s. First, it reclaimed land from the ocean to create room for expanding a crowded central business district. Other cities, such as Hong Kong and Tokyo, simply extended their shorelines outward, encapsulating older waterfront structures behind walls of new development. Singapore, instead, left its waterfront in place and created a ring of projects around a new bay. Three themes shaped the development: "explore," providing new central living options; "exchange," doubling the size of the business district and making it a global hub; and "entertain," establishing new performance venues and cultural opportunities.

The original Marina Bay Development Plan, prepared in 1996 by Singapore's Urban Redevelopment Authority (URA), laid down a grid of forty-five blocks, each kept deliberately small to encourage diverse projects. Waterfront areas were reserved for pedestrian promenades and cultural uses. Detailed design guidelines stipulated that views to the bay should be maintained and buildings have a harmonious character. A new mass-transit line was installed to connect Marina Bay developments with the existing city, and a common services tunnel was created to provide all necessary infrastructure in a location easily reached. Singapore reserved more than half of the reclaimed land for recreation and cultural uses, including the new Gardens by the Bay, an extraordinary tropical arboretum and botanical garden. While the development plan was refined over the years, it has remained remarkably true to its original intentions.

The government's second important decision was to promote integrated resorts as a way of expanding the attractiveness of Singapore as a visitor destination. Integrated resorts are based on the idea that there are synergies to be gained by combining hotels, casinos, and convention and meeting spaces, along with shopping and cultural uses. In less than a decade, Singapore has made lands available for two such resorts, soliciting proposals from international developers and operators with the capability to assemble the capital and human resources to make them a success.

Design Requirements

The Singapore Tourism Board worked closely with the URA to frame the expectations for the six blocks allocated to the integrated resort at Marina Bay. They required it to be "an iconic development that is unique and differentiated from other existing properties in the region," containing "a compelling mix of unique anchor attractions such as theater shows and/or themed attractions, as well as MICE facilities (meetings, incentives, conventions, and exhibitions), hotels, food and beverage, retail and entertainment facilities." The board was seeking a complex dynamic enough to "support Singapore's ambition to be the knowledge exchange capital of the world." Proposals would also be judged by the track record of their developers and architects, the quality of designs submitted, the financial arrangements offered, the economy-wide multiplier benefits, and the career opportunities they provided—especially for residents.

The design regulations were even more specific, running to over thirty pages. Nothing escaped the attention of the URA. The authority established overall height limits for each of the project's blocks—245 meters for those beside the garden, 50 meters for those fronting on Marina Bay—to ensure unobstructed water views from the inland parcels. It prescribed minimum and maximum floor areas, limited the size of the gaming area, and provided incentives to increase the allowed floor area if the project met sustainability goals. Guidelines set the width of the streets and the waterfront promenade, and pinpointed vehicular access and drop-off points. Materials to be used on streets and promenades were not left to chance, and the size and location of signage were tightly restricted.

Of the dozens of requirements the design team needed to address, several had a formative influence on the site. Marina Bay had been planned as a pedestrian-friendly district, and the URA mandated that it have walkways belowground, at street level, and over the streets between the waterfront promenade and the Gardens by the Bay. An indoor connection was needed between the site and the planned Marina View MRT station nearby. Most important, the URA wanted the development to maintain two view corridors through the low-rise blocks to keep the waterfront

Top: Marina Bay Sands and
Singapore's Central Business District

Bottom: Project view from the north

140

visible from Bayfront Avenue. These stipulations led to pedestrian activity on at least three levels, and ultimately, the design team went even further, creating fourth and fifth levels along the promenade.

An interesting footnote: the design guidelines imagined a landscaped roof deck, about three stories high, to house swimming pools, concessions, and other activities, and to give visitors a fine prospect of the garden and bay. This proved difficult to achieve because of other demands on roof space. In the end, the architect had a better idea about how to meet this requirement.

What the Architect Brought to the Project

This is not the first large or complicated project that Moshe Safdie has designed, although it was a unique opportunity to consolidate many ideas he had experimented with on earlier buildings. The Marina Bay Sands program was sprawling and multifaceted, and required a sophisticated repertory of organizational and formal ideas to get all its parts working in unison. In its completion, it is one of the largest building complexes ever created, almost equaling the planned square footage of New York's new World Trade Center. Safdie believes that the cues for every building's form can be found in a deep understanding of its purposes. Meaning and purpose are intimately connected.

Beginning with his first project, the design of Montreal's Habitat '67, Safdie has demonstrated an abiding preoccupation with sunlight as a force for human life and inspiration. He has mastered the many ways the sun can be exploited: direct sunlight in gardens and outdoor spaces, brilliantly achieved in the terraced houses of his new town of Modi'in in Israel (1989). Filtered sunlight that changes color through the course of the day in indoor atria, as seen in Safdie's Peabody Essex Museum, in Salem, Massachusetts (2003). Indirect light in the large indoor spaces so ably designed in the Skirball Cultural Center in Los Angeles (final phase completed in 2013). Reflected light at the edges of water at the Crystal Bridges Museum of American Art, in Bentonville, Arkansas (2011). And, finally, the dramatic contrasts of light and darkness memorably realized at the Yad Vashem Holocaust Museum in Jerusalem (2005). Animating the huge complex at Marina Bay required a full vocabulary of light.

Safdie has always approached the design of buildings as an act of urban design. When a project is viewed in its larger context, even a small building helps form a street, while a large building can create the framework for an entire city district. His two magnificent public libraries, in Vancouver and Salt Lake City, are organized along new pedestrian zones that attract people, commerce, and other uses into their midst, while being tightly connected to the surrounding pattern of streets and spaces. Safdie's National Gallery of Canada in Ottawa (1988) is the counterpart in form to the nearby parliamentary complex and, with its glass perimeter public spaces, draws the rugged Canadian landscape into the experience of every visitor. His architecture makes the museum an even more fitting setting for the display of early-twentieth-century paintings by the so-called Group of Seven, whose work celebrated the Canadian wilderness.

Yet while his architecture is unfailingly respectful of its context, Safdie also recognizes the obligation to produce buildings that are memorable on their own terms and to create a context for future structures. His thirty-year involvement with the design of the Mamilla Center in Jerusalem is very much about creating a new vocabulary for modern functions in a sandstone city 2,500 years old. Whenever possible, he finds inspiration for a building's forms in the traditional materials and shapes of a place, but he is not afraid to respond to the emerging forces of change. With the advent of digital technology, his designs have become more expressive, bringing an excitement and freshness to the places he creates. His modernist side has been liberated. Safdie is especially fascinated with creating curvilinear glass structures, exploiting the potential that glass offers to layer space and animate outdoor public areas with scenes of people moving indoors.

Translating Guidelines into a Plan

The three-dimensional puzzle presented by the URA design stipulations could have been solved in many ways, with better or worse results. While the guidelines were strict, the outcome was not inevitable. The genius of the Marina Bay Sands scheme is that it not only met the requirements but also invented possibilities the planners could never have imagined. That is the mark of inspired design.

Moshe Safdie's mentor, Louis I. Kahn, emphasized the distinction between form and design. "Form is 'what,'" Kahn argued. "Design is 'how.'" Form grows out of the program and circumstances of a site, and finds its expression in the diagram of how the parts of a building or complex

Illustration of waterfront promenade

are positioned and relate to each other. Once the form is established, design is the process of making it a material reality. Kahn believed that while there can be many legitimate design expressions for a building, its form should be deeply rooted in the institution and locale. Good buildings have a sense of "rightness."

Establishing the form of the Marina Bay Sands complex began by recognizing its context. Connected to Singapore's historic waterfront by the DNA Bridge, the site offered the potential for a steady flow of residents and visitors walking the circuit around Marina Bay. The promenade on the bay was the logical place to situate the important cultural attractions and spaces where visitors congregate. The two other main frontages suggested other uses—Bayfront Avenue is the main point of arrival to the resort by car or bus, while the edge along the gardens was the logical place for outdoor extensions of the hotel and the ideal face for rooms with balconies for enjoying the green space. Responding to this varied set of opportunities, and respecting the required view corridors between Bayfront Avenue and the waterfront, the organizing framework for the complex became clear.

Next came the question of how to orient the large components of Marina Bay Sands—the MICE, two performing arts theaters, a museum, and a large casino, among the most difficult elements to fit into any urban setting. Customarily, such venues turn their backs on streets, siphoning off activity into lobbies and indoor spaces. Thinking as an urban designer, Safdie decided to wrap the large spaces with retail shops, making a seamless connection with Bayfront Avenue and the waterfront promenade. Coupled with this was his decision to create three levels of uses belowground, accommodating all service docks, parking, and several levels of retail activity. This removed distractions from the street and created the opportunity to locate the main retail level underground, where many pedestrians would arrive from buses and the hotels. Creating a five-level basement in marine clay was like excavating toothpaste, but it proved well worth the effort and expense.

Often, retail promenades along waterfronts fail because they have only a single line of shops without enough energy to attract customers. Safdie created three levels of retail lining the waterfront, anchored at the northern end by a skating rink, museum, and performing arts center, and at the southern by the public spaces that spill out of the convention center. The waterfront Event Plaza is the venue for large outdoor gatherings, complemented by displays and performances on lower levels of the retail area. A remarkable five-story, curved, glass arcade creates an indoor promenade paralleling the outdoor walkway, while glass-covered retail arcades connect to Bayshore Avenue. At Marina Bay Sands, the pedestrian is celebrated.

The form of the hotel provided other challenges. Most large resort lodgings are lumpy blocks with miles of dark indoor corridors totally disconnected from lobbies, amenities, and ground-level activities. Marina Bay Sands turns this formula on its head: a 150-meter-long wedge of light and space, organized as a street, connects hotel walkways to restaurants, shops, and activities. The decision to create three separate hotel towers allowed Marina Bay Sands to tap a different segment of the resort marketplace in each structure. By separating the towers, Safdie also reduced their overall mass and allowed sunlight to penetrate to the center of the street.

Coming into the complex at the vehicle entrances at either end is like setting foot in a secular cathedral. Shafts of light draw visitors along the hotel street. There is visible activity above and below. A third-level bridge thrusts through the space, connecting the gaming and cultural venues with the public gardens on the opposite side of the hotels. Escalators lead to two generous, below-street walkways for those headed for shopping and other activities. The walkway is generously planted with large trees, as if an extension of the public gardens outside. And to ensure this remains a civic space, the Singaporean government maintains a 2-meter easement that makes the indoor walkway open to all pedestrian traffic twenty-four hours a day.

That the final element in the complicated structure of Marina Bay Sands is visible from a distance but invisible from inside the hotel only adds to the anticipation of getting there. The SkyPark, too, is a uniquely public and private space, with one set of elevators from the hotel blocks for guests and another from the street for other visitors. Its form is hard to pin down. Seen from across the bay, it appears as some kind of altar offering humans to a sun god—Surya, Apollo, or Amun-Ra. Or perhaps it is the mythical solar boat constructed for Amun-Ra himself. Yet as one walks across the DNA Bridge, the SkyPark looks different, more like a giant skateboard drawing air. None of this is of any concern, of course, from within the SkyPark, where pleasure and awe mingle at the top of the world.

Design of the Complex

The form of Marina Bay Sands indeed has rightness about it, matched by the creative design that brought form into material reality. It stretches the limits of the possible, nowhere more than in the design of the SkyPark, which spans three separate structures and cantilevers 65.5 meters at its northern edge. Supporting the pool and platform is a massive truss, which during construction was hoisted up along the sloping concrete walls of the hotel towers. The boatlike profile of the park obscures the technical gymnastics needed to contain water in the pool, yet allows individual towers to sway up to 25 centimeters in wind and 50 centimeters in an earthquake.

Concrete, steel, and glass are the primary palette of Marina Bay Sands. Concrete is the instrument of height; steel makes daring spans possible; and glass provides the transparency that connects the complex to the surrounding streets, gardens, water, and sky. Digital technology made the design possible, liberating forms from the orthogonal box, allowing them to be shaped into expressive plastic elements. The three hotel towers are, on closer inspection, splayed like clothespins, reducing their apparent bulk and opening their interiors to light. The gentle curve of the waterfront glass arcade provides a continuously changing vista—how much better than a straight shot along the water. And the ArtScience Museum on the waterfront is a remarkable lotus form, elevated on columns and reaching up like a blossom that captures the sun and draws it down the walls of the galleries inside.

Curved metal roofs cover the three blocks of activities lining the waterfront. Their shape was partly dictated by the need to cover fly lofts in the theaters and large exhibition and ballroom spaces in the MICE facilities, but, in truth, they are expressive elements that help unify the blocks. Their design also recognizes that every building has five important facades, and that the view of rooftops is probably the most important aspect for hotel guests, visitors to the SkyPark, and occupants of the tall office buildings across the bay in the Singapore business district.

Top: Skating rink and retail area

Bottom: SkyPark Infinity Pool and gardens overlooking Singapore

Retail canal boats

This same thoughtful plasticity carries through to the forms of the large interior spaces. The four-story height of the casino is a welcome contrast to the usual low-ceilinged, noisy gaming rooms that characterize most resorts. Undulating balconies rise above the main floor, providing access to other table games, celebrity restaurants, and high-limit spaces. At its ceiling, the area is lit by pleated bands of reflected light, echoing the elegance of the greatest art deco movie houses. The two theaters, subtly different in form, both have cascading seats that put the audience in intimate touch with performers. The flowing movement inside the theaters extends out into the lobbies, where curving mirrored walls multiply the sense of activity, making even a lightly filled space seem crowded and bustling.

While the large spaces of Marina Bay Sands are expressively shaped, the retail areas are more tightly ordered, providing an antidote to the chaos that can result from each outlet importing its branded format. The coordinators of the retail zones struggled to find a middle ground, prohibiting projecting signs or storefronts and forcing merchants to design their shops to fit into a structural grid. They may have pressed too hard, however, and generally the retail areas are less interesting than they might have been if the shops had been allowed to venture into the public space. The most animated retail areas surround the main water feature, where restaurant tables spill out into the pedestrian zone. Perhaps more events, and programmed use of the space, will bring life to the retail arcades.

As inventive as many of the spaces are, art commissioned for the project adds further depth of character to Marina Bay Sands. Seven artists contributed creative responses to the architecture and spaces. Antony Gormley's remarkable matrixlike sculpture floats above the hotel atrium, emphasizing its height and openness. Zheng Chongbin's oversize ceramic tree vessels line the hotel street and extend into the adjacent outdoor spaces. Their 3-meter height is scaled to the huge space they occupy, but every visitor can understand them in reference to ordinary flowerpots, these gorgeously glazed in colors drawn from traditional Asian ceramics. Shimmering aluminum screens, created by Ned Kahn, cover the large glass areas between the hotel towers, a featherweight chain mail that enlivens the facade while filtering the sun. James Carpenter's glass-and-LED-lit facade on the Bayshore Avenue entrance to the casino and retail area comes to life as the sun sets and helps transform Marina Bay Sands into a bright nighttime attraction.

The landscape design of the complex, created by PWP Landscape Architecture, is also essential to the experience of Marina Bay Sands. It helps make the SkyPark an oasis, with palm trees providing just enough cover to temper the bright sun, while also making the space seem rooted. Along the promenade, rows of magnificent cabbage palms offer shade to pedestrians as they browse the shops and cultural attractions, while smaller ornamental gardens present a respite for those who wish to linger. A lower walkway, decked in yellow balau wood, stretches near the water's edge. The climax of the promenade is the grand, ceremonial Event Plaza, designed with stage segments that can be raised or lowered to suit performances ranging from rock concerts to dance to sound-and-light shows. Offshore, Marina Bay has been fitted with fountains and lights that can be programmed to music for daytime or evening events. As the landscape matures and traditions of events develop, the promenade will surely become an important part of Singapore's civic realm. The public art projects and performance venues also remind us that memorable spaces have many authors, some when buildings are constructed, others during their use over time. The installations that leave the deepest impressions resulted from close collaboration between the artists and Moshe Safdie, and they capture and extend an essential quality of the place. Similarly, the most successful performances will be those that could only be created at the edge of Marina Bay.

A feat of design and engineering innovation, Marina Bay Sands is quickly becoming a destination for residents of Asia and beyond and should serve as a prototype for new integrated resorts elsewhere in the world. Its lessons are in its basic precepts: large complexes need to be integrated rather than separated from their surroundings. Pedestrian streets can unify a complex and uplift the experience of moving through them, even if they are enclosed to deal with harsh climates. Natural daylight is critical to the character of places. Multilevel retail and activity spaces can provide the density to promote continuous activity. And, not least, rooftops can be much more than gardens or observation decks.

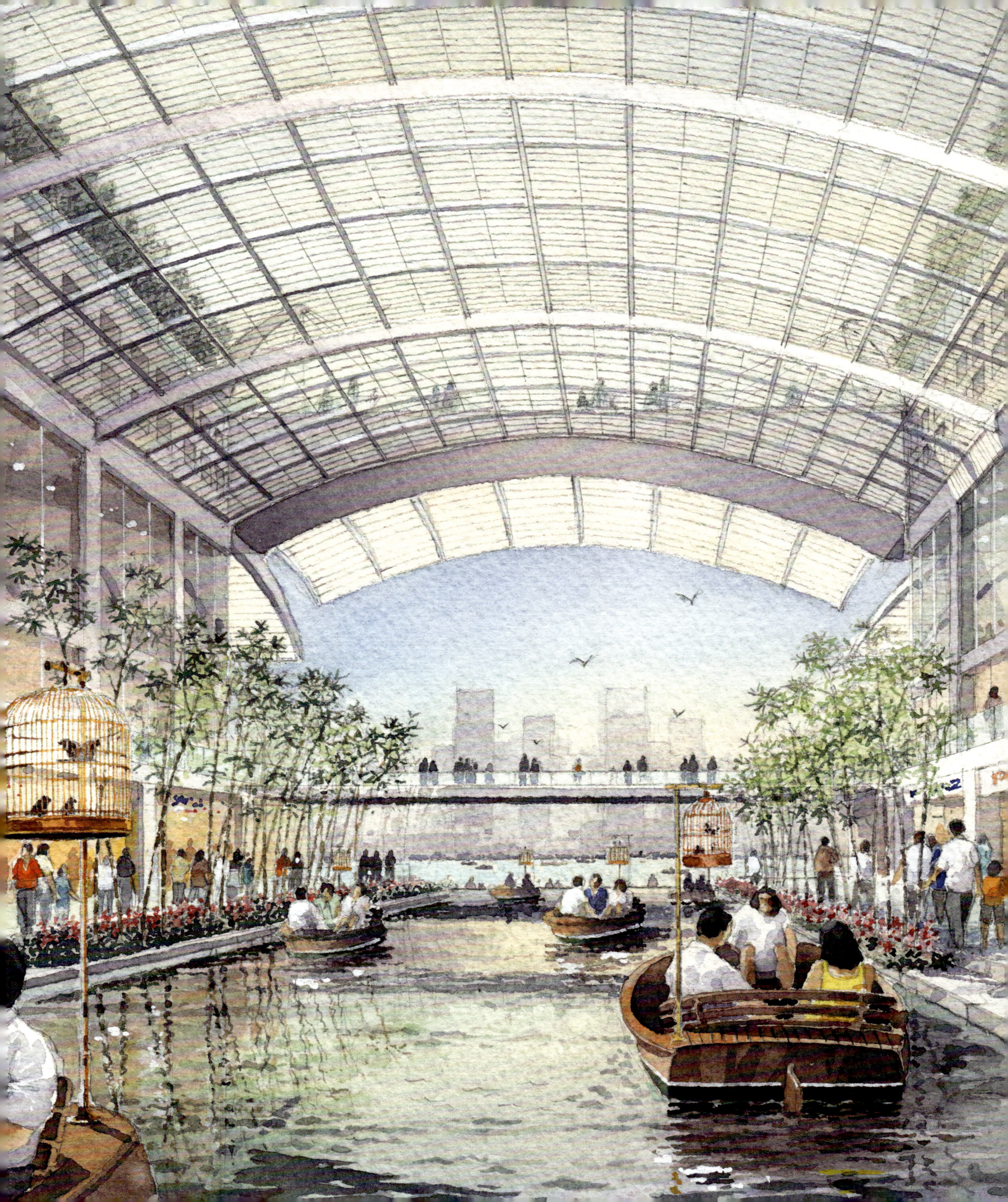

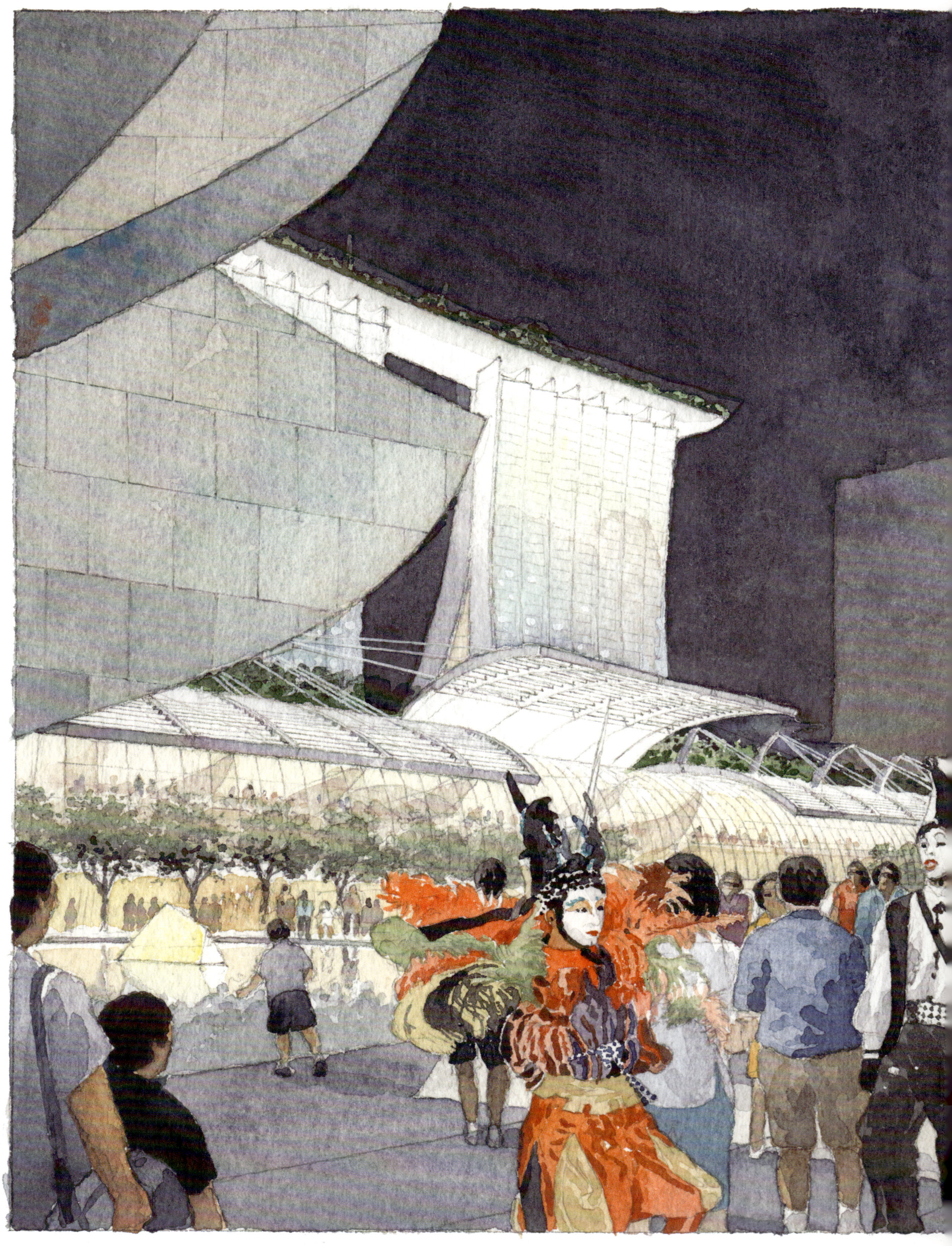

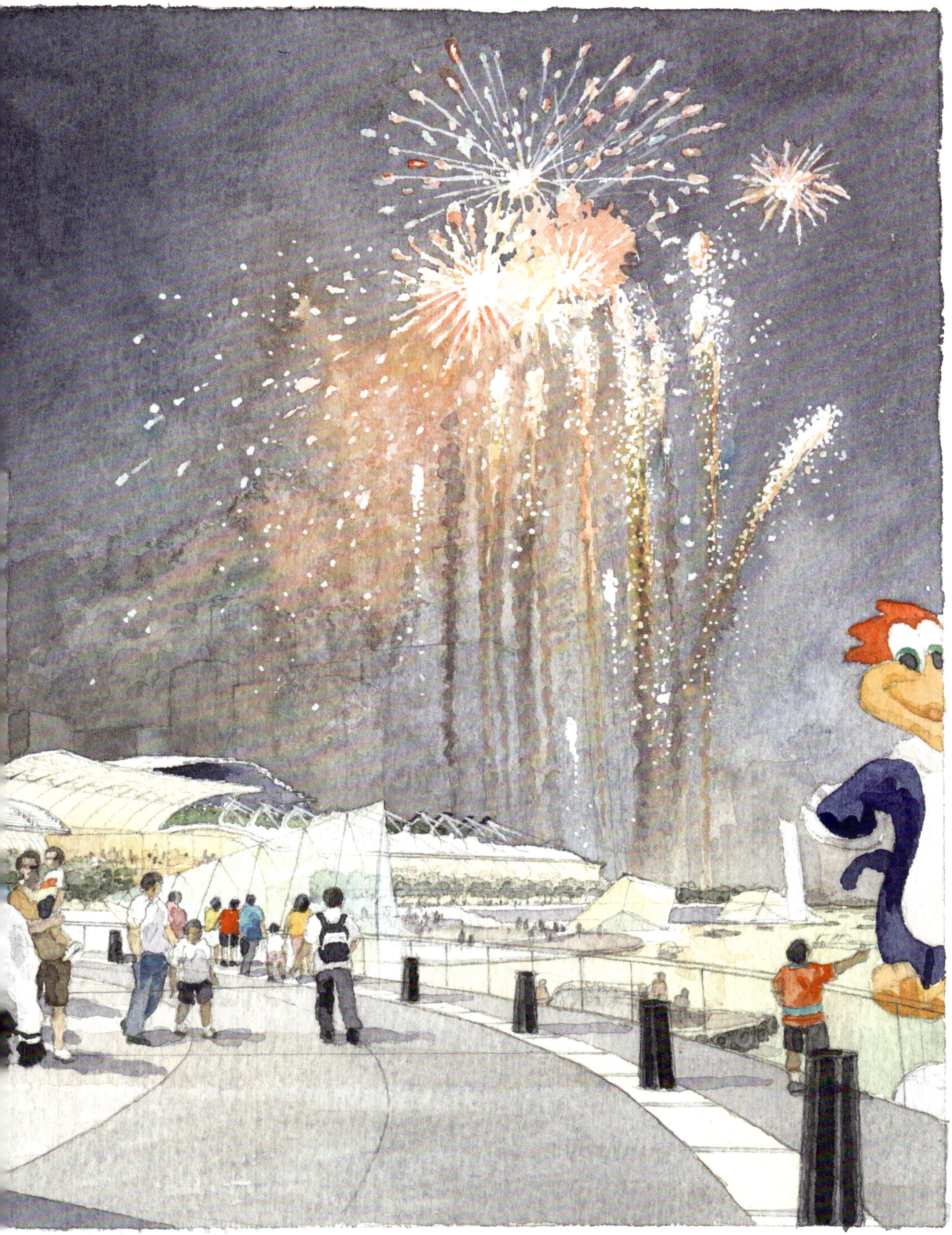

PART 4
A CLOSER LOOK

MARINA BAY SANDS

THE PUBLIC REALM

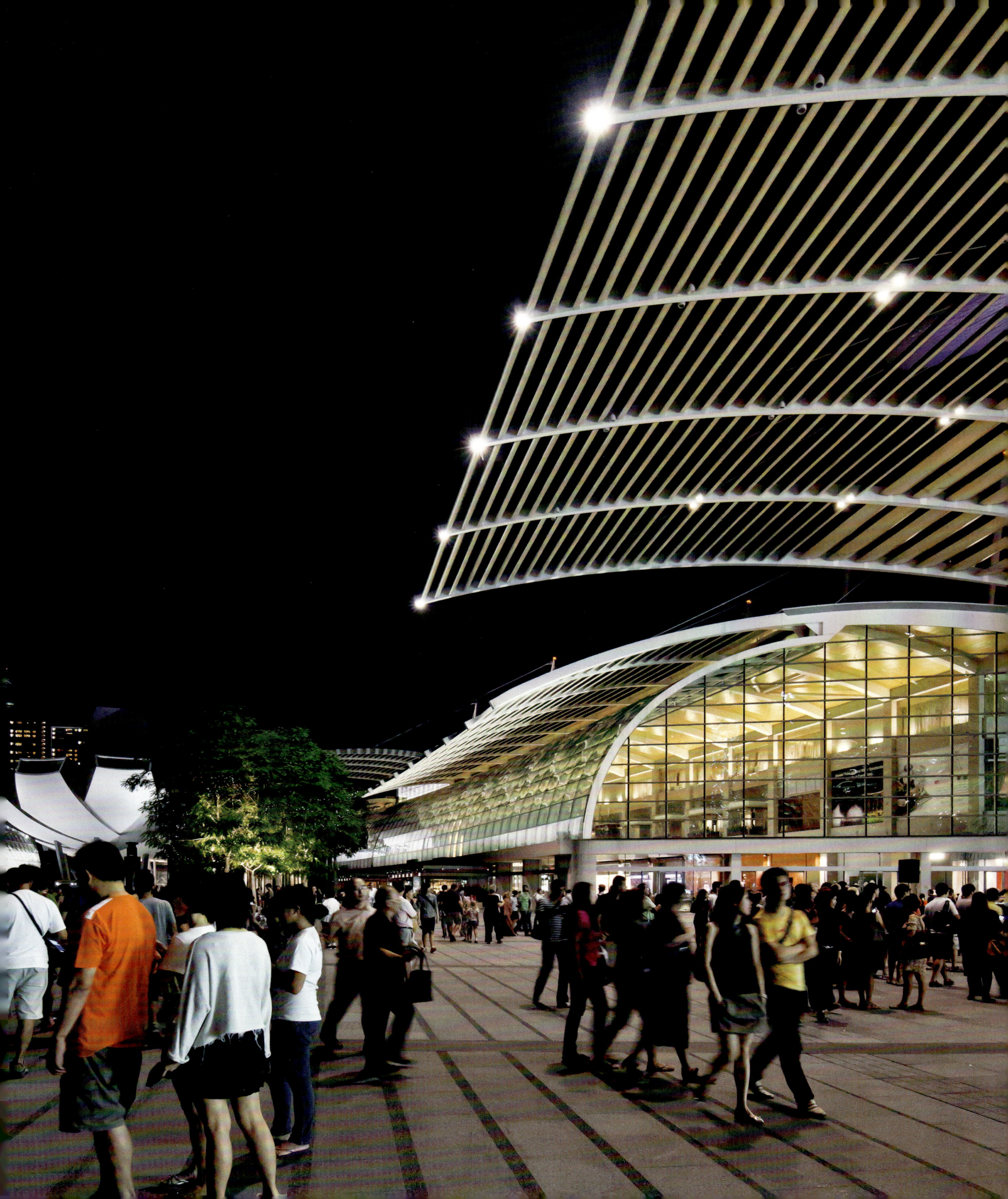

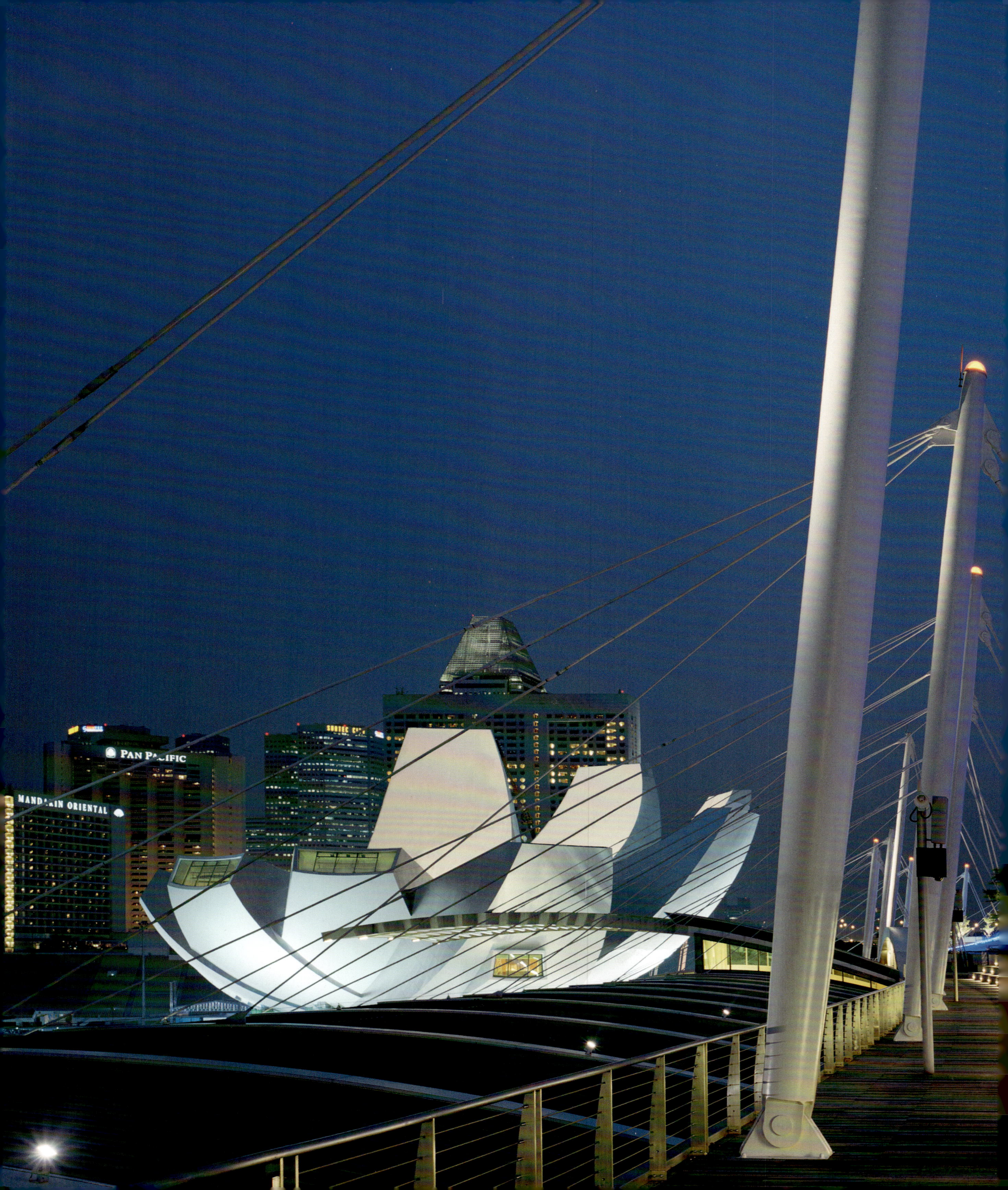
PAN PACIFIC
MANDARIN ORIENTAL

Level 4 garden terrace, with view of ArtScience Museum

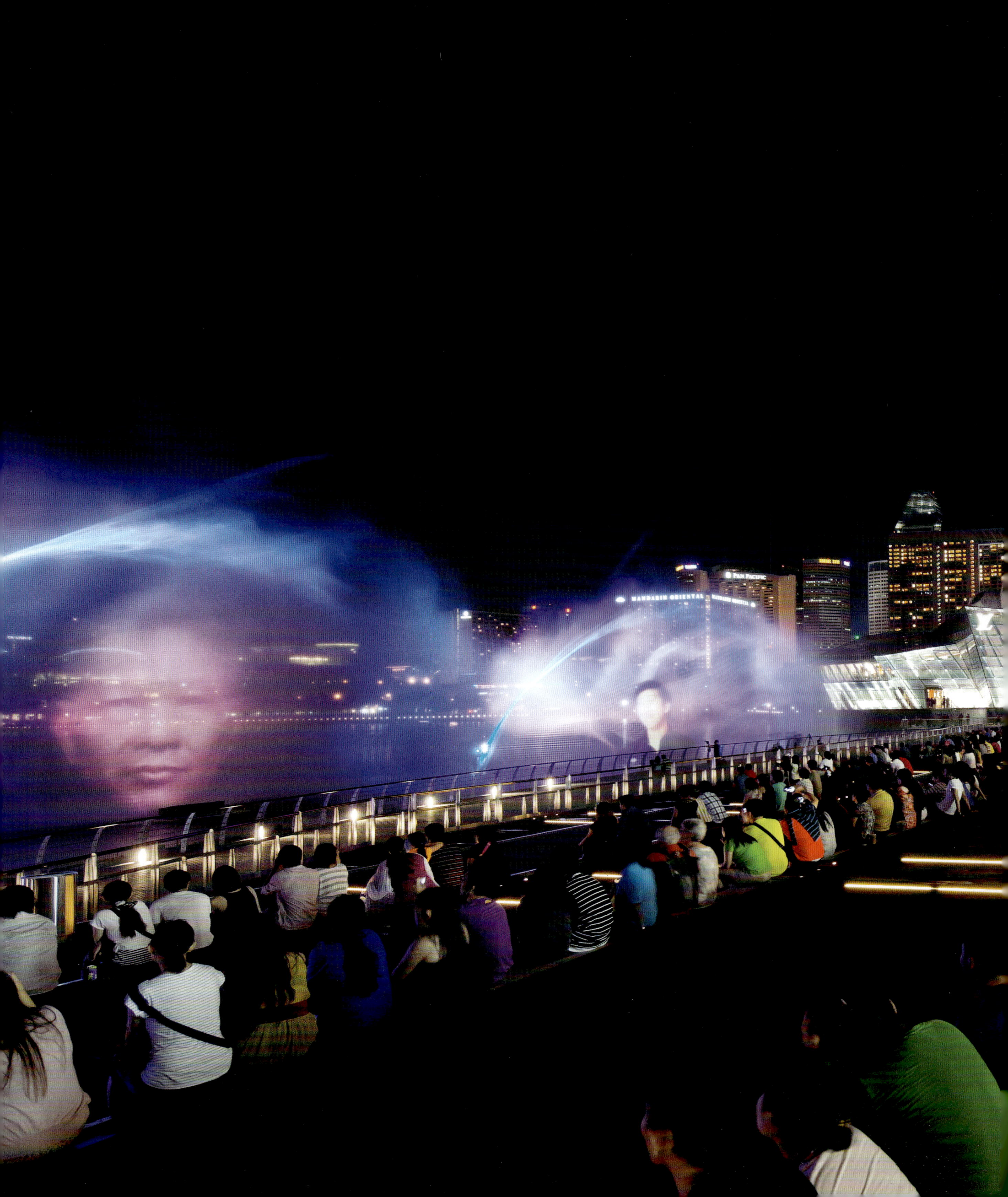
PAN PACIFIC
MANDARIN ORIENTAL

Event Plaza light-and-water show

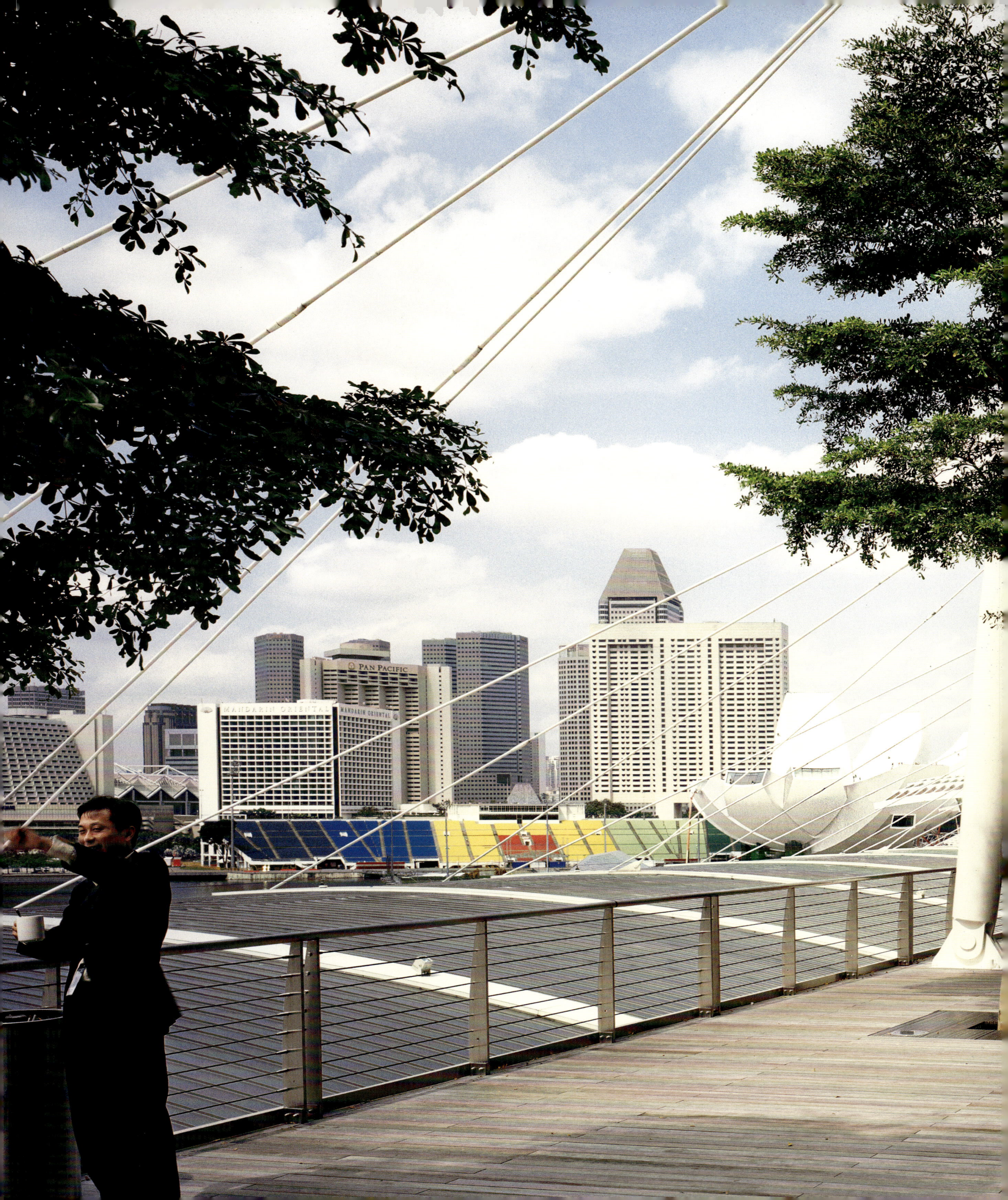

Level 4 terrace off convention space and meeting rooms

Retail canopy shading in- and outdoor spaces

Top: Waterfront promenade shaded by retail canopy

Bottom: Food kiosks accessible from retail arcade and waterfront promenade

Nighttime activities along waterfront promenade

Downtown view from Grand Arcade retail area

Natural light fills multilevel retail view corridor.

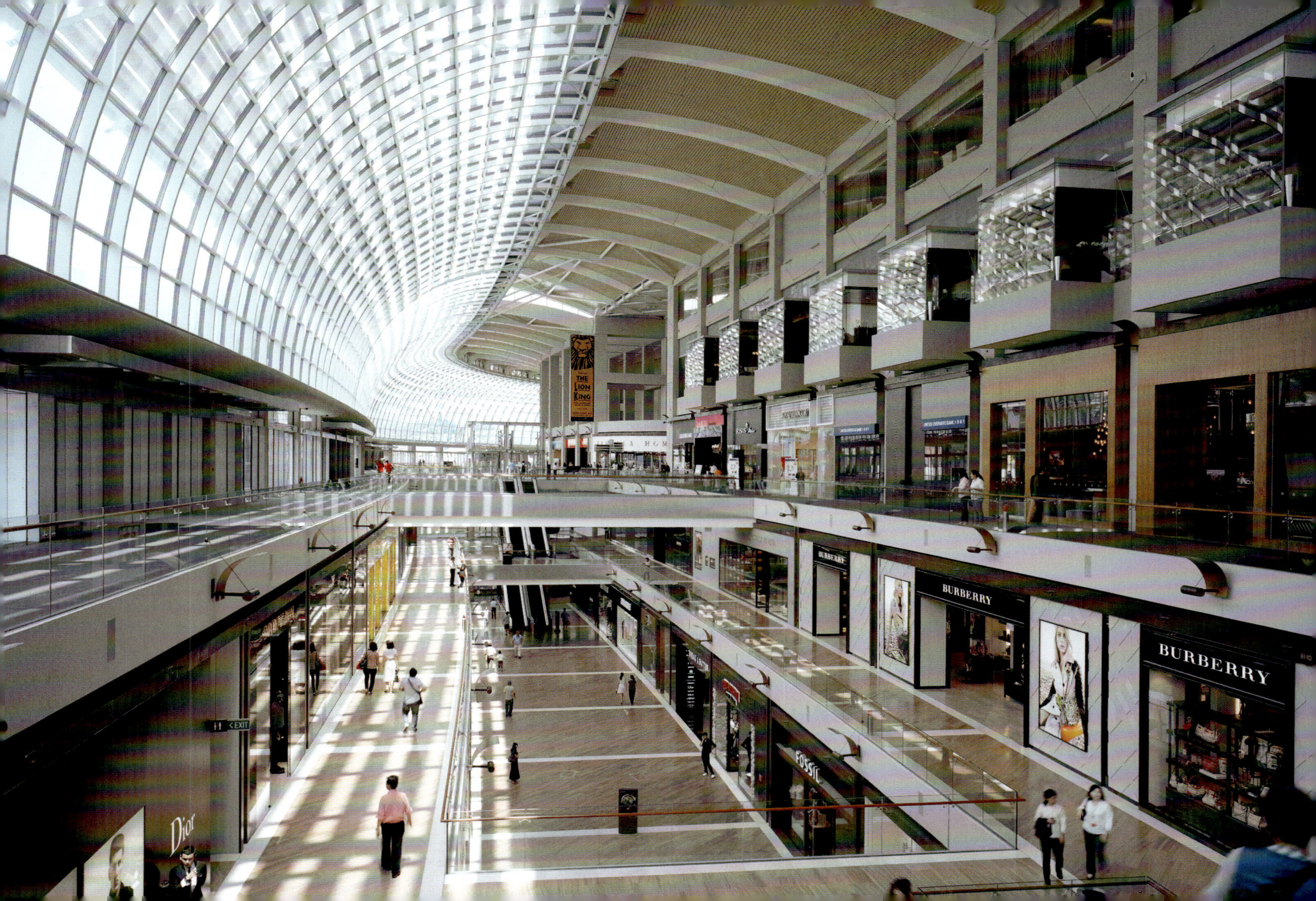
THE LION KING
BURBERRY
BURBERRY
FOSSIL
Dior
EXIT

Disney
THE
Lion
King
THE LANDMARK
MUSICAL EVENT

OCBC CARDS

OPENS MARCH 2011
TheLionKing.com.sg

Marina Bay Sands retail space

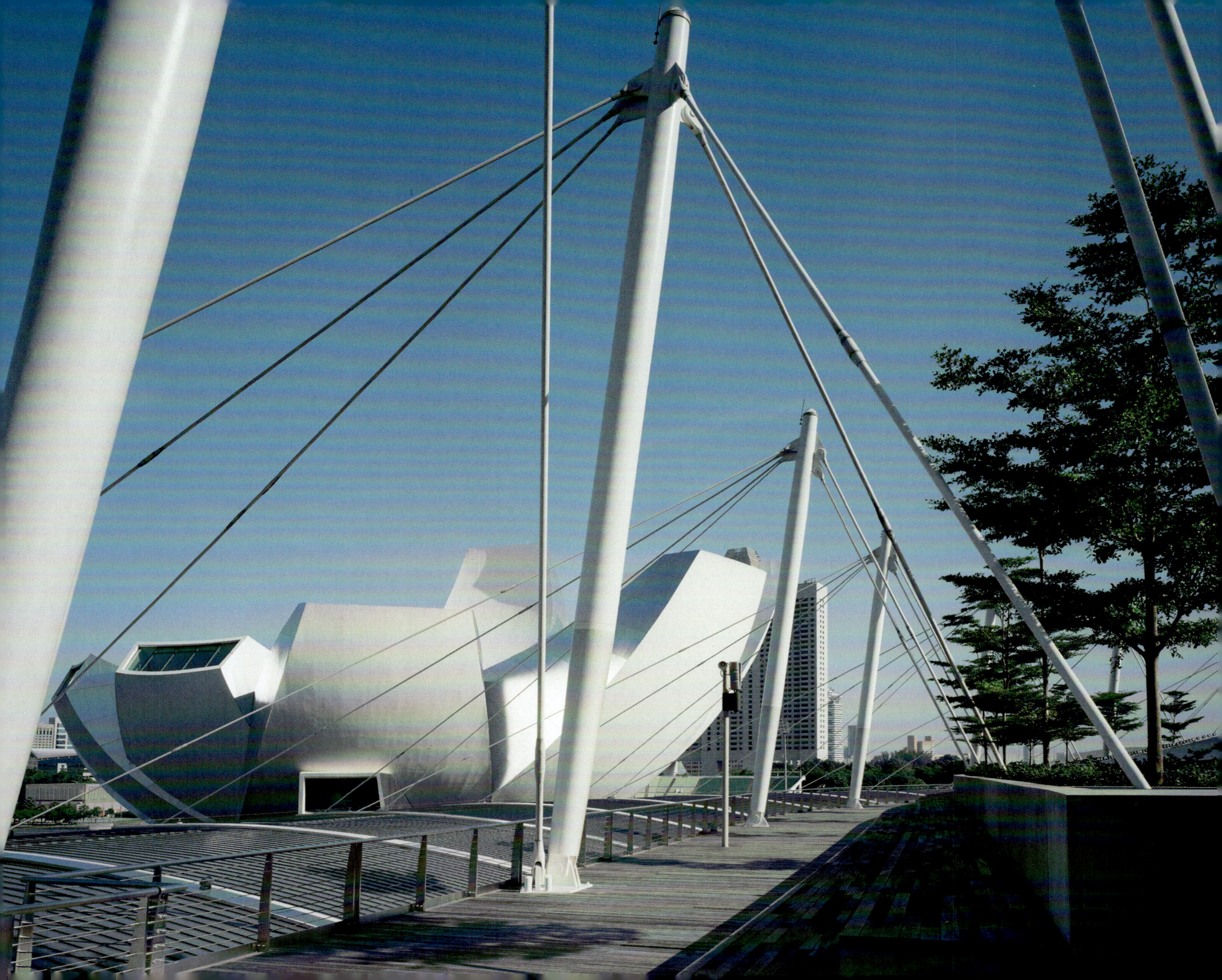

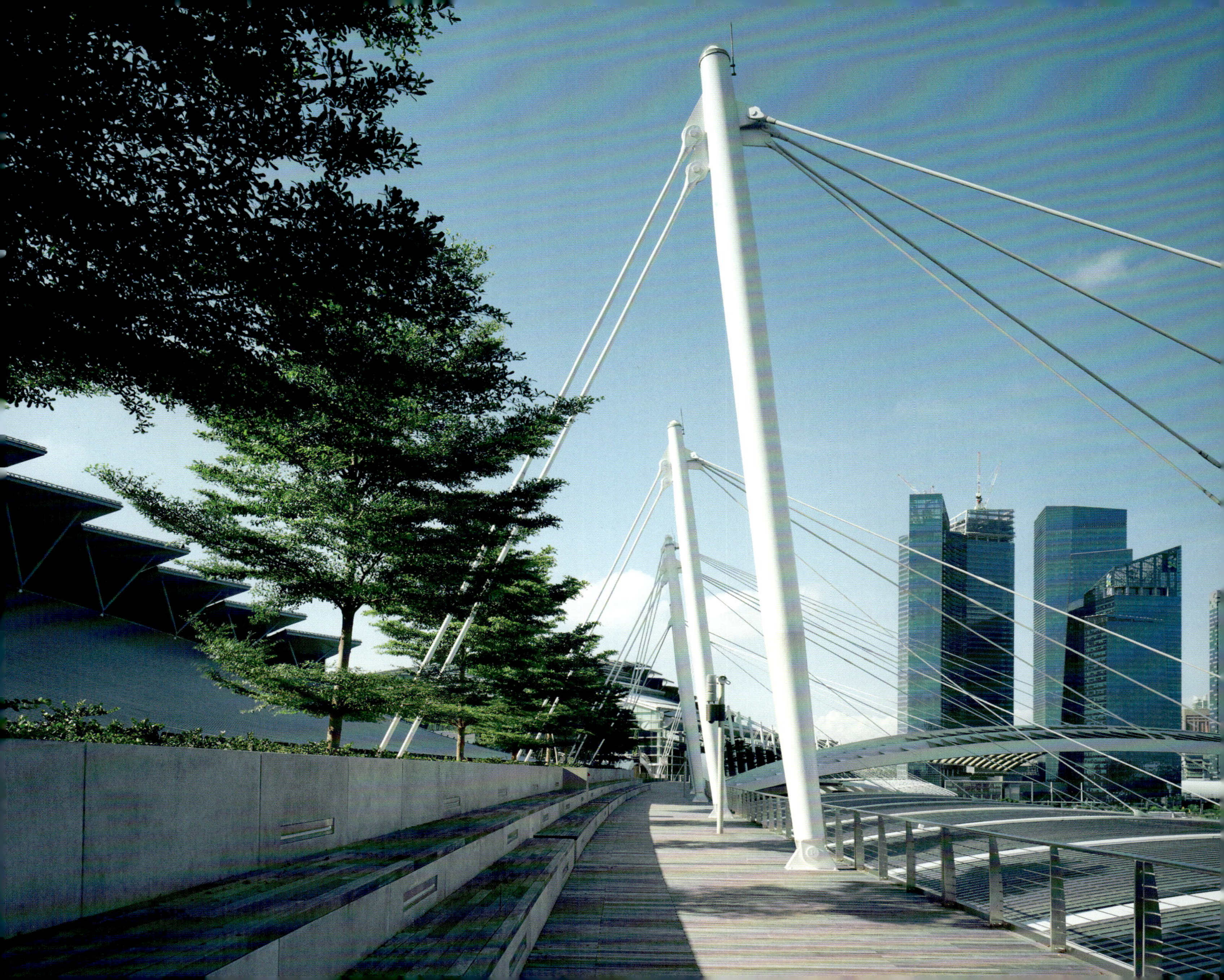

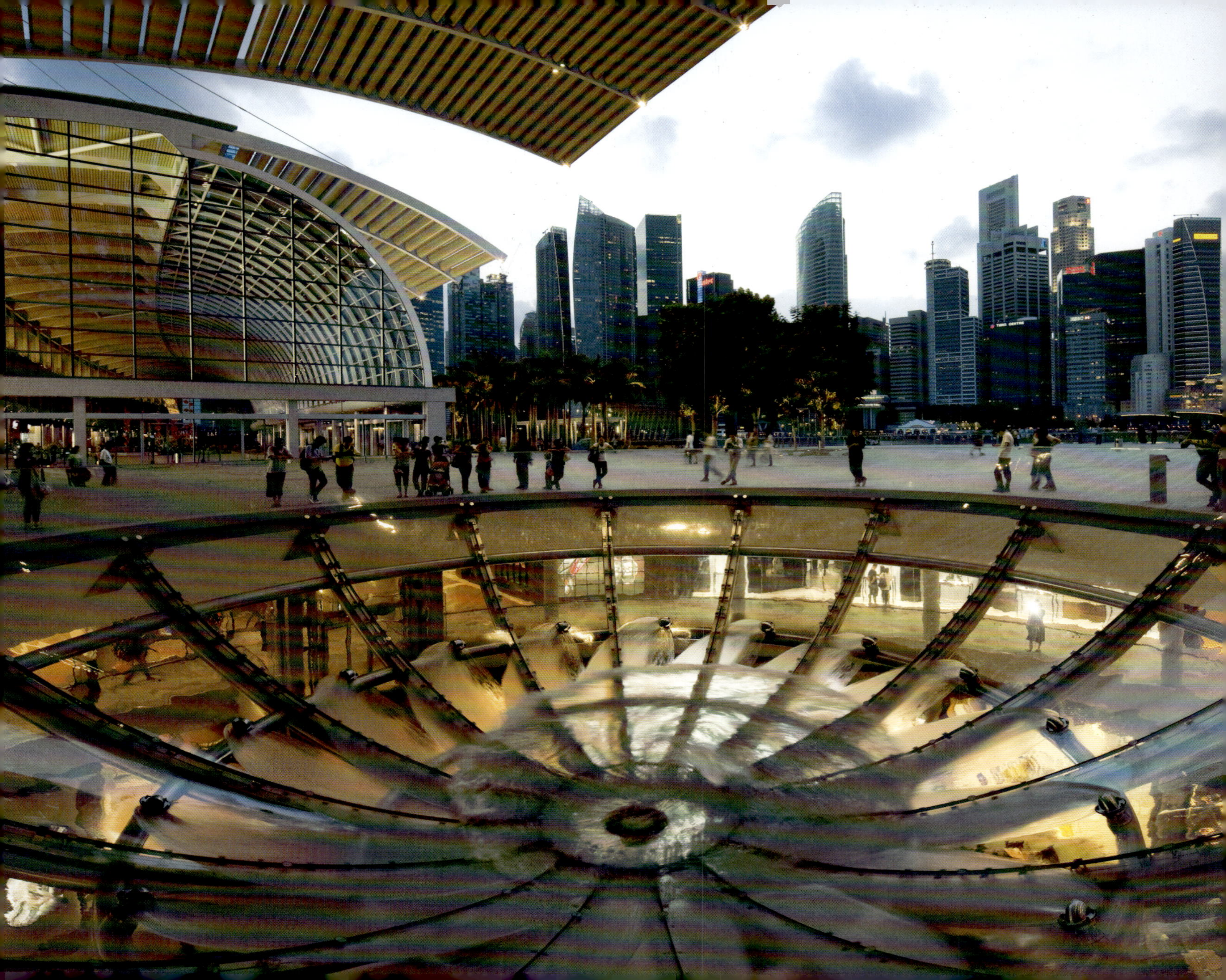

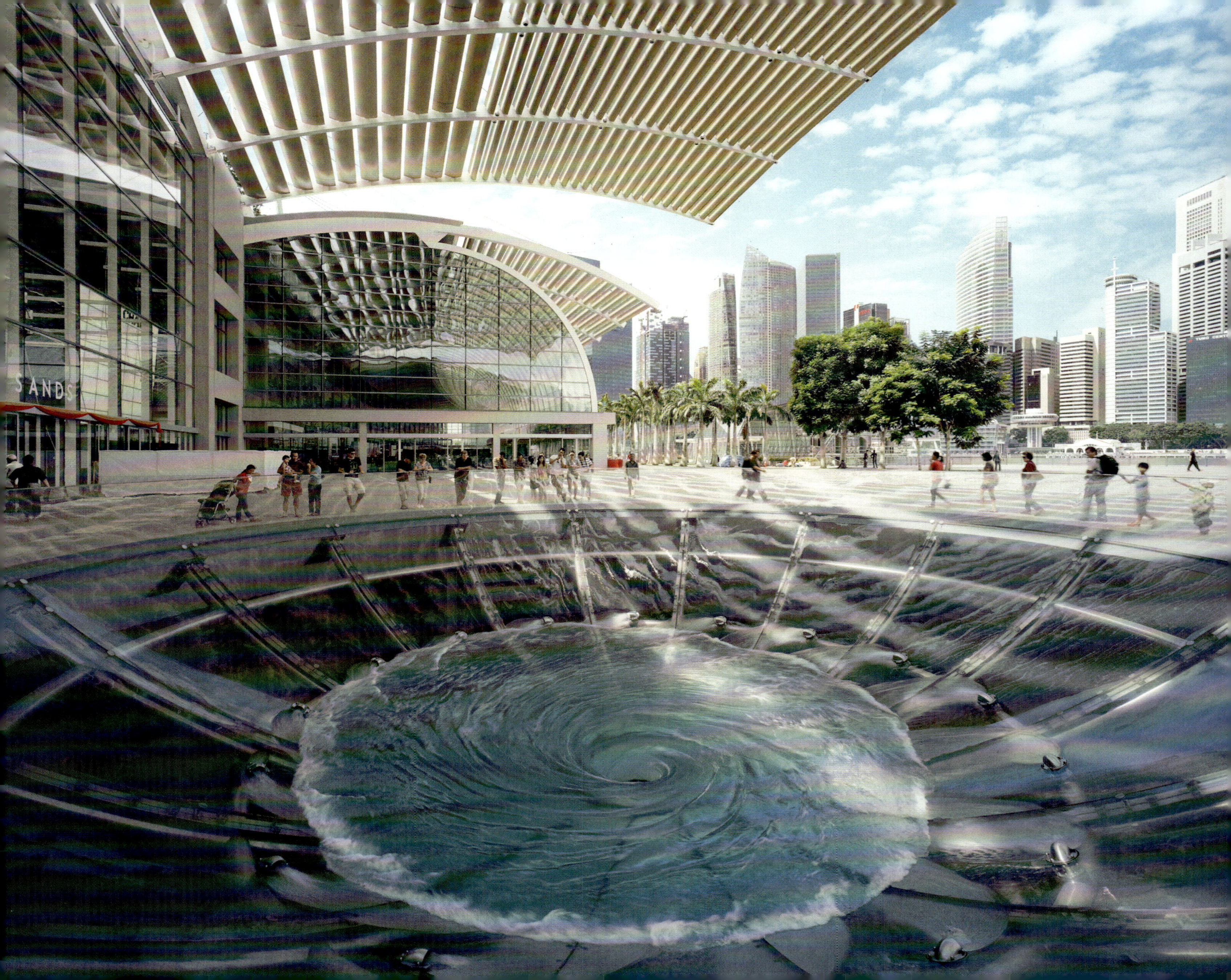
SANDS

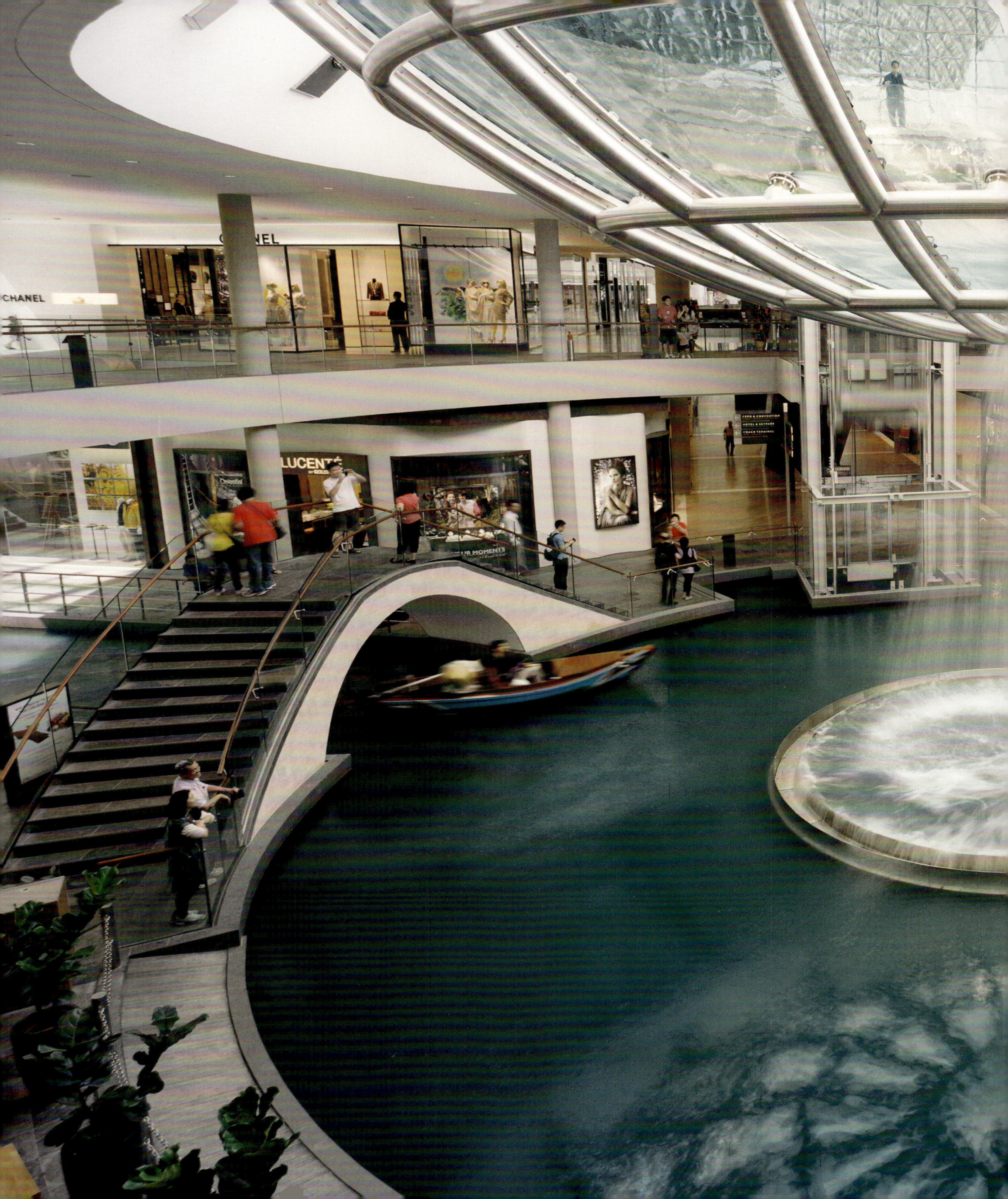
CHANEL
LUCENTÉ

Water from the *Rain Oculus* splashes down into retail corridor canal.

HOTELS, ATRIA & SKYPARK

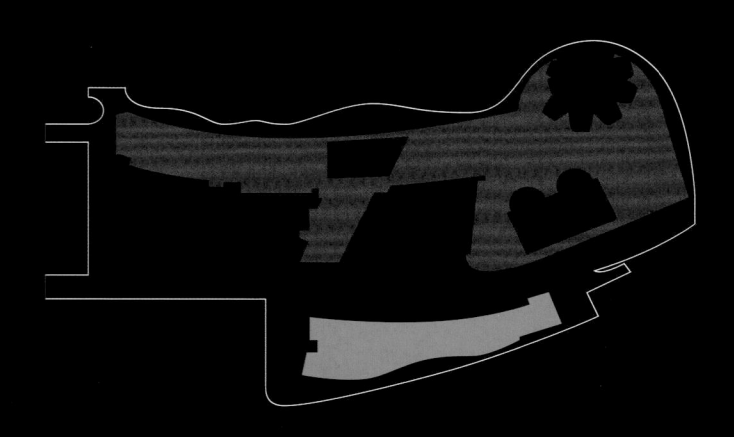

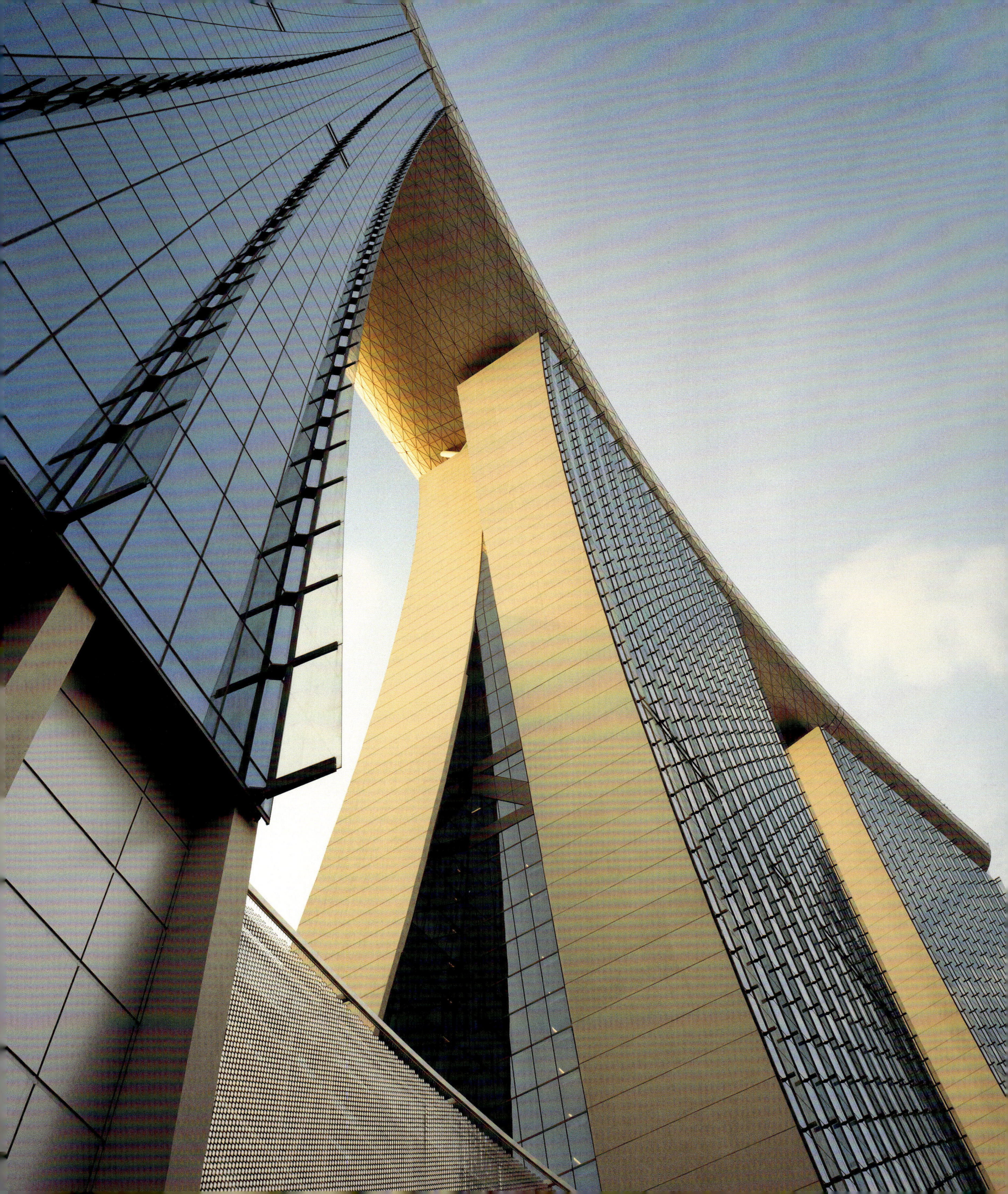

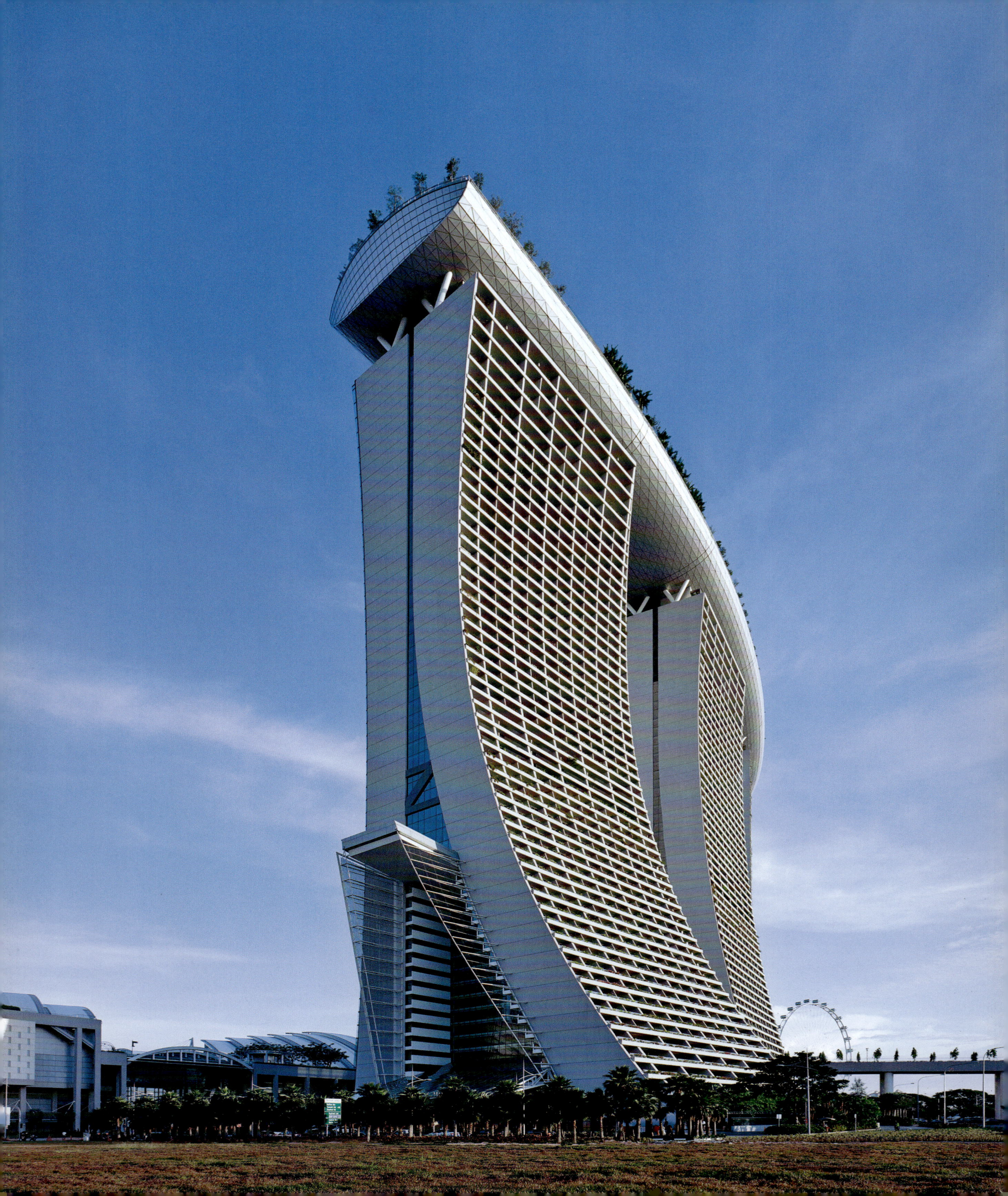

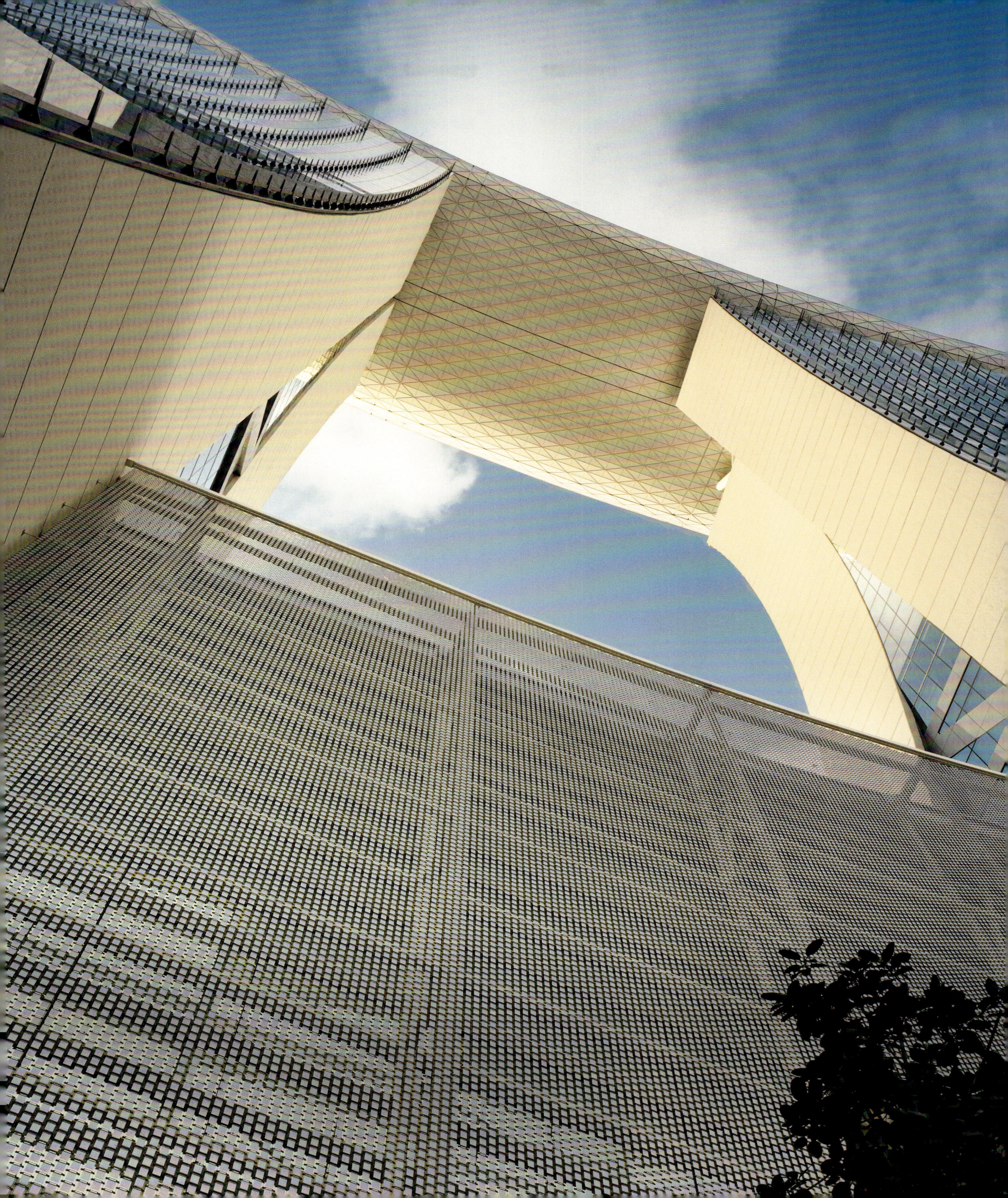

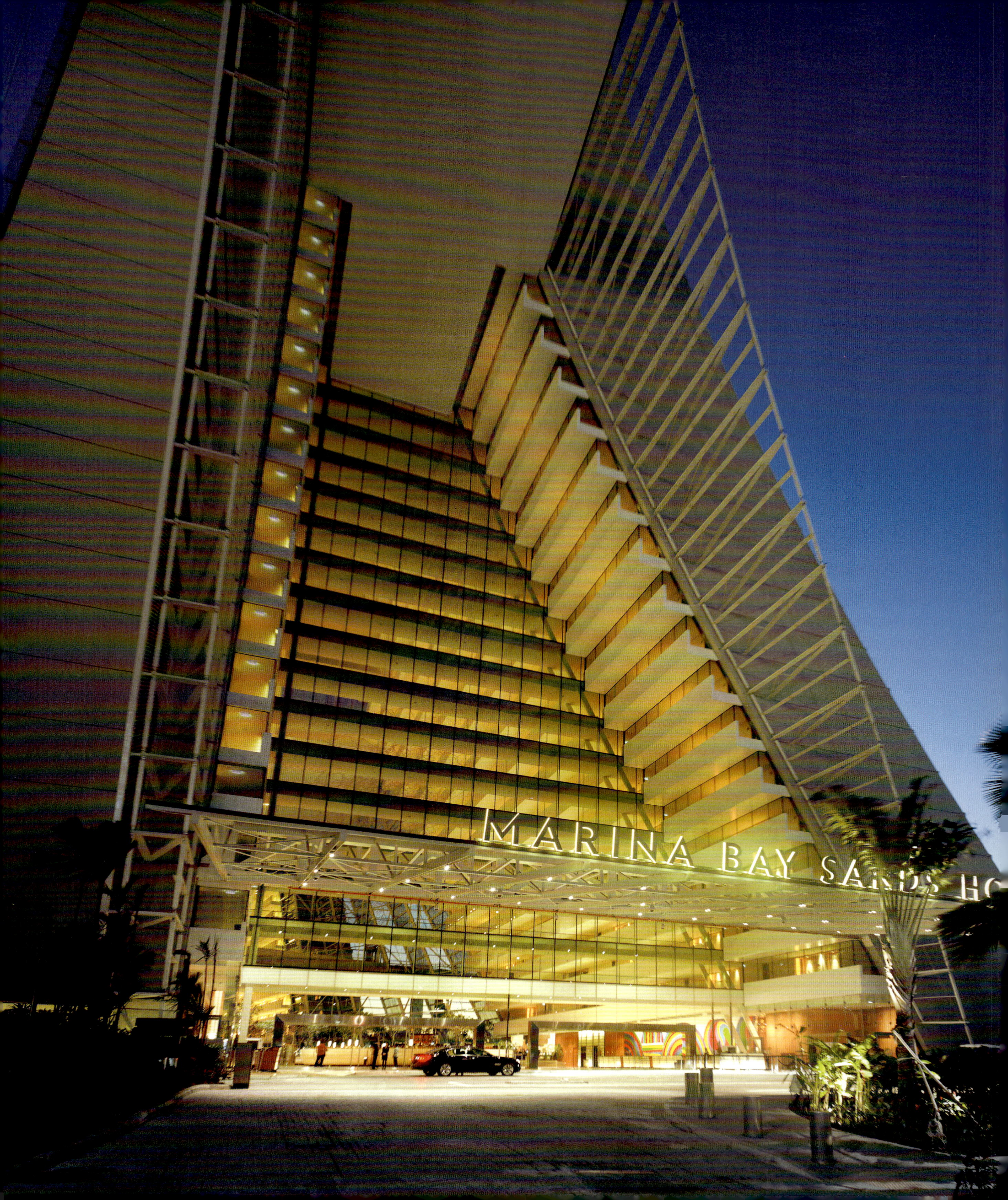
MARINA BAY SANDS

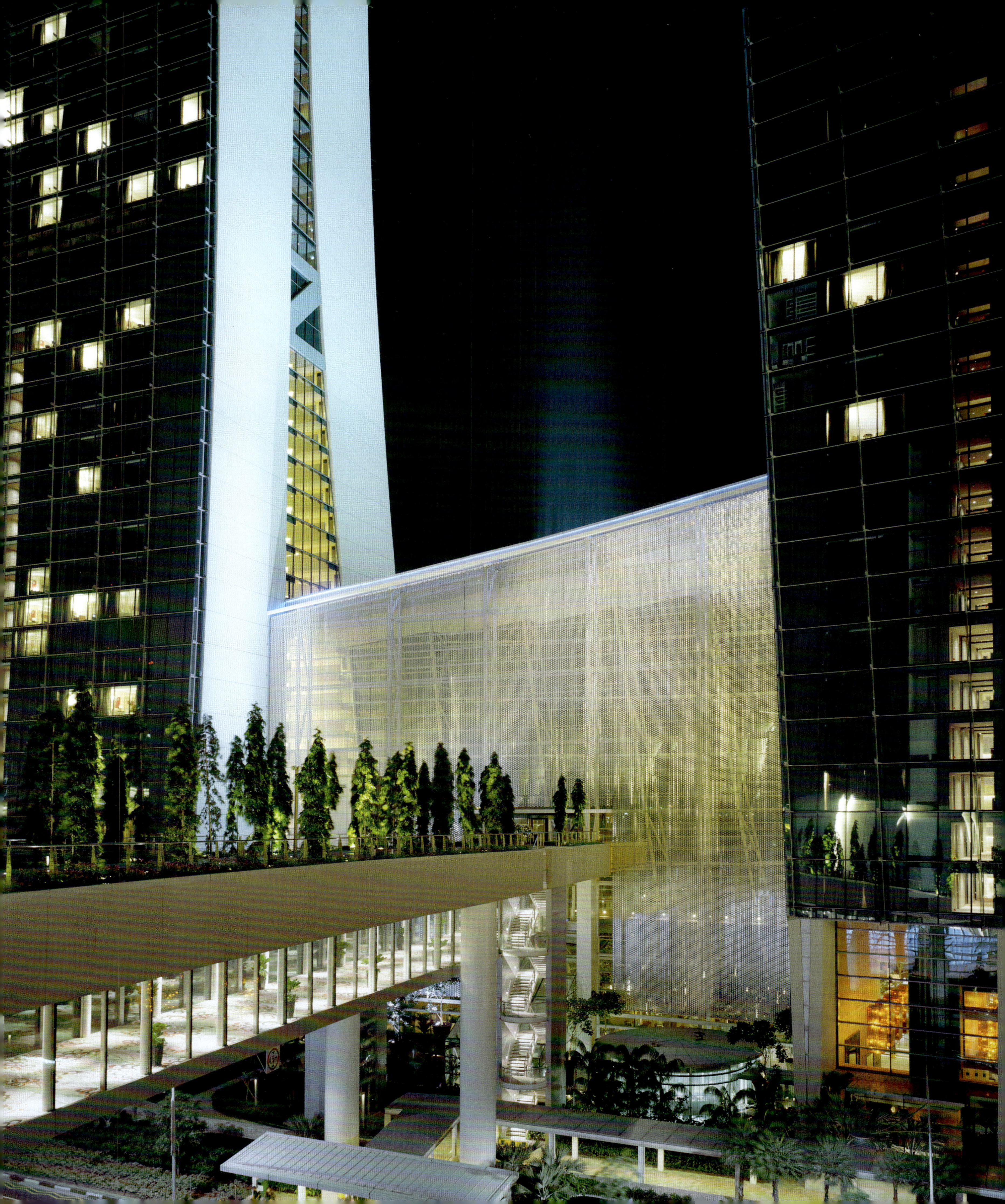

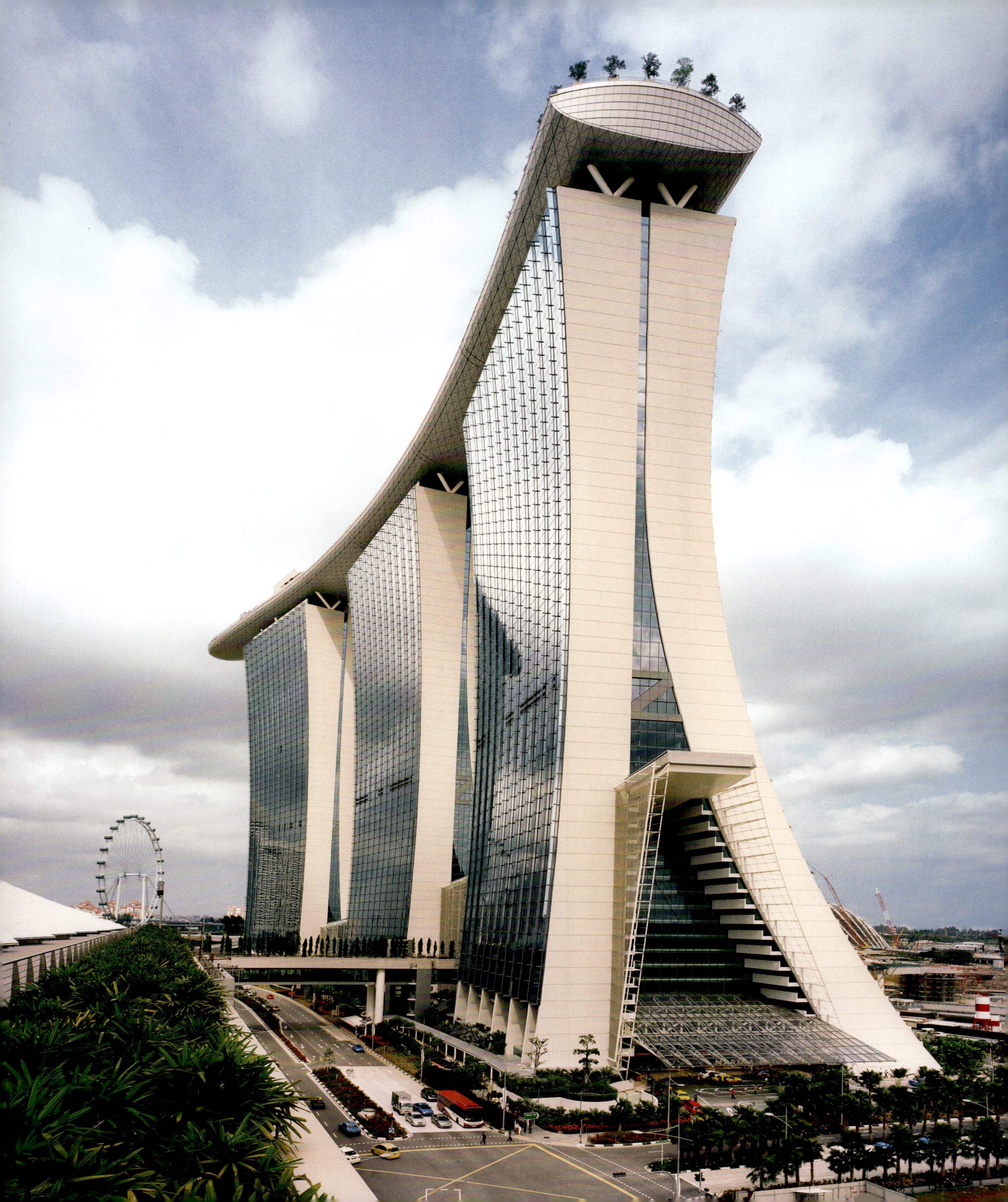

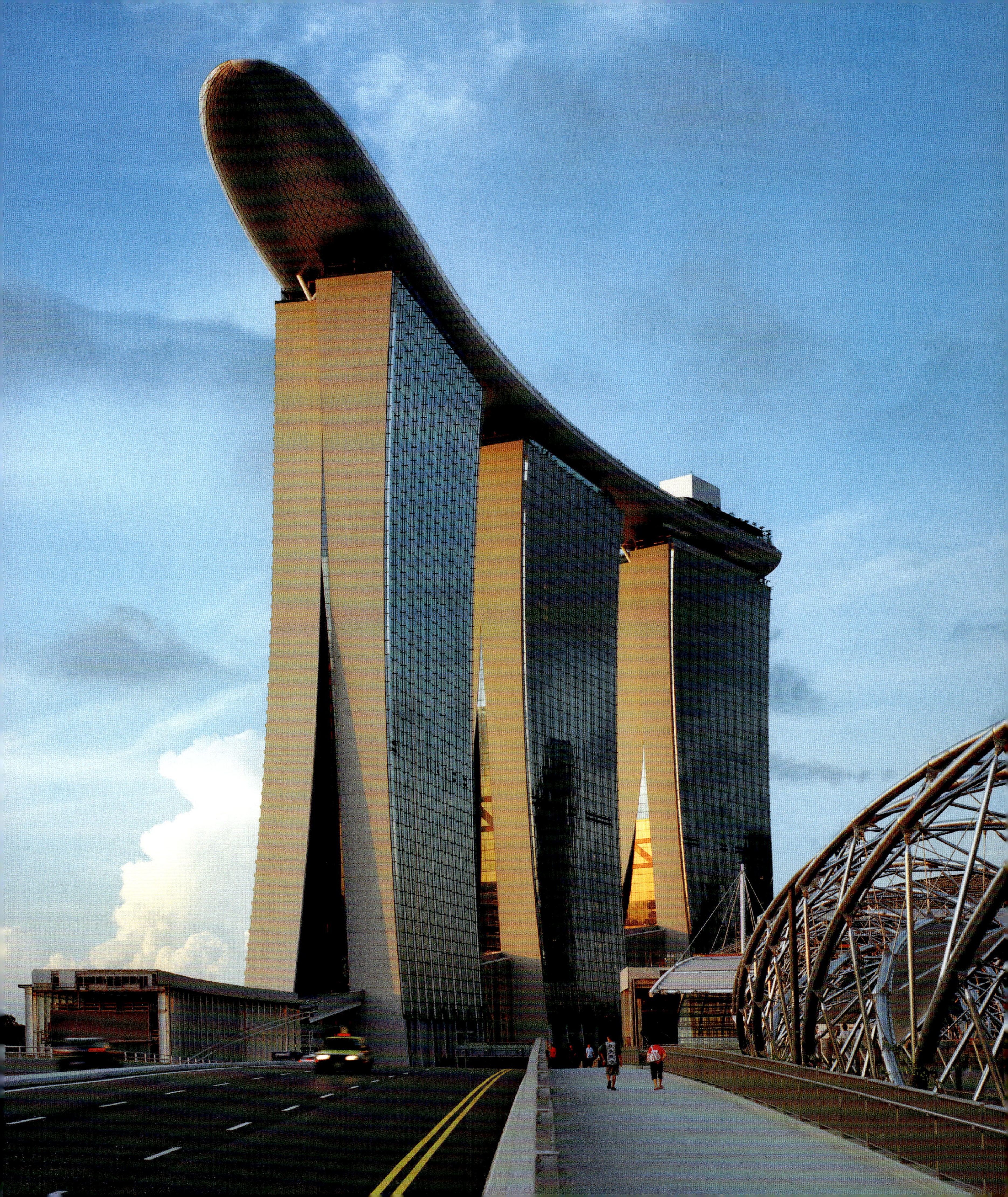

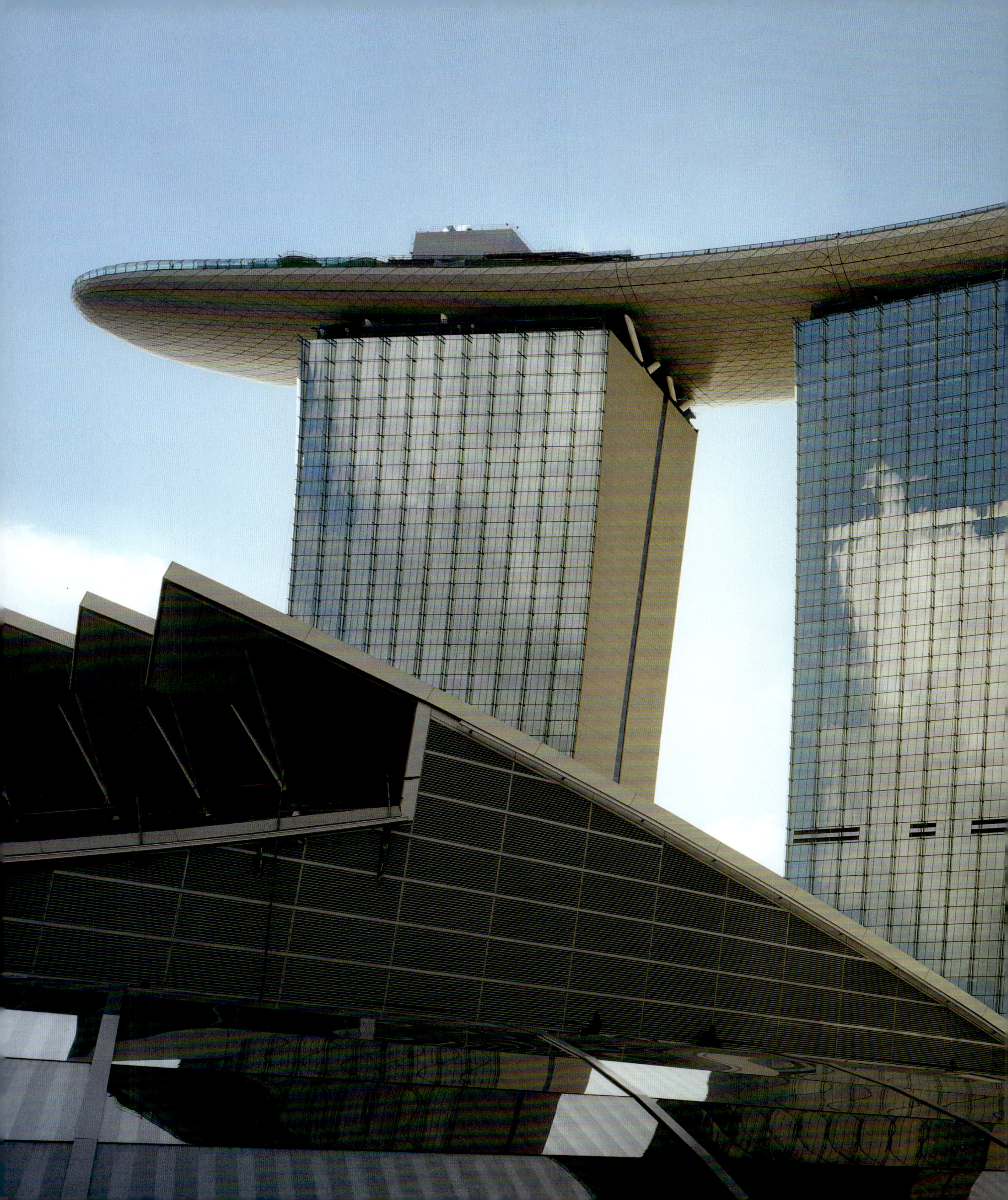

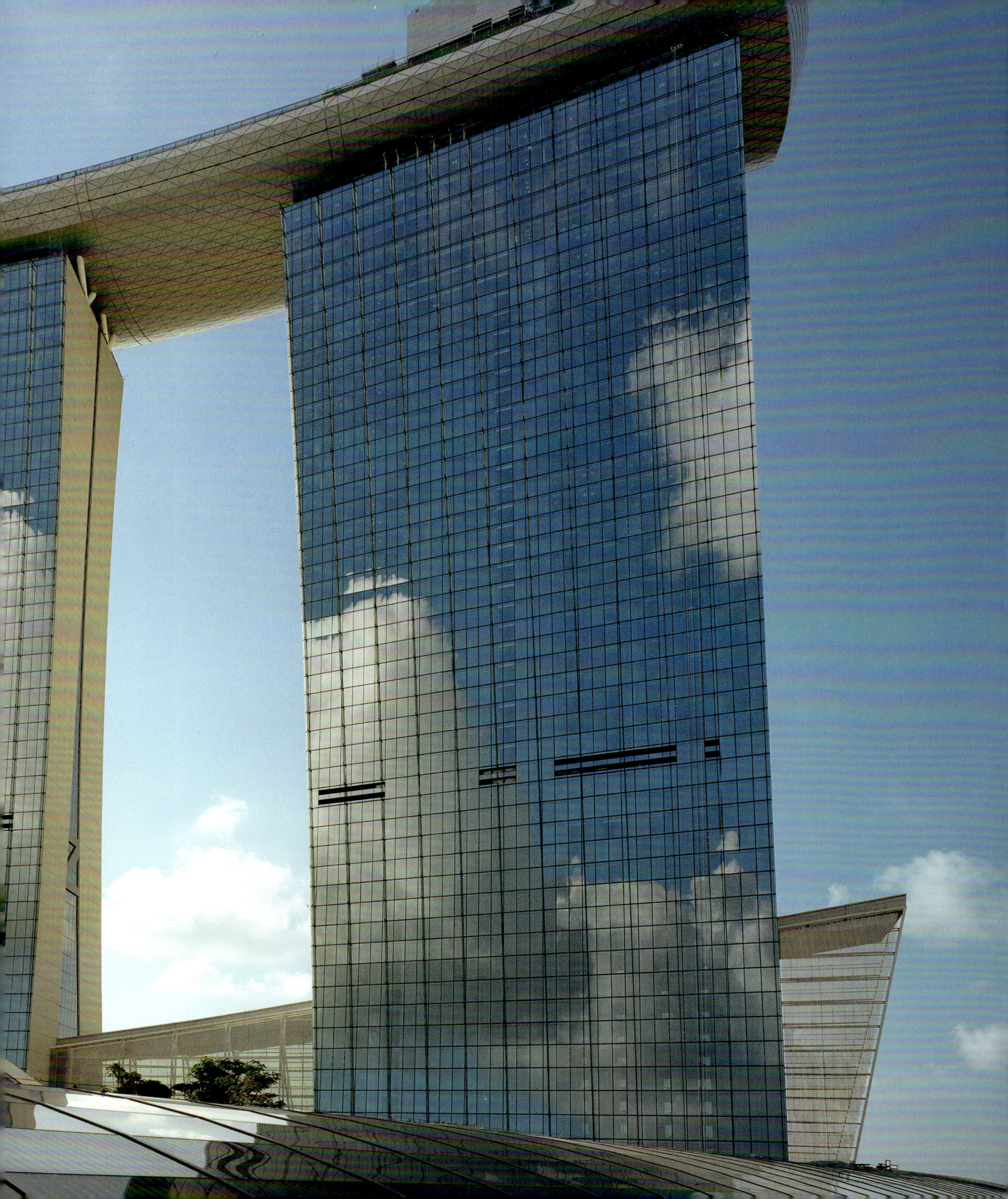

SkyPark viewed from below. Bougainvillea planted on the hotel's eastern exterior creates a fifty-five-story vertical garden.

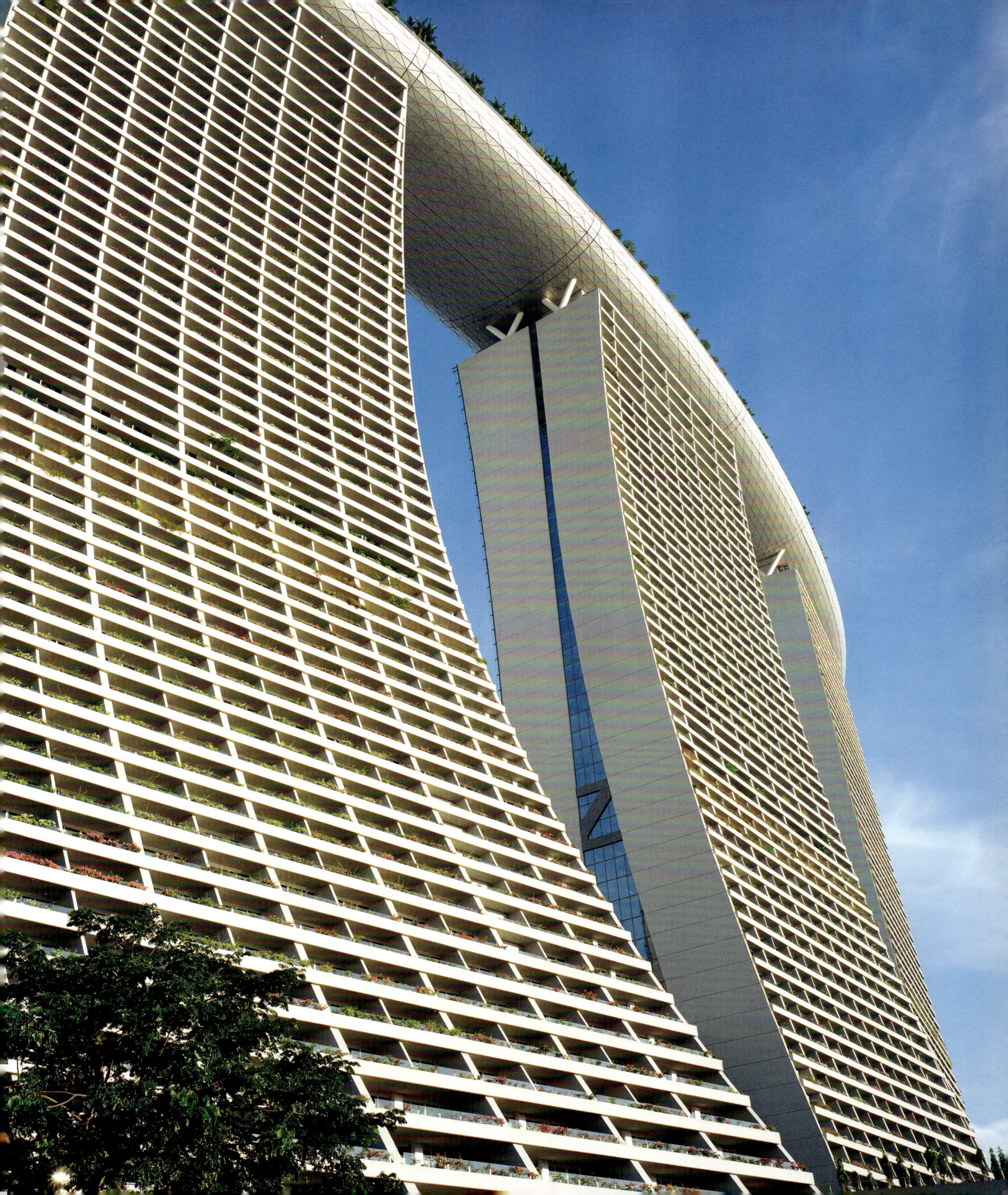

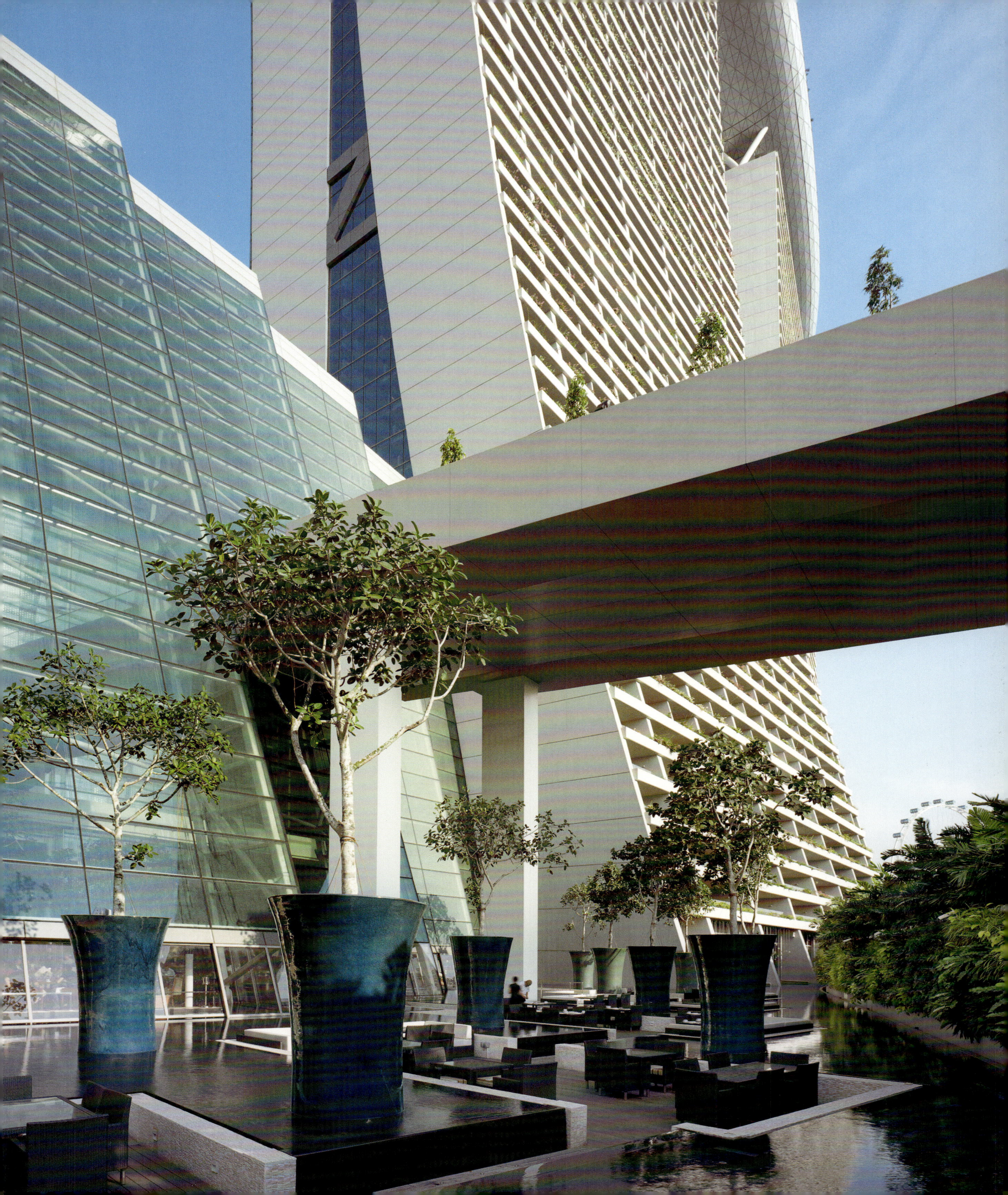

Underside of SkyPark

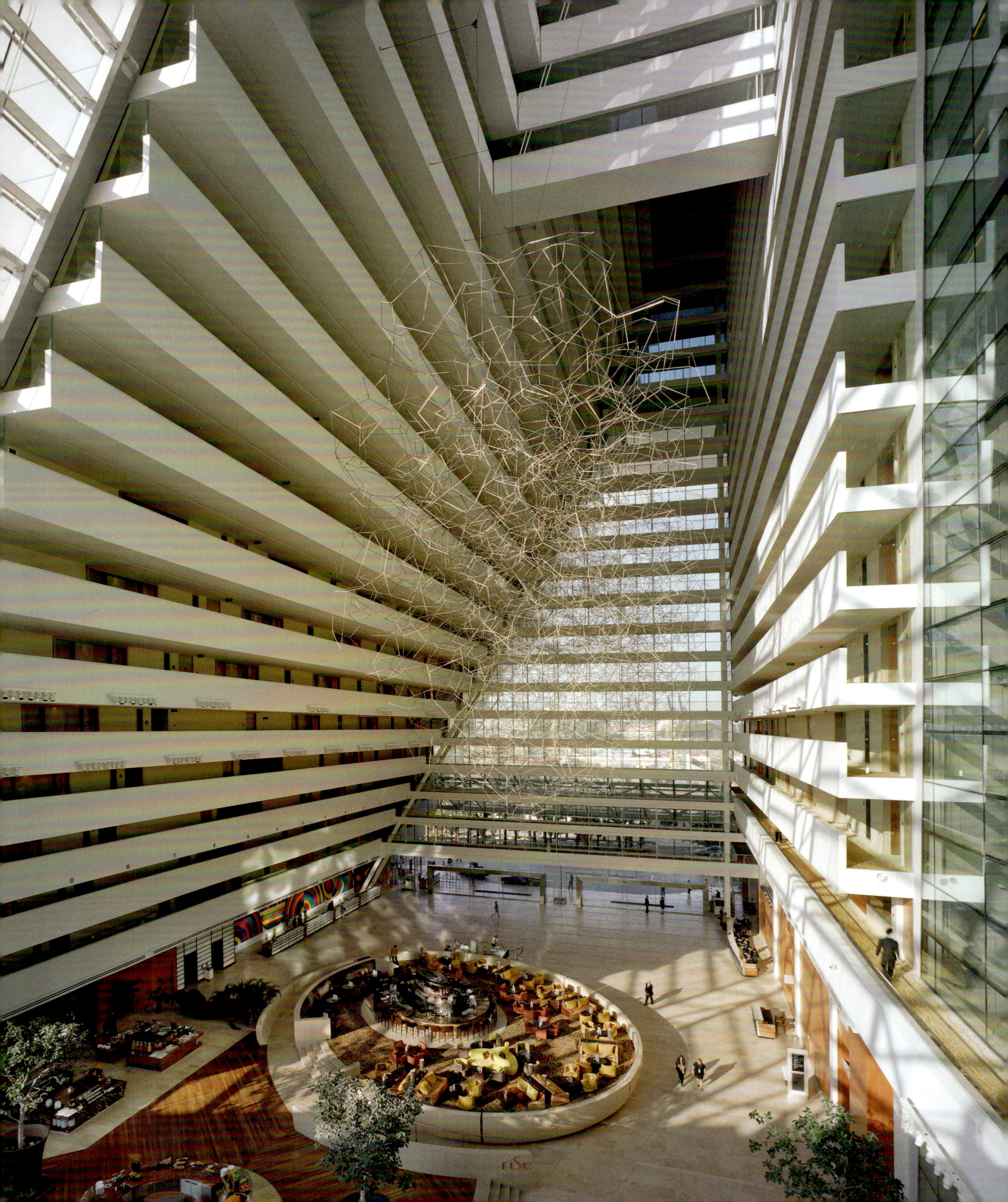

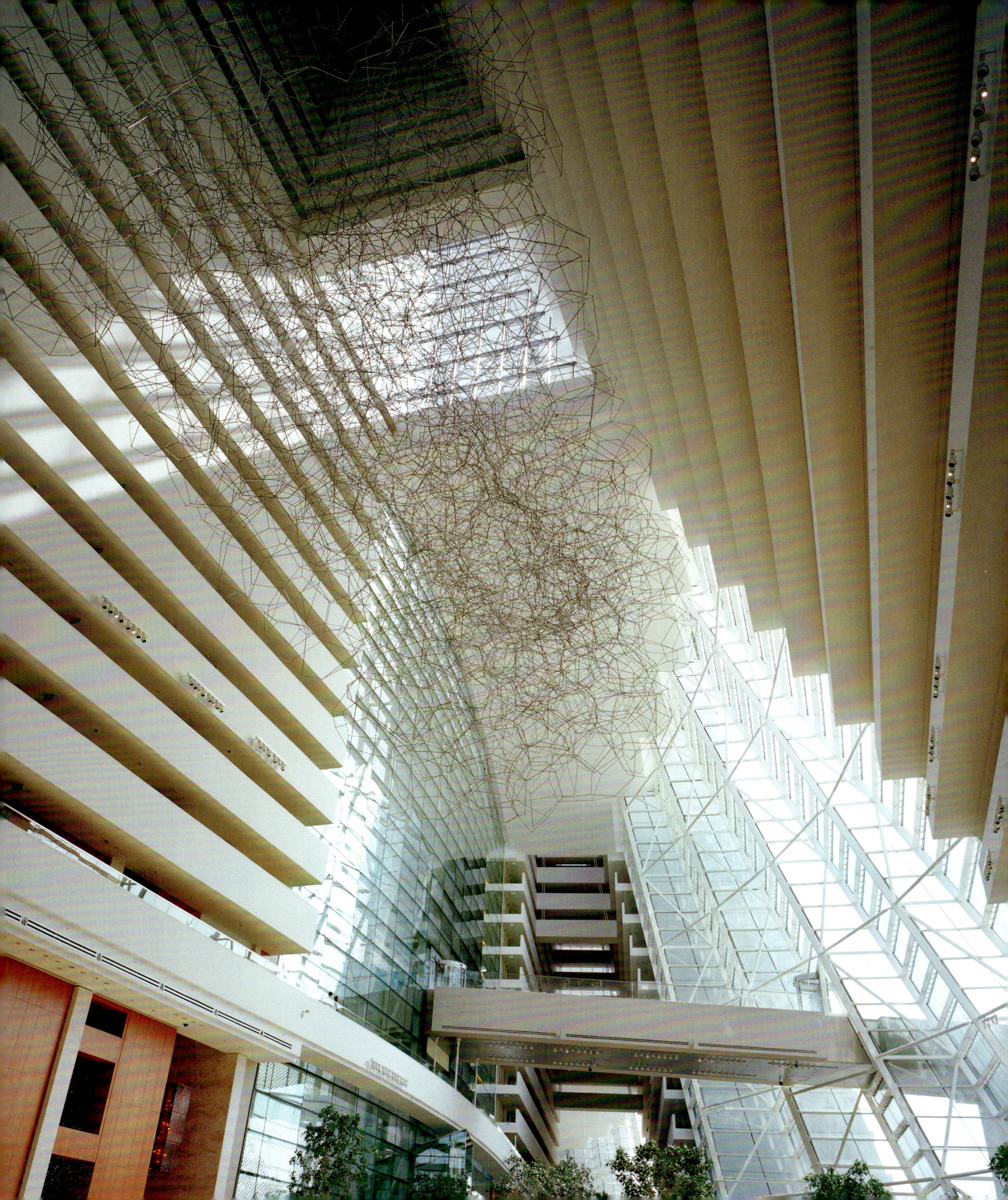

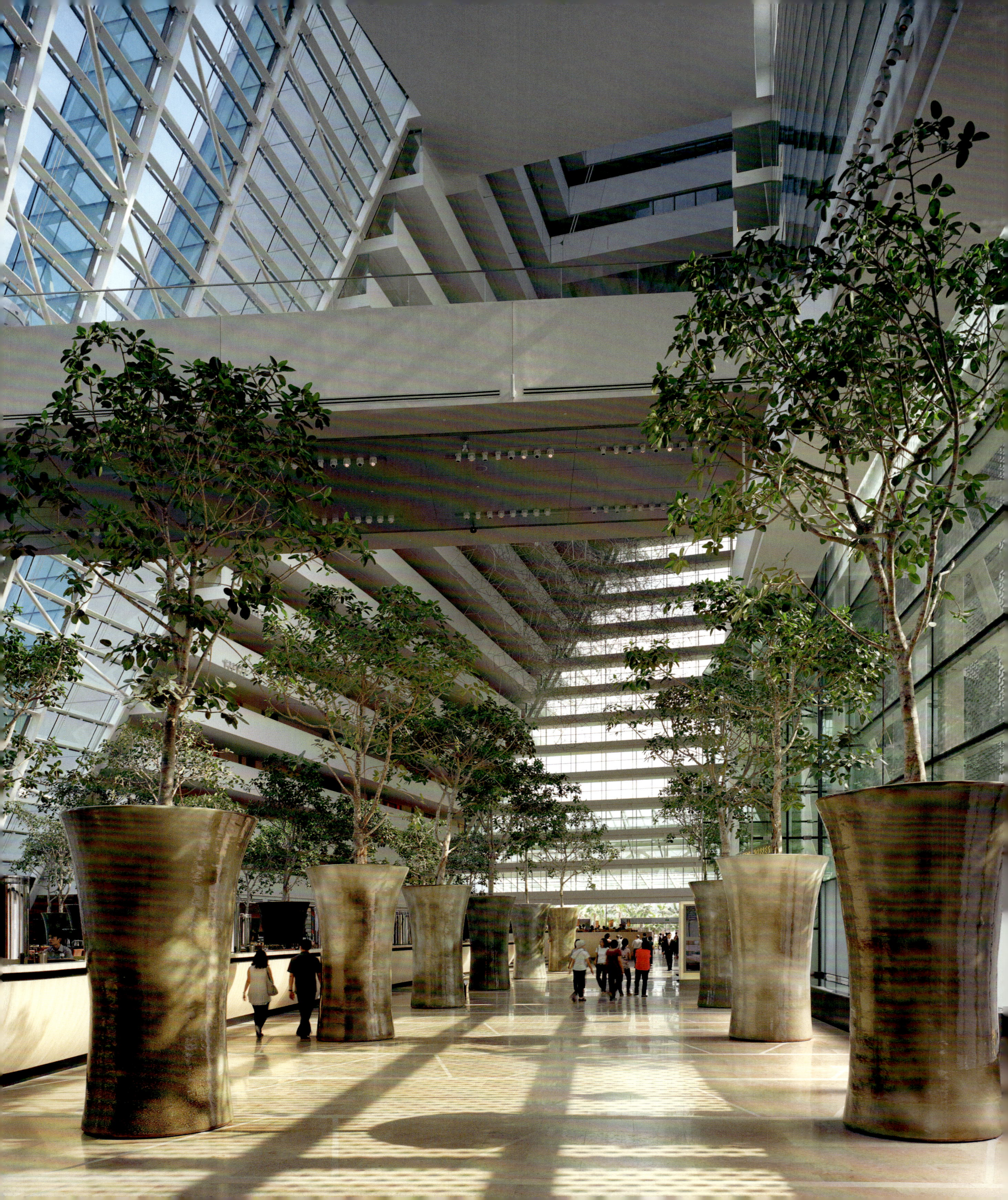

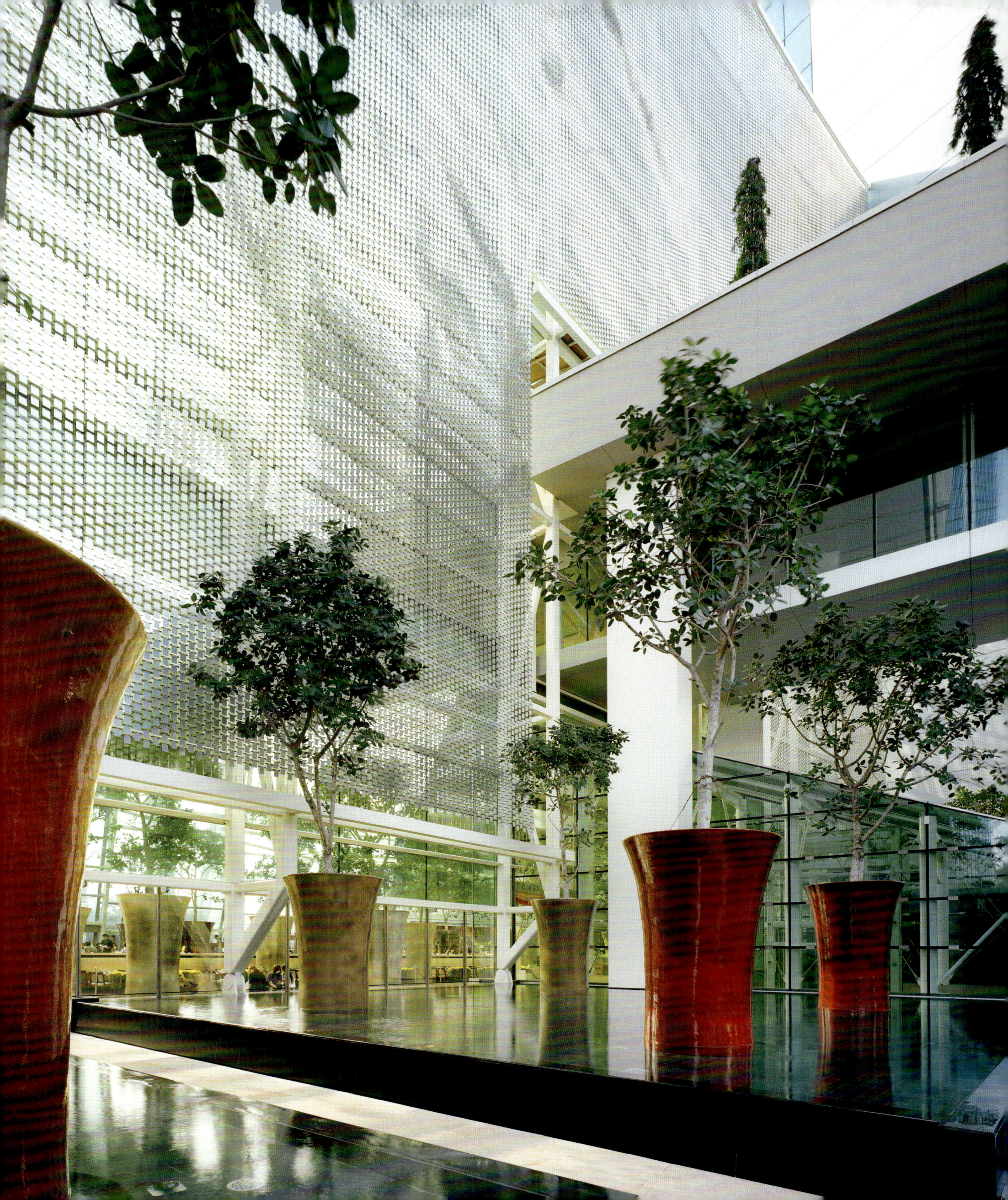

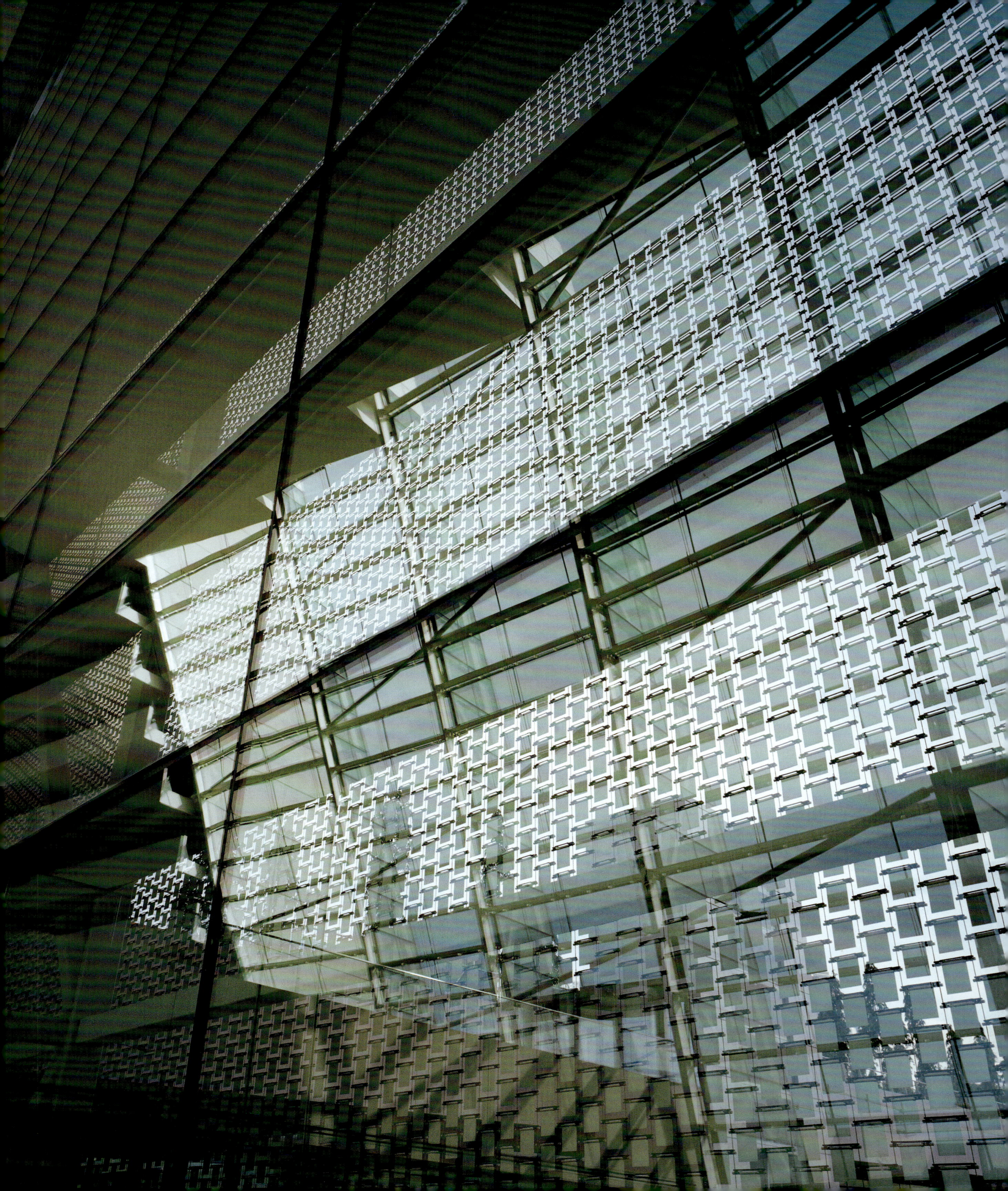

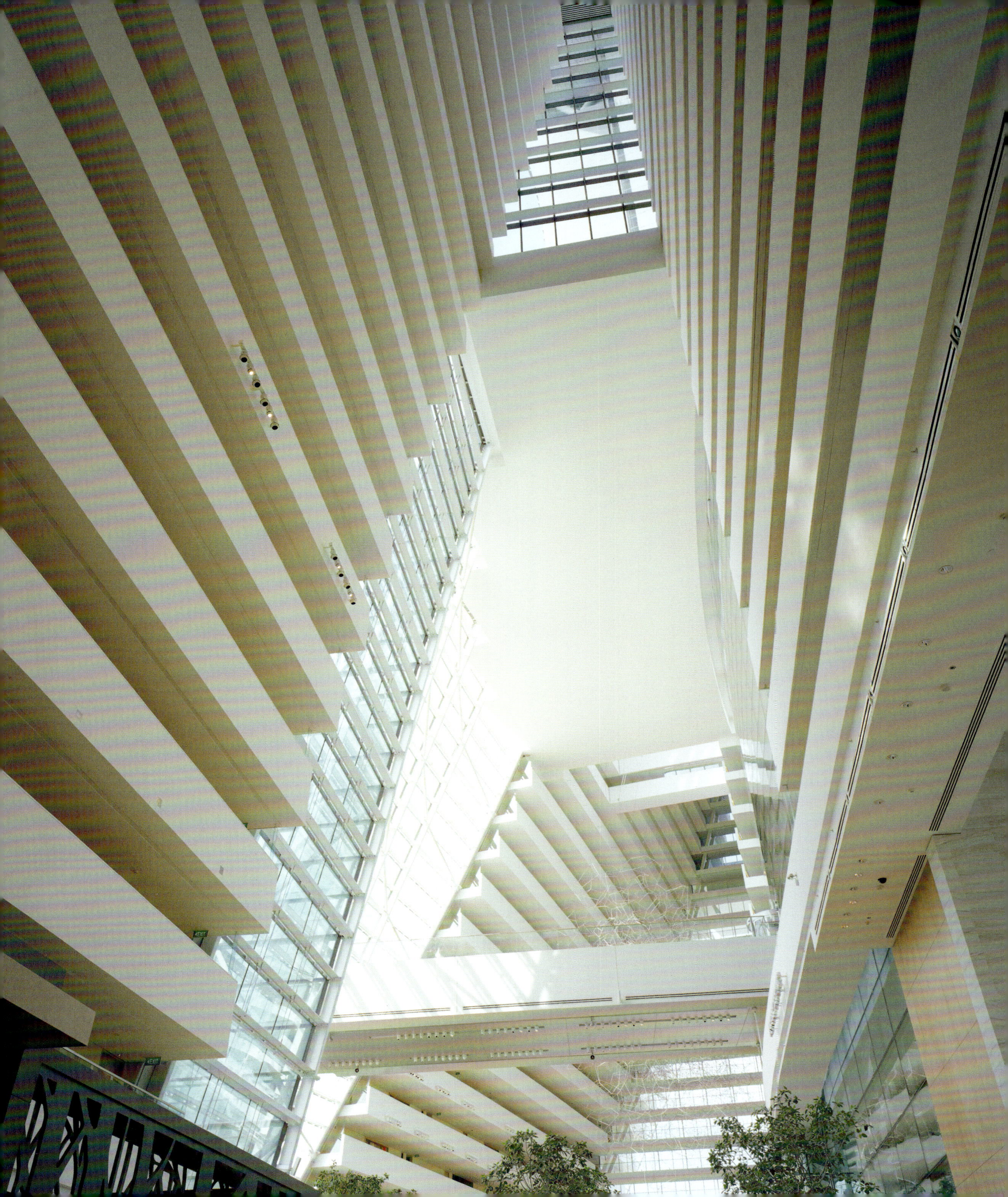

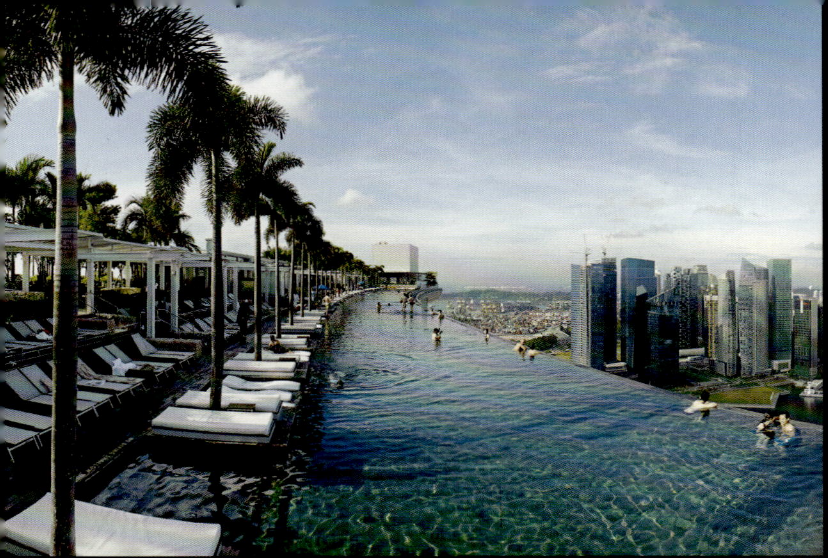
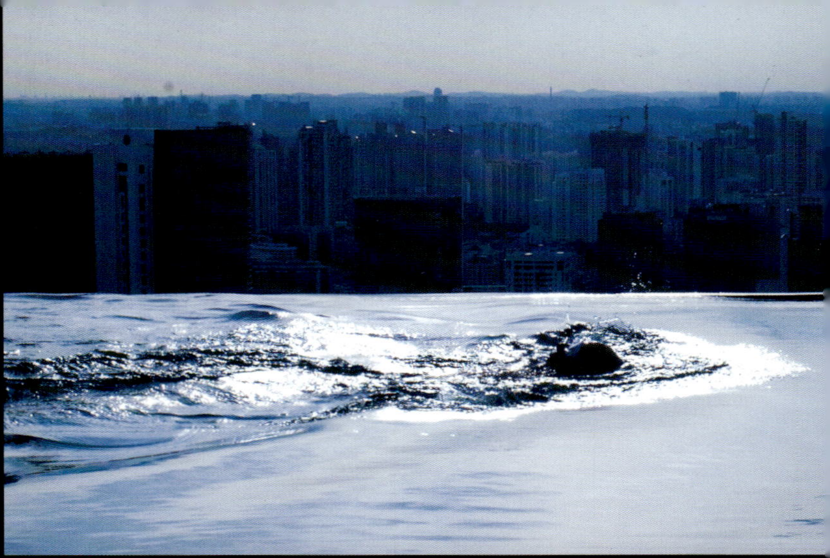
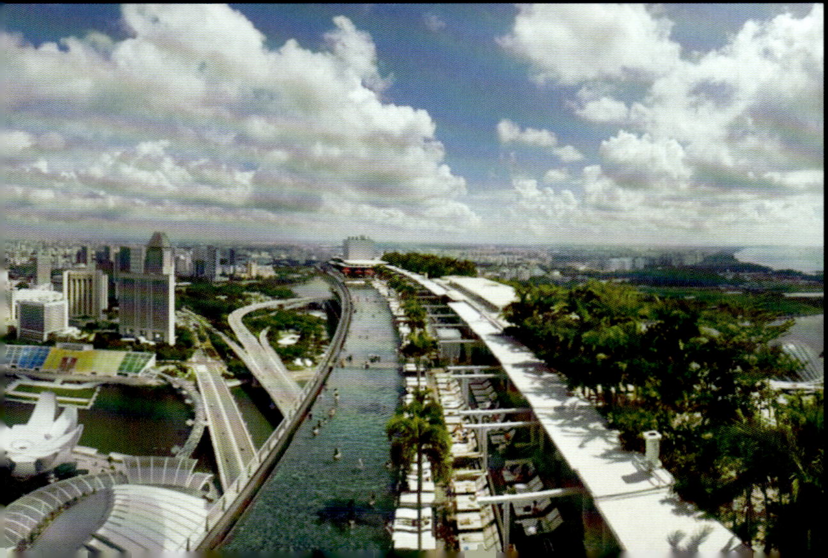
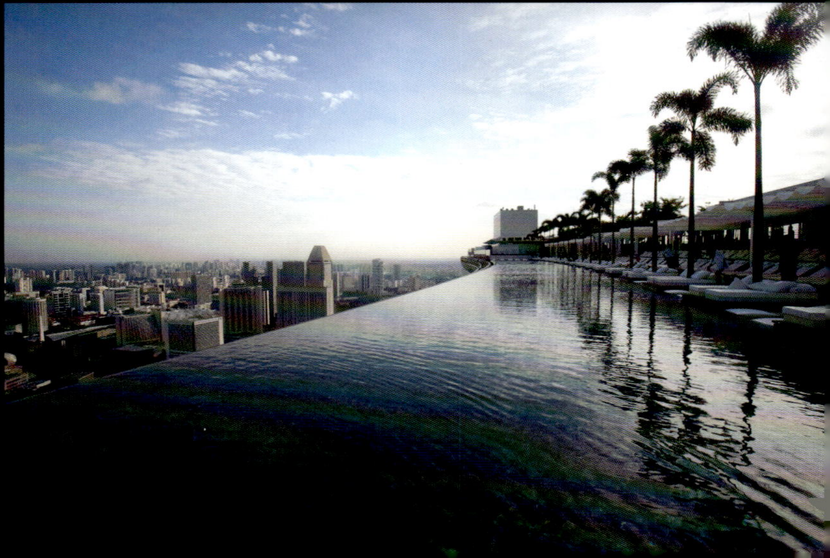

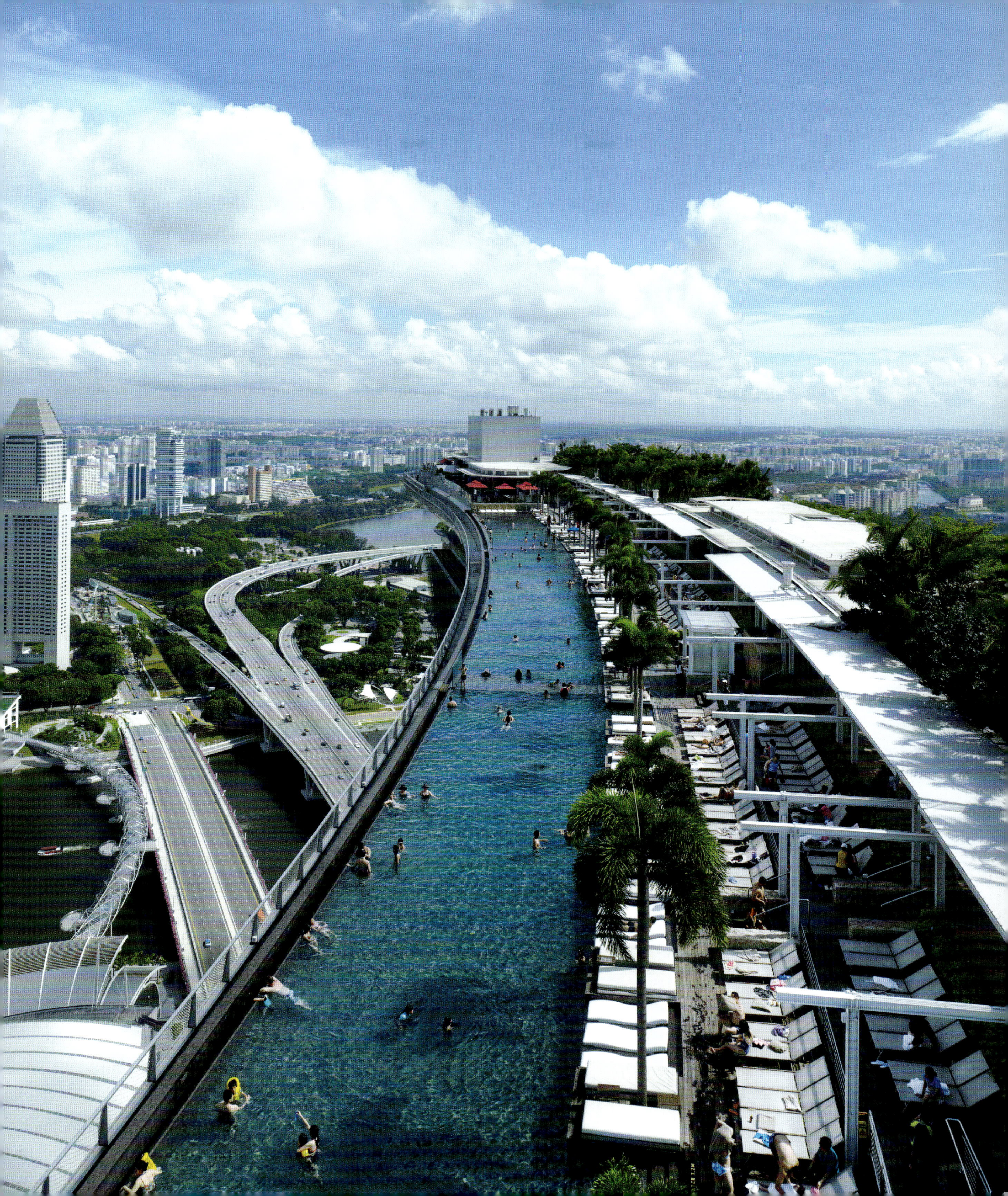

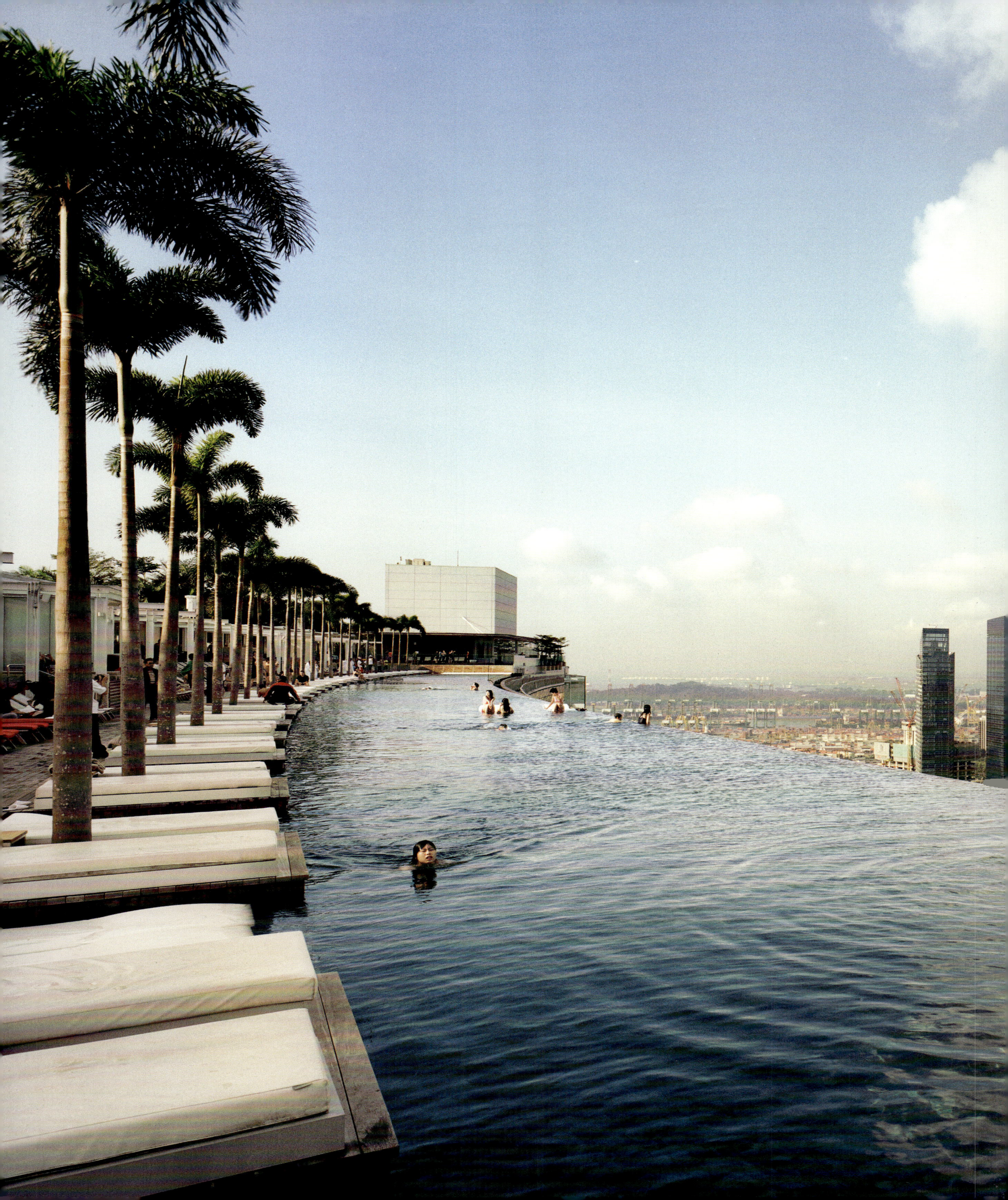

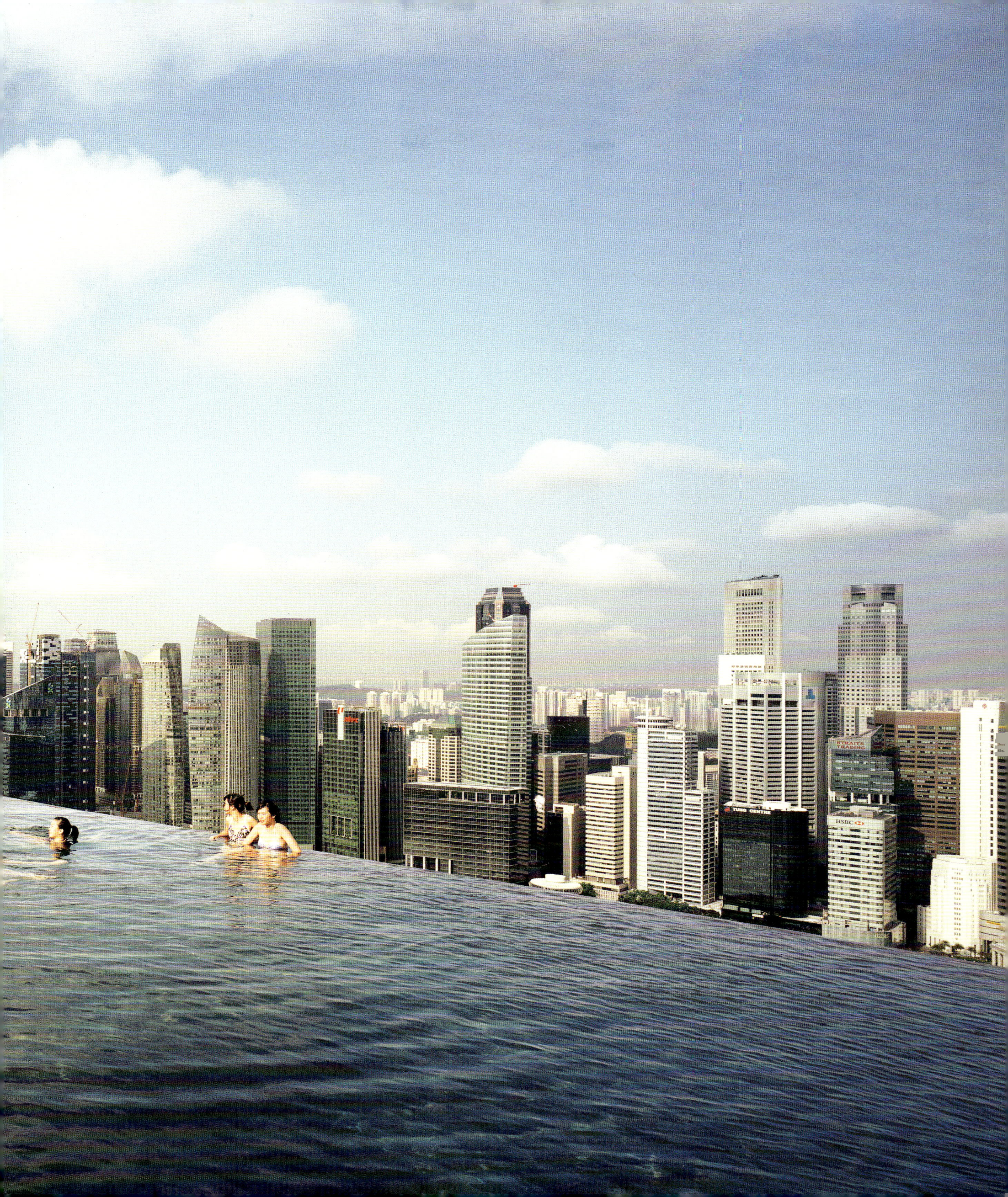
STRAITS TRADING
TUNG CENTRE
HSBC

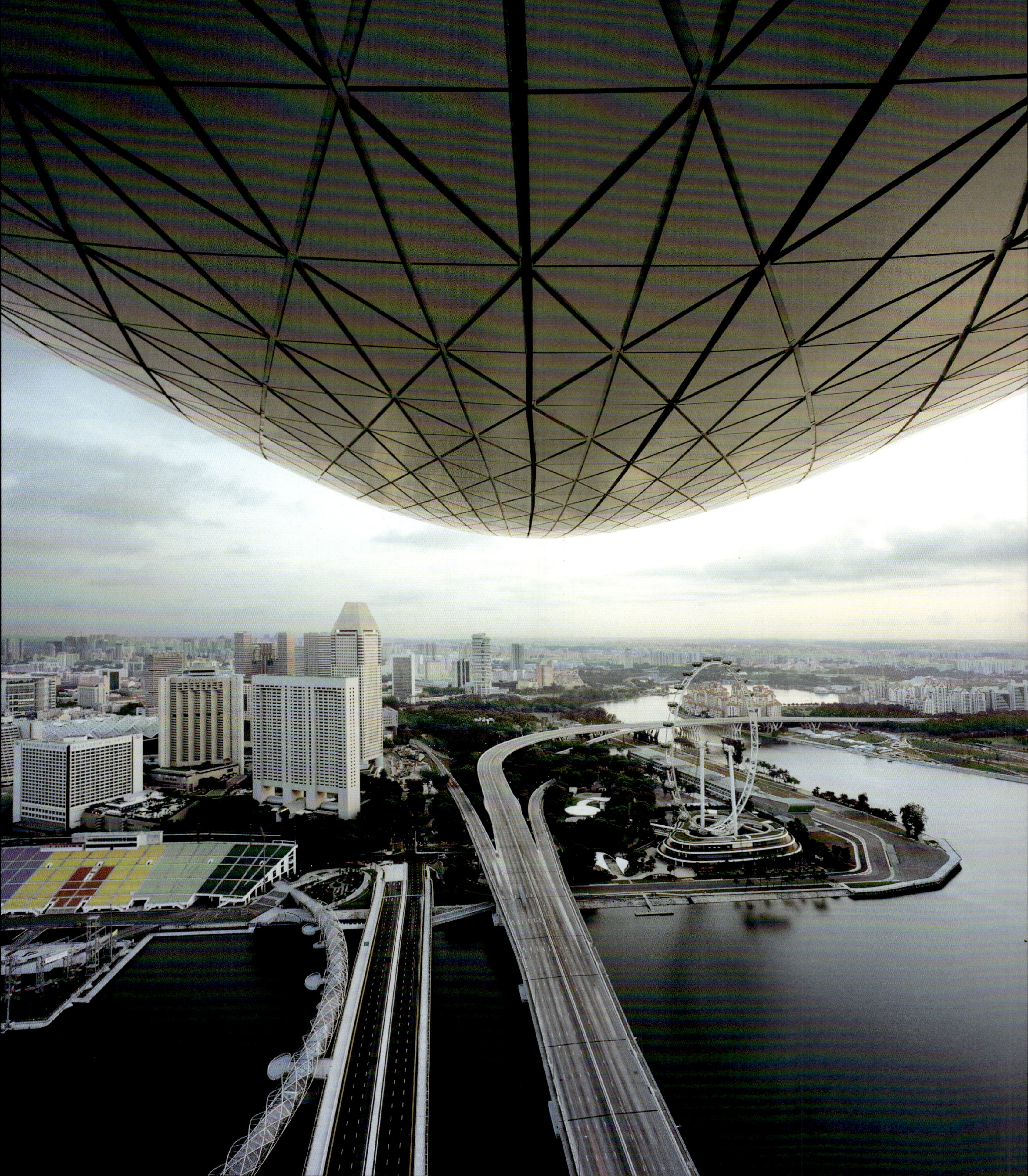

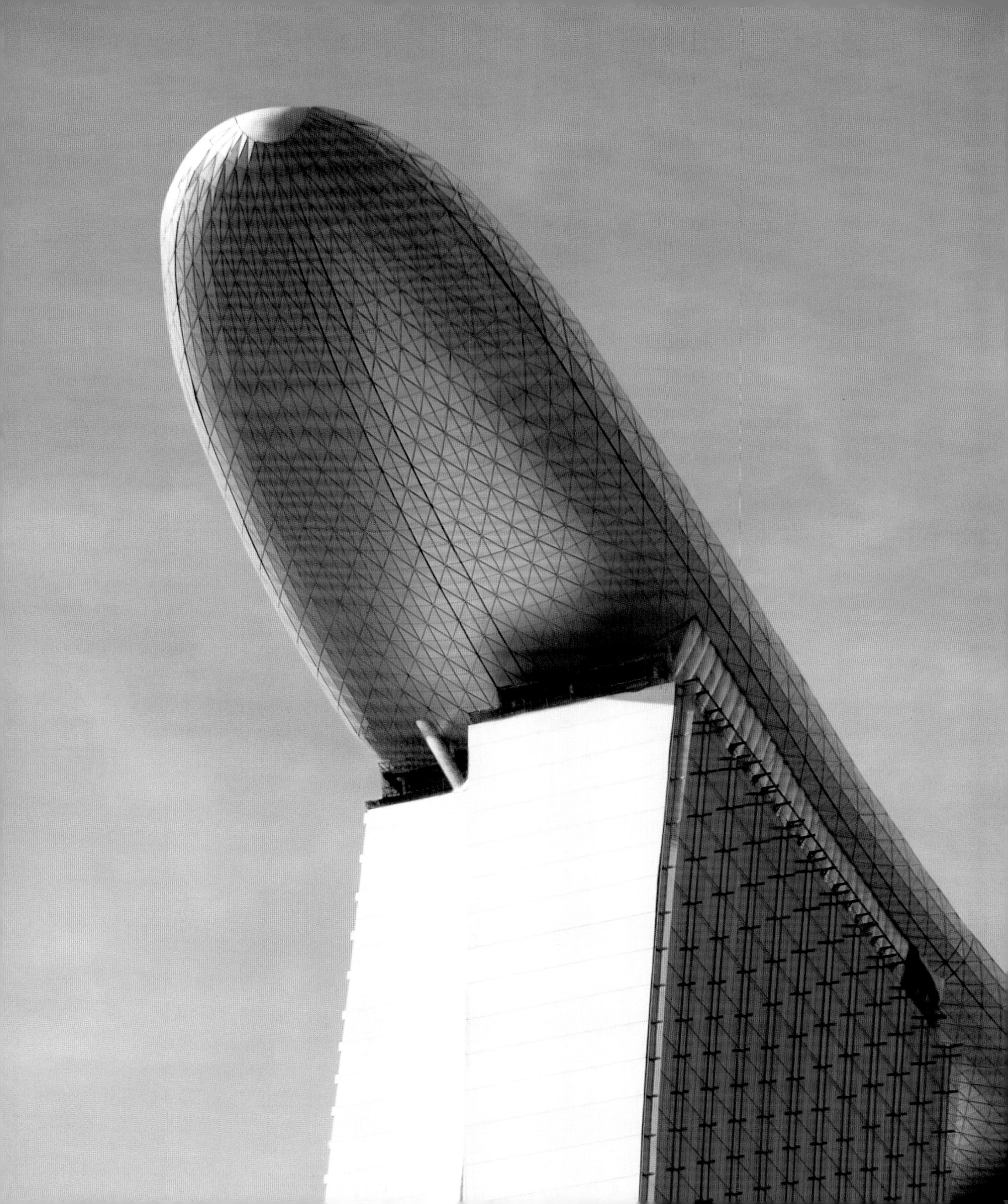

CASINO, THEATERS & CONVENTION

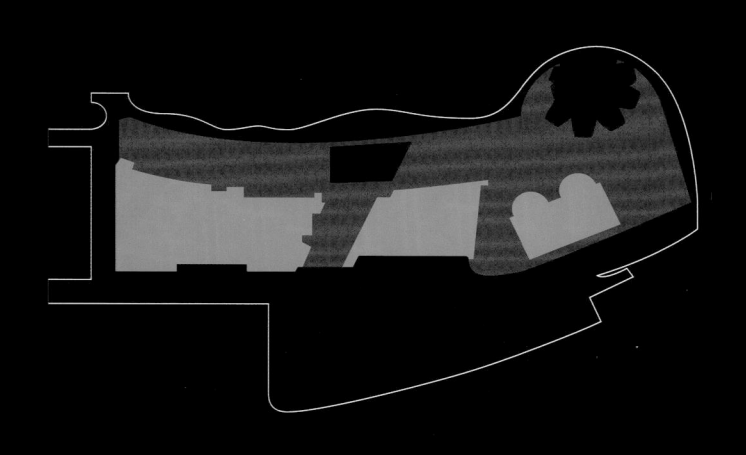

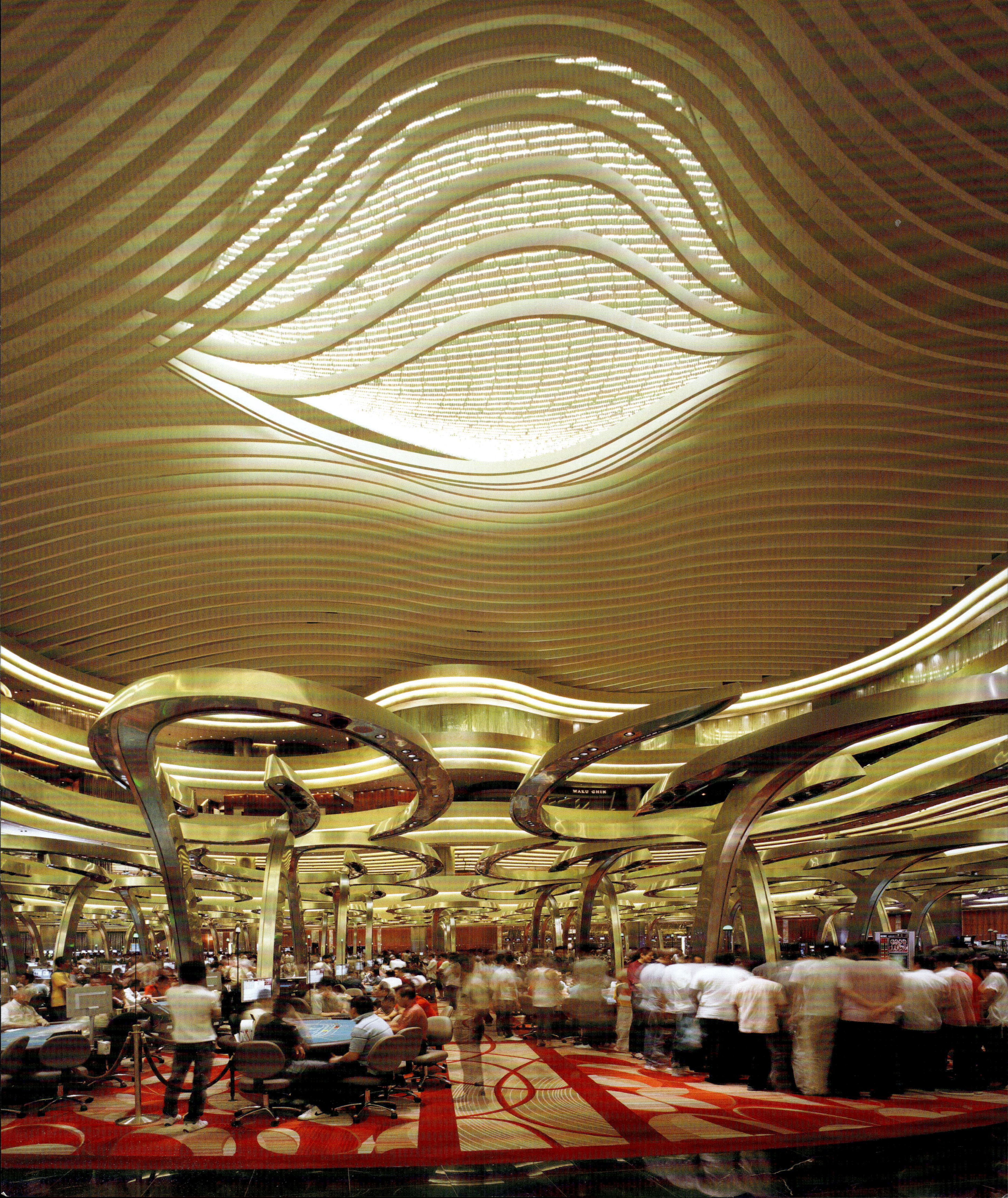

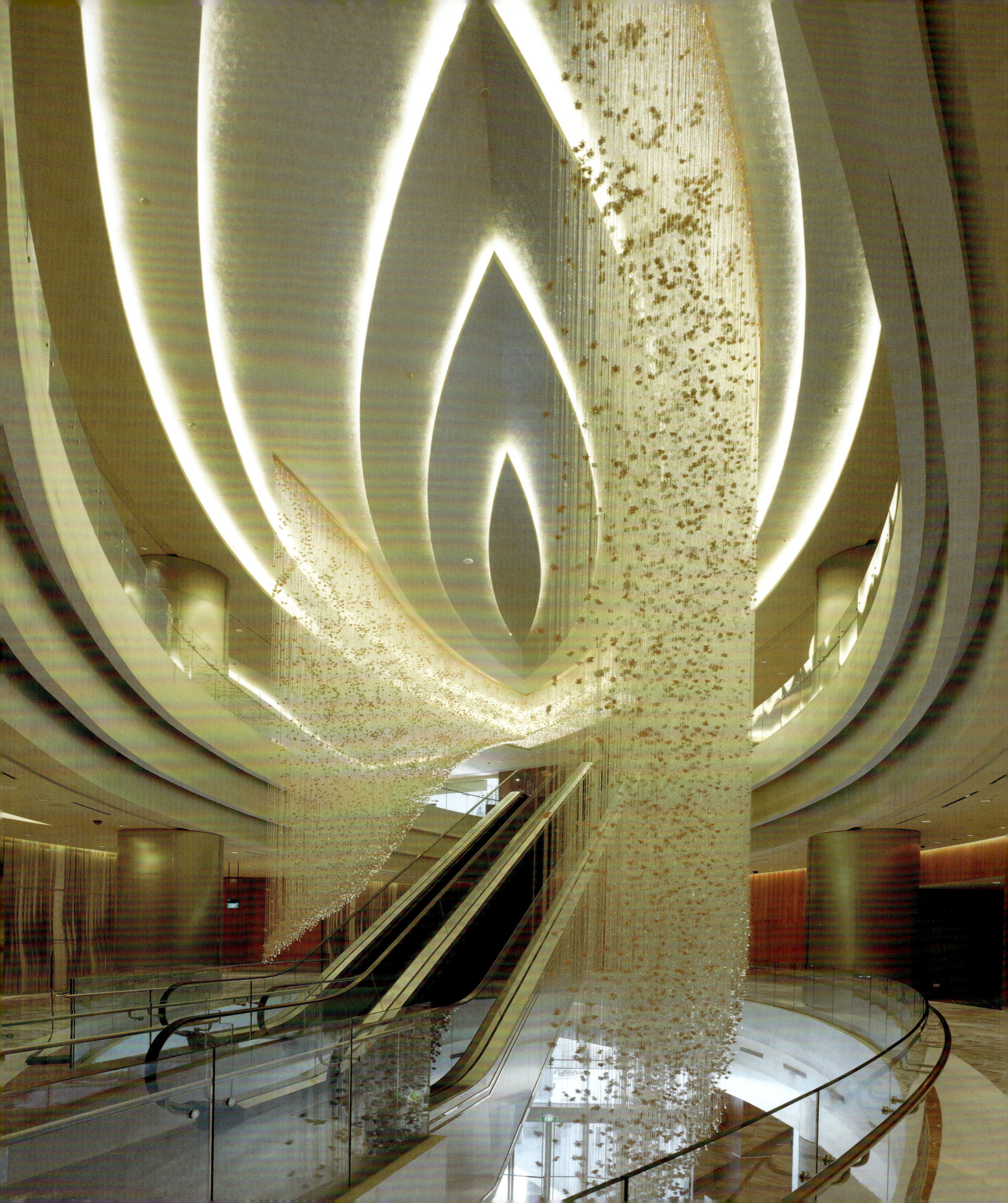

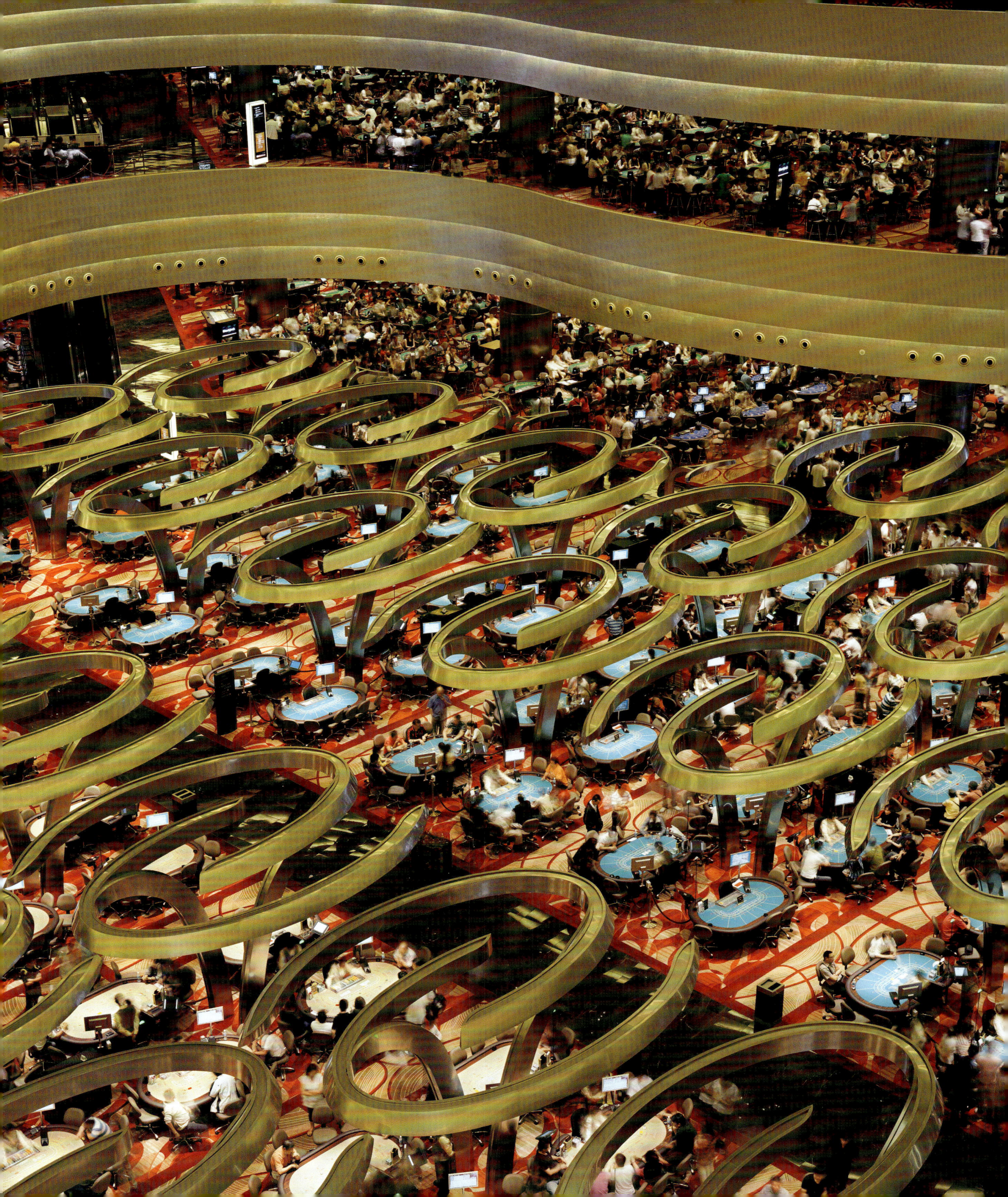

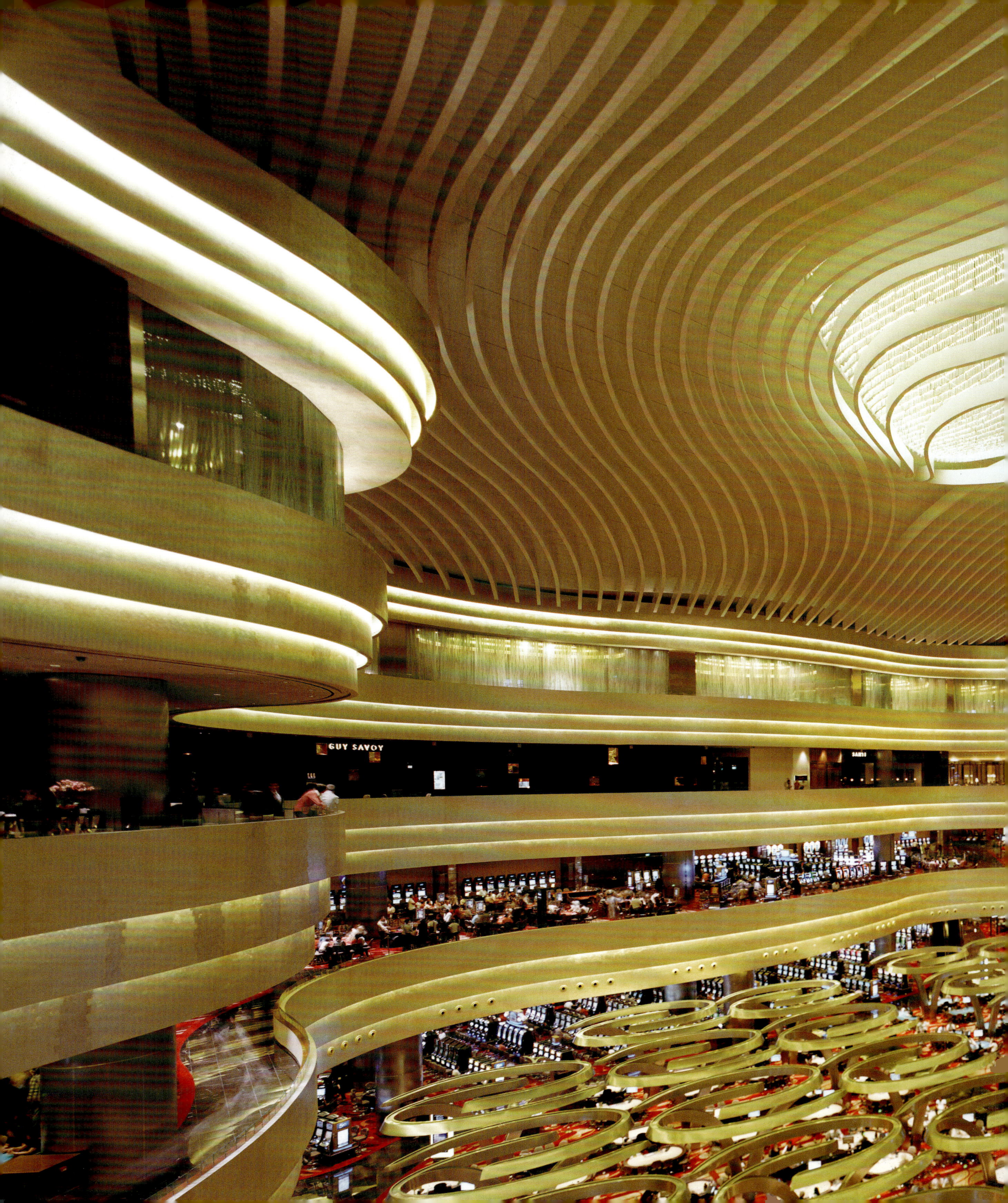
GUY SAVOY

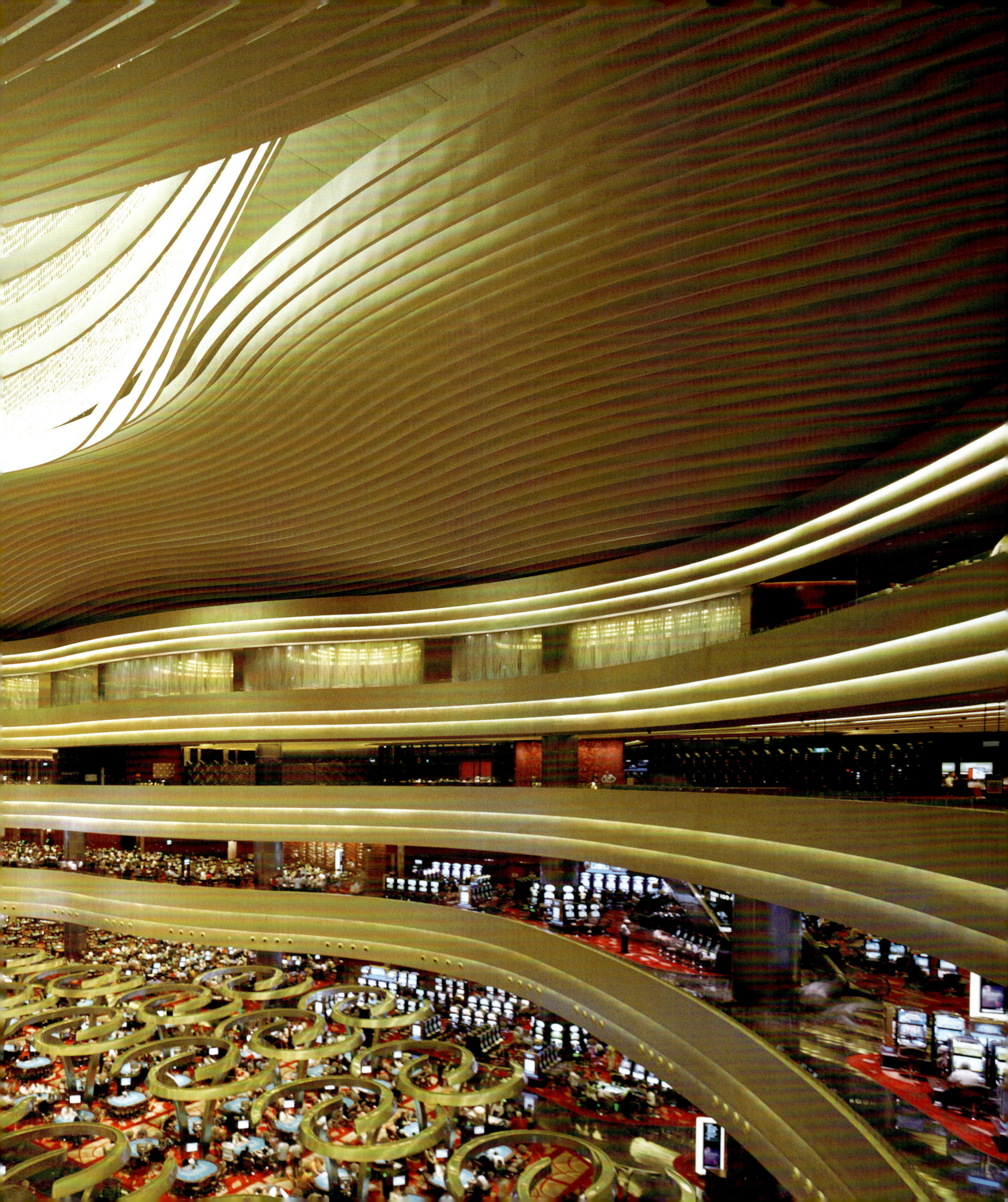

DRESS CIRCLE

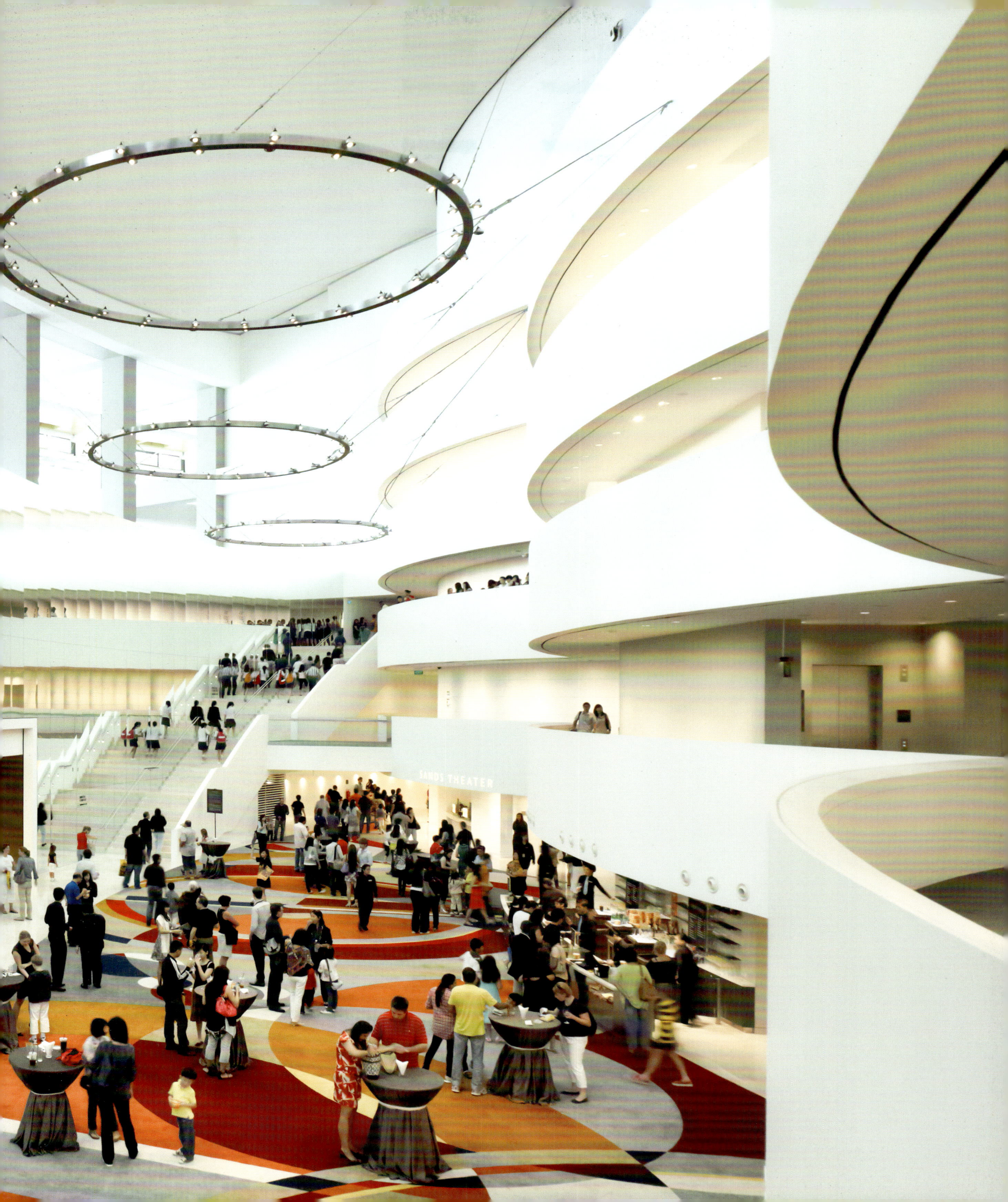
SANDS THEATER

Grand Theater house

Sands Theater

CRYSTAL PAVILIONS

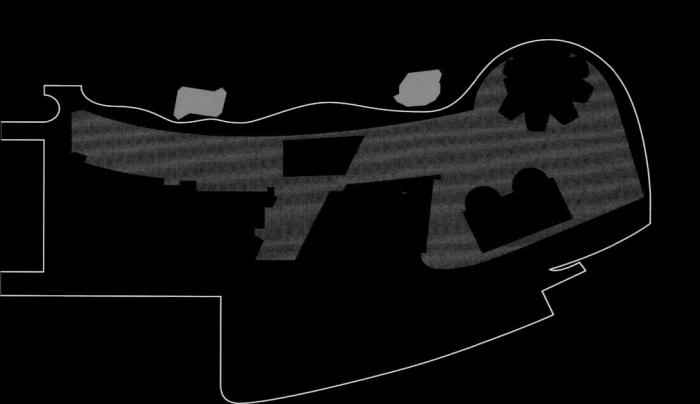

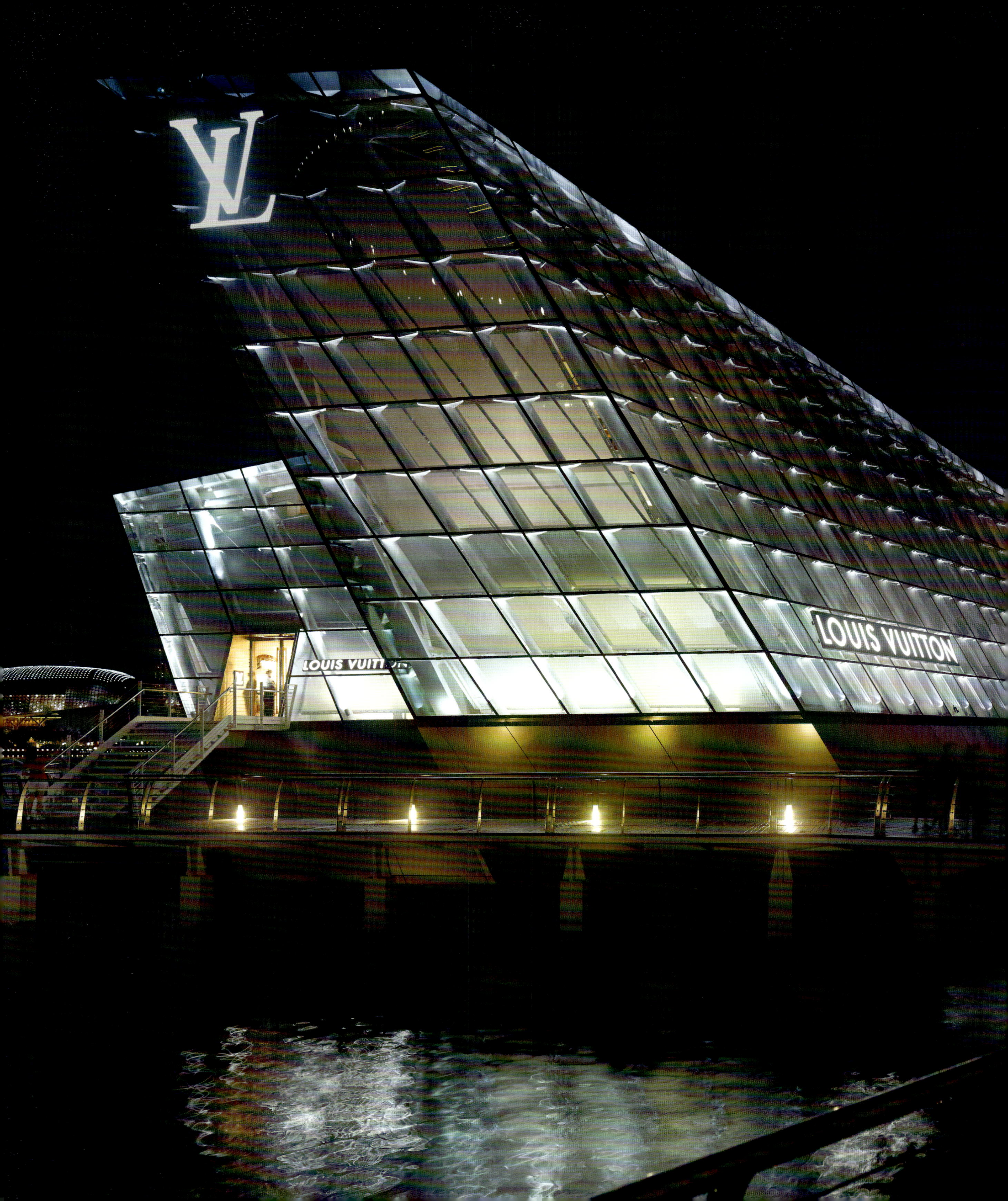
LOUIS VUITTON
LOUIS VUITTON

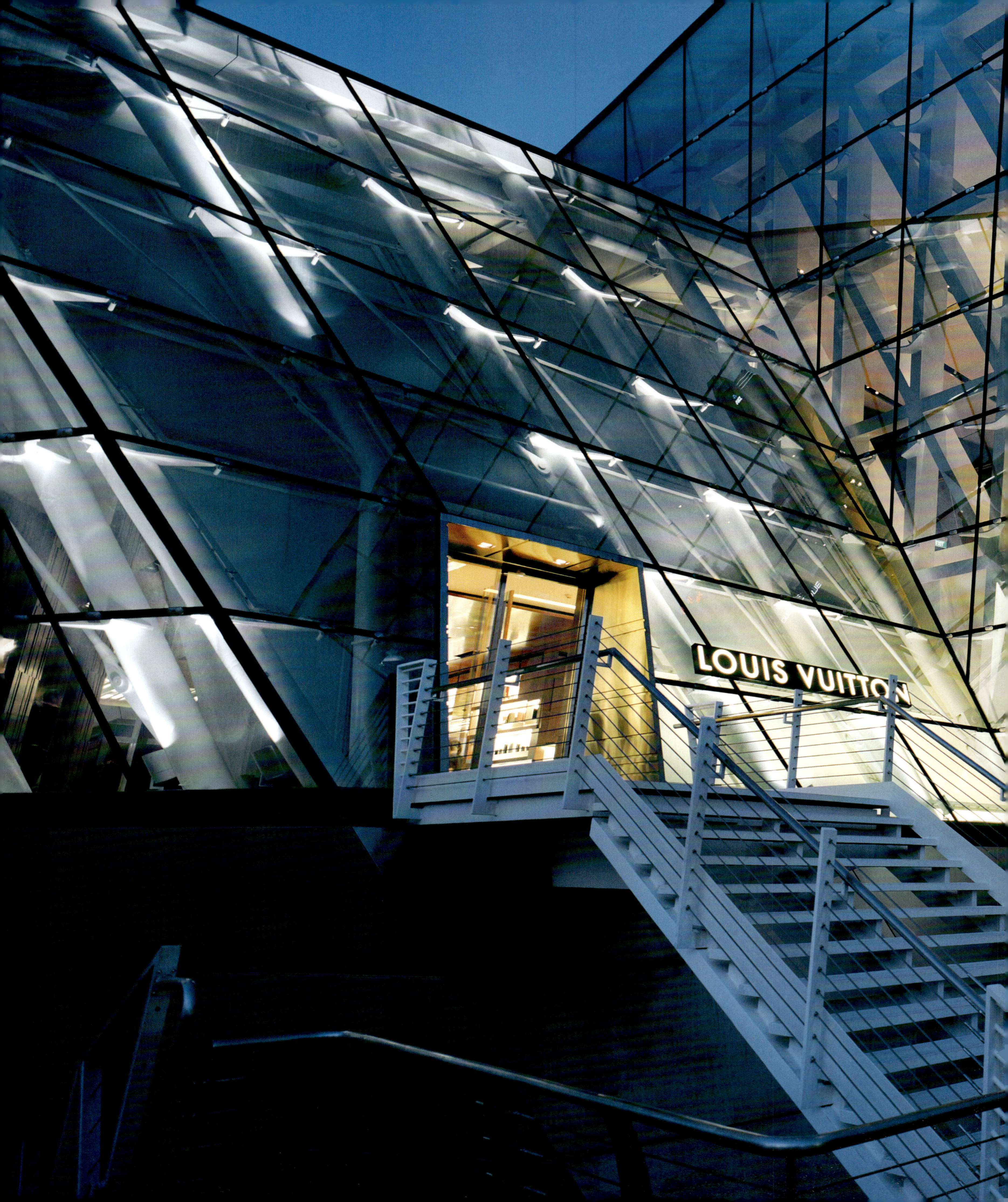
LOUIS VUITTON

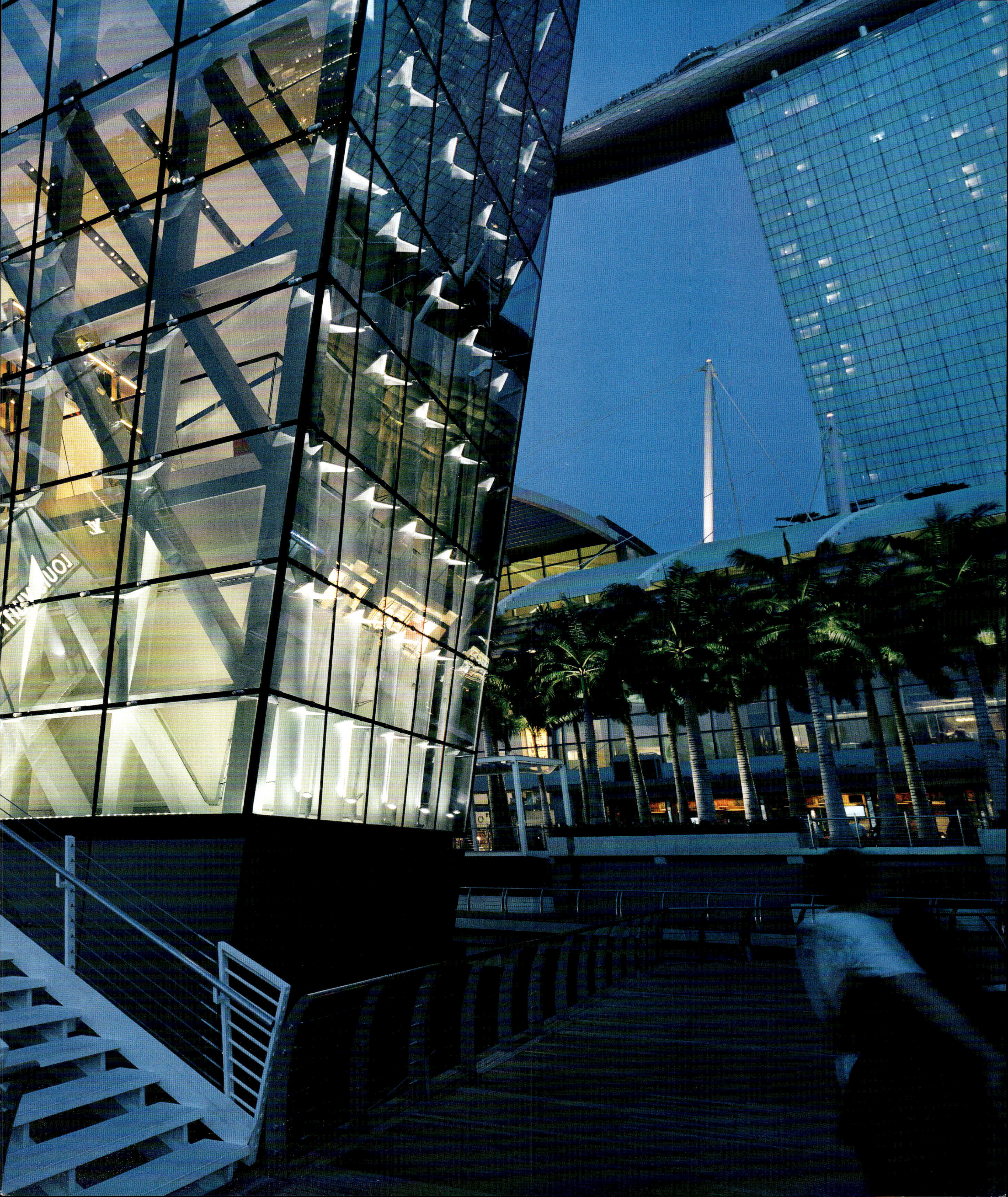

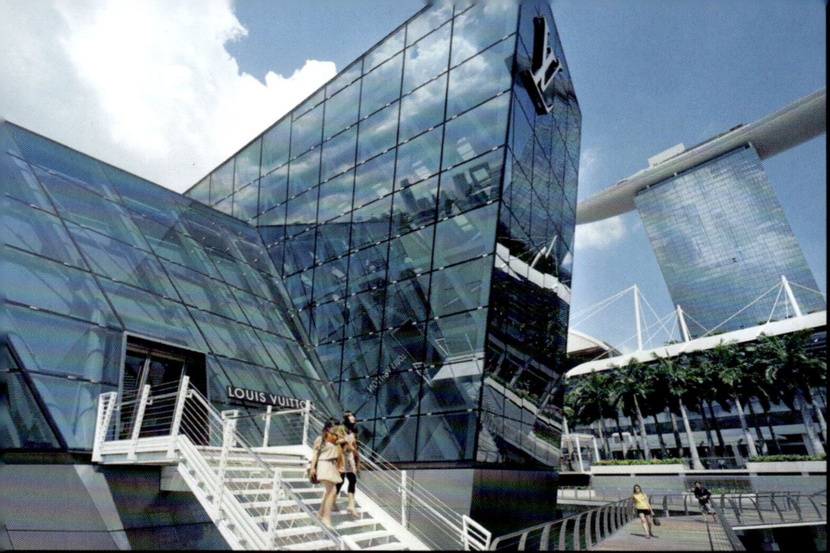
LOUIS VUITTO
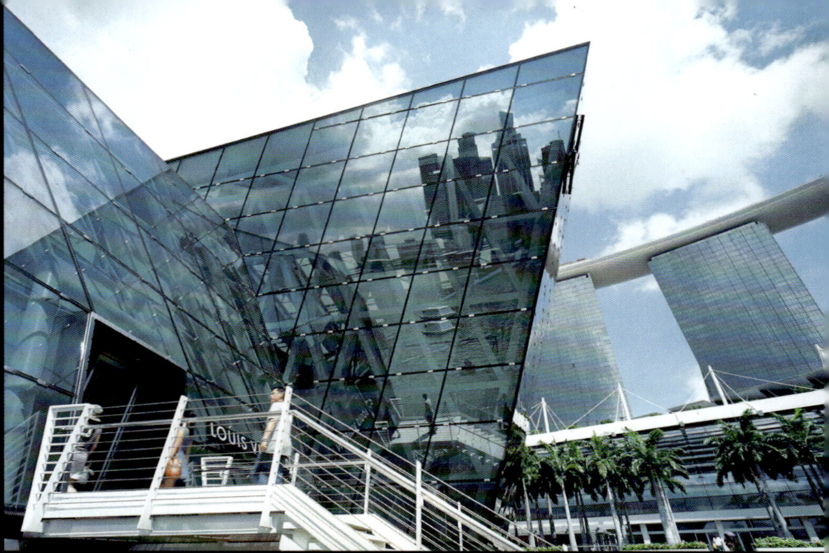
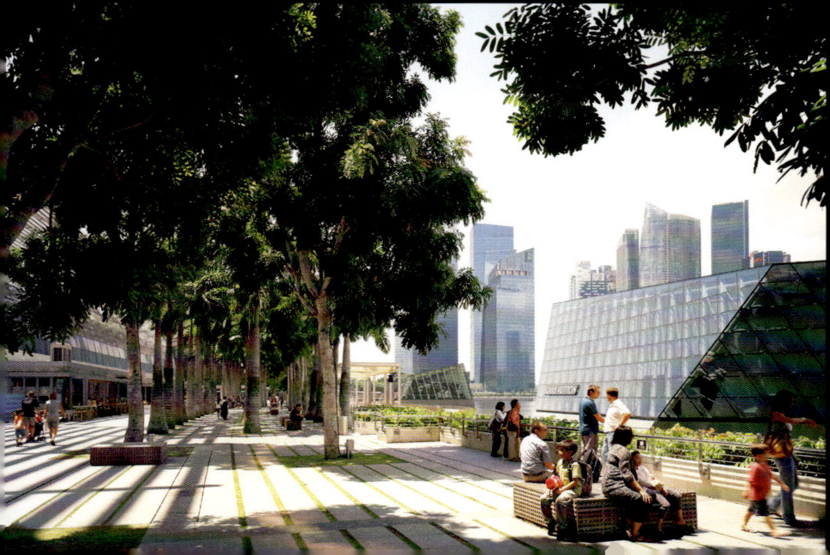
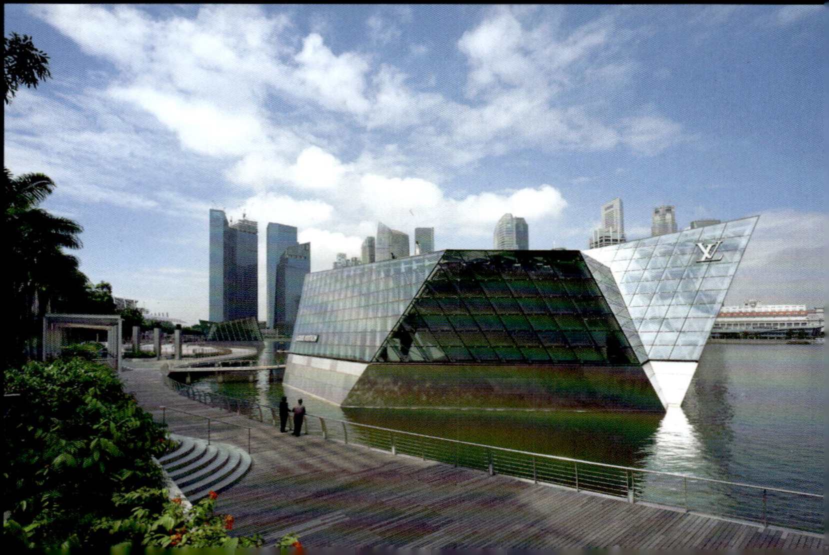

The Crystal Pavilions reflect sky and water during the day and

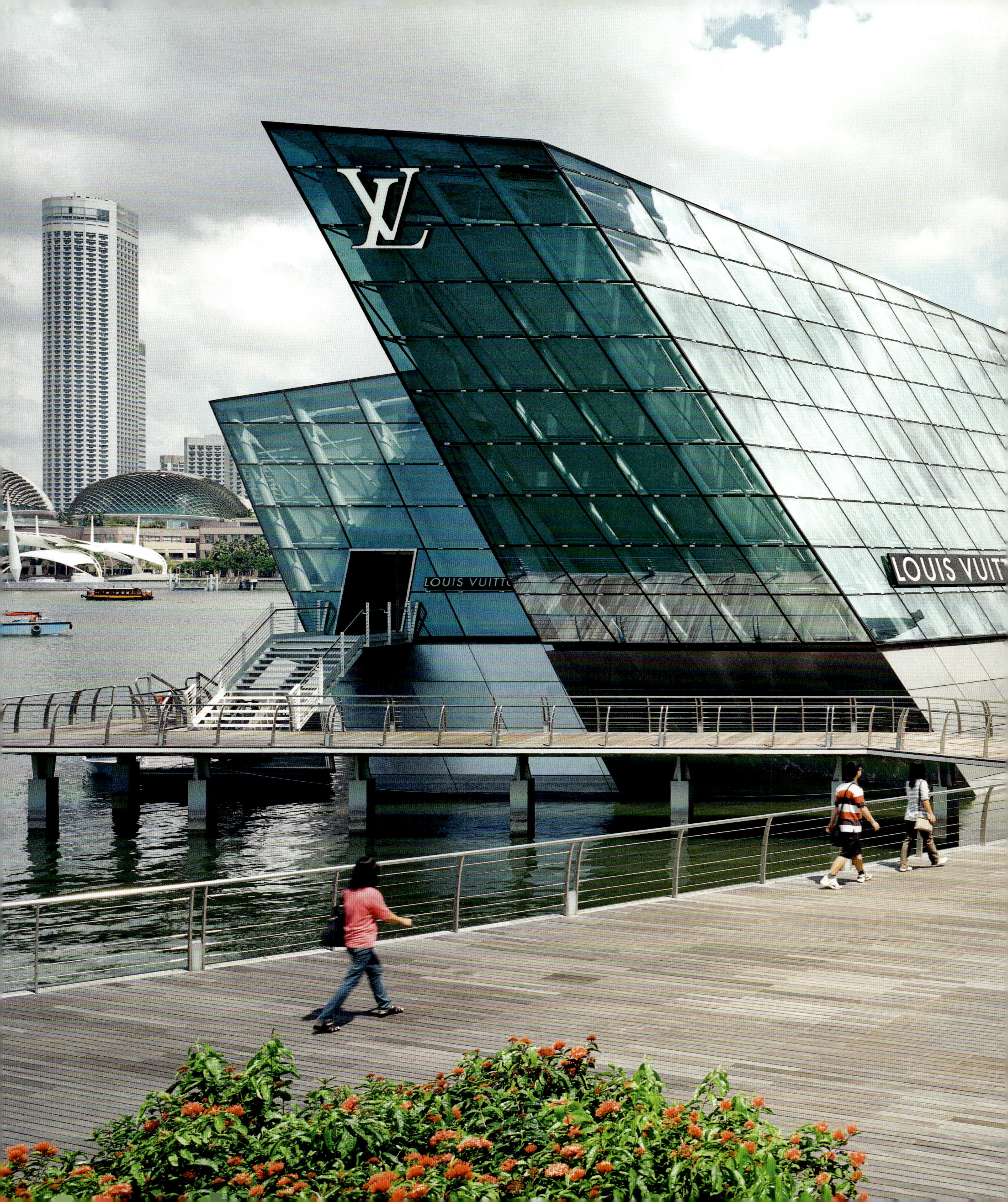
LOUIS VUITTON
LOUIS VUITT

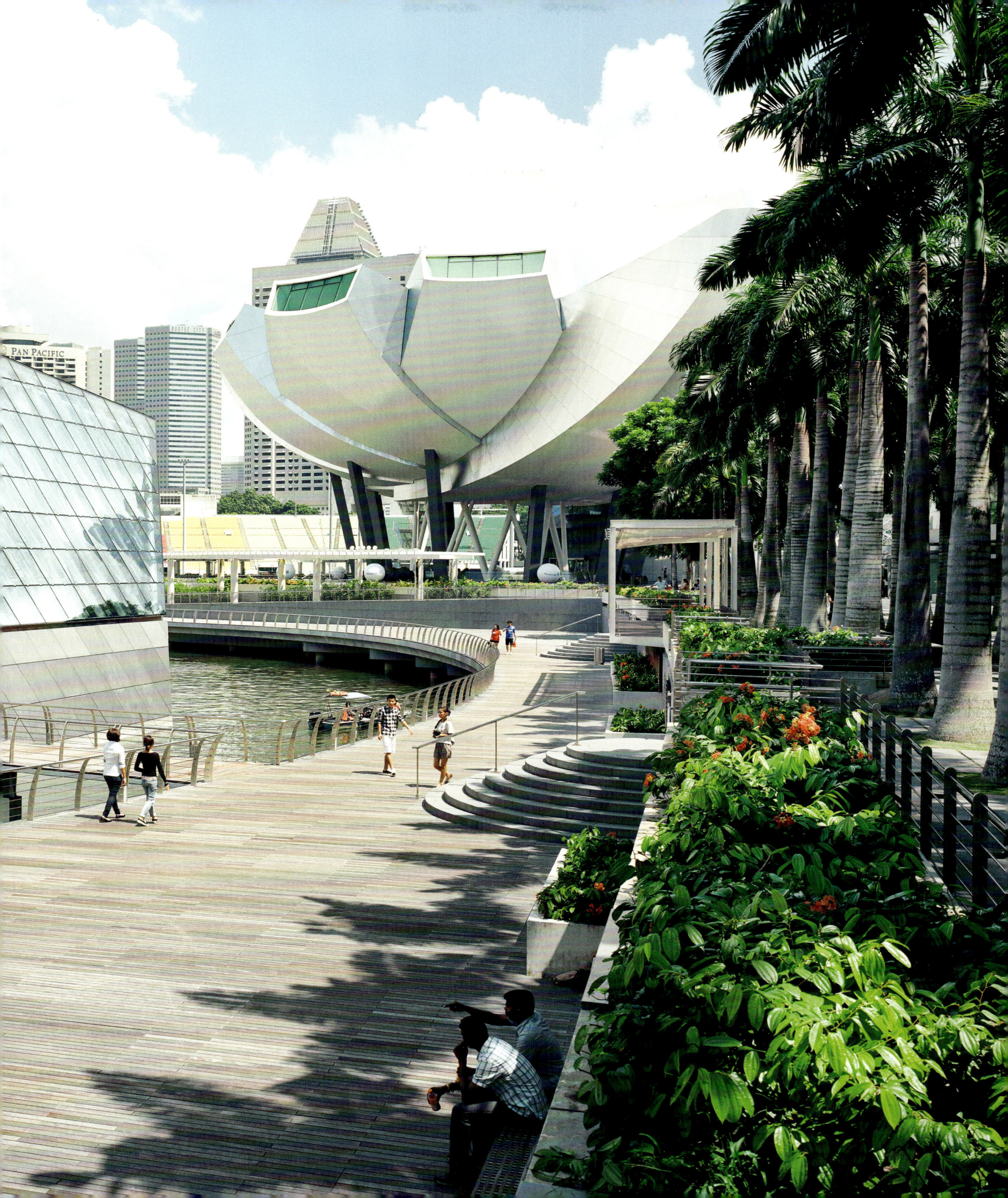
PAN PACIFIC

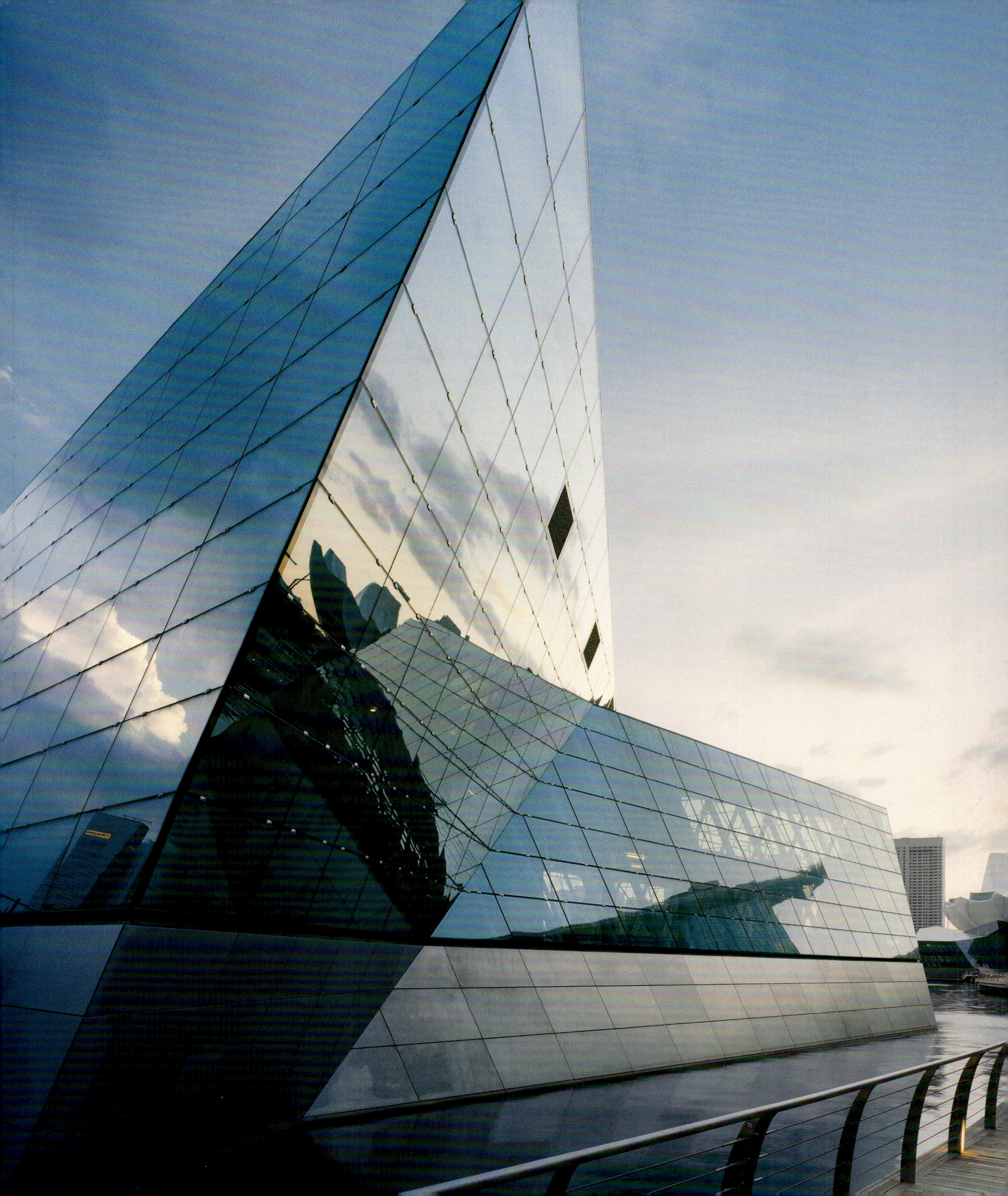

Boardwalk animated by
Pavilions, ArtScience M
and seating areas

ARTSCIENCE MUSEUM

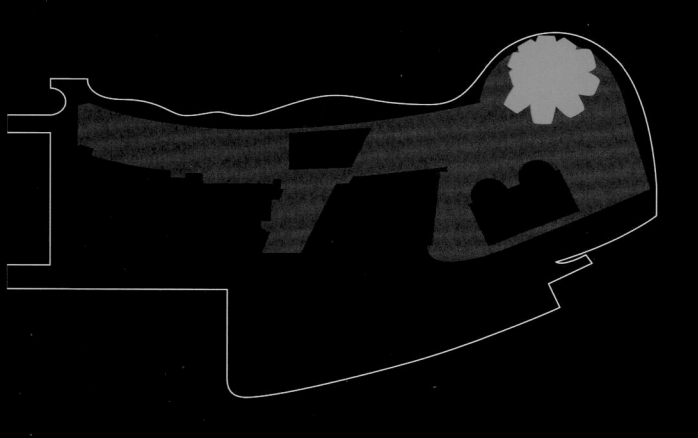

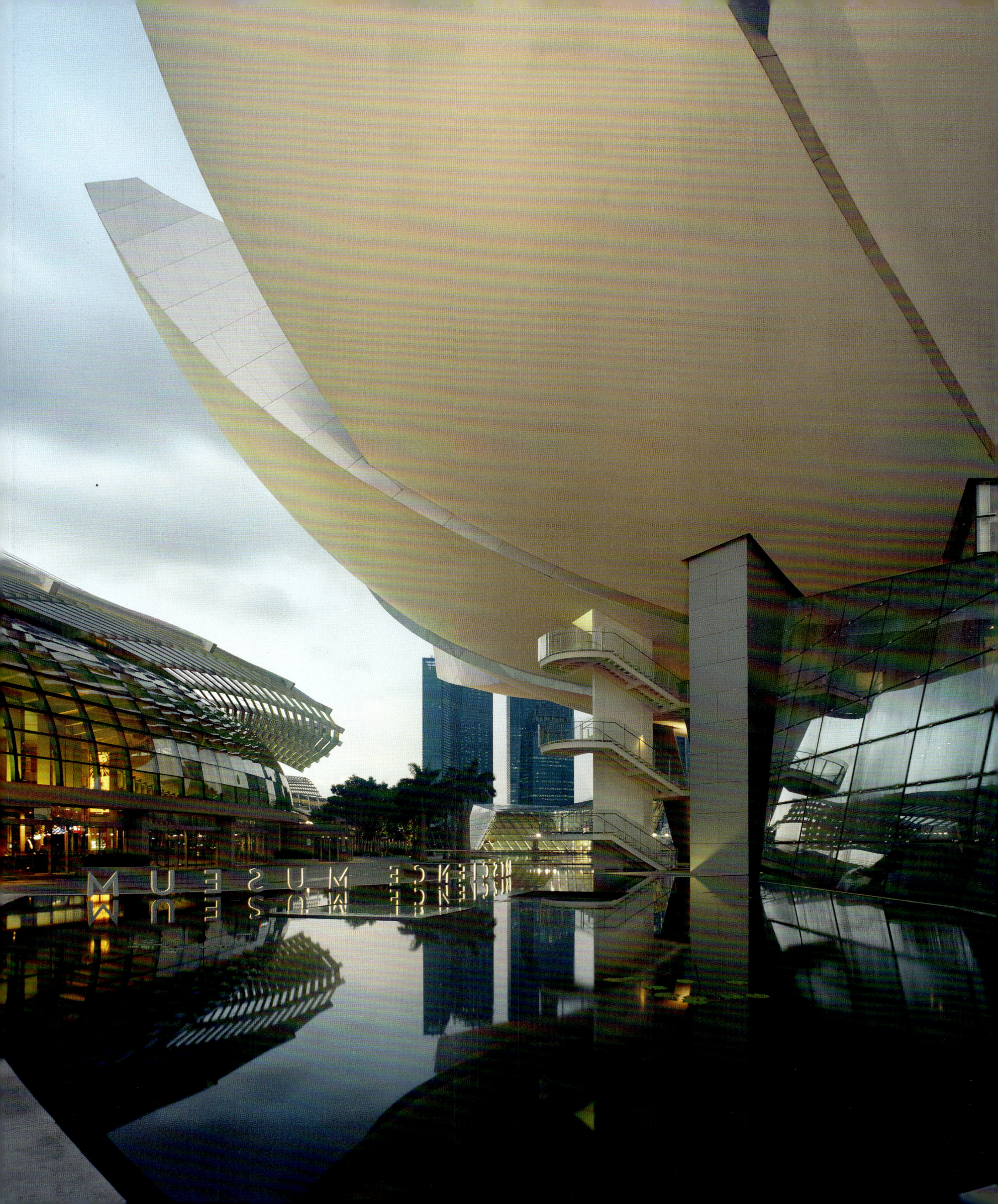

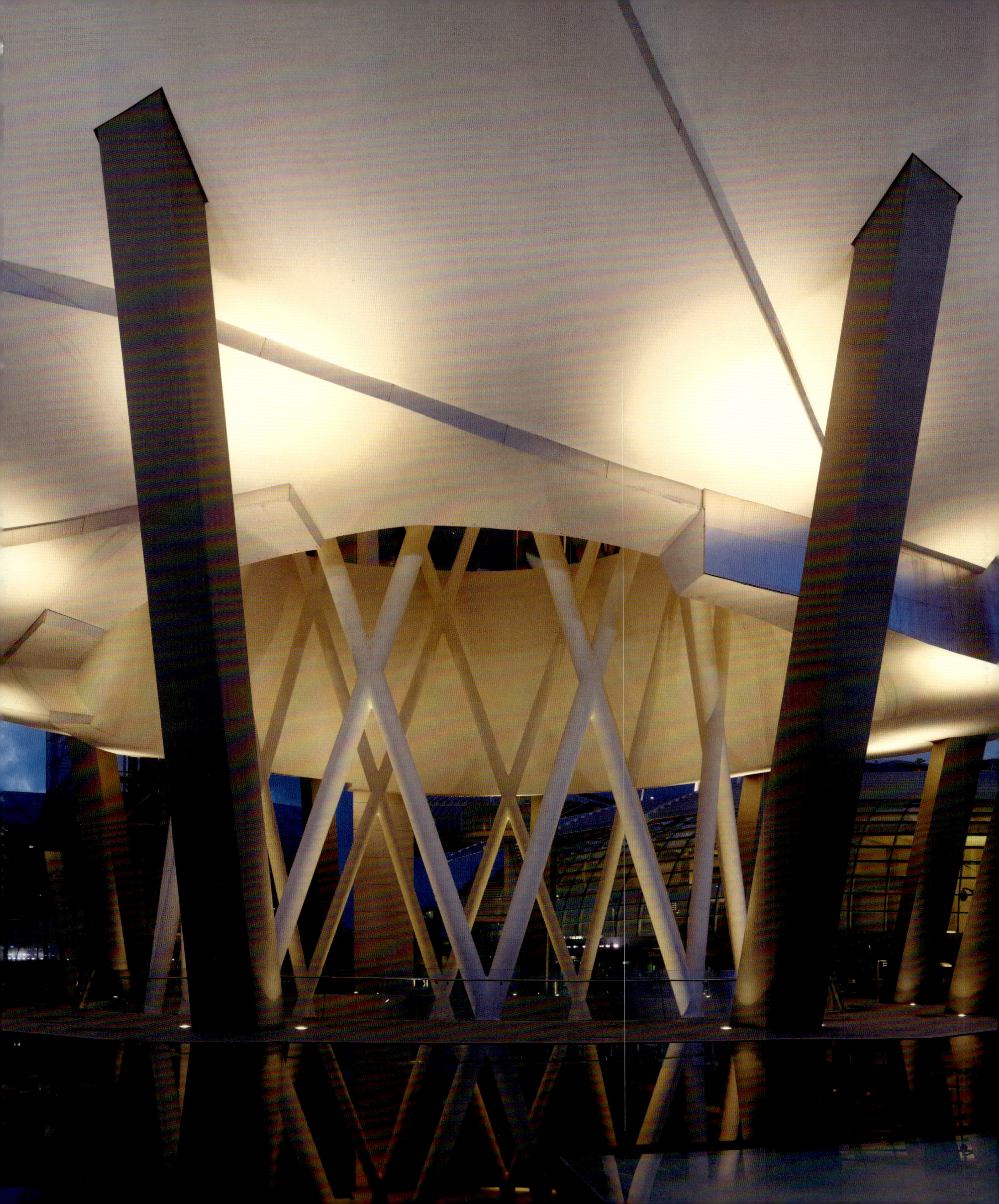

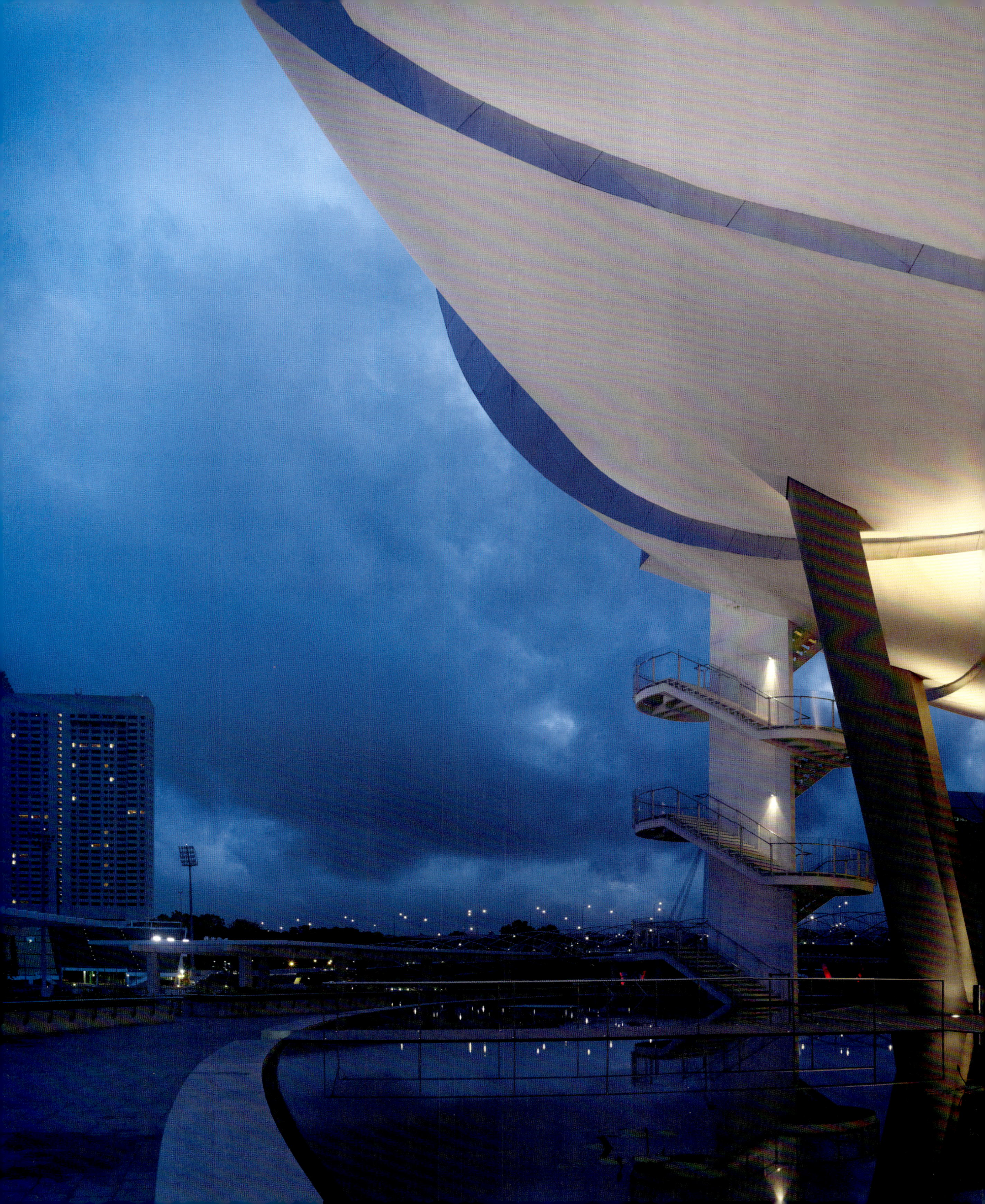

The museum's complex geometry resembles a lotus floating above the promenade. Its white shell changes character during the day.

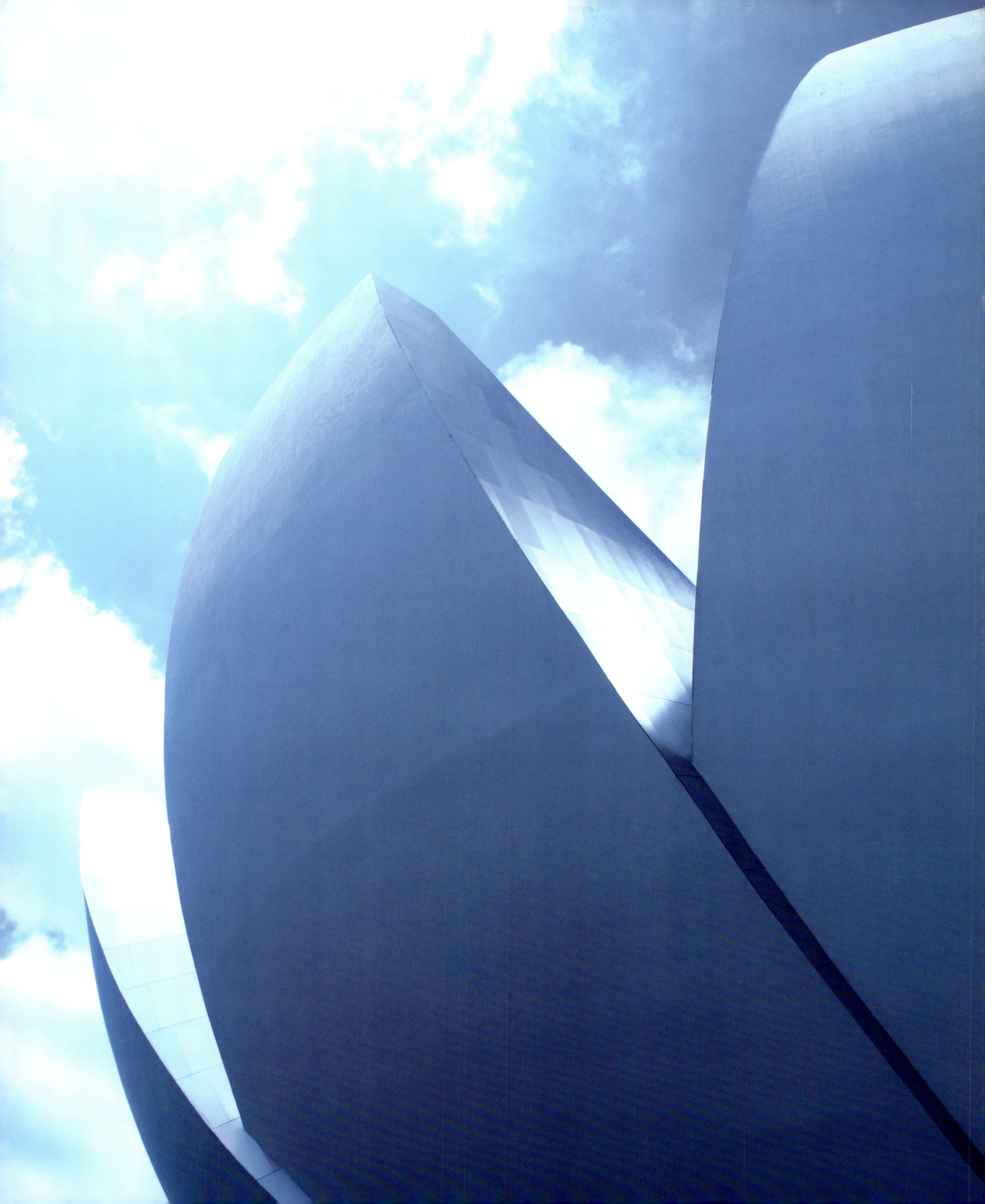

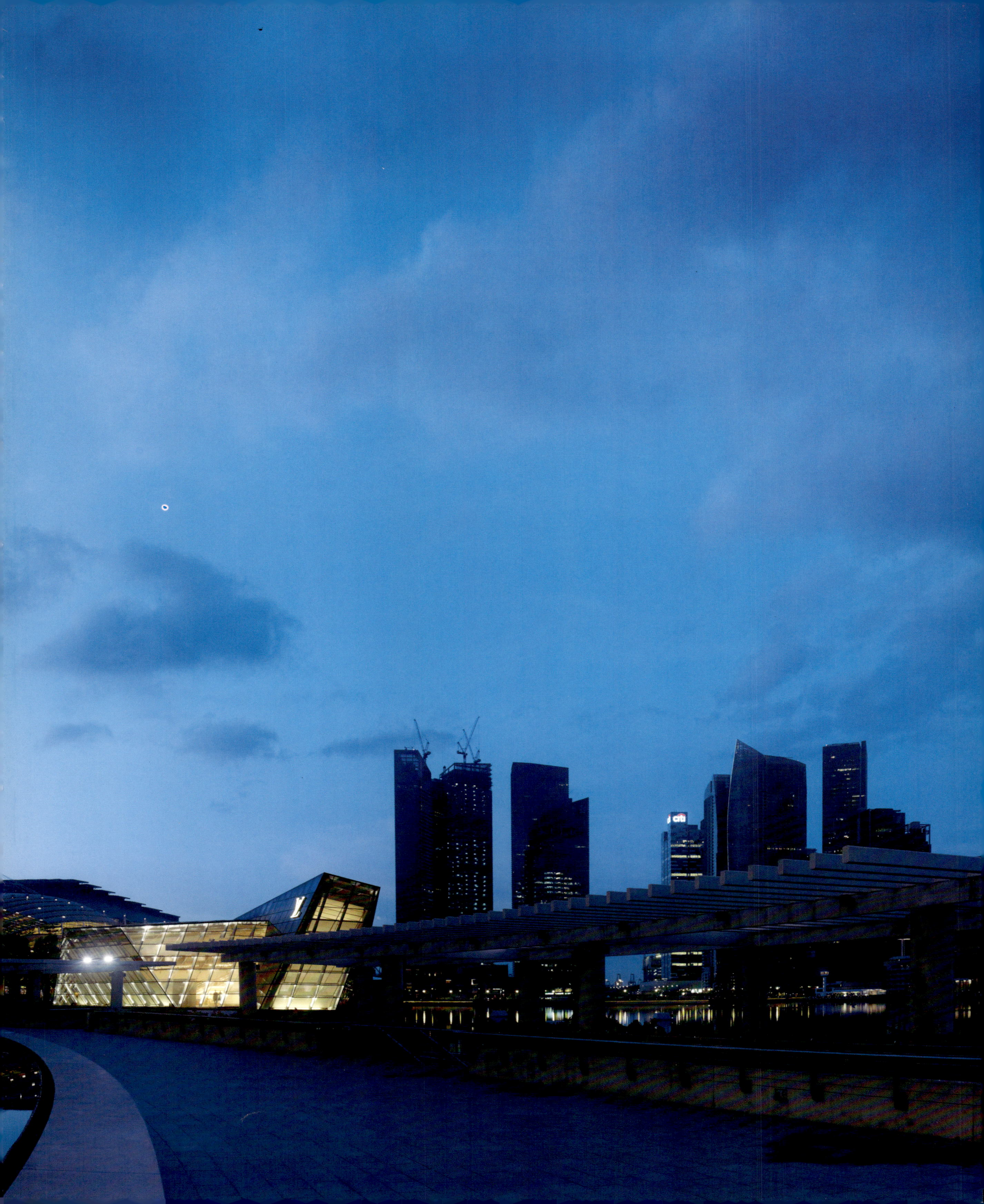

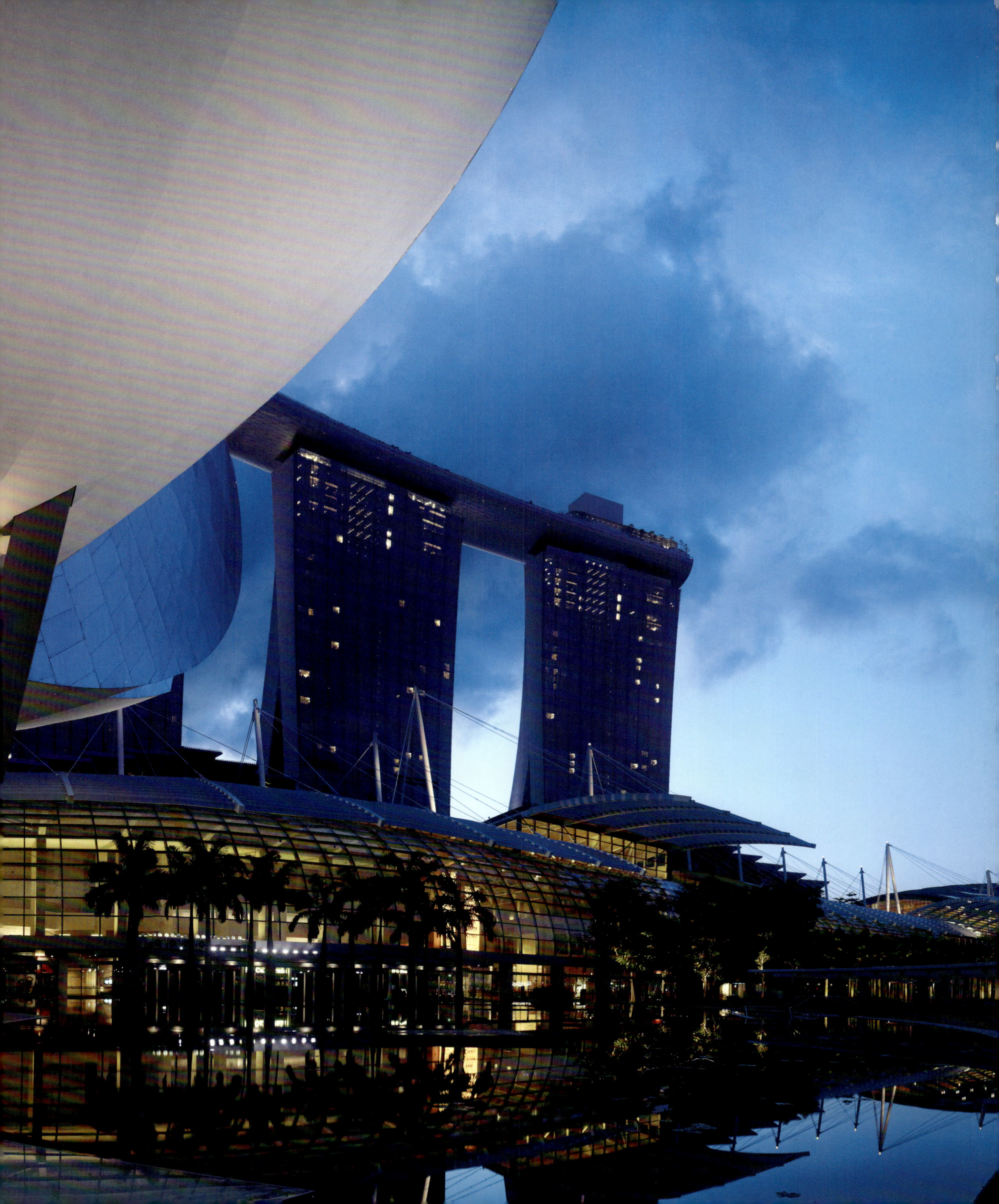

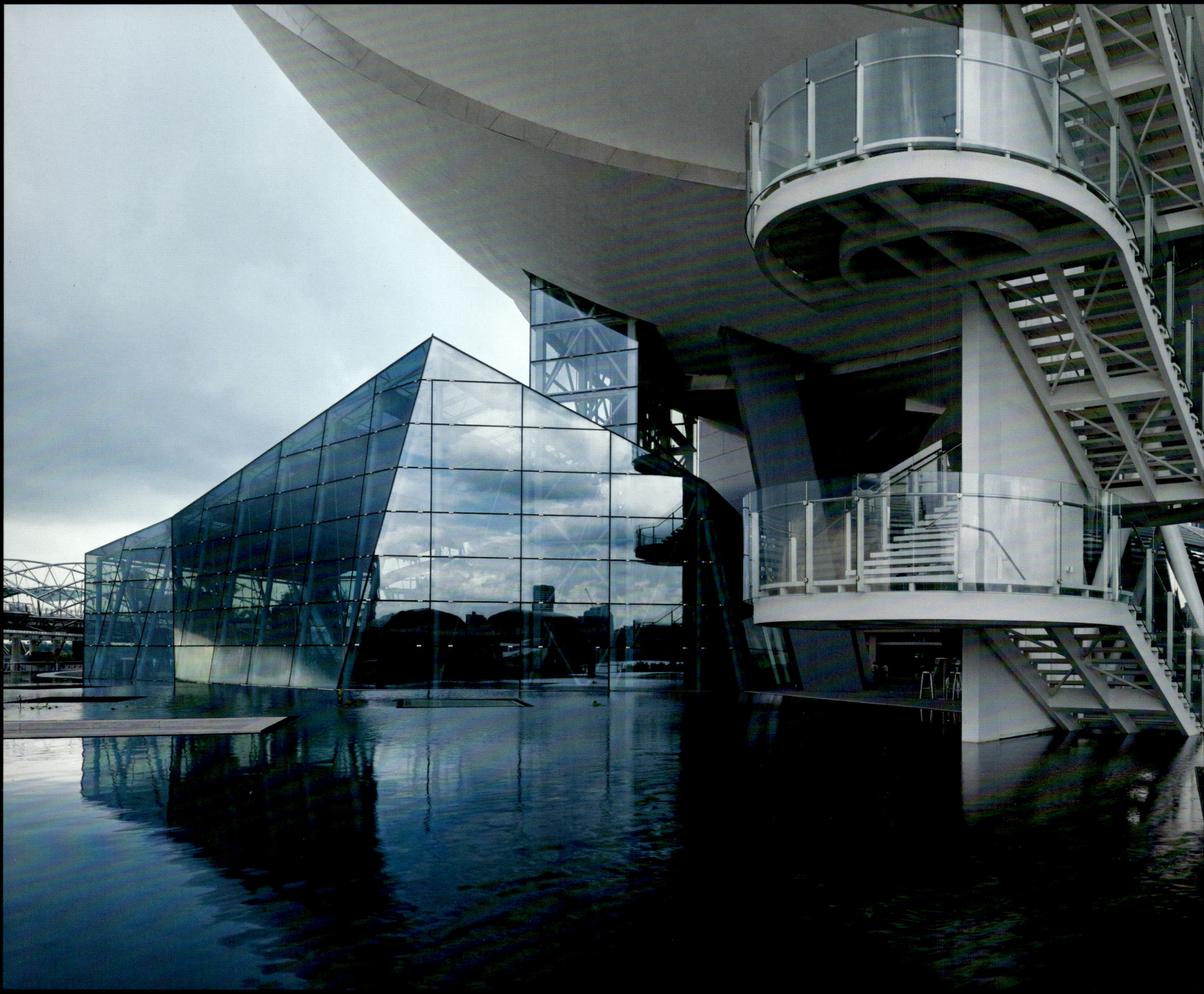

Museum atrium evolving from reflective to transparent

The ArtScience Museum hovers over a reflecting lily pond and frames the skyline.

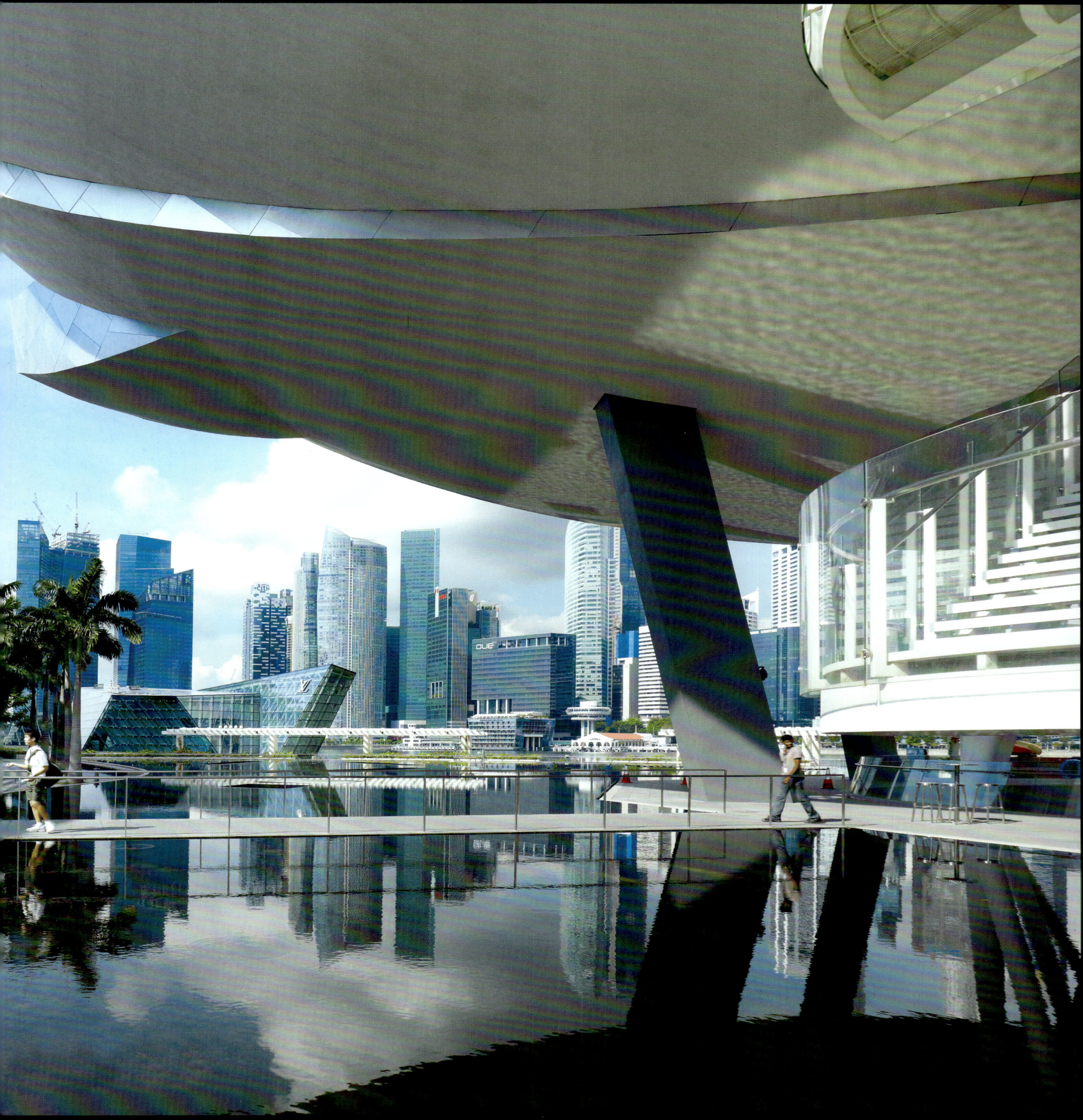

Water falling through museum oculus into the atrium

Reflecting pool at the lower gallery level

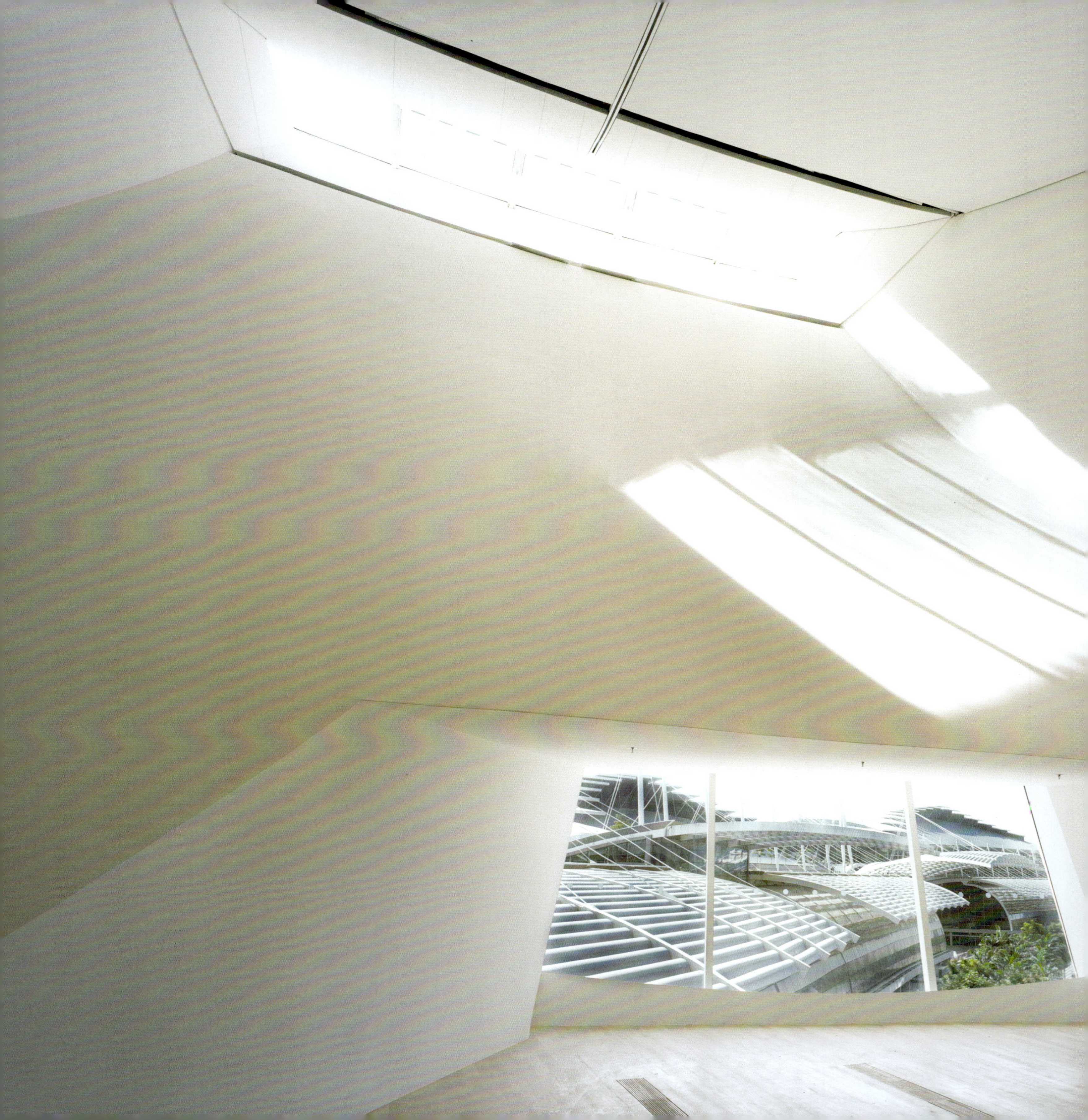

Workers perfecting the matte white finish of the interior gallery walls

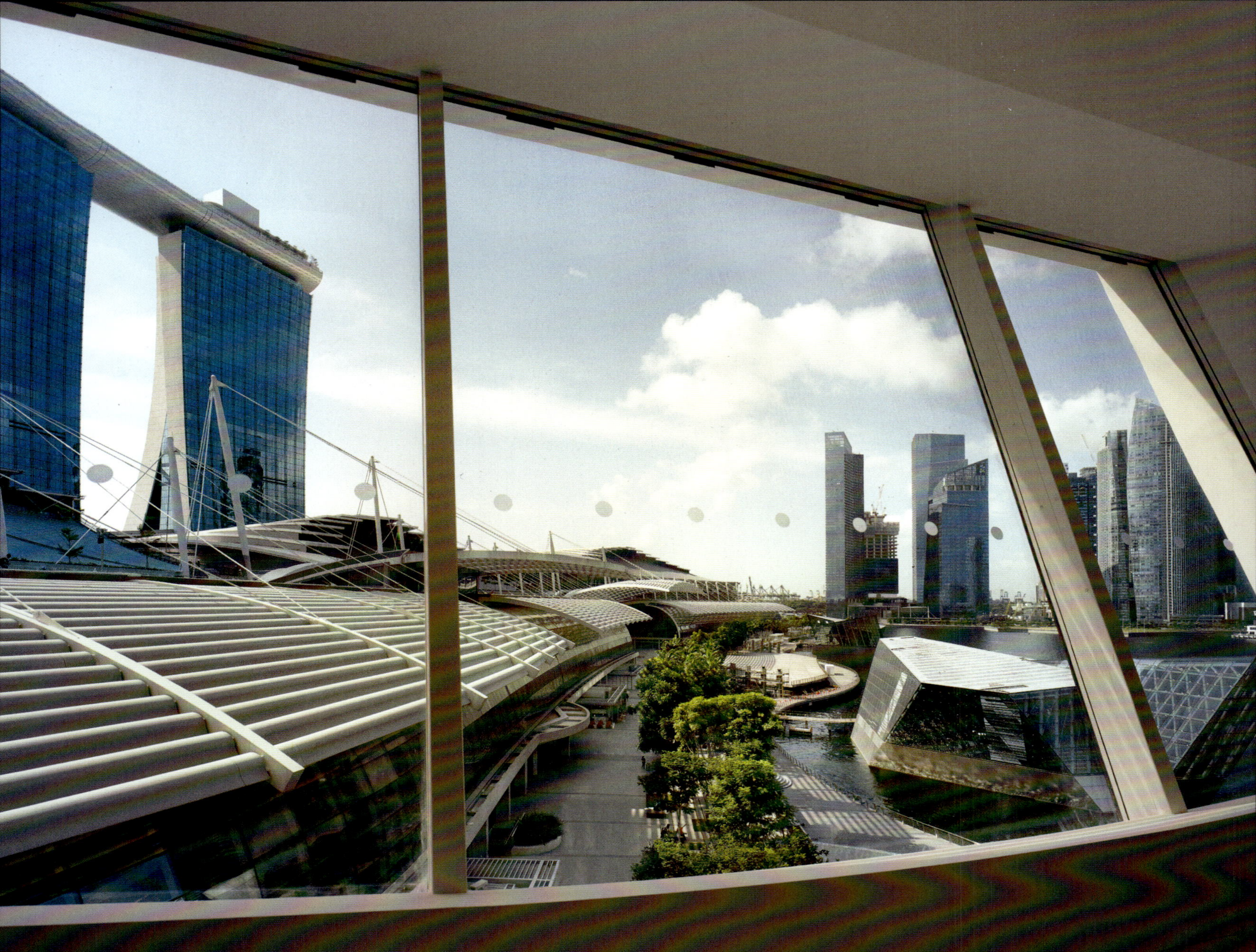

An upper-level gallery window offers a view of the waterfront promenade to the south

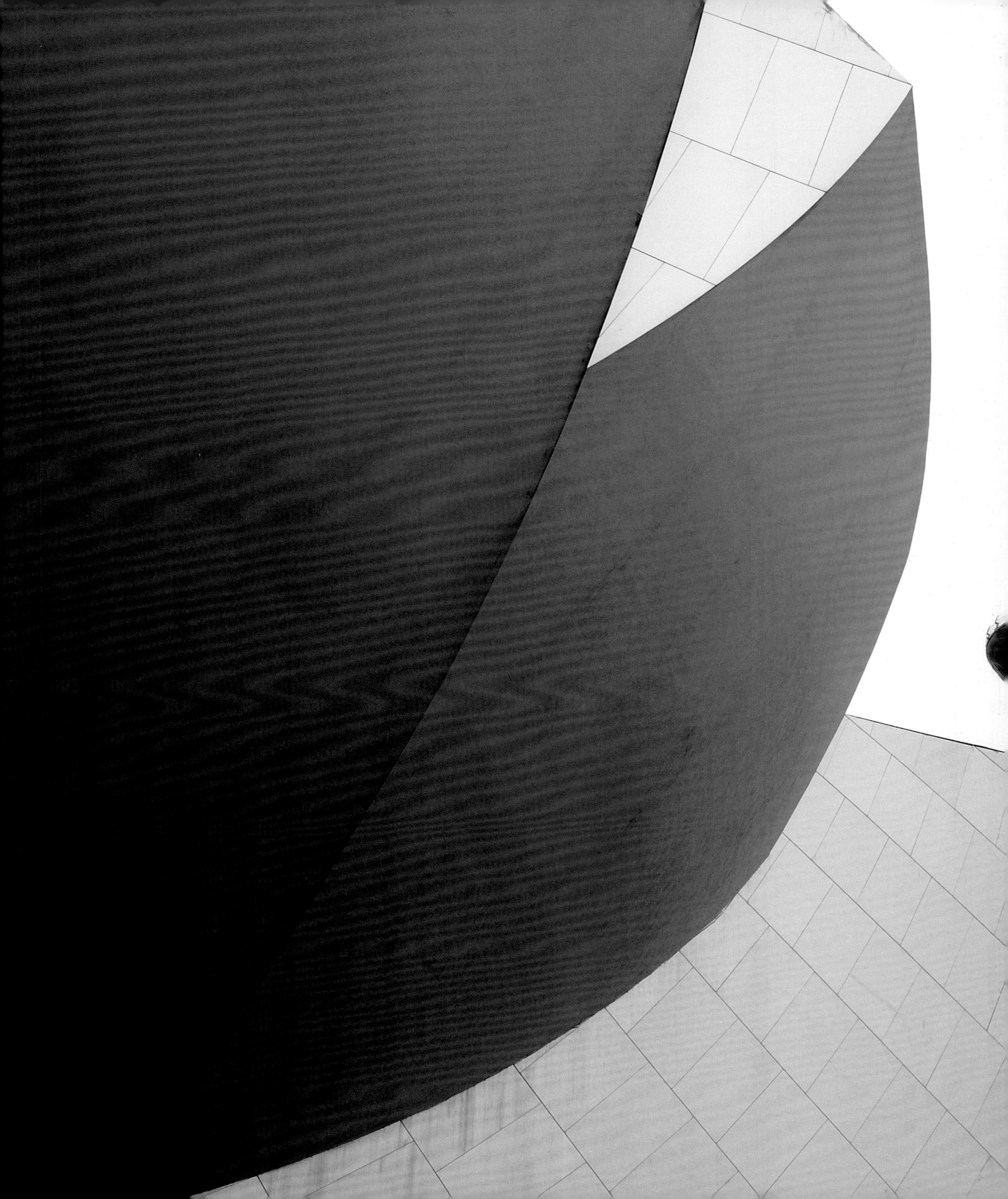

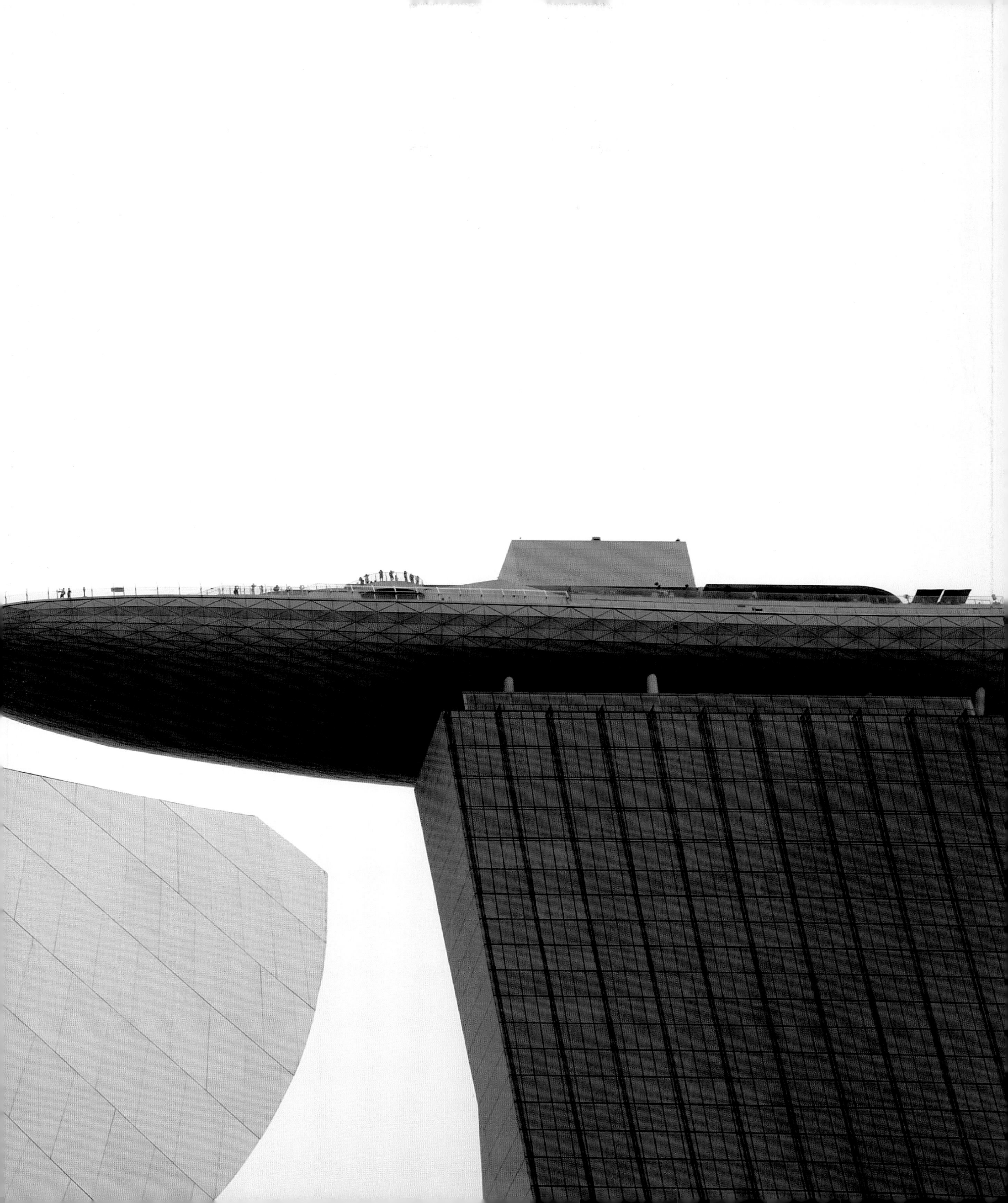

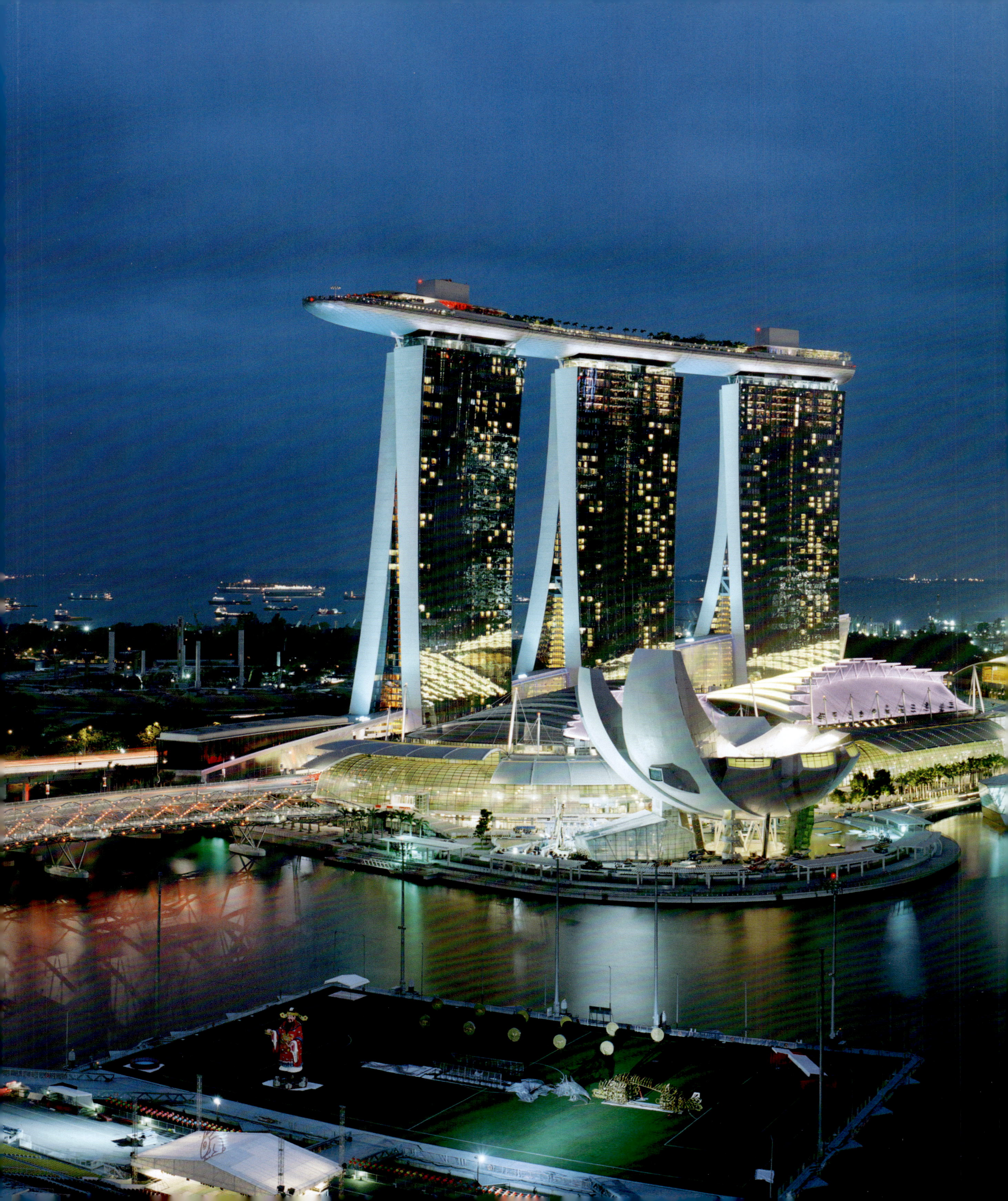

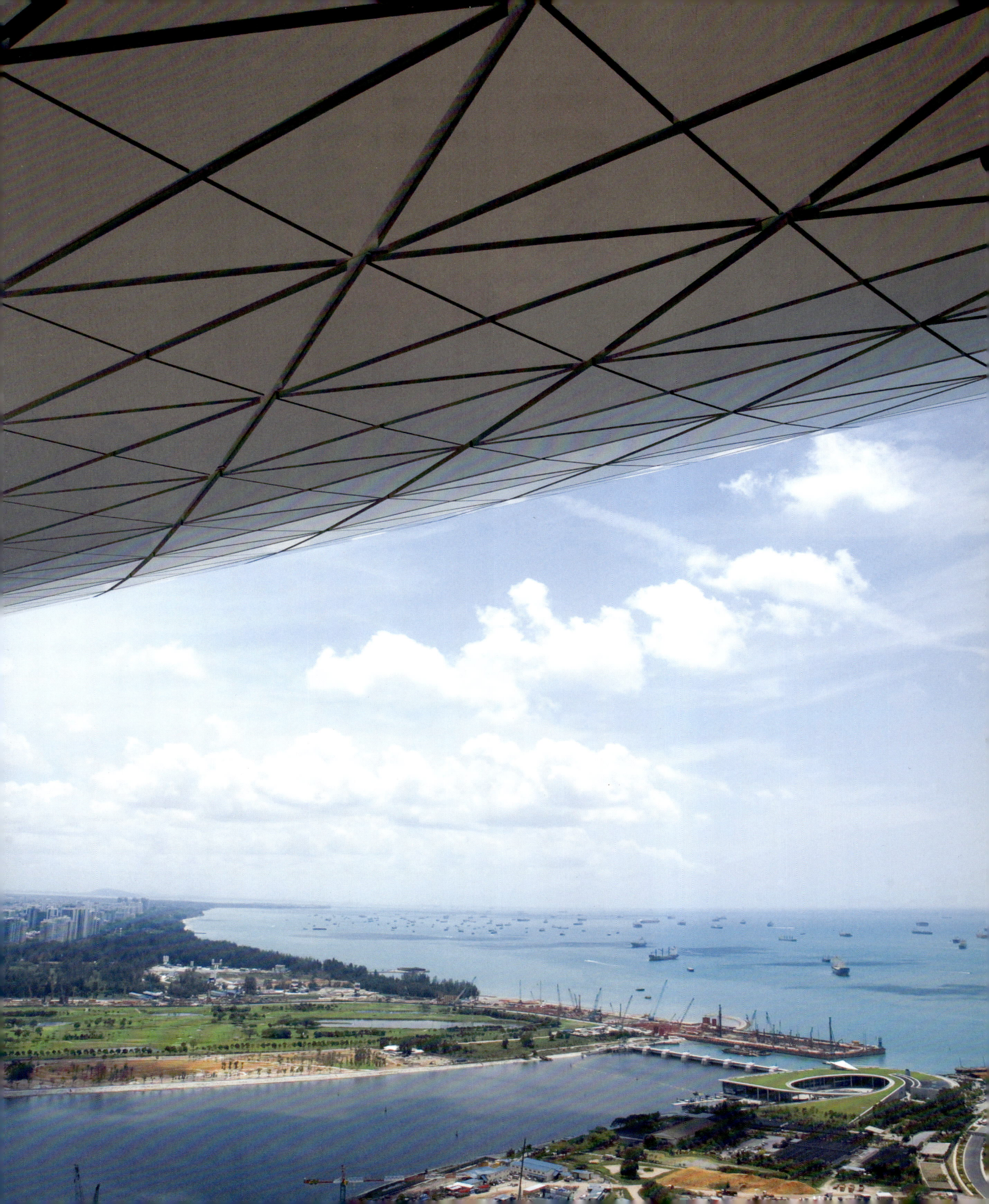

STRAITS TRADING
STRAITS TRADING
Maybank
HSBC
THE FULLERTON HOTEL

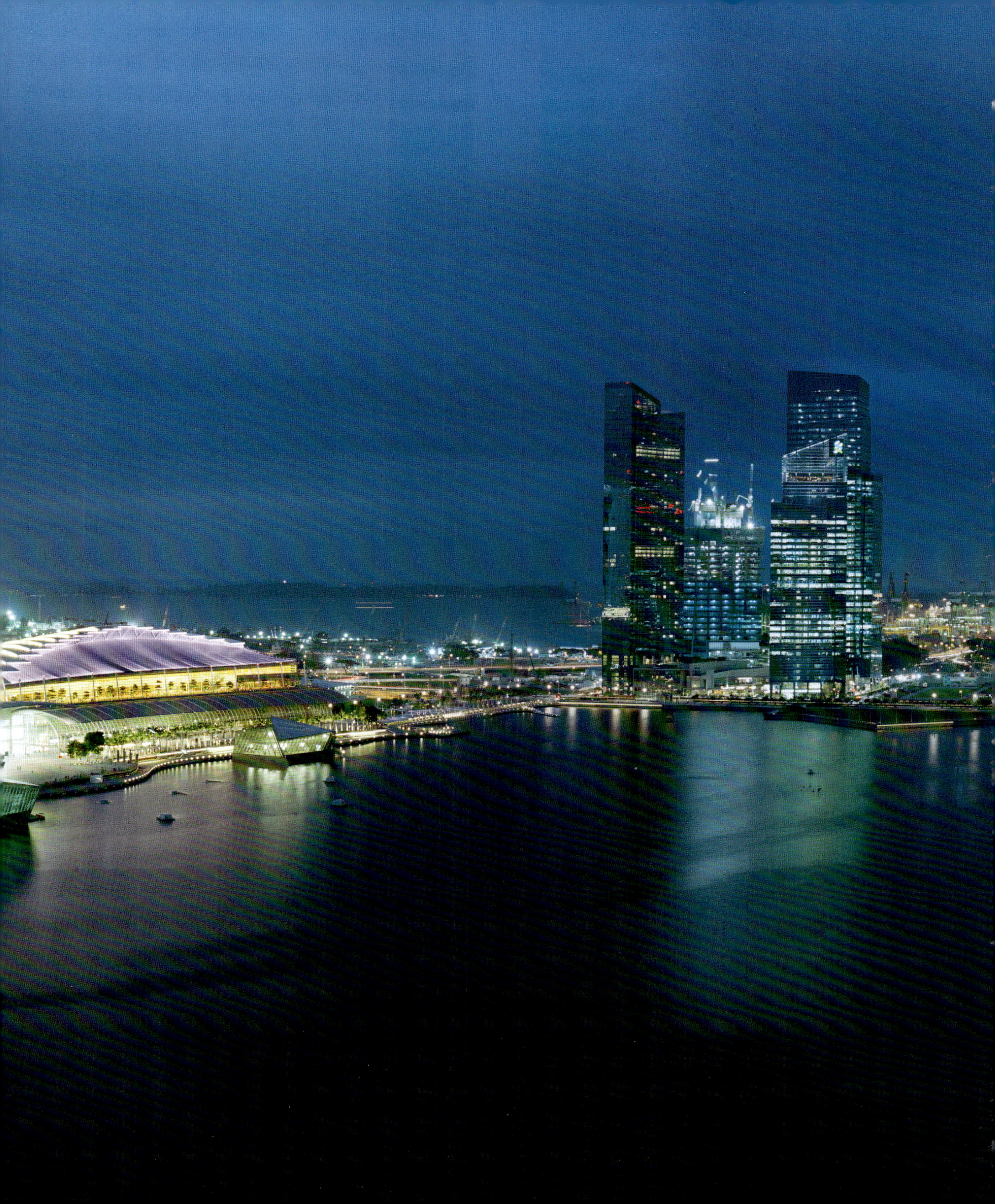

ART AT EVERY TURN: THE MARINA BAY SANDS ART PATH

BROOKE HODGE

Visitors to Marina Bay Sands encounter art immediately, whether they arrive by car at the hotel or the Shoppes or by airport bus in the transit bay under the lobby. While the resort's spectacular triple towers provide the powerful, and enduring, image that draws visitors from near and far to Marina Bay Sands, the more subtle integration of eleven remarkable site-specific art installations, both inside and outside the resort's buildings, is no less powerful.

For architect Moshe Safdie, art and architecture are virtually inseparable. He believes that art plays an essential role in the public's experience of any built environment and over the years has made the incorporation of art with architecture a major hallmark of his practice. Early in his thinking about Marina Bay Sands, Safdie envisioned a program of unique commissioned art works as being a key part of the vast resort. The result is a selection of spectacular installations by seven internationally renowned artists: American glass and structural artist James Carpenter; British sculptor Antony Gormley; Israeli sculptor Israel Hadany; American environmental artist Ned Kahn; Chinese painter Zheng Chongbin; the late American conceptualist Sol LeWitt; and Chinese sculptor Zhan Wang. Accessible to resort guests and the public alike, the Art Path at Marina Bay Sands gives visitors the opportunity to enjoy world-class artworks at a single destination, just as they would in a museum of contemporary art.

Safdie himself has designed many of the most acclaimed museum buildings of our time, including the National Gallery of Canada, in Ottawa (1988); the Peabody Essex Museum, in Salem, Massachusetts (2003); the Yad Vashem Holocaust History Museum, in Jerusalem (2005); and the Crystal Bridges Museum of American Art, in Bentonville, Arkansas (2011). His deep appreciation and understanding of art is unmistakable, and he often works with artists early in his design process. For Safdie, art is integral to the creation of a space, as opposed to being an adornment, something to be added later. This approach underlines his belief in the importance of art not only in his life but also in the lives of those who work in or travel through his buildings. At Toronto Pearson International Airport's new Terminal 1—a

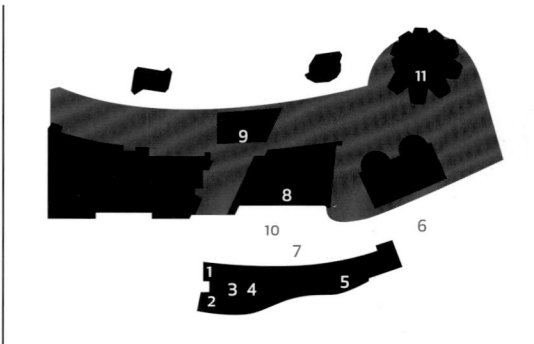

1. Sol LeWitt, *Wall Drawing #915*
2. Sol LeWitt, *Wall Drawing #917*
3. Antony Gormley, *Drift*
4. Israel Hadany, *Motion*
5. Zheng Chongbin, *Rising Forest*
6. Ned Kahn, *Tipping Wall*
7. Ned Kahn, *Wind Arbor*
8. James Carpenter, *Blue Reflection Facade with Light Entry Passage*
9. Ned Kahn, *Rain Oculus*
10. Zhan Wang, *Artificial Rock #159*
11. ArtScience Museum

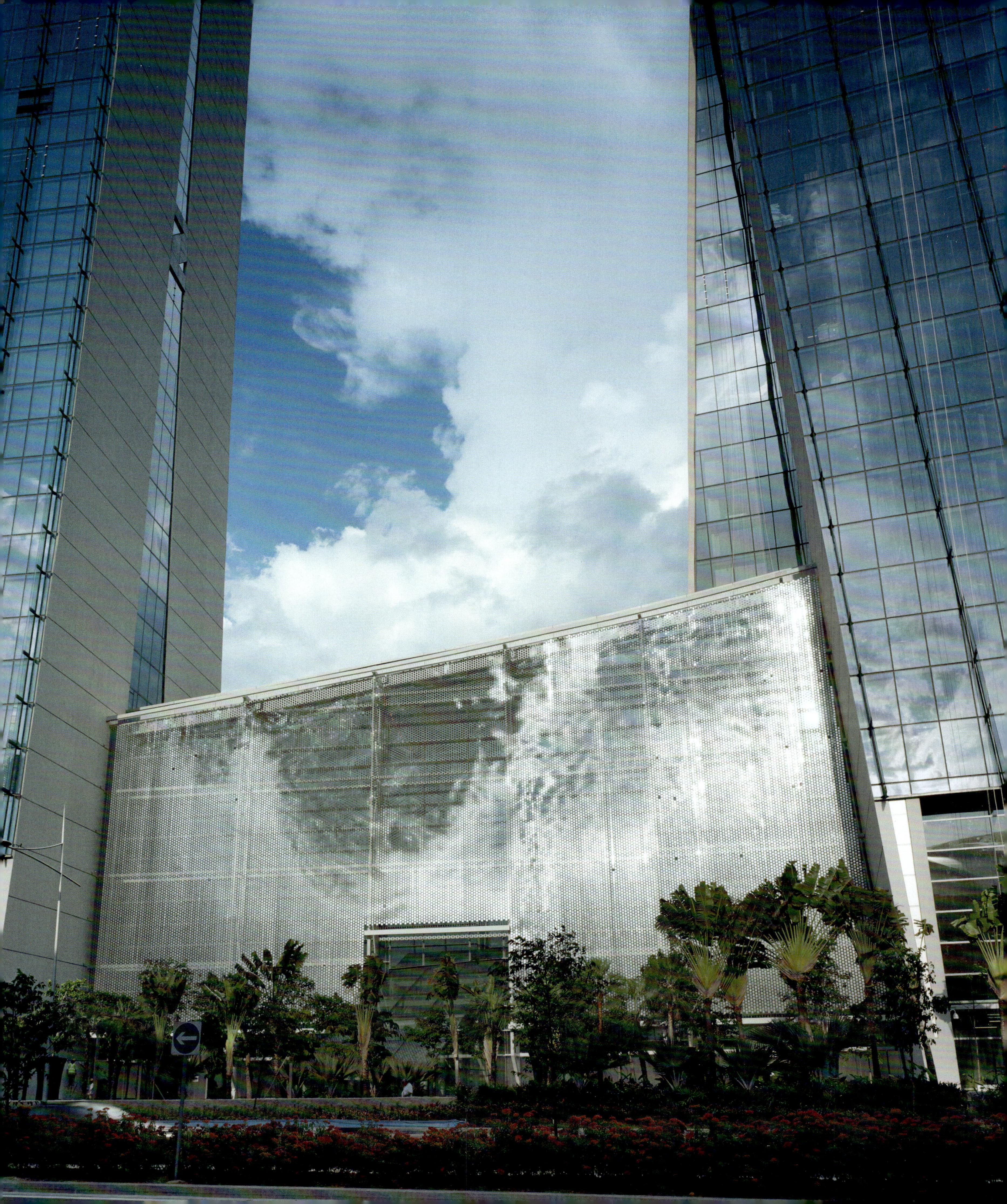

Top: Sol LeWitt wall drawing at Toronto Airport

Bottom: Richard Serra sculpture at Toronto Airport

vast complex his firm designed in 2007 in collaboration with Skidmore, Owings & Merrill and Adamson Associates under the moniker Airport Architects Canada—Safdie worked closely with Elsa Cameron, president and chief curator of Community Arts International, to weave eight commissioned artworks into the airport's striking architecture. Safdie brought this experience to Singapore and Marina Bay Sands.

Developer Sheldon Adelson and his wife, Dr. Miriam Adelson, have also made the integration of art an important element of the other Sands properties. In Las Vegas, Adelson commissioned Dutch architect Rem Koolhaas to design a jewel-like gallery, clad in Cor-ten steel and nestled in the lobby of the Venetian, to house a selection of masterpieces from Russia's renowned Hermitage Museum. The Solomon R. Guggenheim Museum became involved, resulting in what is now the Guggenheim Hermitage Museum at the Venetian. This inclusion of major international art museum franchises, designed by well-known architects, was something new for Las Vegas, adding another layer of sophistication to the activities for which the city's casino hotels are better known and putting Vegas on the map as an art destination.

While art was important to both client and architect from the start, the presence of site-specific works in all the major public spaces of the resort was made possible by a third interlocutor: the government of Singapore. Like other countries and cities around the world, Singapore has an arts incentive program, established in 2005, that mandates that a percentage of a project's overall budget be allocated to the creation of public art. According to the guidelines of Singapore's Urban Redevelopment Authority (URA), which oversees the program, such works must be permanent in nature, integrated with the architecture, and freely accessible to the public. Safdie admits to having had mixed experiences with such incentive programs, which are frequently administered by independent selection committees according to a particular agenda. Often the art is selected for its political correctness or thematic link to a project—think of the bronze statues of public figures that stand guard outside a police headquarters or other civic building. In some cases, the committee-chosen art can be very foreign to the architect's vision. In this instance, however, Safdie himself—with the full trust of his client, and working again with Cameron and Community Arts International—was able to personally invite a roster of internationally recognized artists to participate in developing an arts program extraordinary in size and ambition. Because of the scope of Marina Bay Sands, the percentage of its price tag earmarked for public art amounted to close to 50 million dollars. Since at the outset of the project no one on the developer's team would have conceived of spending such a sum on art, it is to the credit of Safdie and his firm's work with Singapore's URA that museum-quality commissions became such a significant element of Marina Bay Sands.

The Hotel Lobby

The Art Path at Marina Bay Sands begins just inside the resort's main entrance at Tower 1. Upon passing through the front doors, guests are surrounded by the work of some of the world's greatest contemporary artists—whether they know it or not. A brilliantly colored Sol LeWitt wall drawing beckons visitors to the reception desk. A massive stainless steel sculpture by Antony Gormley hovers overhead, high in the soaring atrium. And an installation by Zheng Chongbin, composed of eighty-three giant ceramic vessels holding a canopy of trees, marches down the length of the hotel's atrium, appearing in- and outside the majestic space.

From the earliest stages of the design process, Safdie and his associates collaborated closely with each artist to choose the right location for his commission. LeWitt, who died in 2007, had worked with Safdie on projects including the United States Federal Courthouse in Springfield, Massachusetts (2008), and Toronto's Terminal 1, and the architect knew that one of the late artist's works would be a perfect fit for Marina Bay Sands. LeWitt, considered a master of minimalist art, is known for his deceptively simple geometric sculptures and brightly colored, almost psychedelic, muralsize wall drawings and paintings. A frequent traveler to Italy during the 1970s, the artist moved to Spoleto with his wife in 1980 and lived there for many years. He had always been interested in the Renaissance painters, and the frescoes he saw in Italy—particularly those of Giotto in the Arena Chapel, in Padua, and of Piero della Francesca in the Basilica of San Francesco, in Arezzo—were an extraordinary inspiration to him. It was there that the mature form of his now-renowned wall drawings truly developed. "I would like to produce something that I would not be ashamed to show Giotto," he once said.

Wall Drawing #917, Arcs and Circles (1999)—a joyous arrangement of two rainbowlike semicircles flanking a circle filled with vertical and horizontal stripes—displays the vivid use of color characteristic of LeWitt's later work. The bold composition, nearly 4.5 meters high by

Installation of Sol LeWitt wall drawing in Marina Bay Sands Hotel lobby: a tent protected the work and artists while the piece was painted in-situ.

247

Moshe Safdie and Antony Gormley review a study for *Drift* in the artist's London studio.

20.5 meters long, fills the wall behind Tower 1's reception desk with radiating stripes and arcs, some straight, some wavy, in hues of green, red, blue, orange, yellow, and purple. LeWitt wall drawings of this scale can take weeks to produce, as teams painstakingly follow directions set out by the artist. While a drawing may be installed many times, and in different locations simultaneously for temporary exhibitions and permanent commissions like those at Marina Bay Sands, it may vary only slightly in size and never in format. Safdie worked closely with art advisor Cameron on all of the Art Path's commissions, and she ascertained that LeWitt's estate had three wall drawings that were large enough and had the necessary horizontal orientation for the project. Safdie knew the artist's daughter Sofia from his previous collaborations with her father, and together they chose two wall drawings for Marina Bay Sands. The second, *Wall Drawing #915, Arcs, Circle, and Irregular Bands* (1999), is sited in the underground pedestrian network connecting Marina Bay Sands to the Bayfront Mass Rapid Transit (MRT) Station. Artists Takeshi Arita and Gabriel Hunter, who worked with LeWitt for many years, executed the wall drawings, assisted by four local artists chosen by Singapore's Tyler Print Institute.

Even more of a challenge to install was *Drift*, Antony Gormley's three-dimensional stainless steel sculpture, seven stories tall, which hangs inside the atrium of Tower 1 like a cloud above the earth. It appears delicate, airy, and lightweight. In fact, it is a web of more than 16,000 rods and more than 8,300 nodes, slightly smaller than ping-pong balls, formed into packed polyhedra that follow bubble matrix geometry. Approximately 40 meters long, 23 meters high, and 15 meters wide, it was one of the most complex of the art commissions to produce and is one of the artist's largest works to date.

For the main lobby, Safdie wanted something to complement the character of the atrium and its soaring atmosphere, a work that would occupy but also create space. Gormley—best known for public projects such as *Habitat*, a giant humanoid sculpture in Alaska; *Event Horizon*, a group of thirty-one statues in his own likeness (and naked, to boot) scattered for several months around London in 2007 and New York in 2010; and *Asian Field*, an array of 180,000 terra-cotta

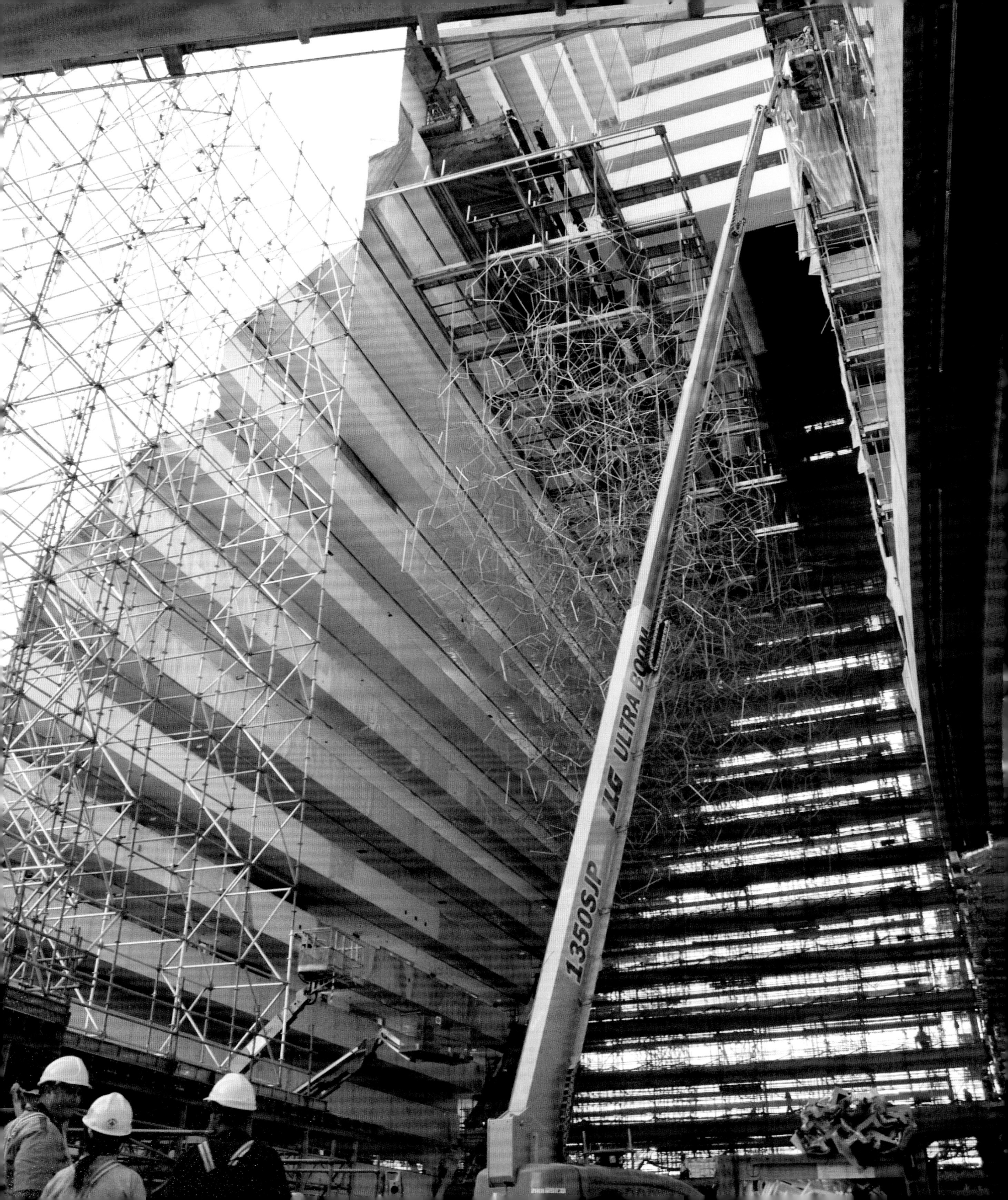
ULTRA BOOM
1350SJP

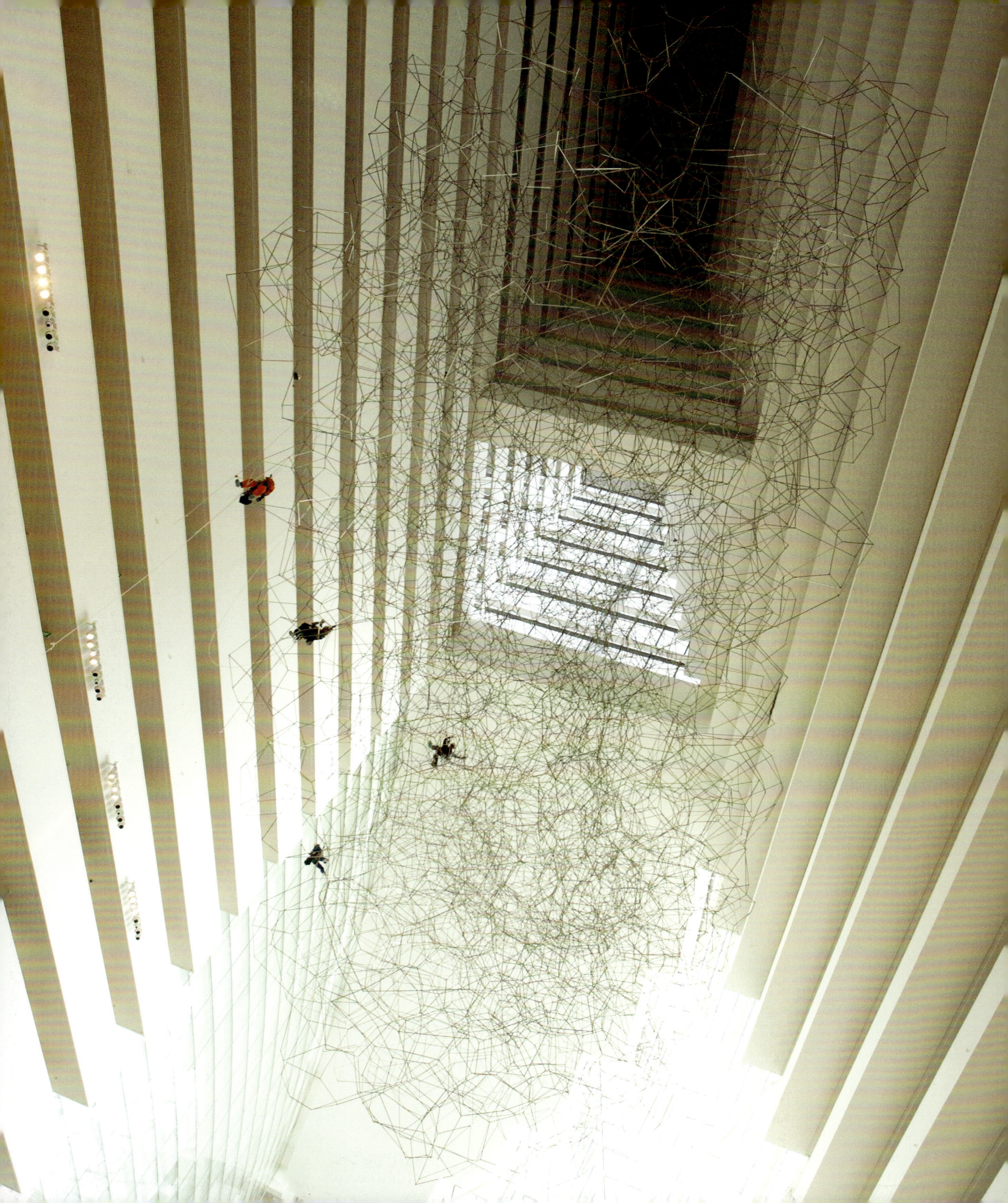

Workers cleaning *Drift* before Marina Bay Sands opening

figurines commissioned for the 2006 Sydney Biennale—makes figurative and abstract sculpture that explores the relationship of the human body to space in both large-scale installations and singular, smaller pieces. He was a natural choice for this important commission.

Safdie visited Gormley many times in his sprawling London studio, just north of King's Cross station, during the development of this complex sculpture. The artist, whose works are often described as three-dimensional drawings in space, builds models to test the spatial and physical effect of his projects. The architect recalls: "Gormley and I spent a lot of time lying on his studio floor, looking up at various mock-ups suspended from the ceiling, so we could imagine the experience visitors would have with *Drift* once it was installed at Marina Bay Sands."

"*Drift* exists somewhere on the cusp between a drawing and a thing," says Gormley. "Seen from a distance, it appears as delicate as a line drawing, yet it has the mass to be described as an object and even occupies a large enough field to be considered a place." His idea was to internalize the external conditions of weather, referencing an emergence of form from chaos that is both cosmological and biological. *Drift* engages and activates the space of the atrium in such a way that visitors, in moving their bodies, contemplate their personal relationships with space. Because of its vast expanse, the sculpture has no singular vantage point. Different locations provide different views and experiences. Looking down or across the atrium, one can see the linked open cells of the work in long sight lines running through the connective geometry. From below, one senses the cloudlike *Drift* overhead. From the upper guest-room corridors facing the atrium on both sides, one can almost inhabit the cloud.

While the architects and engineers worked closely on-site with all of the Art Path artists, John Downs, the Marina Bay Sands project architect, says that, "figuring out how to install *Drift* was especially complex and challenging because of its sheer size and many, many individual parts." Downs and his team worked closely with Gormley and his engineer, Tristan Simmonds, to realize the artist's vision. Because of the monumental scale of the sculpture, its elements were assembled off-site, and Gormley visited often to oversee the process. The team determined that the best way to install *Drift* was to break it down into eight horizontal slices, each approximately 3 meters tall, and transport them to Marina Bay Sands. Describing the process, Safdie notes: "I will never forget the day I walked into a big factory of steel fabricators and the Gormley sculpture was being assembled—layers and layers of it, and bandaged to protect the steel. Even in that stage, I could tell that it was a great work of art." In the end, it took more than sixty workers, each with a different expertise, from engineering to welding, to assemble and mount *Drift* in the atrium. Most visitors will never know the extraordinary effort that went into creating this ethereal yet monumental work, which appears to hover so effortlessly over the buzz of activity below.

One way to view the Gormley is by engaging with yet another site-specific installation—sculptures by Jerusalem-based artist Israel Hadany that function as benches. Shimmering aqua glass plates create the impression of water rippling over large stones, and each stone has a smooth ledge that invites people to sit. From the vantage point of this artwork, titled *Motion*, visitors can see *Drift* above, the LeWitt behind the Tower 1 reception desk, and three other Art Path installations in the distance. Unlike these pieces, however, *Motion* was conceived not during but after the design and construction of the resort complex. Hadany, therefore, had the unique opportunity of creating a work in response to the Marina Bay Sands architect and also to some of the project's other artists.

Hadany is perhaps best known for his many large-scale outdoor public sculptures, including the *Arthur Rubinstein Memorial*, in Aminadav Forest, Israel (1984); *Twisted Arch*, in Williamsport, Pennsylvania (1978); and *Light Tower*, at the Virginia Center for the Arts in Sweet Briar, Virginia (1988). His smaller-scale works, made from multilayered laminated plywood, reside in the collections of museums around the world, and it was one of these sculptures that captured Safdie's attention. During a 2003 visit to the Israel Museum in Jerusalem, the architect spied Hadany's *Ephesus* (1999) as he strolled through the galleries with a colleague. He was intrigued by the work's ambiguity, unable to discern whether it was abstract or figurative, anthropomorphic or architectural. "It links themes from myths and Egyptian, Mesopotamian, and Greek art, yet remains totally architectural," Safdie recalls. His experience of the sculpture moved him to visit Hadany in his studio the next day to see more of his work, and their conversation continued with the opportunities provided by Marina Bay Sands.

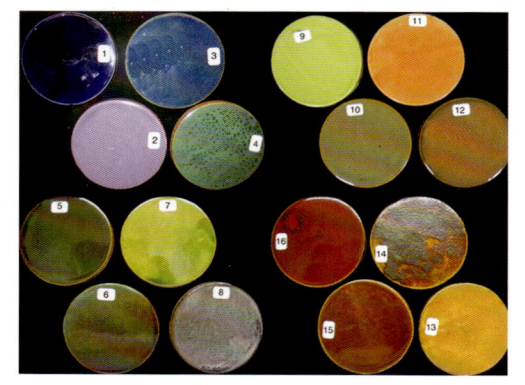

Top: Zheng Chongbin measuring ceramic vessels for *Rising Forest*

Middle: Glazing samples for *Rising Forest*

In 2010, Safdie invited Hadany to create a sculpture that would function as seating—an installation that would allow people to pause, to rest, to enjoy the art and architecture—yet still enable fluid circulation of visitors through Tower 1. "I flew to Singapore with certain ideas in my mind but had to carefully study the spatial, physical, and human behavior within the lobby space," says the artist of his first visit to Marina Bay Sands. "I learned that the lobby functions as an 'urban piazza', where passing and gathering people create an intense dynamic movement." Hadany's task was a sensitive one: he had to make something bold enough to hold its own in the soaring atrium yet low enough not to compete with the works by Gormley and LeWitt already in place.

Hadany says he titled the work *Motion* because: "It is a visual metaphor of a flowing river, a symbolic attempt to bring nature into an architectural environment, a 'natural' landscape constructed of rigid materials, glass and stone, brought into motion by a mysterious wind." Safdie notes that the Israeli sculptor never stops surprising his audience and that, in his contribution to Marina Bay Sands, he both accommodates and defies gravity. "He deploys geometry—recurrent themes in nature, layers, terraces, interpenetrating and overlapping curvatures. At the same time, this geometry evokes spirituality, memory, myth. While drawing on the past, Hadany's sculptures leap into the future."

Of all the works in the resort complex, the Chinese artist Zheng Chongbin's *Rising Forest* was perhaps the most controversial, because, at first, Singapore's URA questioned whether the proposed installation of eighty-three monumental glazed stoneware vessels was indeed art and not merely decoration. Safdie and his team prevailed, convincing the URA of Zheng's acknowledged stature as a world-renowned artist and of *Rising Forest*'s merit as public art. Zheng, who currently divides his time between San Rafael in northern California and Shanghai, is best known for his ink brush paintings but also works frequently in ceramics. For *Rising Forest*, he initially explored several approaches: one focused on pots made of porcelain; a second involved pots with patterned glazes. In the solution Safdie and the artist chose to pursue, the pots are glazed in a range of solid colors, in warm and cool shades, with a watery, almost shimmery finish. Each vessel holds a tree, creating a green canopy across the interior and exterior atrium spaces of Towers 1, 2, and 3. PWP Landscape Architecture, the landscape designer for the entire resort complex, recommended ficus, which can survive indoors and out; firm representatives personally selected each individual tree.

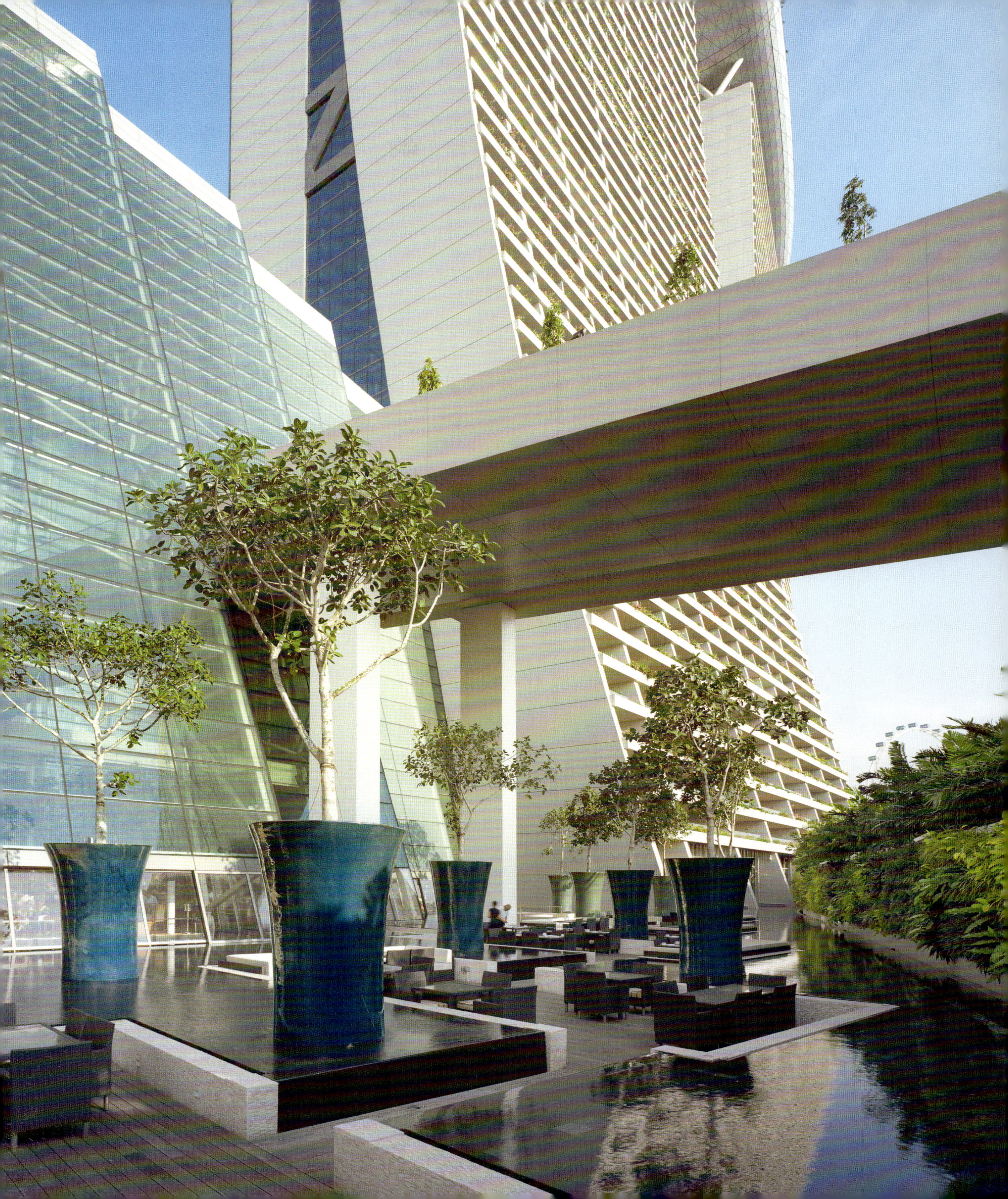

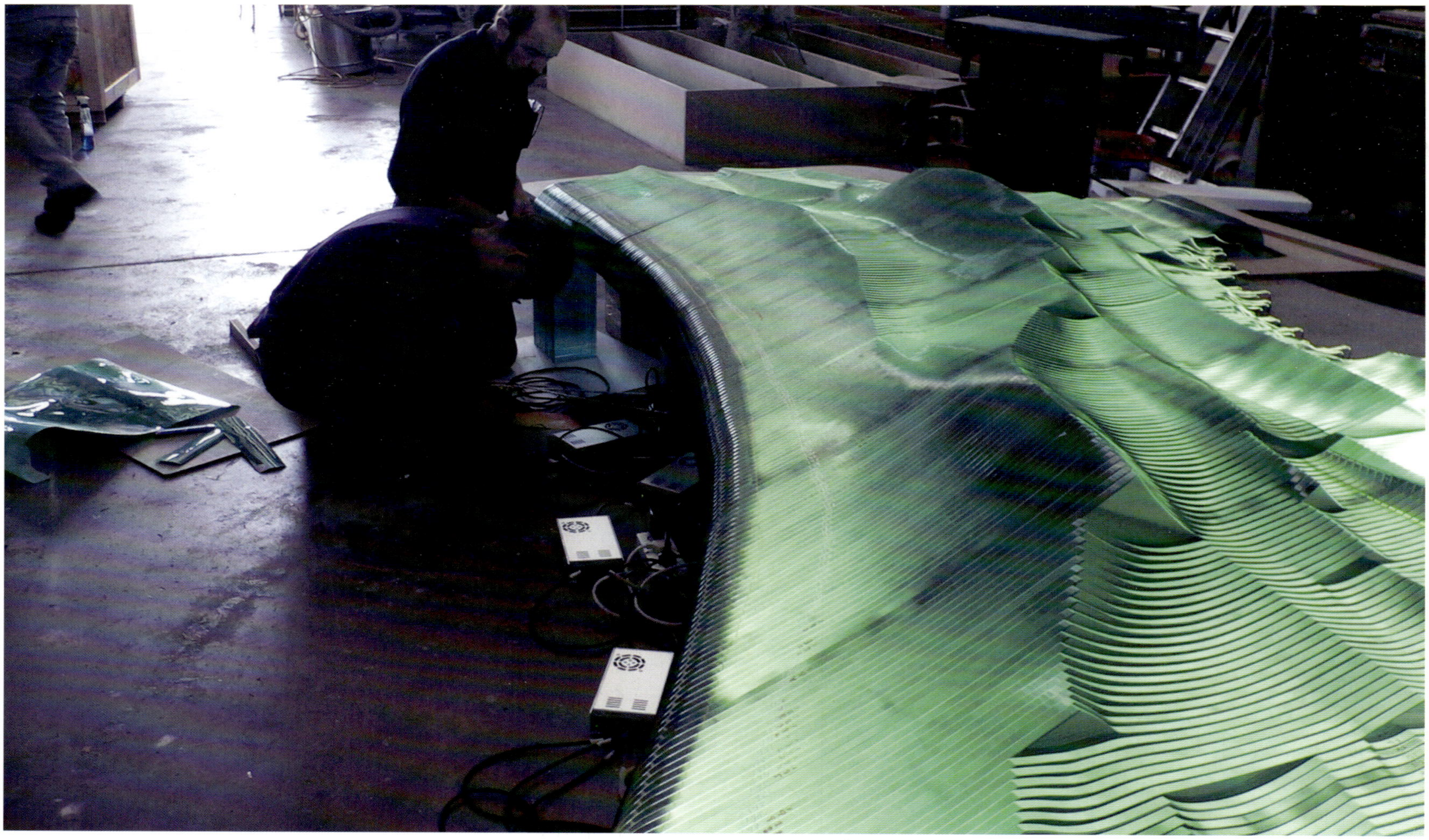
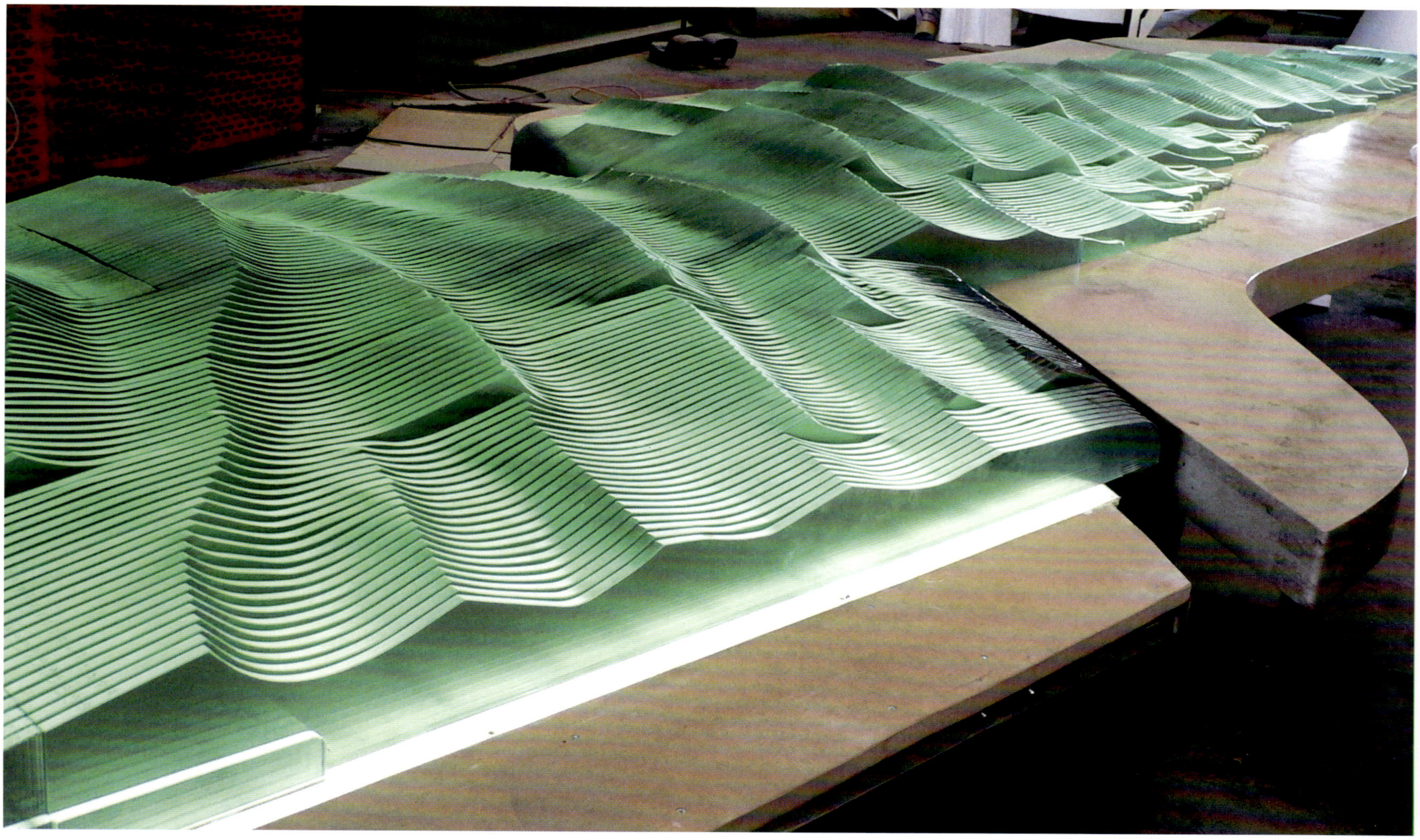

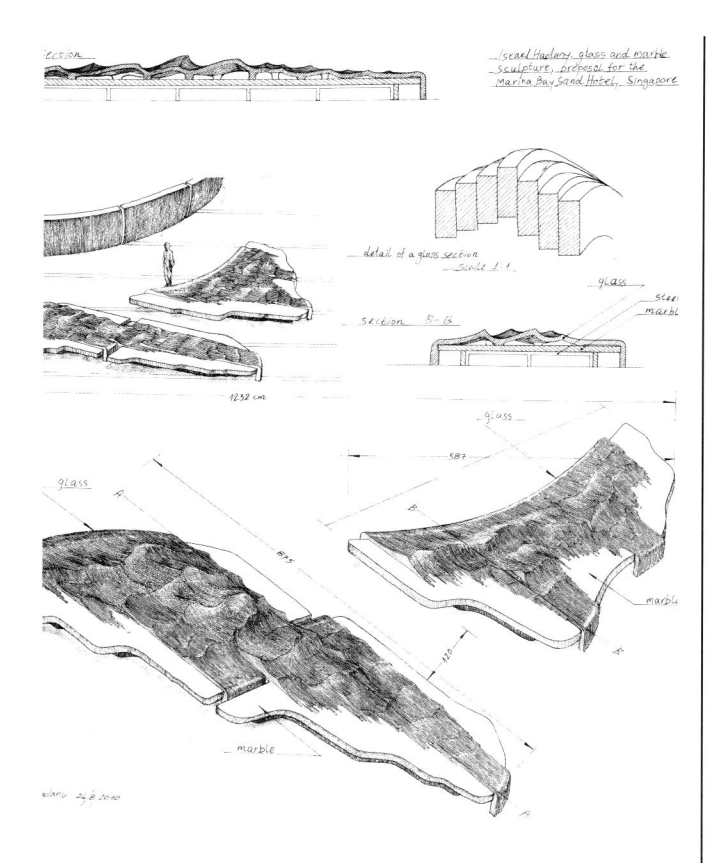

Preparatory sketch of Motion, by Israel Hadany

Zheng's installation, like Gormley's, had its own particular challenges. Because the ceramic pots are so large—each 1,200 kilograms and 3 meters tall—the artist had to build four custom kilns the size of small buildings to fire them. Zheng and his team of artisans made each pot by hand using the traditional coil method, stacking rings of clay until they achieved the desired height and shape. *Rising Forest* represents a major breakthrough in ceramic art, marking the first time in history that such a large-scale work has been fired in one piece. It took more than a month to complete just one stoneware vessel, including the application of the glazes, which the artisans brushed on by hand, much as Zheng would produce one of his signature ink paintings.

Safdie worked closely with Zheng to select the color palette for *Rising Forest*. While the glazes are characteristic of traditional Chinese pottery, the artist was also inspired by Josef Albers' color theory—outlined in his seminal book *Interaction of Color*—which asserts that colors function optically in relationship to each other and need one another to form a unified visual statement. The palette of *Rising Forest* moves from cool to warm (or vice-versa, depending on the direction from which one approaches the work), and the colors exert a mutual influence, with lighter-hued vessels appearing larger in scale and darker ones smaller. "They are a visual symphony," Zheng declares, "singing both color and form as they stand together."

Although each vessel is unique, for Zheng, the individual units compose a single sculpture. He and his team made the pots in Yixing, China, a region renowned for ceramic artistry since the eleventh century. The clay was mined from a special quarry in Yellow Dragon Mountain and aged for five years before it was ready for use. During production, Zheng maintained a rigorous quality-control process, making many extra vessels to ensure that the ones selected for *Rising Forest* could be as perfect as possible. "I chose to create eighty-three pots," says Zheng, "because numbers are very symbolic in Chinese culture. Eight plus three equals eleven, which is a number of great strength and power, and the idea of oneness is integral to my concept for *Rising Forest*."

While the ceramic vessels loom over visitors to Marina Bay Sands, their sheer size, combined with the canopy of trees, allows the installation to mitigate the soaring height of the hotel atrium, bringing nature inside at a scale familiar to all. In certain spaces of Tower 1's atrium, Zheng's forest almost meets Gormley's hovering cloud. Zheng describes *Rising Forest* as a repetitive object that works through serial progression: "It is an energy field that spans an interactive space between the inner and outer atria. From every perspective, the work changes depending on the viewer's physical location and perspective, looking up or down, left or right. The work creates transformation by color, the notion of its abstraction, gradation, and the seasons." Zheng's minimalist approach has created a masterful contemporary interpretation of ancient Chinese traditions.

Indoors and Out

The installations on the Marina Bay Sands Art Path are not intended only for hotel guests. In fact, part of what qualifies all these works as public art is that they can be seen and experienced by anyone at any time. Safdie and the Marina Bay Sands team commissioned several of the artists to create works so seamlessly integrated with the resort's buildings that, at first glance, one might understandably think they're part of the architecture. Ned Kahn, an environmental artist and sculptor based in Sebastopol, in northern California, is responsible for three such commissions.

Kahn is known for striking installations that capture an ephemeral aspect of nature, such as wind, water, or fog. From 1982 to 1996, he designed educational exhibits at San Francisco's Exploratorium, where he apprenticed with the center's founder, Frank Oppenheimer, the brother of renowned atomic physicist J. Robert Oppenheimer. In the late 1980s, he began developing his own independent work, frequently conducting lab experiments and analyses to test his ideas. Often sited in public or institutional settings, Kahn's work, much like that of fellow artist Olafur Eliasson, blurs the distinction between art and science and reveals his engagement with atmospheric physics, geology, astronomy, and fluid motion. His keen interest in natural elements, how they interact and behave independently, is the foundation of all of his projects. No less important to Kahn is how visitors respond to his work—that they first experience its effects as natural and only later realize they were constructed artificially. He often conceals the technical expertise and high-tech materials behind the complex "natural" systems at play in his work, foregrounding instead the engagement of the audience. In recognition of his intriguing and groundbreaking work, Kahn won a prestigious MacArthur Fellowship—or "genius grant"—in 2003, and in 2004 received a National Design Award from the Smithsonian's Cooper-Hewitt, National Design Museum.

Artist Ned Kahn reviews mock-up of *Wind Arbor*

For Marina Bay Sands, Kahn created two installations that animate particular exterior surfaces of the resort's architecture. His third piece, *Rain Oculus*, is a signature feature inside the retail mall. Like many of the other artists, Kahn had worked with Safdie before, designing *Quantum Wave* for the Bureau of Alcohol, Tobacco, and Firearms headquarters, in Washington, D.C. (2008) and *Rainbow Arbor* for Los Angeles's Skirball Cultural Center (final phase completed in 2013). Marina Bay Sands was, in fact, their fifth collaboration, and Kahn remembers Safdie asking him to imagine works large enough to complement the resort's grand scale. Of the five he proposed, Safdie accepted three. "Moshe told me to 'just go for it,'" the artist recalls, "and a couple of ideas seemed really compelling to us, because we realized that my work could help solve particular architectural or environmental issues involved with the project."

One of these dual-function artworks is Kahn's *Wind Arbor*, the largest and most visible commission on the Art Path: at more than 6,800 square meters, it is equivalent in size to the surface area of five-and-a-half Olympic swimming pools. The sculpture covers the entire western facade of the Marina Bay Sands Hotel atrium and is not only beautiful but also practical, concealing some of the building's mechanical systems and providing much-needed shade from the intense Singapore sun. Kahn devised a screenlike surface of 260,000 aluminum "flappers," which ripple and oscillate when caught by the wind, sculpting the facade into a shimmering surface that from afar looks almost as if water were washing over it. The featherweight flappers, mounted on hinges and hung from steel cables so they can move independently, respond to even the subtlest changes in the wind. At times, the whole wall appears to move. Viewed up close, the aluminum screen is reminiscent of the iconic dress of connected metal disks by fashion designer Paco Rabanne (who, coincidentally, originally trained as an architect). Kahn has created other sculptures that respond to air currents, but *Wind Arbor* is his largest such piece to date and was among the first Art Path commissions. Because energy conservation was an important consideration for the entire Marina Bay Sands project, Kahn's wind-animated facade is doubly important for its contribution to the sustainable aspects of the resort's architecture. The panels bounce back 50 percent of the sunlight that hits them, thus decreasing the heat load on the air-conditioning system.

Tipping Wall, which conceals the cooling tower adjacent to the southern end of the hotel, greets visitors arriving by car at the quieter Tower 3 of the hotel complex. Kahn's kinetic sculptural surface features 7,000 mechanical polycarbonate channels attached to a glass-reinforced concrete wall that is nearly as large as a basketball court. Water running down the wall fills the white channels. Each tips right or left like a seesaw, spilling water into the channels below and creating a chain reaction fascinating to watch. The water pools in a catchment area below the tippers and recirculates so the whole process can begin again. To test his idea for *Tipping Wall*, Kahn designed a smaller freestanding version in 2008 for the Sebastopol Center for the Arts. In the prototype, the artist connected the polycarbonate channels to steel cables strung inside a circular frame. Water running down the steel cables fills the channels and triggers the tipping and spilling. "As each channel fills with water, it must 'decide' to tip either left or right

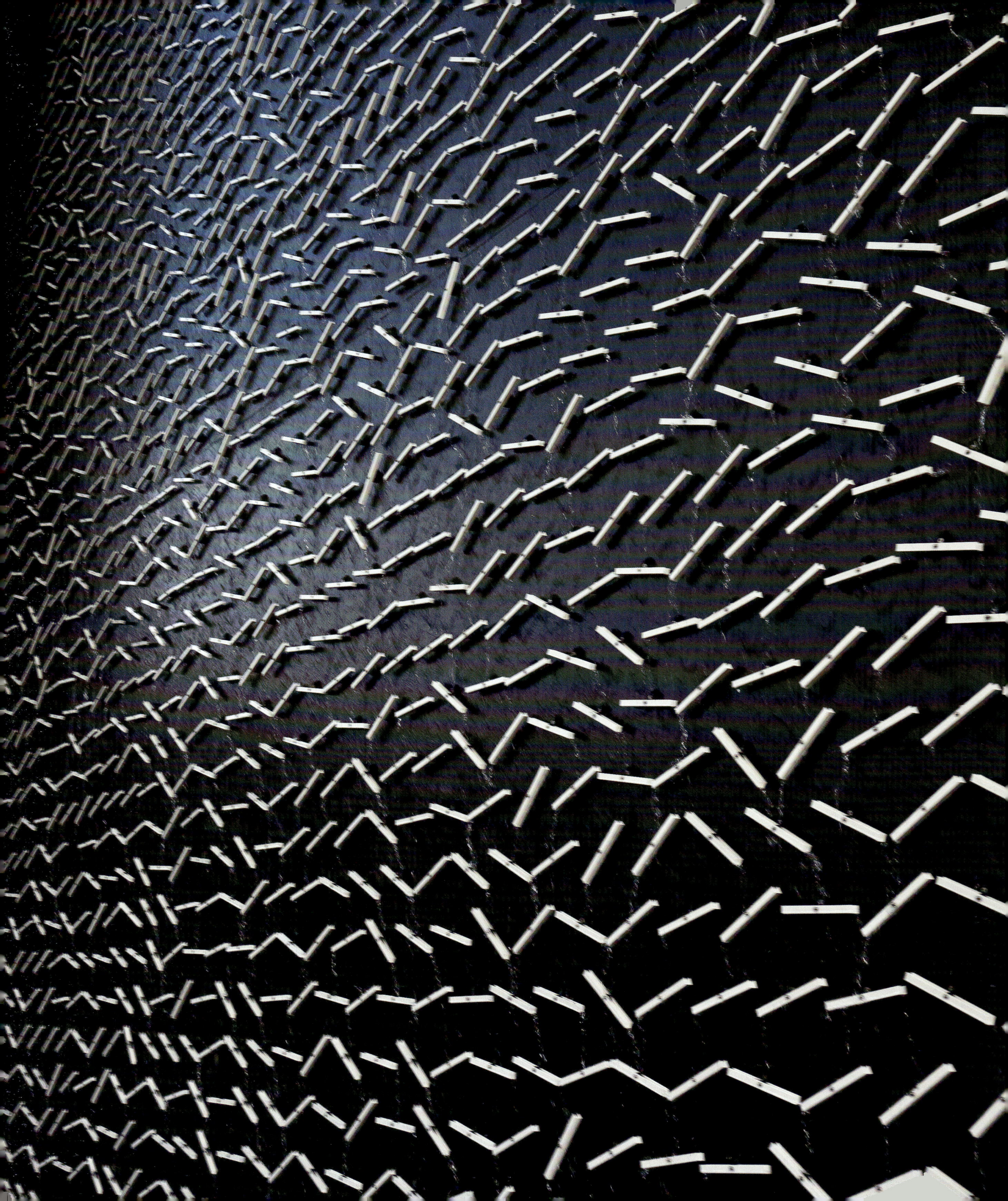

Top: Construction image of *Rain Oculus*

Bottom: Kahn's inspiration for *Rain Oculus*

and spill water into either of the two channels below. Thus, the entire array becomes an interrelated web of water decisions," says Kahn. At Marina Bay Sands, *Tipping Wall* takes on a different form at night, as lights bouncing off the water animate the facade with a shifting pattern of shadows from the tilting channels.

Rain Oculus, the third of Kahn's site-specific works at Marina Bay Sands, delights visitors, old and young alike, to the resort's vast retail mall. As with *Tipping Wall*, Kahn uses water to create a dramatic and somewhat mysterious effect. At the central location where the mall and waterfront promenade intersect, a large transparent bowl becomes a dynamic, water-filled skylight. Water roils and churns to create a whirlpool inside the skylight, building up enough pressure for it to gush out through a hole in the center. The rainlike torrent falls into a pool two stories below at the mall's promenade level. It is not uncommon for people to wait patiently for the next awe-inspiring "rainfall." As usual, Kahn hides the sophisticated technology used to create the marvelous illusion of nature at work, emphasizing instead the audience's experience. The mechanics of *Rain Oculus* consist of a 22-meter-diameter acrylic bowl mounted on top of a basketlike tubular stainless steel superstructure. The combined weight of the bowl, or oculus, and superstructure is 90 tonnes. Water rushes into the bowl at 22,700 liters per minute. As soon as the water reaches the maximum weight the bowl can hold, or 200 tonnes, it rushes down into the mall. Just as in his other site-specific installations at Marina Bay Sands, the artist uses a natural force to create a sculptural effect.

Like Ned Kahn, James Carpenter—one of the most respected architectural glass artists in the world—is deeply interested in enriching the viewer's relationship with natural phenomena in urban environments. Also like Kahn, Carpenter was honored, in 2004, with a MacArthur Fellowship for his innovative and evocative work. For Marina Bay Sands, the artist and his New York–based firm, James Carpenter Design Associates, created an elegant site-specific work for the casino. *Blue Reflection Facade with Light Entry Passage* transforms the upper and lower concrete outer walls of the venue, which might otherwise be somewhat monotonous, into shimmering reflective surfaces. Both Kahn's and Carpenter's exterior installations are so well integrated with Safdie's architecture that they are not as immediately recognizable as art works as LeWitt's wall drawings or Gormley's *Drift*. Yet, they are perhaps almost more significant, because they enliven the more functional corners of the resort's architecture, transforming areas primarily devoted to service and engineering—vehicular bays, cooling towers, mechanical systems—into spaces no less glamorous than the Marina Bay Sands Hotel lobby.

On the front of the casino, Carpenter's installation nods to Las Vegas with a clever spin on Sin City's flashing lights and LED signage. Carpenter, who received his architecture degree from the Rhode Island School of Design, works with light. His projects straddle the fields of art, architecture, and engineering, ranging from sculptural installations to unique structural designs. Most recently, he and his firm completed the planning and design of five new buildings for the Israel Museum in Jerusalem (2010). Of his projects in general he says: "Light in transmission, reflection, and refraction as it is perceived is the work's initial inspiration and becomes a guiding principle, whether designing a site-specific work or a complete architectural project."

His treatment of the casino exterior has two sections, as suggested by the work's title. The "passage" refers to the recessed pedestrian-level entrance, which Carpenter sets aglow with a frosted-glass wall backlit by blue LED lights. On the three stories above the entrance, he wraps the casino's serpentine facade with a series of vertical, louverlike fins of glass and stainless steel to create a luminous "blue reflection" that changes depending on the hour. Light and airy by day, it mirrors the bright blue Singapore sky; dramatic by night, it reflects the blue beams of giant spotlights below. Carpenter's installation transforms a dark and nondescript space into something majestic. For visitors in vehicles or on foot, the work's dynamic visual layering signals the entrance to the casino.

Unlike the other works on the Art Path, Chinese sculptor Zhan Wang's *Artificial Rock #71* and *Artificial Rock #86* were not commissioned by Moshe Safdie but instead acquired by Sheldon Adelson. These works represent Zhan's engagement with the scholar's rock, which, long revered for its complexity and beauty, occupies a place of honor in gardens and courtyards throughout China. Inspired by these natural forms, Zhan intends his highly reflective abstract sculptures to represent his rapidly changing country. Here, located on the Garden Bay Bridge, their mercurial, mirror-finish surfaces reflect, as well, the rapidly changing image of Marina Bay and Singapore. Zhan, based in Beijing, is best known

Rain Oculus in operation

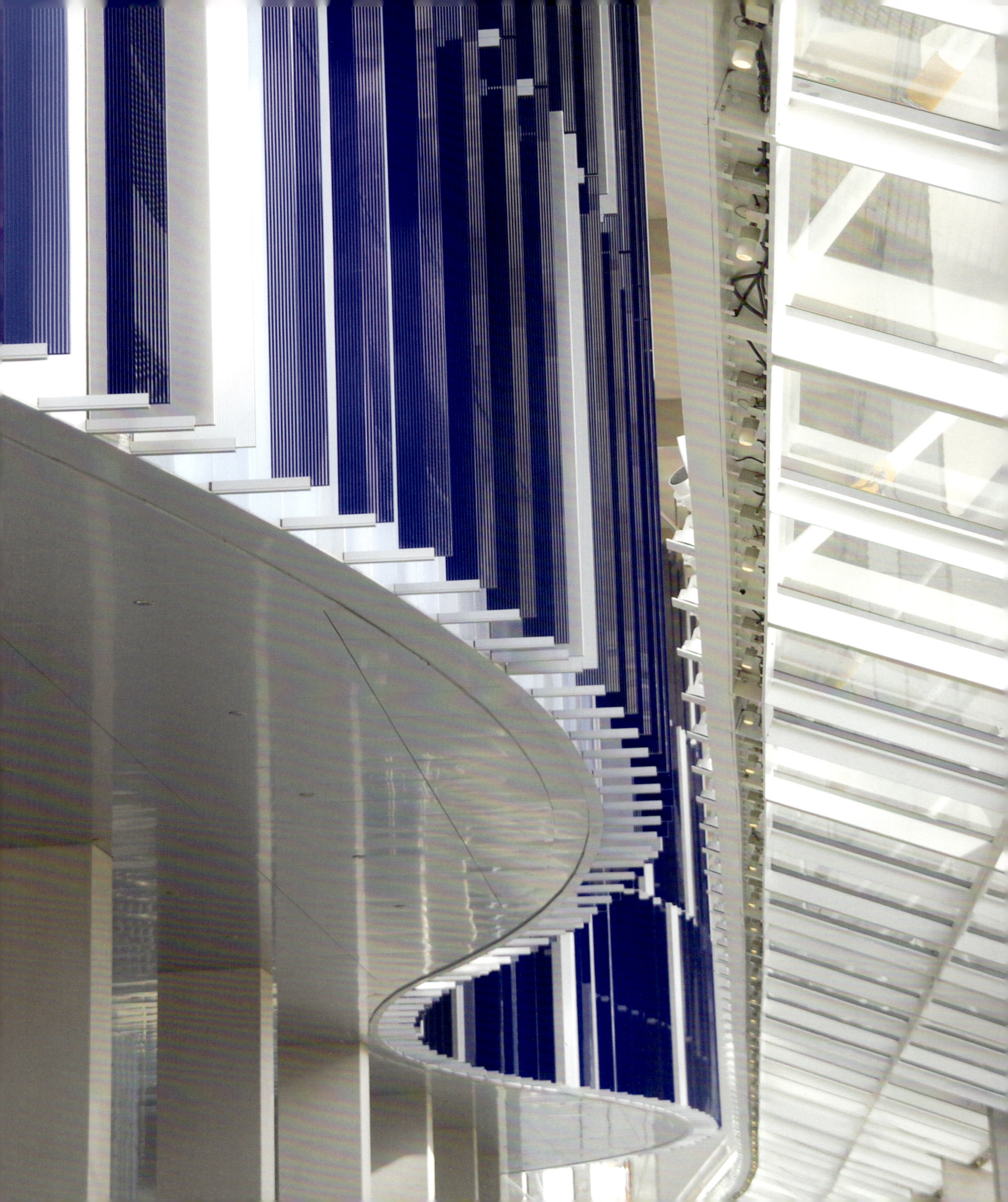

James Carpenter's Blue Reflection Facade with Light Entry Passage

in the West for his monumental *Artificial Rock #59*, which, in 2008, towered over visitors in the Great Court of London's British Museum.

Filling out the Art Path's portfolio is quite possibly the resort's largest and most spectacular work of art: Moshe Safdie's ArtScience Museum. The building's striking white sculptural form, which resembles the open hand of Buddha or a lotus in full flower, floats on a reflecting pool and, visible from near and far, has become both a symbol of Marina Bay Sands and a fitting metaphor for the commitment of all involved in the inclusion of art at the resort. The Art Path at Marina Bay Sands is a rare and remarkable achievement on many levels. Never before has a commercial development embraced such a complex, varied, and integrated public art program. The Art Path is the result of an ambitious and inspiring collaborative process that unites art with architecture in a dramatic setting accessible to all. Together, architect and client, working closely with the Singapore government, have created an extraordinary collection of works by world-renowned artists that, for years to come, will delight visitors at every turn.

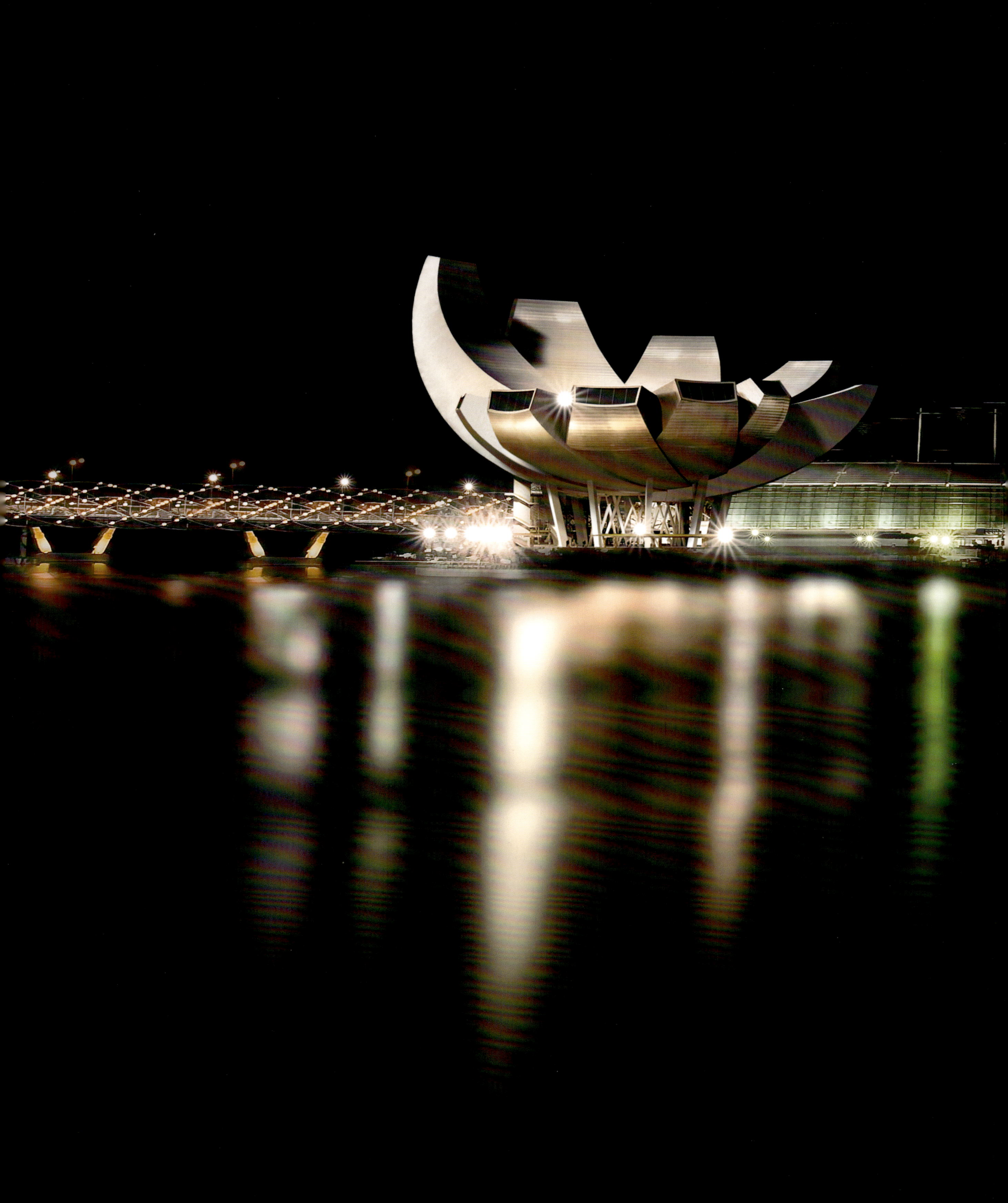

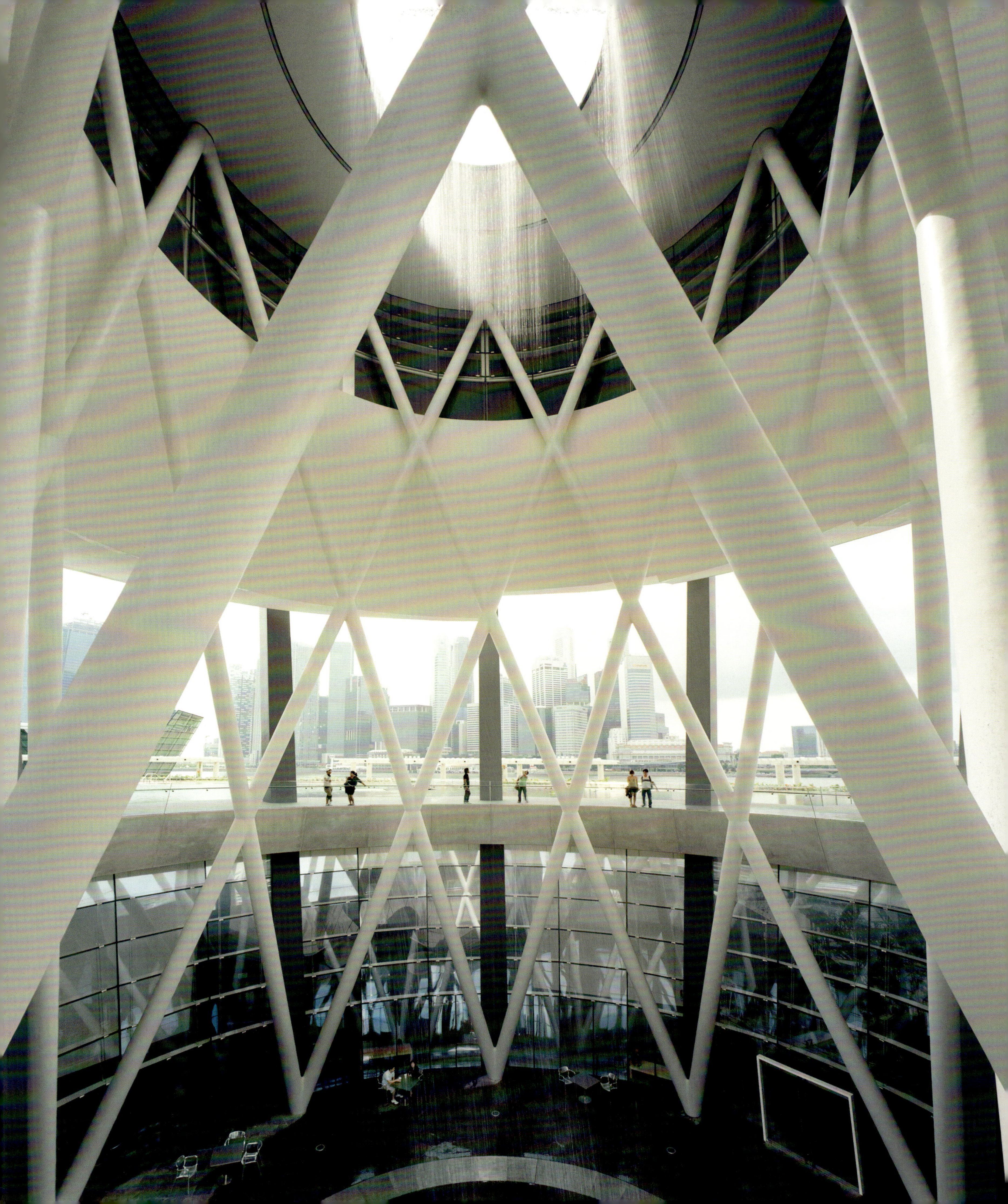

PART 5
A PLACE FOR THE PEOPLE

MARINA BAY SANDS

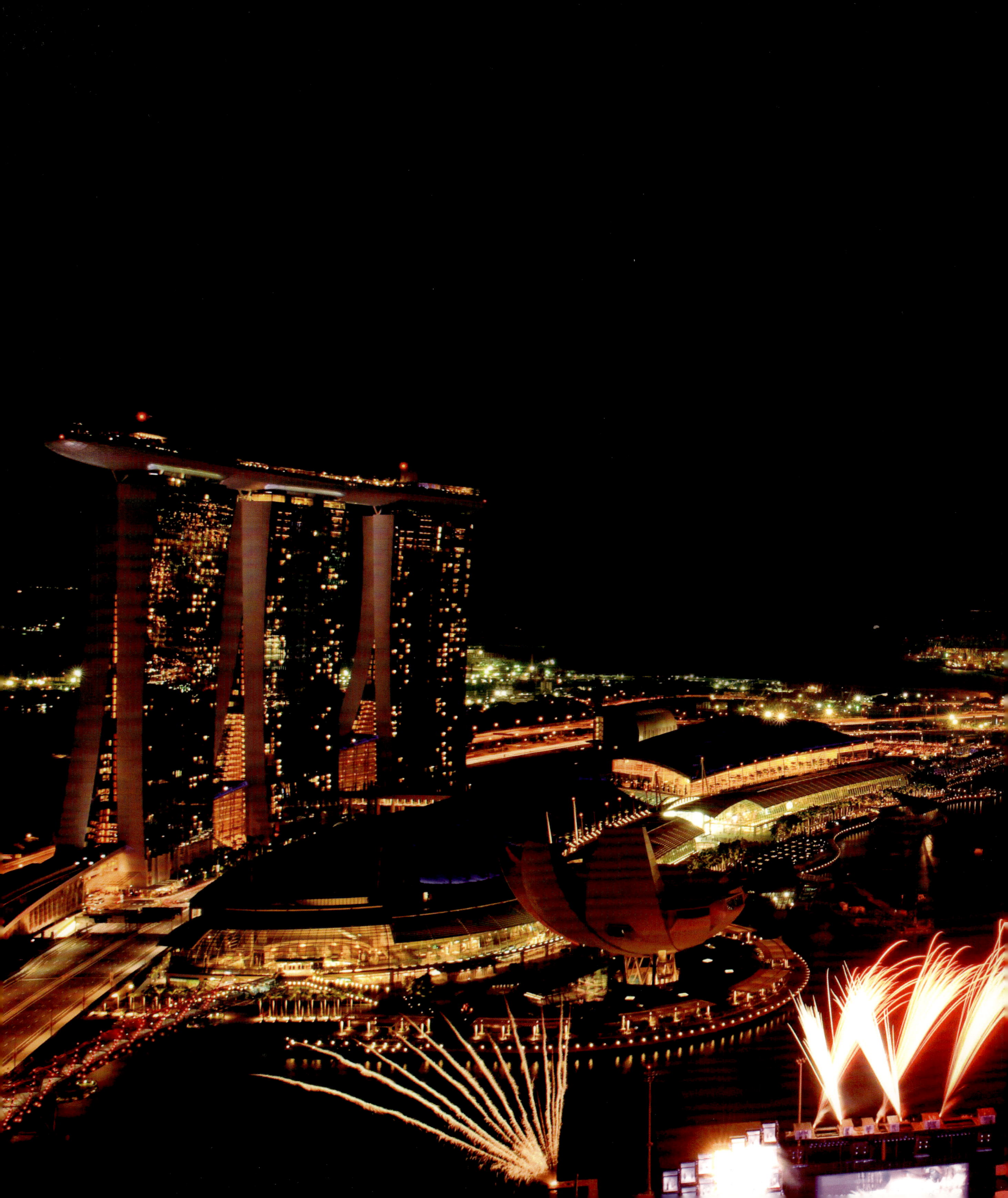

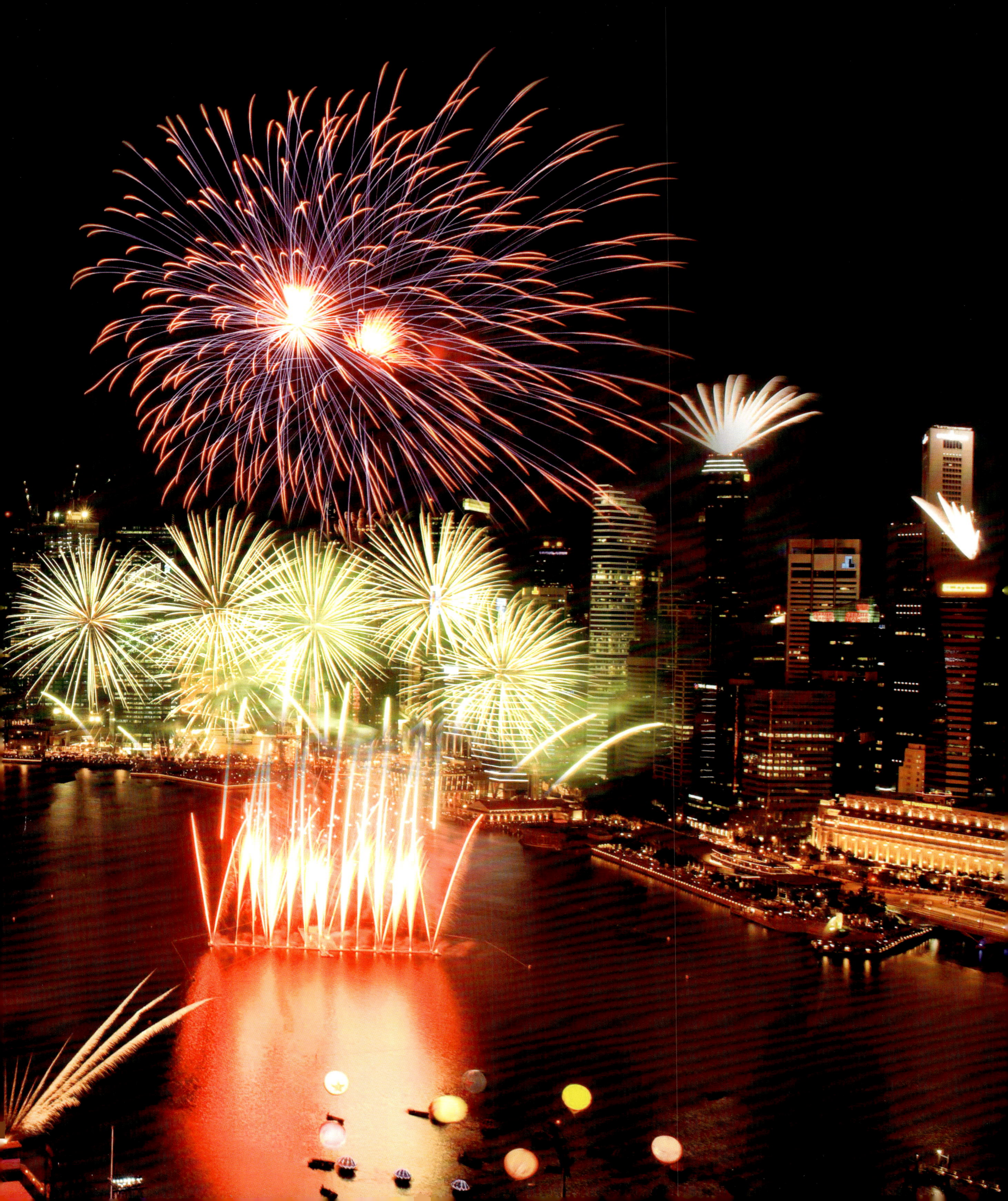

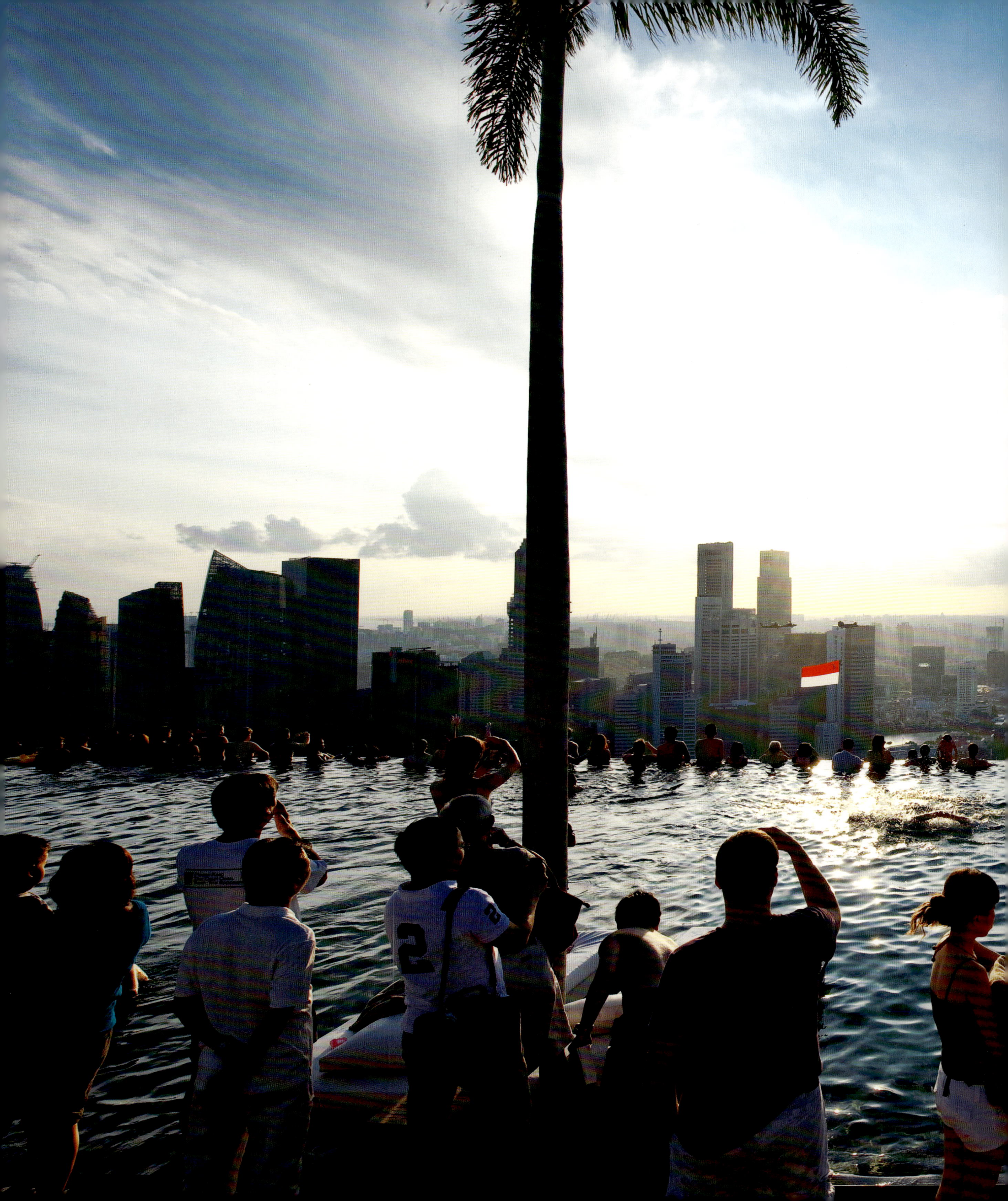

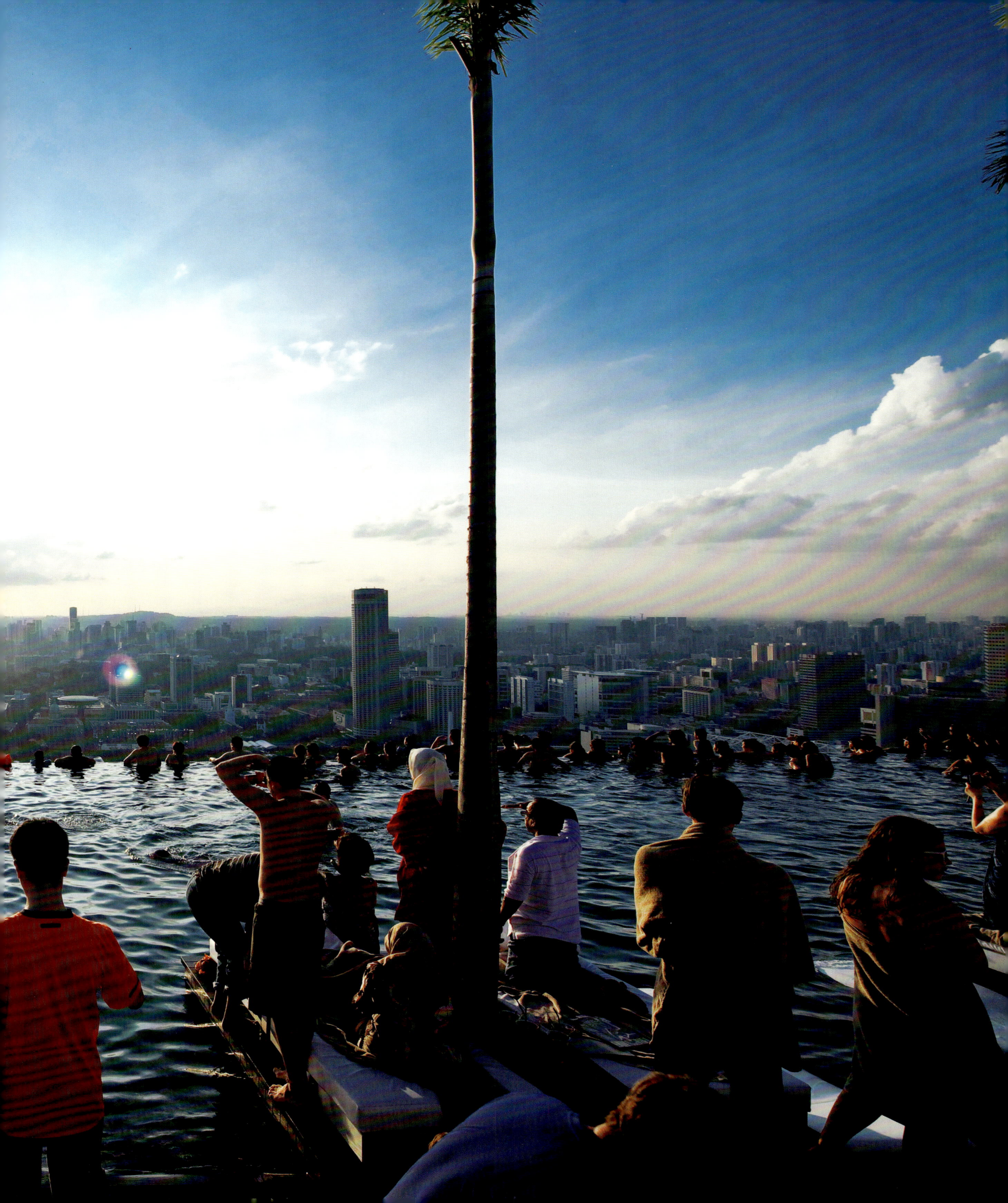

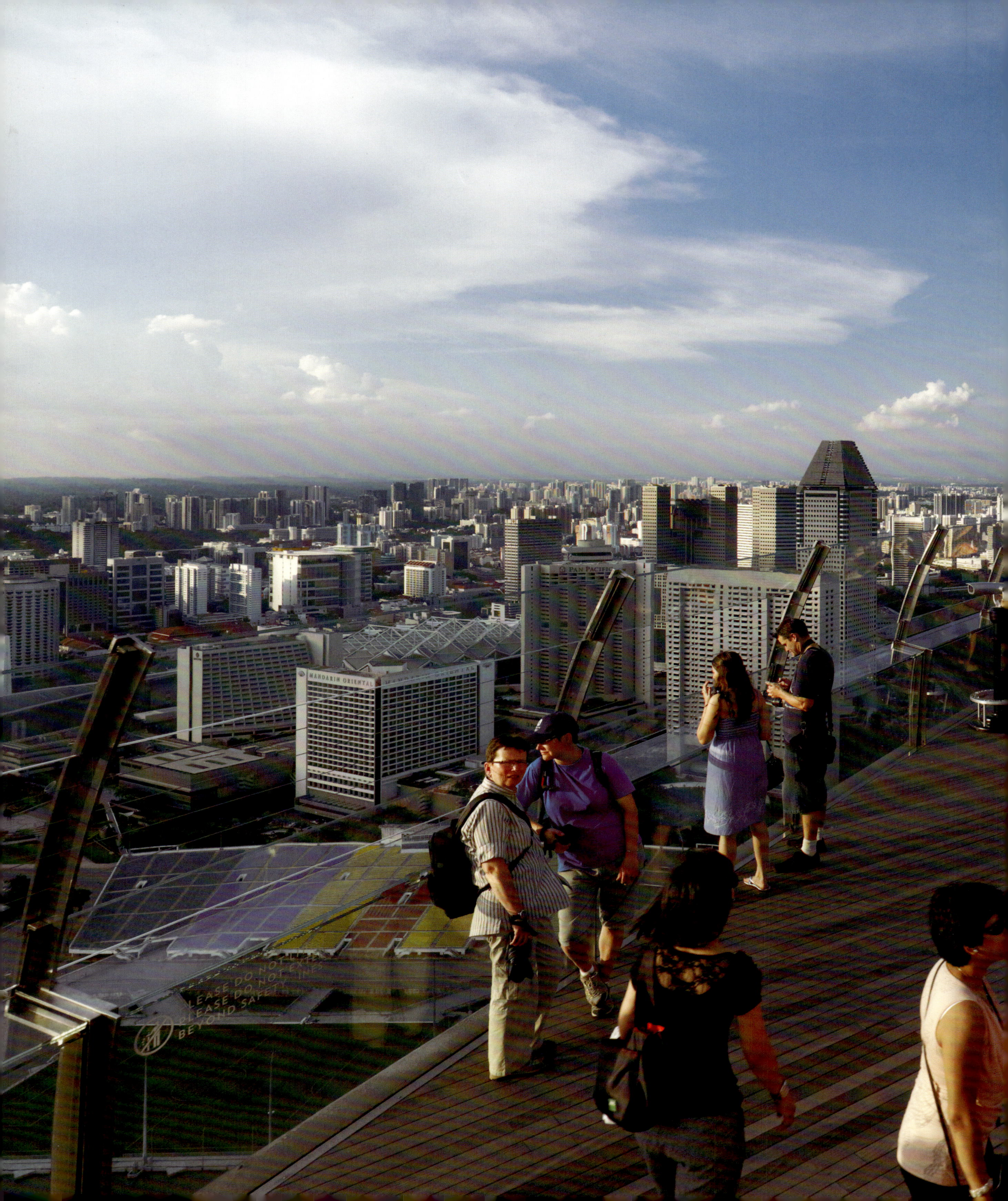
PAN PACIFIC
MANDARIN ORIENTAL

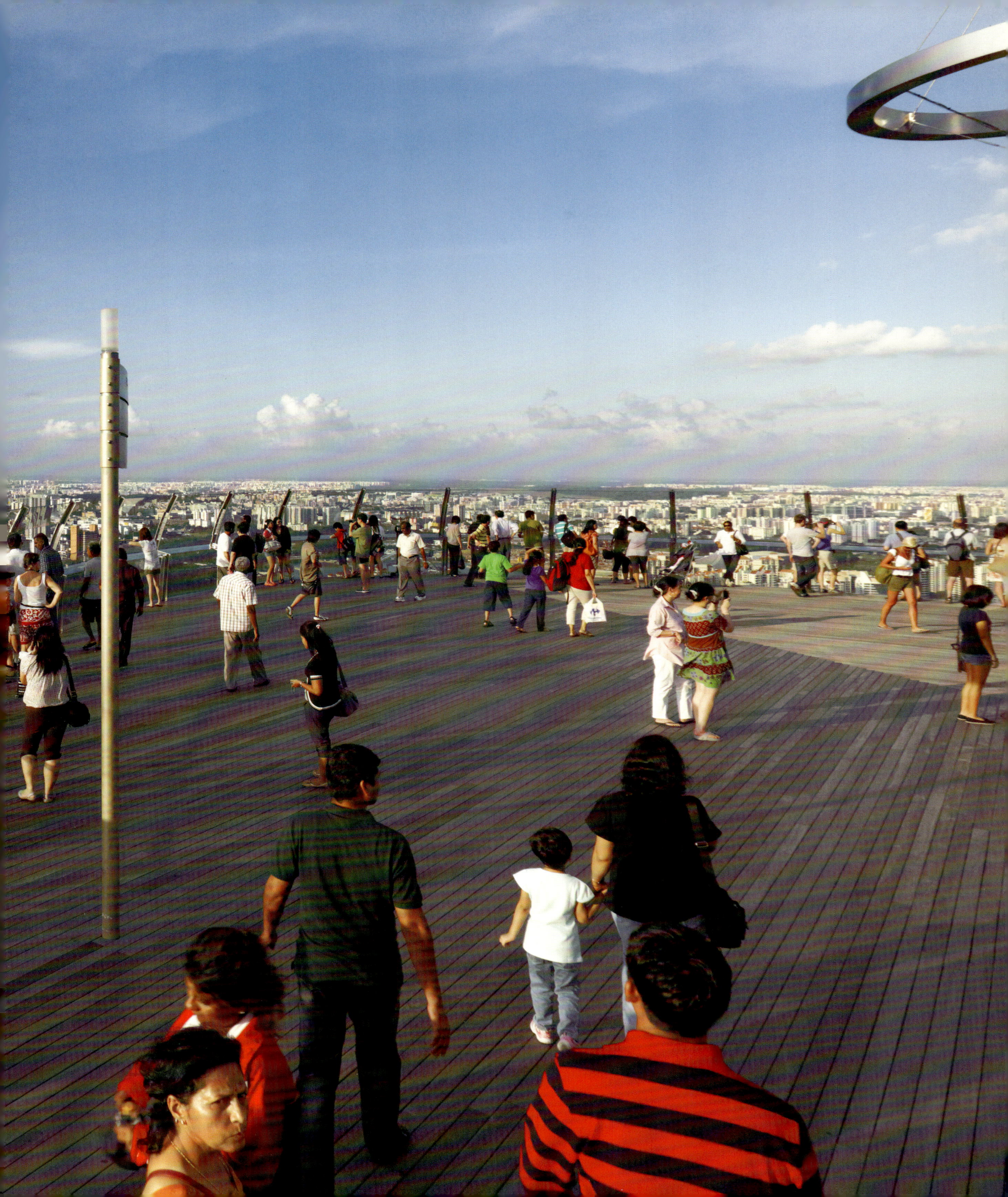

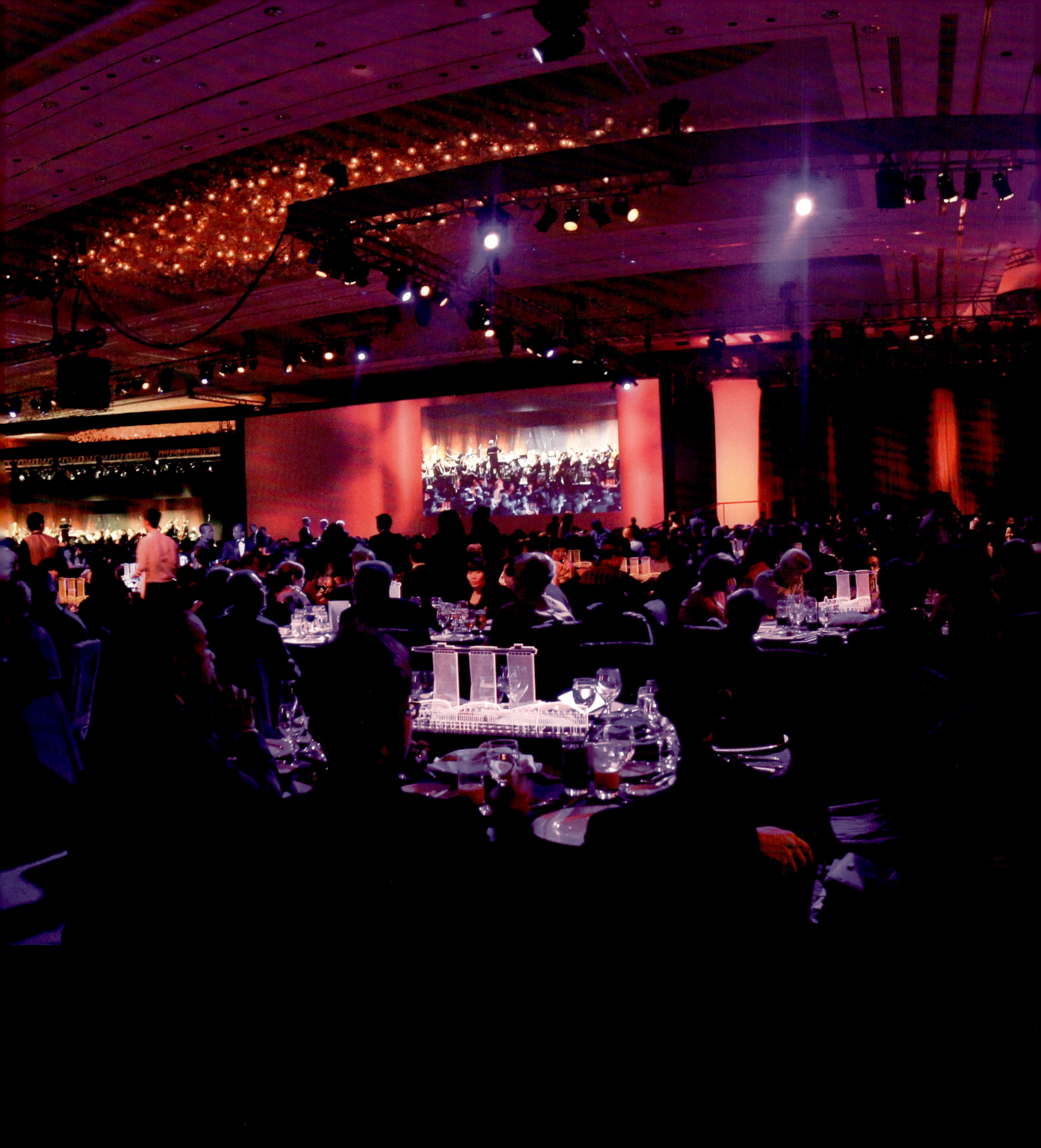

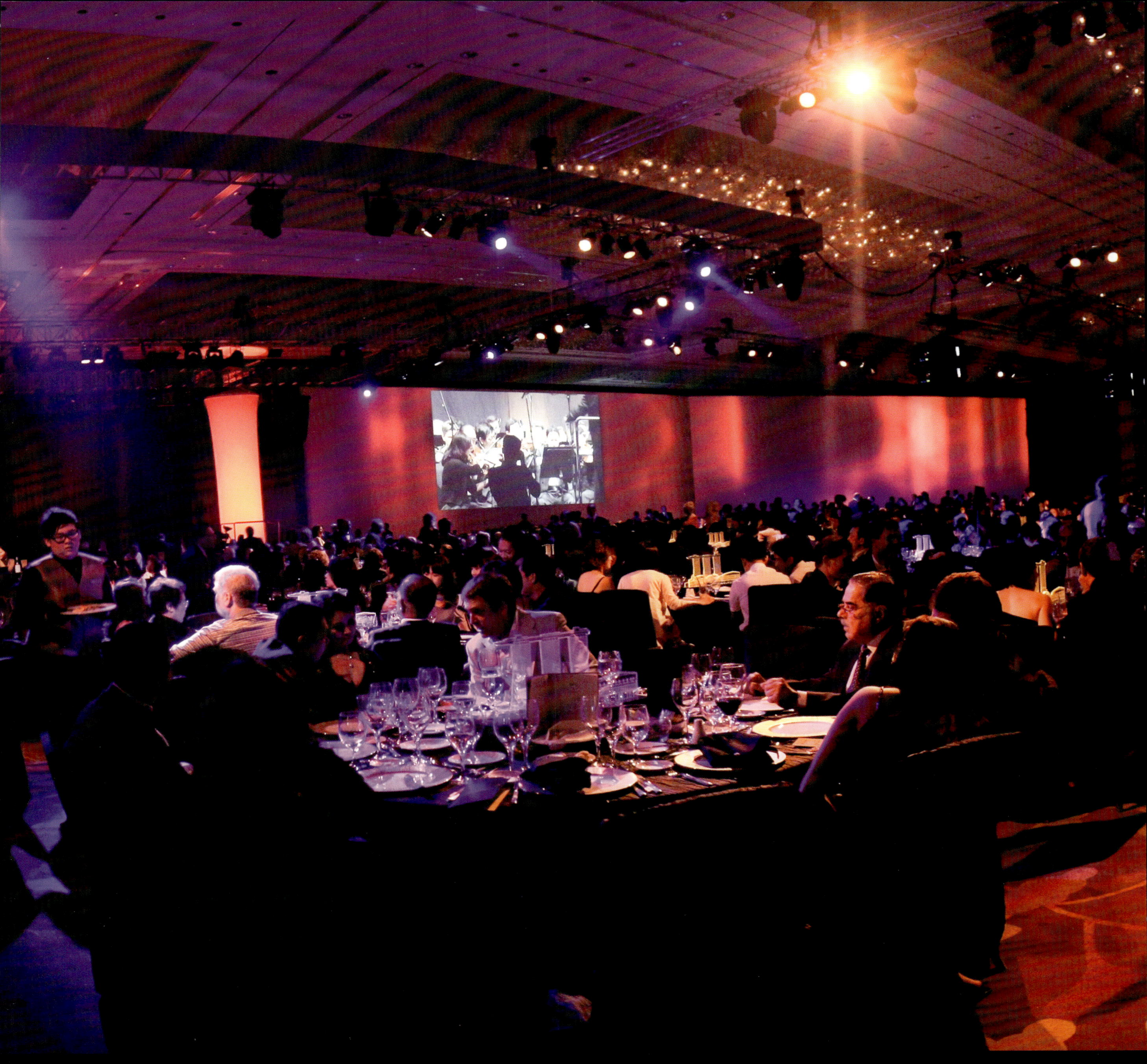

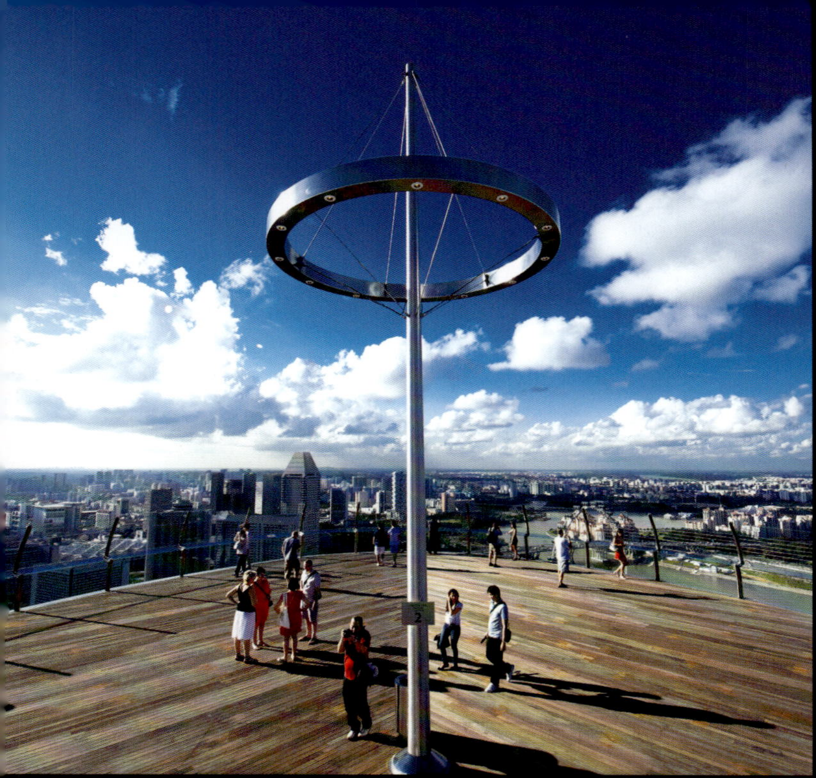

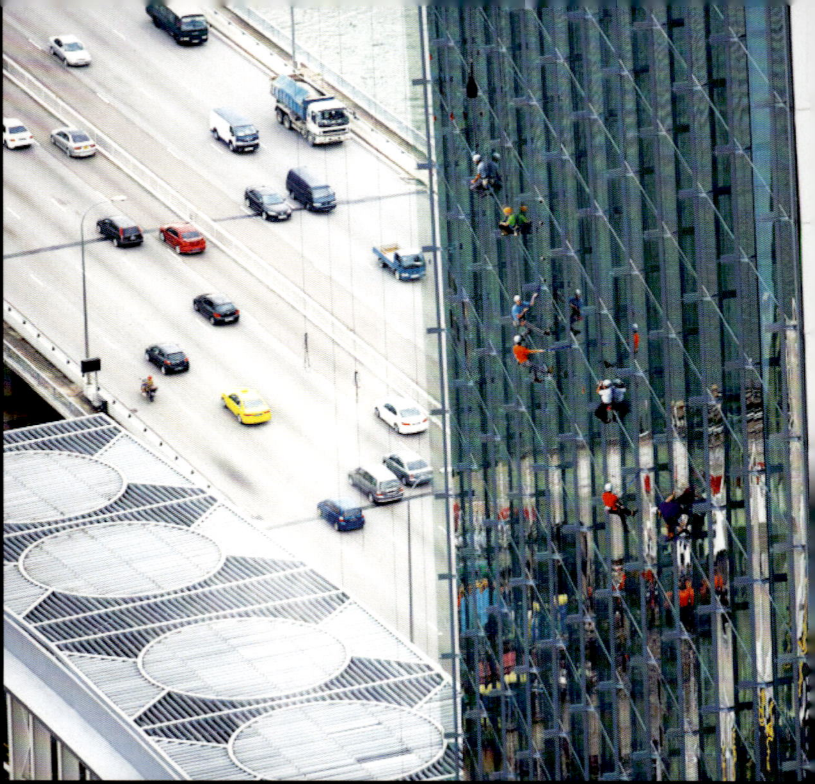

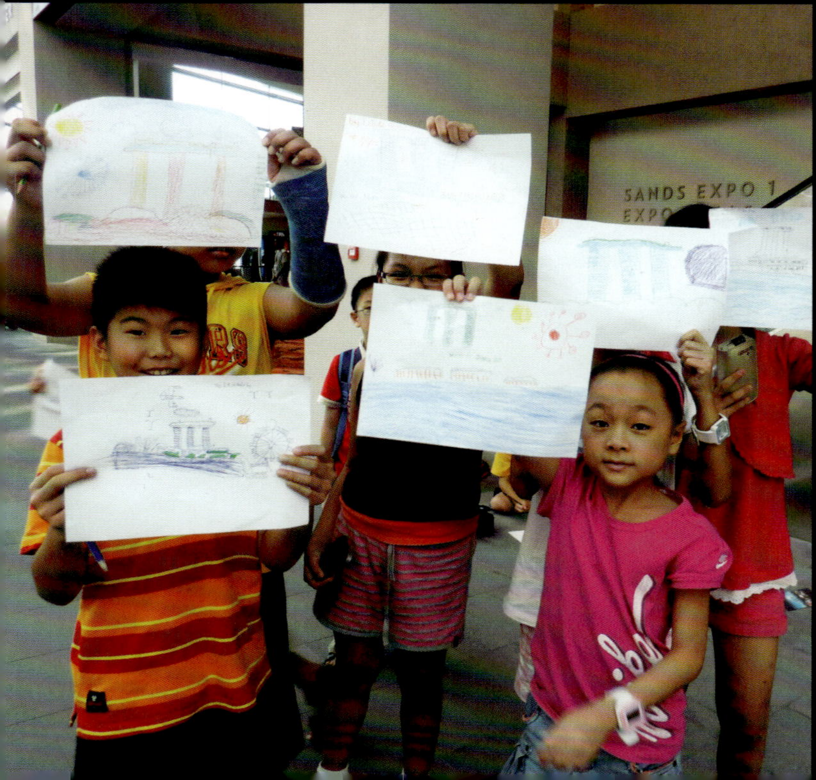
SANDS EXPO 1

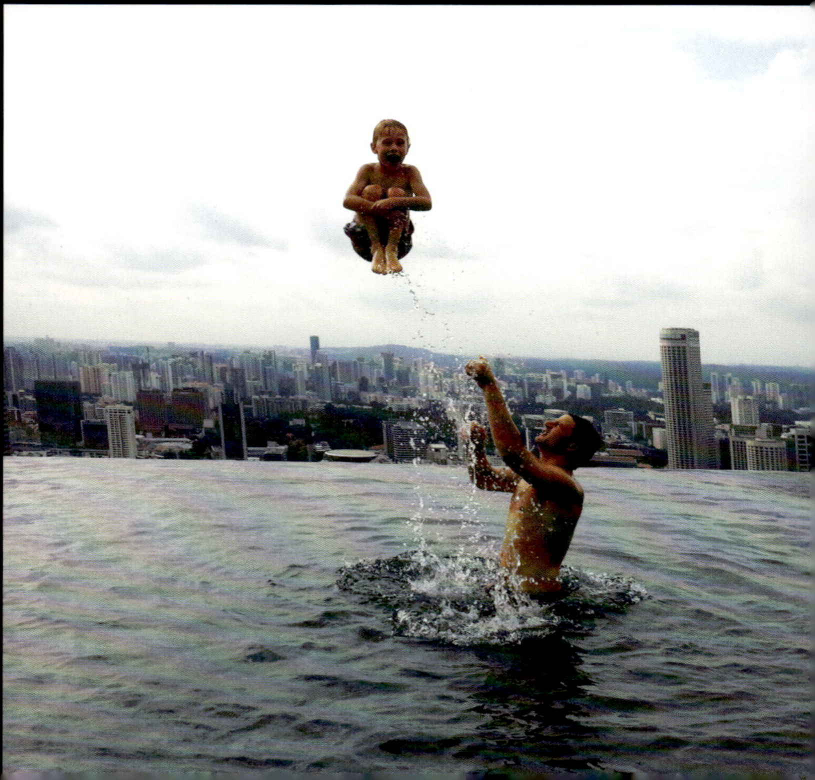

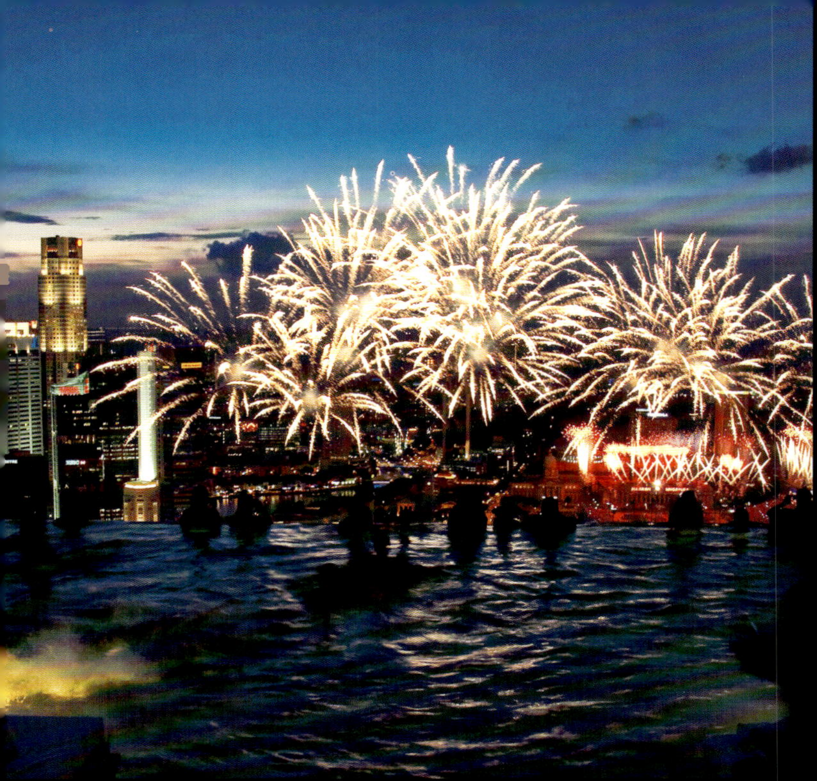

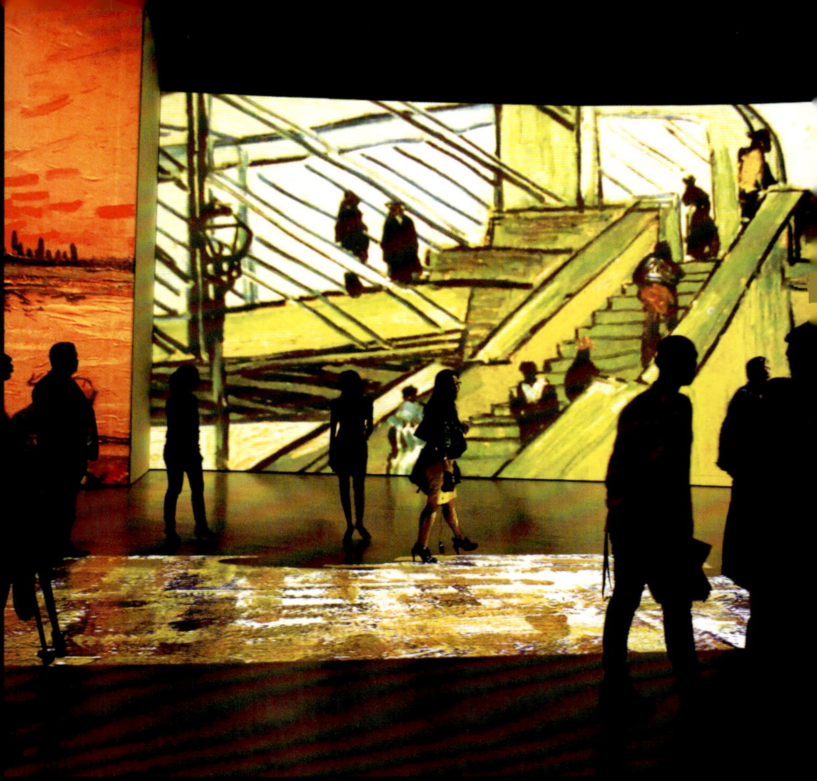

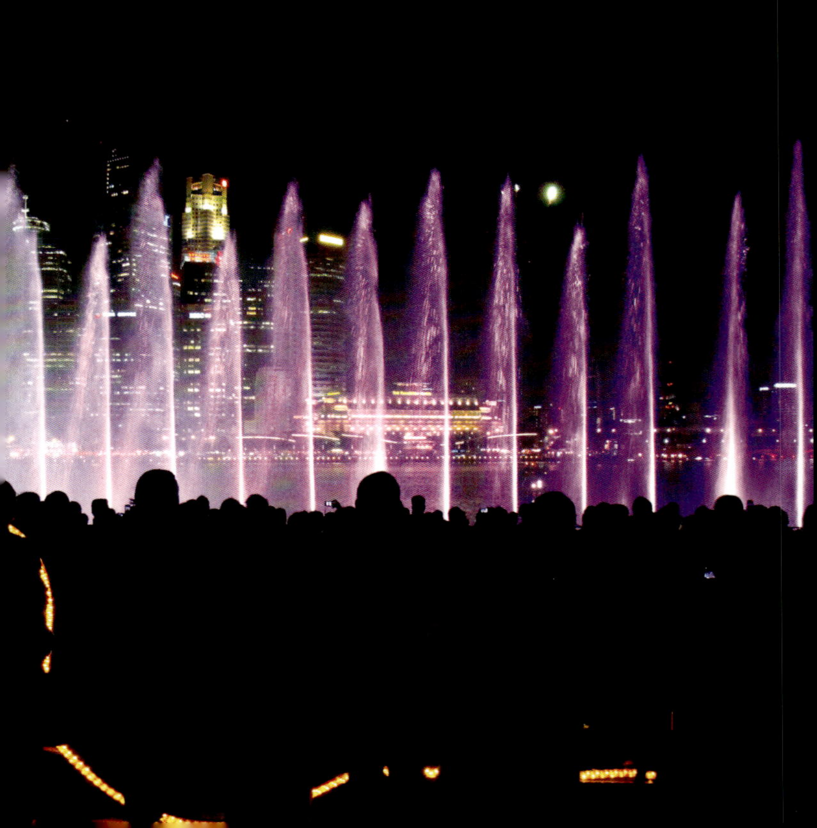

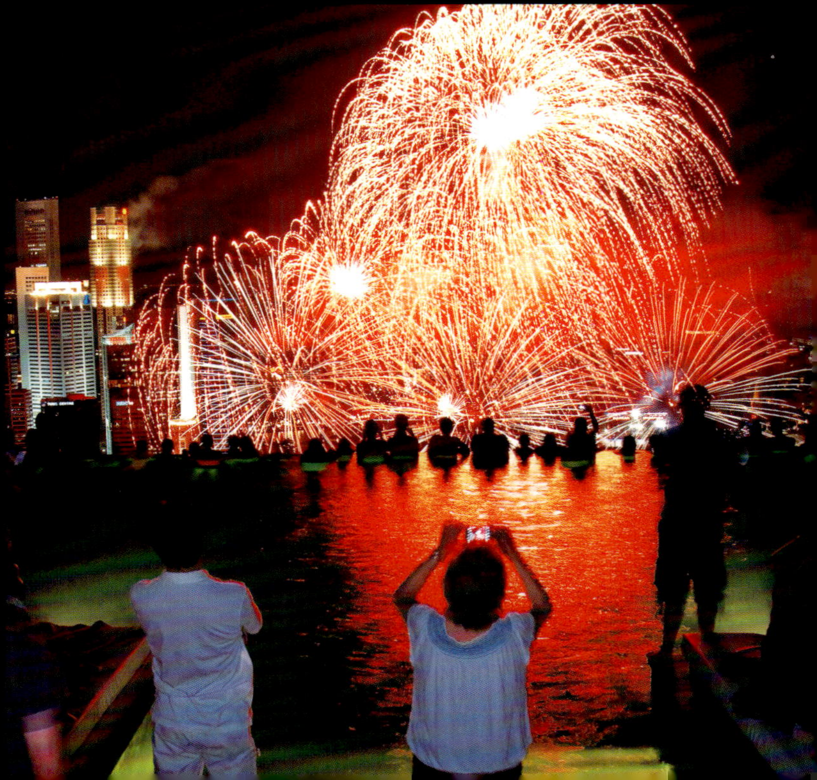

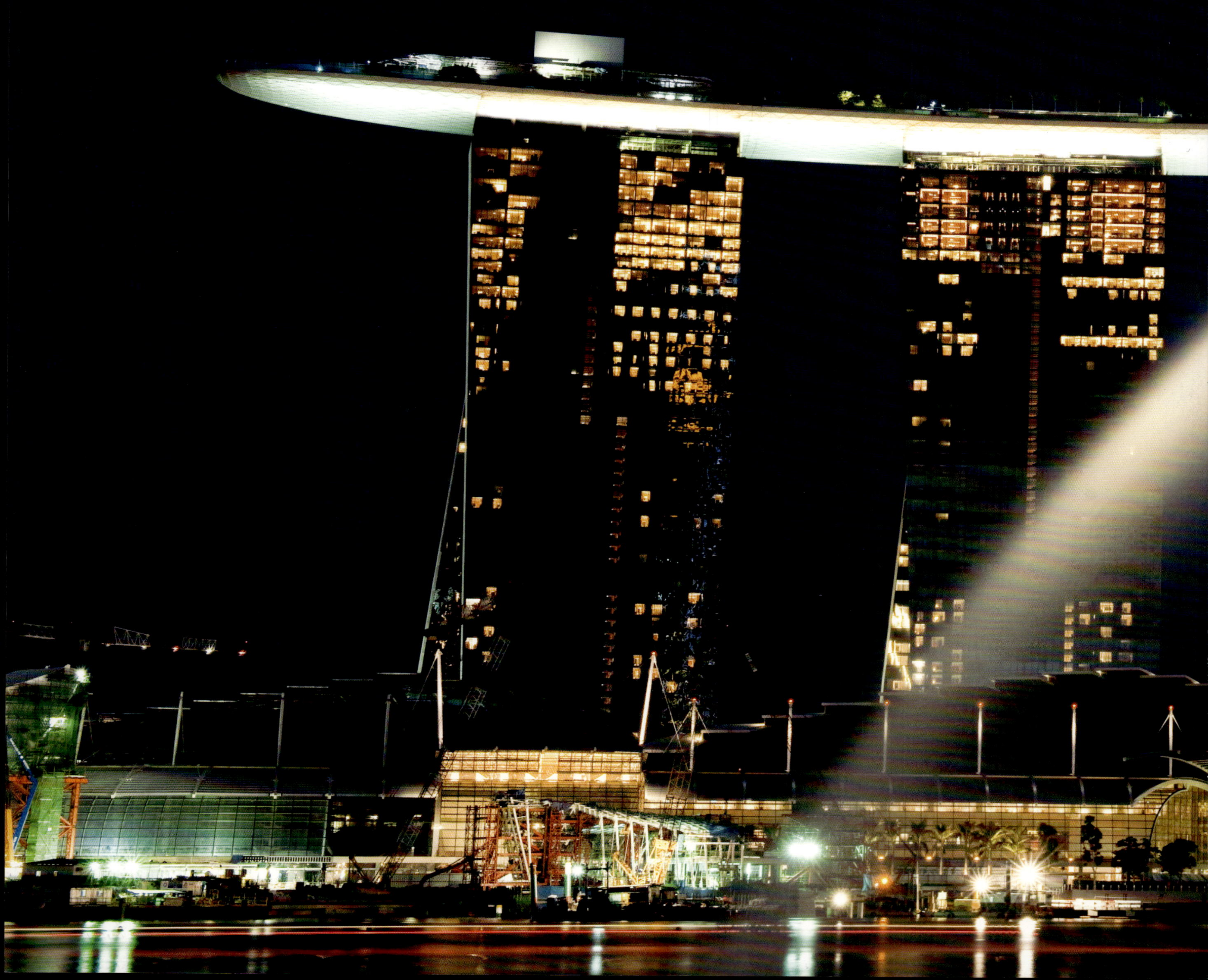

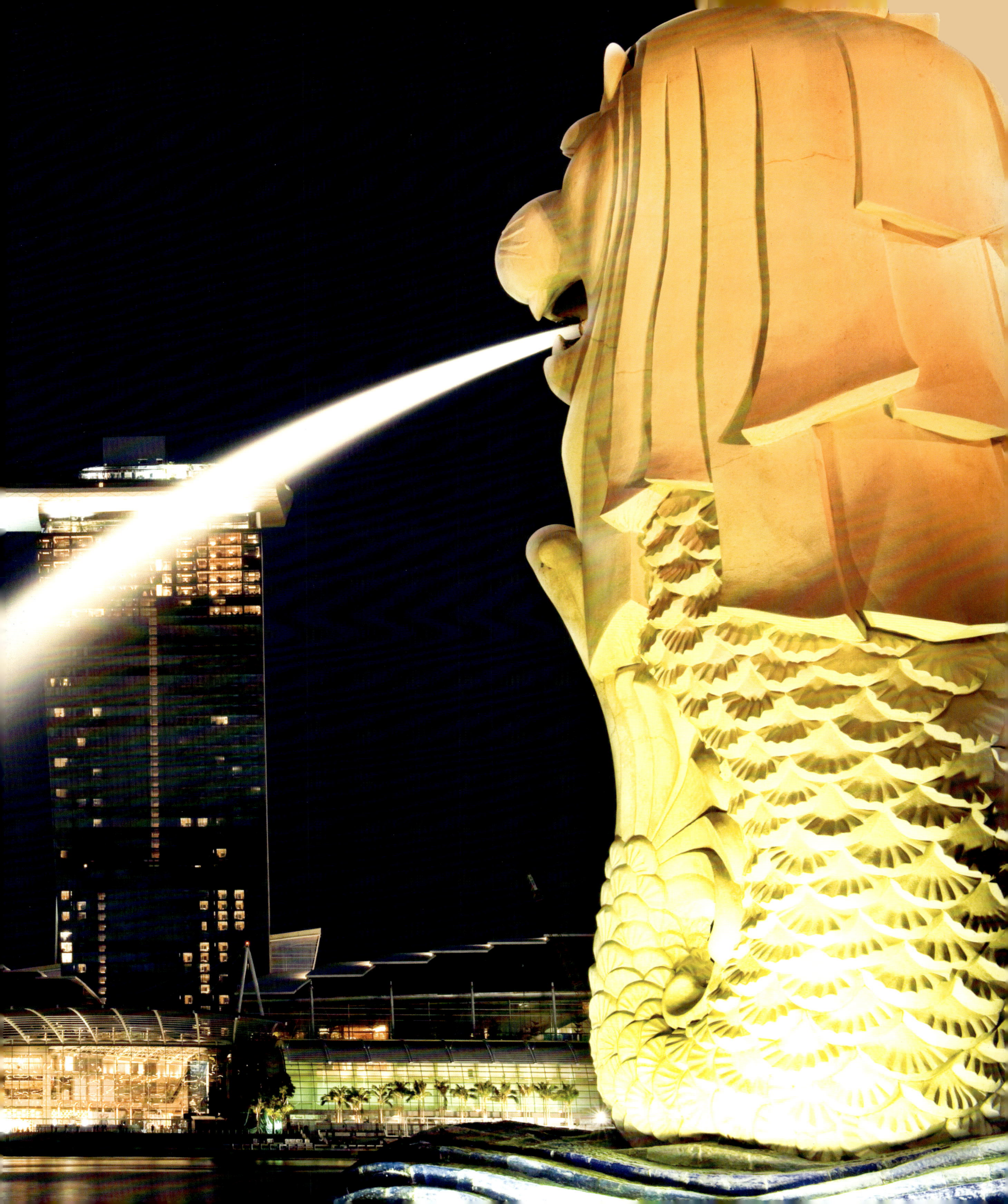

About the Contributors

Sheldon Adelson is chief executive officer and chairman of the Las Vegas Sands Corporation, whose properties include the Sands and Venetian resorts in Las Vegas and Macau, and the Marina Bay Sands integrated resort in Singapore.

Peter Bowtell is a principal of Arup, the global firm of designers, planners, engineers, and consultants. He is responsible for a broad range of building projects in Asia, Europe, and the United States, as well as the Australasia region. During his thirty-year career, Bowtell has led large multidisciplinary engineering design teams for major structural and civil engineering projects; he has particular experience in the design of museums, libraries, sports-and-leisure facilities, retail complexes, casinos and hotels, and embassies. Passionate about the difference good design and innovation can make to our built environment, Bowtell creates teams of interdisciplinary talent from around the Arup world to deliver better project outcomes for clients and the community. Long-term sustainability is a key focus of his projects.

Dr. Cheong Koon Hean is chief executive officer of Singapore's Housing and Development Board. She oversees the development and management of approximately one million public housing units and has formulated a roadmap for developing better designed, more sustainable, community-centric towns. She also serves as a deputy secretary in Singapore's Ministry of National Development. Formerly, Cheong was chief executive officer of the government's Urban Redevelopment Authority, where she was in charge of strategic land use planning and the conservation of built heritage. She played a key role in the development of Marina Bay and other major growth areas. Cheong is a board trustee of the Urban Land Institute, an eco-advisor to China's Tianjin-Binhai New Area, and serves on several international advisory panels on sustainability and strategic planning. In 2011, she received the Women Who Make a Difference Award from the International Women's Forum, and in 2010 she was given the Convocation Medal for Professional Excellence from Australia's University of Newcastle, her alma mater. Cheong also has received several national honors, including the 2010 Meritorious Service Award for outstanding public service.

Adam Greenspan directs design at PWP Landscape Architecture with Peter Walker. He has been the lead designer on a wide range of projects including estates, public parks, campuses, and design competitions, among them the Marina Bay Sands integrated resort; the Transbay Transit Center Park, in San Francisco; Glenstone in Potomac, Maryland; and the Newport Beach City Hall and Park, in Newport Beach, California. Greenspan's diverse background in sociology, studio art, landscape architecture, and horticultural practice allows him to conceive and develop projects from many angles, including the integration of regenerative and sustainable principles.

Gary Hack is professor and dean emeritus of the University of Pennsylvania School of Design. He has prepared urban design plans for more than fifty cities in Asia, Canada, and the United States, including the redevelopment of the Prudential Center, in Boston; waterfront planning for New York City's West Side; urban design guidelines for the redevelopment of the World Trade Center site in New York; and the metropolitan plan for Bangkok, Thailand. He is the co-author of *Site Planning*; *Urban Design in the Global Perspective*; *Local Planning*; and *Global City Regions: Their Emerging Forms*.

About the Contributors

Brooke Hodge is director of exhibitions and publications at Los Angeles' Hammer Museum. From 2001 to 2009, she was curator of architecture and design at the Museum of Contemporary Art in Los Angeles, where she organized major exhibitions on the work of architect Frank Gehry and car designer J. Mays, as well as Skin + Bones: Parallel Practices in Fashion and Architecture, a groundbreaking thematic exhibition on the relationship between contemporary fashion and architecture. Hodge writes "Seeing Things," an ongoing column for the T Magazine blog of the *New York Times*, and is a contributor to the *Los Angeles Times Magazine* and *Wallpaper**.

Martin C. Pedersen has served as executive editor of *Metropolis* magazine since 1999. In addition to his editing duties, he also writes for the magazine and website. He is co-author of *Robert Polidori's Metropolis*. Prior to working at *Metropolis* magazine, he was editorial director at *Graphis*, the international graphic design magazine. Pedersen lives in New Orleans with his wife and two children.

Moshe Safdie is an architect, urban planner, educator, theorist, and author. He is committed to architecture that is informed by the geographic, social, and cultural elements that define a place, and that responds to human needs and aspirations. Safdie has designed and realized a wide range of projects: cultural, educational, and civic institutions; mixed-use urban centers and airports; and master plans for existing communities and entirely new cities. Major projects under construction or recently completed include the Mamilla Center, a forty-acre development adjacent to the Old City in Jerusalem; the Marina Bay Sands integrated resort in Singapore; Khalsa Heritage Center, the national museum of the Sikh people in India; the Kauffman Center for the Performing Arts, in Kansas City, Missouri; Crystal Bridges Museum of American Art, in Bentonville, Arkansas; and Golden Dream Bay, a residential and retail complex in Qinhuangdao, China. Many of Safdie's buildings have become regional and national landmarks, including Habitat '67 in Montreal; the Salt Lake City Main Public Library, in Utah; the National Gallery of Canada, Ottawa; and the Holocaust History Museum at Yad Vashem, in Jerusalem.

Peter Walker has exerted a significant influence on the field of landscape architecture through his teaching, lectures, and writing over a five-decade career. He also has served as an advisor to numerous public agencies. With a dedicated concern for urban and environmental issues, his designs shape the landscape in a variety of geographic and cultural contexts in Europe and the United States, and in Australia, China, and Japan. Walker is the founder of Spacemaker Press, and his writing has been extensively published in Asia, Europe, and the United States. He is a fellow of the American Society of Landscape Architects and the Institute for Urban Design, and has received the Honor Award of the American Institute of Architects; Harvard's Centennial Medal; the University of Virginia's Thomas Jefferson Medal; the ASLA Medal; and the IFLA Sir Geoffrey Jellicoe Gold Medal.

Team Credits

Project Team

Clients
Las Vegas Sands Inc/
Marina Bay Sands Pte Ltd

Architect
Safdie Architects

Singapore Architect
Aedas Pte Ltd

Geotechnical, Civil, Structural, Facade, Fire and Blast Engineering; BIM, Acoustics, Audiovisual and Security Consultant
Arup

Landscape Architect
PWP Landscape Architecture/
Peridian Asia Pte Ltd

Building Services Engineers
Parsons Brinckerhoff Pte Ltd/
Vanderweil Engineers

Quantity Surveyor
EC Harris/Rider Levett Bucknall

Casino Design
Safdie Architects with The Rockwell Group

Hotel Contractor
SsangYong Engineering & Construction Ltd/
Lian Beng Construction Pte Ltd

SkyPark Contractor
Yongnam & JFE Engineering Corporation JV

ArtScience Museum Contractor
Penta Ocean

MICE/Retail Steelworks Contractor
Alfasi Constructions Singapore Pte Ltd

Casino and Theater Steelworks Contractor
Singapore Jinggong Steel Structures Pte Ltd

Foundations Contractors
Soletanche Bachy Singapore Pte Ltd/
Sambo Geo-Tosfoc Co Ltd/
L&M Foundation Pte Ltd

South/North Podium Excavation and Reinforced Concrete Contractors
KTC Civil Engineering & Construction Pte Ltd/Yau Lee Construction Pte Ltd/
Sembawang Engineers and Constructors Pte Ltd

ArtScience Museum Cladding Contractor
DK Composites Sdn Bhd

Retail Canopies Contractor
DK Composites Sdn Bhd

Retail Canopies Contractor
YKK Architectural Products Inc

Tenant Fitout in South Crystal Pavilion
Pure Projects Singapore Pte Ltd

Theater Planning and Engineering Design Consultant
Fisher Dachs Associates

Wayfinding and Signage
Pentagram/Entro

Lighting Design
Project Lighting Design/Laservision

Performance Sound, Video, and Production Communications Design Consultant
Specialized Audio-Visual Inc

Signage Subcontractor
Crimsign Graphics Pte Ltd

Artists
James Carpenter, Antony Gormley,
Israel Hadany, Ned Kahn, Sol LeWitt,
Zhan Wang, Zheng Chongbin

Team Staffs

Las Vegas Sands Inc
Development Team
George Tanasijevich, Bradley H. Stone,
Jim Beyer, Frank Santagata,
Michael Gebhard, Paul Gunderson,
Pim Robberechts, Nicholas Rumanes,
Mark Signorio

Marina Bay Sands Pte Ltd
Project and Construction
Management Team
Matthew Pryor, John Downs, Dale Chadwick,
Will Cornish, Craig Glover, Mark Avery, Mike
Barton, Rudy Bethshoga, Nick Boekel,
Daniel Boh, Frank Brown, Darren Bull,
Patrick Condon, Luke Conrick, Stephen
Dale, Rob De Wesselow, Peter Dooley,
Samantha Drummond, Au Ka Fai, Marcel
Finlay, Veronica Formenti, Darren Gannon,
Heiko Gold, Raghu Gopalan, Peter Gutman,
Helen Harjanto, James Holman, Justin
Hotton, Kit Johnstone, Simon Kavarana,
Scott King, Silas Kingscott, Ho Kye, Mathew
Lamb, Michael Long, Ted Mahoney,

Team Credits

Tony McKee, David Meade, Andrew Metcalf, Leong Chiu Ming, Leong Chee Mun, Pat Murray, Jan Oebeles, Luke Quinn, Andrew Reeves, Peter Reeves, Jason Rimmer, Remy Rossi, Tolu Sanni, Thiam Seng, Serina Shong, Colin Soh, Graham Stephenson, Melissa Galoy Sy, Kurt Vella, Robert White

Singapore Urban Redevelopment Authority
Design and Management Team
Dr. Cheong Koon Hean, Mrs. Koh-Lim Wen Gin, Andrew Fassam, Linda Lui
URA staff, Design Advisory Panel

Safdie Architects
Architect and Design Principal
Moshe Safdie

Project Directors
Gene Dyer, Easley Hamner, David Robins, Carrie Yoon

Singapore Team
Rafael Acosta, Karlo DeGuzman, Dorothy Dyer, Todor Enchev, Tunch Gungor, Sean Guinan, Jeffrey Huggins, Jeff Jacoby, Charu Kokate, Jaron Lubin, Tiger Shen, Leo Waible, Jean Wang, Siebrandus Wichers

Boston Team
Nina Adams, Anahita Anandam, Marcelo Arjona, Rindala Awad, James Bailey, Adam Balaban, Jane Baldini, Alastair Battson, Ronen Bauer, Howard Bloom, Gary Branch, David Brooks, Shawn Canon, Lauren Cawse, Todd Cahill, Jean-Francois Champoux-Lemay, Gary Chen, Daniel Cho, Jean Cotton, Joseph Dahmen, Anthony DePace, Aneesha Dharwadker, Andrey Dimitrov, Lian Eoyang, Leslie Ford, James Forren, Isaac Franco, AIA, Robert Gagne, Michael Guran, Ori Guy, Yinette Guzman, Justin Harmon, Milena Haskovec, Colleen Higgins, Ryan Hill, Michael Hinchcliffe, Matthew Ibarguen, Nuno Jacinto, Mario Jaime, Chae Lee, Wade J. Lewis, Andrew Longmire, Yuliang Lu, Eugenia Magann, Steven Mager, Velimir Manjulov, Warren Mathison, Oriana Merlo, Andrew Mikhael, John Moran, Stefan Nedelcu, Christopher Mulvey, Kate Murphy, Jungmin Nam, Robert Noblett, Stephen O'Brien, Dana Pasternak, Sara Ossi, Marshall H. Peck III, Chris Polaski, Rafael Ramirez, Tessa Reist, Ryan Renshaw, Jorge Ribera, Ori Rittenberg, Jeremy Schwartz, Henry Sedelmaier, Damon Sidel, Allan Sifferlen, Temple Simpson, Steven Snyder, Dan Spiegel, Virginie Stanley, Craig Steele, Victoria Steven, Charles Stewart, Kyle Sturgeon, Toshihiko Taketomo, Dana Tanimoto, Trevor Thimm, Wayde Tardif, Raffi Tomassian, Casey Tosti, Douglas Tuttle, Juan Villafane, Sarah Walker, Jean Wang, Winifred Wang, Michael Ward, Angie Winston, Tyrone Yang, Shiu Chie Yokoyama, Jing Yu, Stacey Zielinski, Jane Zimmerman

Aedas Pte Ltd
Project Directors
Gruffudd Ab Owain, Tony Ang, Simon Mark Griffiths, Kevin Marshall Jose, Soo Sing Low, Alen Nikolovski, Jose Silva, Ian Charles Murray Wigmore

Project Team
Gomes Goncalves Da Silva Alcoforado, Jecelyn Arimado Almonia, Bin Abdul Hamid Badar, Dragan Bojovic, Agnes Montenegro Bukuhan, Carmichael Tiongson Castillo, Derrick Jin Quan Chan, On Yee Olivia Chan, Ying Kiet Dennis Chan, Rui Fen Chen, Chi Ho Cheung, Joo Gaik Julie Chew, Tat Wai David Chim, Shi Shi Serene Chow, Lin Kiat Frederick Chua, Allan Coltart Curr, Amalia Tizon Da Vera, Samuel De Vera De Guzman, Roel Rotaeche Nolasco Eipodes, Wang Kwoon Eng, Alodia Perez Espanol, Joo Khim Goh, Meiqin Guo, Michael Greville, Way Chiang Harold Hee, Cheong Meng Eric Hoong, Natasha Ilic, Fahmi Ismail Syarif, Mohammad Haizad Bin Johari, George Sagaya Kamagasingam, Peter Vincent Langan, Mei Liew, Siew See Lee, Sok Mei Marjory Liew, King Leong Tony Lim, Qiu Yun Karen Lim, Yew Lee Grace Lim, Kenzie Hin Sze Lo, Delilah Endozo Manalo, Ma Victoria Marimta Marcaida, Kenneth Paul McGuire, Anna Rose Echeo Pastor, Jamaludin Bin Rahamat, Mousumi Roy Chowdhury, Neeraj Sharma, Chai Yan Tan, Hong Kwan Vivian Tan, Jin Hua David Tan, Kim Eng Teh, Lim Teck Teo, Princess Beluang Teopez, Roy De Guzman Tolosa, Yan Lun Daniel Tsoi, Fiona Cheuk Chi Wong, Li Lian Eileen Wong, Mohammad Farek Bin Mohammad Yacob, Jingwen Yang, Renato Paras Yanga, Natalie Yue, Yongli Zang, Xinyi Zhang

Arup
Project Directors
Peter Bowtell, Dan Brodkin, Va-Chan Cheong, Wah-Kam Chia, Russell Cole, Peter Hoad, André Lovatt, Patrick McCafferty, Brendon McNiven, Edwin Ong, Jack Pappin, Larry Tedford, Wijaya Wong

Project Team
Joy Aclao, Nur Liyana Ahmad, Ian Ainsworth, Graham Aldwinckle, Jarrod Alston, Evan Amatya, Joseph Amores, Richard Andrews, Christine Ang, Ling Ling Ang, Siow Ting Ang, Christopher Anoso, Easy Arisarwindha,

Team Credits

Mark Arkinstall, Feng Bai, Jaydy Baldovino, Warren Balitcha, Venugopal Barkur, Rachel Baylson, Dan Birch, Hay Sun Blunt, Greg Borkowski, Sarah Boulkroune, Nick Boulter, Ashley Bracken, Claire Bristow, Jessica Cao, Neil Carstairs, Matt Carter, Kartigayen Poutelaye Cavound, Chee Wah Chan, Chris Chan, George Chan, Kam-Lam Chan, Ken Chan, Marco Chan, Michael Chan, Tat-Ngong Chan, Wayne Chan, Yun-Ngok Chan, Renuga Chandra, Angela Chen, Carrie Chen, Chi-Lik Chen, Melissa Chen, Harold Cheng, Cecilia Cheong, Joy Cheong, Patrick Cheong, Kenny Cheung, Henry Chia, Reve Chin, Clyfford Ching, Park Chiu, Derek Chong, Sok Poi Chong, TS Choong, Henry Chow, Hee Kung Chua, Wee Koon Chua, Rene Ciolo, Richard Clement, Ranelle Cliff, Lyonel Cochon, Yimin Cong, George Corpuz, Joseph Correnza, Anne Coutts, Robert Coutu, Raymond Crane, Josh Cushner, Richard Custer, Yang Dang, Bruce Danziger, John Davies, Lauren Davis, Ethelbert Derige, Antonio Diaz, Mike DiMascio, Ran Ding, Nick Docherty, Graham Dodd, Matt Dodge, Andrew Douglas, Pierre Dubois, Andy Ellett, David Farnsworth, Garth Ferrier, Kai Fisher, Raymond Fok, Clarice Fong, Raymond Fong, Vivien Foo, Kathy Franklin, Feng Gao, Chris Gildersleeve, Gina Goh, Gladys Goh, Ian Grierson, Ken Guertin, Liana Hamzah, James Hargreaves, Rotana Hay, Donal Hayward, Eric He, Zheng-Yu He, Grace Hendro, Kok Hui Heng, Argi Hipolito, Andy Ho, Chong Leong Ho, Don Ho, Kent Ho, Stanley Ho, Wee Keong Ho, Dennis Hoi, Martin Holt, Anna Hon, Andrew Hulse, Sarah Huskie, Philip Iskandar, Mellissa Ismail, Sha Mohamed Ismail, Anthony Ivey, Frank Jeczmionka, Steven Jenkins, William Jimenez, Hong Geng Jin, Matt Johann, Carl Jones, Steven Jones, Edmond San Jose, Chak-Sang Kan, Yiu-Fai Kan, Man Kang, Subash Kathiresan, Teng Chong Khoo, Amanda Kimball, Ben Kirkwood, Henrik Kjaer, Sing Yen Ko, Duraibabu Damodaran Kothanda, Jeyatharan Kumarasamy, Viann Kung, Kin-Kei Kwan, Chris Kwok, Henry Kwok, Nelson Kwong, Andrew Lai, David Lai, Kristin Lai, Otto Lai, Philip Lai, Raymond Lai, Alvin Lam, Clement Lam, Ernest Lam, Joe Lam, Derek Lau, Eric Lau, James Lau, Jeffrey Lau, Tony Lau, Wai-Lun Lau, Henry Law, Michelle Lazaro, Bill Lee, Budi Lee, Cheryl Lee, Chris Lee, Chung Hei Lee, Davis Lee, Francis Lee, Gordon Lee, Hiang Meng Lee, John Lee, Kin Shang Lee, Nicholas Lee, Patrick Lee, Peter Lee, Sebastian Lee, Serena Lee, Yi Jin Lee, Kevin Legenza, John Legge-Wilkinson, Steven Lenert, Tino Leong, Wing-Kai Leong, Erin Leung, Koon-Yu Leung, Sam Leung, Stephen Leung, Stuart Leung, Vivian Leung, Ben-Qing Li, Chi-Shing Li, Lei Li, Shawn Li, Zhuo Li, Alex Lie, Jenny Lie, Keithson Liew, Kim Hoe Liew, Christina Lim, Deyuan Lim, Keong Liam Lim, Patricia Lim, William Lim, Angie Lin, Jonathan Lindsay, Brett Linnane, Rudi Lioe, Amy Liu, Charlie Liu, Chris Liu, Xi Liu, Franky Lo, Sin Ching Low, Danny Lui, Jack Lui, Kwok-Man Lui, Marcellus Lui, Kok Mun Lum, Malcolm Lyon, Michael Macaraeg, Juan Maier, Alex Mak, Brian Mak, Dylan Mak, Louis Mak, Louise Mak, Martino Mak, Dexter Manalo, Mukunthan Manickavasakar, Anand Mariyappan, Sean McGinn, Maciej Mikulewicz, Wing Sze Mo, Junaidah Mohd, Martin Mok, Polly Mok, Lydia Mokhtar, Andrew Mole, Rodel Moran, Jon Morgan, Dean Morris, Samir Mustapha, Vaikun Nadarajah, Bob Nelson, Andrew Neviackas, Derek Ng, James Ng, Jason Ng, Ka-Yuen Ng, Peck Nah Ng, Andrew Nicol, Phamornsak Noochit, Alison Norrish, Ada Oh, Janice Ong, Natalie Ong, Khine Khine Oo, Kamsinah Osman, Ayca Ozcanlar, Jin Pae, Priya Palpanathan, Jack Pan, Kathy Pang, Stuart Pearce, Alan Philp, Maggie Puvannan, Chris Pynn, Jie Qian, Virgilio Quinones, Jim Quiter, Nizar Abdul Rahim, Mohan Raman, Rey Redondo, Adrian De Los Reyes, Archie Ricablanca, Darlene Rini, Peter Romeos, Ian Del Rosario, Alex Rosenthal, Ken Roxas, Matthew Ryan, Emily Ryzak, Richard Salter, Katherina Santoso, Majid Haji Sapar, Haico Schepers, David Scott, Lin Ming See, Richie See, Janice Sendico, Bee Lian Seo, Kartini Shabani, Henry Shiu, Margaret Sie, Michael Sien, Chris Simm, Nick Simpson, Kenneth Sin, Alexandra Sinickas, Jimmy Sitt, Nathan Smith, Andrew Snalune, Penelope Somers, Noel Sotto, Charles Spiteri, Jimmy Su, Doreen Sum, Joyce Sum, Daojun Sun, Malar Suppiah, Muljadi Suwita, Jamie Talbot, Hon-Wing Tam, Jonas Tam, Winfred Tam, Kok Yong Tan, Mac Tan, Suan Wee Tan, Vicky Tan, Rajesh Tandel, Johnson Tang, Joyce Tang, Lim Mei Tang, Willis Tang, Brendan Taylor, Sean Teo, Ming Jong Tey, Nithi Thaweeskulchai, Andra Thedy, Kia Ling Tho, Helen Tolentino, Michael Tom, Roberto Tonon, Roland Trim, David Tse, Jeff Tubbs, Mart Umali, Richard Vanderkley, Karthik Venkatesan, David Vesey, Henry Vong, Doug Wallace, Delu Wang, Qian Wang, Ekarin Wattanasanticharoen, Toby White, Garry Wilkie, Huw Williams, Ashley Willis, Berlina Winata, Ian Wise, Alex Wong, Ambrose Wong, Dick Wong, Joseph Wong, Kin-Ping Wong, Ling Chye Wong, Mary Wong, Ruth Wong, Suman Wong, Tim Wong, Joanne Woo, Andrew Woodward, Colin Wu, Gin Wu, Louis Wu, Tao Wu, Wendy Wu, Xiaofeng Wu, Takim Xiang,

Team Credits

David Xiong, Jingfeng Xu, Dai Yamashita, Frances Yang, Zhi-Qiang Yang, Wison Yang, Seven Yau, Mehdi Yazdchi, Yanli Ye, Sam Yeung, Victor Yeung, Wing-Cheong Yeung, Yiu-Wing Yeung, Reman Yick, Kek-Kiong Yin, Colin Yip, Alan Yiu, Jack Yiu, Heng Yong, Jennifer Yong, Lip Bing Yong, Lily You, Yuki Yu, Zhen Yuan, Matthew Yuet, Carlos Zara, Hai-Tao Zhang, Jing Zhang, Liang-Liang Zhao, Zhi Qin Zhou, Jing Zhuang.

PWP Landscape Architecture
Peter Walker, Adam Greenspan, Julie Canter, Conway Chang, Su Jung Park, Conny Roppel

Peridian Asia Pte Ltd
Neal Samac

Howard Fields Associates International
Howard Fields, Chas Jones, Brent Safley

Project Lighting Design
Douglas Brennan, Stephen Gough

Pentagram
Michael Gericke, Don Bilodeau
Matt McInerney, Jed Skillins

Entro
Wayne McCutcheon

Fisher Dachs Associates
Robert Campbell

Specialized Audio-Visual Inc
Michael Cusick

Illustration Credits

Aedas
213 bottom right

Arup
47, 67 (Joseph Correnza),
68 top/bottom, 69 top,
70 (all), 71 top row/bottom row,
72, 74, 75 (all)

Associated Press Reuters
192 bottom right

Chia Ming Chien
220, 238/239, back cover

Zheng Chongbin
252 top/bottom

Graetz Studio
32 top left

Israel Hadany
254 top/bottom, 255

Timothy Hursley
26, 27, 30 top left/right, 32 top right,
32 bottom, 56 (5, 6, 7, 8), 124/125, 126 (all),
127 (all), 128/129, 130 (all), 131 (all), 151,
152/153, 154/155, 156/157, 158, 159 (all),
160, 161, 162, 163, 164/165, 166, 167, 168,
169, 170/171, 173, 174, 175, 176, 177, 178, 179,
180/181, 182, 183, 184, 185, 186, 187, 188,
189, 190, 191, 192 top left, 192 bottom left,
193, 194/195, 196, 199, 200, 201, 202/203,
204/205, 206, 207, 209, 210/211, 212 (all),
213 (all except bottom right), 214/215,
216/217, 219, 223/225, 226, 227, 228 (all),
229, 230, 231, 232, 233, 234, 235, 236, 237,
240/242, 245, 246 top/bottom, 253, 263,
270/271, 274 top left

JFE/Ssanyong
88 (1-6)

Ned Kahn
256, 257, 258 top/bottom

Alan Karchmer
30 middle row

Marina Bay Sands Visual Media
Cover, 17, 20/21, 23, 50/51, 53, 56(3),
69 bottom, 76/77, 80 (all), 86/87,
88 bottom, 90/91, 92/93, 134/135,
247 bottom, 260, 261, 262, 266/267,
268/269, 272/273, 274 top right,
275 (all), 276/277

Michael McCann
137, 138/139, 140, 142, 144, 145, 146/147

Stéphane Muratet
213 bottom left

Tim Nolan
29 bottom left/right

Cymie Payne
28 left

Frank Pinckers
132/133

PWP Landscape Architects
54, 55, 56, 57, 58/59, 60, 62, 63, 64, 65

Steve Rosenthal
30 bottom row middle

Michal Ronnen Safdie
79, 248

Moshe Safdie
25, 30 bottom row left, 34 bottom,
39, 42 top/bottom, 44 top row left/middle

Safdie Architects
10, 13 top, 28 right, 29 top, 30 bottom right,
34 top, 36, 37, 38, 40 (all), 41 (all), 43,
44 (all), 48/49, 56 (1, 2, 4, 9), 57 (all),
71 middle left/right, 81, 83 (all), 84 (all),
85 (all), 88 bottom left/middle right,
96/97, 98/99, 100/101, 102/103,
104/105, 106/109, 110/111, 112/113, 114,
115, 116/117, 118/119, 120/121, 221,
(Dorothy Dyer) 274 bottom left/right,
(Gene Dyer) 197, (Jaron Lubin), 192 top right,
243, 247 (1, 2, 3, 4), 249, 250, 259,
(Kate Murphy) 46

Singapore Archives
9

**Singapore Urban
Redevelopment Authority**
11, 12 top/bottom, 13 bottom, 14/15

Wikimedia Commons
19 top left, Venky TV on Flickr, 19 top right,
ilovebutter on Flickr, 19 middle left/bottom
left/bottom right, jimg944 on Flickr,
19 middle right, Son of Groucho on Flickr, 35

Acknowledgements

The transformation of Marina Bay is the result of the leadership and vision of the Singapore Urban Redevelopment Authority, under the guidance of Dr. Cheong Koon Hean. We are grateful to the dedicated URA staff members, as well as the capable Design Advisory Panel who have worked tirelessly to realize this colossal vision of Singapore.

In addition to the many team members who have contributed their efforts to the success of the project, Safdie Architects would like to thank Marina Bay Sands Visual Media for their valuable contributions to this publication. In particular, we are grateful to Lisa Williamson, Jeremy Ng and Angela Chong for their abiding commitment to collaboration and extended professional courtesies.

This publication would not be possible without the extraordinary photographs by Timothy Hursley. In several trips over an 18-month period, Tim captured the progress and development of Marina Bay Sands' architecture and landscape. For more than 25 years, we have relied on Tim's creativity and skill to capture the spirit of our work.

Finally, we are indebted to the professionals who have generously allowed us to reproduce their fine work in this collection. In particular, we appreciate the contributions of Dorothy Dyer, John Horner, Jenny Lie, Lukito Nugroho, Neoscape Boston, Michael McCann and Michal Ronnen Safdie.

All efforts have been made to trace original source material.

–Safdie Architects, Somerville, Massachusetts

Credits

Published by
ORO Editions
Publishers of Architecture, Art, and Design
Gordon Goff, Publisher
www.oroeditions.com
info@oroeditions.com

Project directors
Diana Murphy and Jaron Lubin
Graphic design
Michael Gericke, Matthew McInerney, Pentagram
Editors
Anne Thompson, Christa Mahar
Color separations and printing
ORO Group Ltd.
Printed in China
Production manager
Usana Shadday

Library of Congress Cataloging-in-Publication Data:
Available upon request

Copyright © 2013 by Safdie Architects, LLC
ISBN 978-0-9819857-6-3
First edition
10 9 8 7 6 5 4 3 2 1

All rights reserved. No part of this book may be reproduced, stored in a retrieval system, or transmitted in any form or by any means, including electronic, mechanical, photocopying of microfilming, recording, or otherwise, without written permission from the publisher.

This book was printed and bound using a variety of sustainable manufacturing processes and materials including soy-based inks, aqueous-based varnish, VOC- and formaldehyde-free glues, and phthalate-free laminations. The text is printed using offset sheet-fed lithographic printing process in 5 color on 157gsm premium matt art paper.

ORO Editions makes a continuous effort to minimize the overall carbon footprint of its publications. As part of this goal, ORO Editions, in association with Global ReLeaf, arranges to plant trees to replace those used in the manufacturing of the paper produced for its books. Global ReLeaf is an international campaign run by American Forests, one of the world's oldest nonprofit conservation organizations. Global ReLeaf is American Forests' education and action program that helps individuals, organizations, agencies, and corporations improve the local and global environment by planting and caring for trees.

For information on distribution please visit www.oroeditions.com.